Analyzing Oppression

Studies in Feminist Philosophy is designed to showcase cutting-edge monographs and collections that display the full range of feminist approaches to philosophy, that push feminist thought in important new directions, and that display the outstanding quality of feminist philosophical thought.

Analyzing Oppression

ANN E. CUDD

OXFORD
UNIVERSITY PRESS

2006

OXFORD

UNIVERSITY PRESS

Oxford University Press, Inc., publishes works that further
Oxford University's objective of excellence
in research, scholarship, and education.

Oxford   New York
Auckland   Cape Town   Dar es Salaam   Hong Kong   Karachi
Kuala Lumpur   Madrid   Melbourne   Mexico City   Nairobi
New Delhi   Shanghai   Taipei   Toronto

With offices in
Argentina   Austria   Brazil   Chile   Czech Republic   France   Greece
Guatemala   Hungary   Italy   Japan   Poland   Portugal   Singapore
South Korea   Switzerland   Thailand   Turkey   Ukraine   Vietnam

Published by Oxford University Press, Inc.
198 Madison Avenue, New York, New York 10016

www.oup.com

Oxford is a registered trademark of Oxford University Press

Library of Congress Cataloging-in-Publication Data
Cudd, Ann E., 1959–
Analyzing oppression / Ann E. Cudd.
    p. cm.—(Studies in feminist philosophy)
Includes bibliographical references and index.
ISBN-13 978-0-19-518743-4; 978-0-19-518744-1 (pbk.)

1. Oppression (Psychology)   2. Social psychology.   I. Title.   II. Series.
HM1256.C83 2005
303.3'3—DC22   2005049873

9 8 7 6 5 4 3 2

Printed in the United States of America
on acid-free paper

For Neal, with love and gratitude

Preface

Human beings suffer myriad kinds of harms. Like all other animals, we wither and die of disease and injury, in pregnancy and childbirth, and from old age. Like some other animals, we sometimes inflict injury and death upon each other. In this, as in many other respects, our abilities are vastly superior to the other animals. Not only can we harm each other one by one, we have systematic ways of uniting to harm whole collections of other humans. We wage war, we annihilate, we execute, we enslave, we retaliate, we punish, we dominate, we terrorize, we tyrannize, we exploit, we coerce, and we oppress. Unlike the other animals, we morally judge our actions that harm each other, justifying some, denouncing others. This book is about one of these kinds of harms that we systematically inflict on persons: oppression.

Although "oppression" is a widely used concept, political philosophers, especially in the liberal and analytic philosophical traditions, have provided little in the way of careful conceptual analysis of the term. Aside from short articles and books on specific instances of oppression, there exist no book-length comprehensive, general analyses of oppression by analytic philosophers, though there are such books on related concepts of coercion and exploitation.[1] This is not to say that there is a dearth of literature on oppression. Quite the opposite: Oppression is a common theme in literature, in memoirs, and in books detailing the history of most of the human past. The books that have been written about oppression would fill a very large library, and it would be impossible for one person to read them all in a lifetime. Oppression is both widespread and deeply felt. Books are difficult to write, but oppression sufficiently motivates many to take on the task, whether to inform, to indict the oppressors, or to bear witness to suffering.

So how could philosophers avoid theorizing oppression? I would offer a few reasons by way of speculation on this question. First, philosophers tend not to come from oppressed groups. Philosophizing is an activity for which one has to have time and space in which one is not pressed by mere physical survival tasks. Oppressed persons typically are so pressed. While one need not suffer oppression in order to see it or to be motivated to write about it, clearly it helps. Consider those philosophers who have written about oppression; the majority are Jews, women, members of colonized nations, or members of racial minorities. Yet these groups, even when taken together, form a minority of the professional philosophers on the planet, and especially among analytic philosophers. If there is a connection between being from a minority or being a woman and writing about oppression, as I think there is, then this could in part explain the dearth of work on it. Second, oppression raises strong emotions, which philosophers tend to shy away from. No one can write about oppression without becoming angry, deeply saddened, or perhaps even defensive. Yet to do philosophy is to apply one's reason to the matter at hand, in what Hume called "a cool hour" of thought and reflection. I have found the writing of this book to be a deeply emotional experience at times, and I have had to put the book aside at times to regain my composure. While I would not want to argue that philosophy cannot or should not be done passionately, it is more difficult to reason objectively when one feels great emotion. Furthermore, philosophers tend to think of passion as unseemly for professional work. Since there are a great many fascinating philosophical issues that do not raise this difficulty, many philosophers simply avoid the issues that do. A third reason for the neglect of oppression is that analytic philosophy has gravitated to the most abstract analyses of human experience, regarding abstraction itself the hallmark of philosophical thought. Since understanding oppression involves considerable empirical exploration, at least much of that work is considered "not philosophy." But this is a mistaken prejudice, perhaps even a rationalization for lazy armchair theorizing. Analytic philosophers of science seem to have outgrown their prejudice for empirical work, and it is time that analytic political philosophers and ethicists do so as well.

A more theoretical reason for the lack of attention by analytic philosophers is that justice has long been the primary concern of political philosophers. Although most consider injustice also important, it has been an abiding prejudice of political philosophers (especially in the liberal, Anglo-American tradition) that injustice is simply the negation of justice. John Rawls's twentieth-century classic *Theory of Justice*, for instance, leaves injustice virtually untheorized.[2] This prejudice is mistaken; justice can fail in many different and nuanced ways, as this book points out.

One of the recurring themes of this book concerns the difficulty of recognizing some forms of injustice. Consider some historical examples. It has not always been easy to recognize that the confinement of women to social roles that entail less access to social resources or greater burdens in the provision of social benefit is unjust. It has not always been recognized that persons forced to work for their pay at rates determined by market forces not of their own making are enslaved unjustly. It is not easy to recognize the difference between just and unjust wars. It is not easy to determine when compensation is owed for past injustice, or to whom. Without a proper theory of oppression, we will not be able to recognize injustice in all its forms, however.

I have come to study oppression for reasons that are both personal and theoretical. I have always seen myself as a feminist and have witnessed and experienced the sting of injustice suffered by my sex. But I was a philosopher before I was a feminist philosopher. My early work was on game theory and philosophy of social science, but I soon saw how those theories might be applied to questions of feminism and oppression.

Feminists have long recognized the oppression of women but have had a hard time convincing others that women are oppressed. One of the main motivations for my work has been to construct a general theory of oppression to demonstrate that women are harmed unjustly in ways that are similar to the unjust treatment of other groups who are generally recognized as oppressed. Likewise, for those who can readily recognize the oppression of women, but not other groups, by showing that there are deep similarities in the cases they can be convinced that there is serious unjust harm going on in these other cases as well.

Injustice, since it necessarily comes at the hands of other persons, is surely one of the most painful forms of harm that a person can suffer. And so we should want urgently to eradicate it. I shall argue in this book that the fundamental injustice of social institutions is oppression, and oppression can best be recognized, explained, and ultimately eradicated by the theories, principles, and methods that underlie the liberal and analytic traditions.

Acknowledgments

I have been working on this book for nearly a decade, and in that time I have accumulated many debts to acknowledge. First, I acknowledge permission to reprint in part four of my previously published works: "Oppression by Choice," published in the *Journal of Social Philosophy*, vol. 25 (June 1994), pp. 22–44 by Blackwell Publishers; "Strikes, Housework, and the Moral Obligation to Resist," published in the *Journal of Social Philosophy*, vol. 29 (Spring 1998), pp. 20–36, by Blackwell Publishers; "Nonvoluntary Social Groups," published in Christine Sistare, Larry May, and Leslie Francis, eds., *Groups and Group Rights*, 2001, pp. 58–70, by the University Press of Kansas; and "Psychological Explanations of Oppression," published in Cynthia Willett, ed., *Theorizing Multiculturalism: A Guide to the Current Debate*, 1998, pp. 187–215, by Blackwell Publishers.

Some of my debts are institutional in nature: The University of Kansas and the Hall Center for the Humanities funded research leaves over three semesters during which I wrote and revised large portions of the manuscript. My colleagues in Philosophy and Women's Studies, especially Rex Martin, Thomas Tuozzo, and Ann Schofield offered good advice on the content of the book and on the publishing process. Nancy Scott Jackson was an early supporter of the project, offering good advice that I sometimes ignored to my later regret. Lara Zoble and Peter Ohlin, my editors at Oxford, have been helpful, patient, and generous in their assessment and acquisition of the book.

Other debts are both philosophical and personal. Tamara Horowitz provided me with the initial education and inspiration required to undertake this project, and I deeply regret that her untimely death means she is not able to read and engage the full book. Her comments on my early work on oppression were invaluable to me; her mentoring and friendship means more to me than I can ever say. Marcia Homiak has been a constant friend in the deep, Aristotelian sense that she has taught me to appreciate and practice. She offered valuable insights and suggestions on the book manuscript, as well as on my earlier articles on oppression. Anita Superson likewise has been a philosophical friend and has offered valuable comments over the years on work that forms this book. Julie Maybee and Cynthia Willett helped me think through this book at an early stage. Claudia Card, Sally Haslanger, and an anonymous reviewer offered challenging criticisms along with encouragement to make the book better.

I have been inspired and challenged by my students, and several deserve particular recognition. Roksana Alavi, Pamela Belman, Pelle Danabo, Stephen Ferguson, Tamela Ice, Pinfei Lu, Xiufen Lu, John H. McClendon, III, Anne Morgan, Jorge Muñoz, Gina Rose, and Almas Sayeed have all helped me in my thinking about the subject and arguments of this book. Pelle also assisted me with the preparation of the final manuscript.

My deepest debts are personal. My mother, Bernice Daniels, has taken care of me and mine, entertained us with wonderful diversions, and modeled for me a life of courage, perseverance, and hard work. My father, Kermit Cudd, has encouraged and supported me always, particularly through the frustrations of academic life. He is always a fountain of wisdom, whether academic, familial, or spiritual, and of love. My brothers, Ben Cudd and Tim Cudd, provide friendship and friendly competition that motivates me. My stepparents, Anne Cudd and Edward Daniels, have loved and supported me most of my life. My sons, Alex and Thomas Becker, have not yet known a time when I was not writing this book. I thank them for the playtime, the love, and the times when they gave me the space and the time to work without resenting my absence. Finally, my husband, Neal Becker, read and critiqued much of the book. Many of the thoughts and ideas of chapter 5, in particular, can be traced to discussions with him over the dinner table or during long driving trips. Neal has been my best friend and closest collaborator for over twenty years. His wisdom, gentleness, generosity, and love sustain me.

Contents

PART I

A FRAMEWORK FOR ANALYSIS

Oppression: The Fundamental Injustice of Social Institutions

1. A Genealogy of "Oppression"

In the 1950s if you asked the average (white) American about oppression they would likely have talked about Hitler, Fascism, Communism, Stalin, North Korea, and, possibly, Joseph McCarthy and the House Un-American Activities Committee. What these regimes of oppression have in common is that they are governmental regimes that deprive people of at least some of their human rights. Fifty years later these names are no less connected to oppression, yet the kinds of terrible oppression that the average American witnesses on TV or reads about in the newspapers and magazines have changed to guerillas in Peru, warlords and the Taliban in Afghanistan, child labor in Pakistan, forcibly veiled women in Iran, the destruction of Palestinian homes by the Israeli army, and sexual slaves in Thailand. Many of these cases of oppression are not new, but they are now being recognized by more of the world, and they are more salient than in the past. The end of the Cold War has changed the way we think of oppression from a state-imposed circumstance to one that is brought about by any great disparity in wealth and power, whether that comes from the legitimate or illegitimate governmental monopoly on the use of force, or from some other illegitimate but effective dominion. This changing perception, however, raises the issue of what oppression is and opens the possibility that legitimate uses of force or power will be mischaracterized as oppression. Indeed, some readers may disagree with the second list, arguing that the Israeli destruction of Palestinian homes is a legitimate response to terrorism. Yet other readers will charge that conspicuous cases of oppression are missing, such as racism and sexism in America. To answer these charges rationally, a theory of oppression is needed.

How shall we go about characterizing and explaining the phenomenon of oppression? Analytic philosophers often begin by looking at how the concept has been used, and then checking those uses against the implications for categorizing various cases when the concept is consistently applied. In this chapter I begin to clarify the concept by examining critically its uses in political and philosophical discussions, and theories that attempt to explain it. From an investigation of the history of the use of the word, we can glean several important things for our investigation of oppression. For the history of the concept of oppression parallels the development of ideas about freedom, equality, and justice, yet unlike those positive notions, oppression has developed mainly, with a few important exceptions that I will note, implicitly and in the shadows of the others. From the genealogy of the concept itself I will formulate a general description of the harm of oppression and a set of paradigm cases. From a survey of theories that attempt to explain oppression, I will formulate a set of questions that should be answered by a theory of oppression, and a survey of possible methodologies to employ in answering those questions.

Looking at how the concept has been applied is only the beginning of a proper analysis of it, however. Conceptual analysis involves more than this. Sally Haslanger (2004b) distinguishes three aspects of a concept that a deep analysis should investigate. The manifest concept is the concept as defined by its dominant meanings in a culture; this concept is to be investigated by asking how the term is typically used in a culture, but not necessarily by those who are doing analysis or theory on the concept. The manifest concept is accessible to us upon reflection on typical use. The operative concept is the role that the concept actually plays in what Haslanger calls the matrix of social practices, and this may be a different concept from the manifest one. She uses the concept of "tardy" as used in the public schools her children attend. While there is an official school district definition of the term, the classroom definition varies considerably from that abstract ideal. It is implicit and guided by ideas about whether and how a particular child should be punished for being late to school on a particular day. Understanding the operative concept requires attention to how the concept's use in a society affects and is affected by the social institutions that it relates to. Although both the manifest and the operative concepts can be gleaned through genealogical research, the operative concept is more subterranean. To see the implicit meanings one has to be willing to see the concept operating in ways that go against its official, explicit meanings. Reflection on the interplay between the manifest and operative aspects of a concept lead us to a third aspect of the concept, what Haslanger calls the normative concept. The normative concept is informed by a social theory of what the concept does and what it means for the society and recommends itself as the preferred use. I take the normative concept to be the right sense of the term, the way that, on reflection, we want to use it given a full assessment of how it is explicitly and implicitly defined and used in the culture. To construct this normative concept we will need to ask what roles the concept is to play in our analysis of society. The term "oppression" plays a rich and complex role in defining a fundamental social wrong. Its complexity will lead us to ask questions about the origin and maintenance of that wrong, as well as how it might be overcome. In this chapter I will begin with a genealogical discussion of the manifest and operative aspects of the concept of oppression and proceed to offering a normative one. Filling out the normative concept of oppression will constitute the major project of the book.

1.1. "Oppression" and Modern Liberalism

Ancient philosophers such as Plato and Aristotle believed in a natural hierarchy of ability among humans that would justify such treatment as enslavement and denial of citizenship, fairness, or equal rights. Oppression did not, as such, become an important topic in political philosophy until the advent of liberalism and the idea that humans are roughly morally equal. It is a distinctly modern notion that persons are in some sense or other equal to each other. The equality thesis has been given various theological, philosophical, and moral interpretations and justifications by different thinkers. Perhaps the most astonishing of all, made by Thomas Hobbes in *Leviathan*, is the claim that persons are in some physical sense equals.

> Nature hath made men so equall, in the faculties of body, and mind; as that though there bee found one man sometimes manifestly stronger of body, or of quicker mind than another; yet when all is reckoned together, the difference between man, and man, is not so considerable, as that one man can thereupon claim to himselfe any benefit, to which another may not pretend, as well as he. For as to the strength of body, the weakest has strength enough to kill the strongest, either by secret machination, or by confederacy with others, that are in the same danger with himselfe. (Hobbes 1985, 183)

This claim, if true, seems to rule out the possibility of long-term oppression; for, if we are equal in the sense that each has the strength and ability to kill the strongest, then how can the strongest keep even the weakest in chains? Why do the oppressed seem to accept or acquiesce to their oppression?

Modern political philosophers differed on the conditions under which persons could be oppressed. For both Hobbes and Rousseau, the rough natural equality of human beings makes the existence of oppression something of a puzzle: How, if we are roughly equal in natural endowments, could one person allow herself to be dominated or enslaved by another? Hobbes, for whom oppression connoted conditions of violence and enslavement, argued that in the absence of a sovereign power to keep the peace, a situation he termed the state of nature, the rough equality of humans led to the war of all against all, and consequently a "solitary, poor, nasty, brutish and short" life. Thus, he argued, we must enter civilized society in order to avoid oppression. "Fear of oppression, disposeth a man to anticipate, or to seek aid by society: for there is no other way by which a man can secure his life and liberty" (Hobbes 1985, 163). Rousseau, who thought of oppression as conditions of enslavement and domination, specifically denies that oppression is possible in the state of nature, however.

> A man could well lay hold of the fruit another has gathered, the game he has killed, the cave that served as his shelter. But how will he ever succeed in making himself be obeyed? And what can be the chains of dependence among men who possess nothing? If someone chases me from one tree, I am free to go to another; if someone torments me in one place, who will prevent me from going elsewhere? Is there a man with strength sufficiently superior to mine and who is, moreover, sufficiently depraved, sufficiently lazy and sufficiently ferocious to force me to

> provide for his subsistence while he remains idle? He must resolve not to take his eyes off me for a single instant, to keep me carefully tied down while he sleeps, for fear that I may escape or that I would kill him. (Rousseau 1987, 58)

For Rousseau, oppression requires the ability for one person to do the work of two and the artifice of money, or a way to store wealth, and these require society. Also, according to Rousseau, oppression could only exist when the oppressed is willing to give up his freedom for some merely apparent reward, a reward that only so-called civilized humans could see as better than freedom.

> Citizens allow themselves to be oppressed only insofar as they are driven by blind ambition; and looking more below than above them, domination becomes more dear to them than independence, and they consent to wear chains in order to be able to give them in turn to others. . . . inequality spreads easily among ambitious and cowardly souls always ready to run the risks of fortune and, almost indifferently, to dominate or serve, according to whether it becomes favorable or unfavorable to them. (Rousseau, 1987, 77)

Oppression then becomes stable and accepted by the institution of laws: "it derives its force and growth from the development of our faculties and the progress of the human mind, and eventually becomes stable and legitimate through the establishment of property and laws" (Rousseau 1987, 81).

John Locke opposed Hobbes's view of sovereign power as a political panacea by arguing that unlimited sovereign power is the cause of political oppression. Locke also opposed Rousseau in thinking that properly limited government and the institution of property rights need not cause oppression (Locke 1980, sec. 93). Thus, Locke argued that a government instituted by the consent of the governed and limited by liberal human rights would maintain its legitimate authority and avoid oppression.

The Enlightenment brought forward the idea that legitimate authority requires the consent (in some sense) of those who are asked to submit to it. Thus, in the modern period (i.e., the sixteenth through eighteenth centuries), in which liberal political theory was initially developed and liberalism took root in many European nations, "oppression" was used by political philosophers to refer primarily to political repression and domination. Less commonly, it was used to talk about a particular person feeling stifled, or to talk of a particular person being overtaxed by the ruler. Hume, for instance, can be seen using "oppression" in these two ways in his *Essays*. I shall not be concerned with this personal sense of "oppression," which I think is a derivative sense of the term. More commonly, "oppression" was used to talk about general sorts of bad treatment by a ruler of his subjects collectively. Locke often used it together with the terms "tyranny" and "violence," though he occasionally uses it to speak of any use of power beyond the bounds of legitimate authority (Locke 1980), and in particular of the imposition of state religion on persons of other religions (Locke 1983).

Particularly beginning in the eighteenth century, "oppression" often referred specifically to economic exploitation of a people by its ruler, either in the form of overtaxation or unequal taxation. Hume, for instance, writes:

> the laborious poor pay a considerable part of the taxes by their annual consumptions, though they could not advance, at once, a proportional part of the sum

required. Not to mention, that property in money and stock in trade might easily be concealed or disguised; and that visible property in lands and houses would really at last answer for the whole: An inequality and oppression, which never would be submitted to. (Hume 1964, 370)

Most generally, "oppression" in the modern period referred to arbitrary or unjust laws imposed on citizens illegitimately that cause material (economic or physical) deprivation. Perhaps the most inclusive list of such "oppressions" in the modern period comes in the Declaration of Independence, where Jefferson named as forms of oppression the kinds of bad treatment that King George had subjected the American colonists to: making bad or unjust laws, interference with elected representatives and their attempts to make law, corrupting the judiciary, overtaxation and over-bureaucratization, trying individuals without due process, the imposition of a brutal, corrupt, standing army, and general brutality and violence against the colonists.

The early liberal political theorists raised important questions about oppression that remain for us to answer today, including: How does oppression originate, and how does it endure over time in spite of humans' rough natural equality of ability? Is oppression an inevitable feature of civil society? Their early uses of the term "oppression" can be summarized by saying that classical modern liberal theorists thought of "domination," "tyranny," and "oppression" as synonyms, connoting rule by an arbitrary or opposing will, and resulting in abrogation of liberal political rights, economic deprivations, and physical brutality. These early liberals limited the scope of human rights to narrow issues and a minority of the existing humans, and hence their understanding of the causes and effects of oppression was correspondingly limited. Cases they considered include those who are ruled by illegitimate governments and persons whose religion is not tolerated by the state. The methodology for understanding oppression was informal empirical observation coupled with philosophical analysis, particularly in the form of state of nature thought experiments.

1.2. Nineteenth-Century Conceptions of Oppression: Four Conceptual Shifts

In the nineteenth century the scope of liberal political rights broadened, and liberalism itself was challenged by the influence of German idealism, especially in the work of Hegel, by liberal works on women's rights, and by the historical materialism of Marx. These movements in political philosophy brought with them new conceptions of oppression. First, we see a shift from a purely political conception of oppression, where the oppressor is the ruler and the oppressed the ruled, to a more social conception of oppression, where oppressor and oppressed are social groups that may be related in a less politically formalized way. We can see a conceptual shift beginning to take place already in the late eighteenth century. In the *Federalist Papers*, written as a series of newspaper columns in 1788 by James Madison, Alexander Hamilton, and John Jay, we see the first explicit use of "oppression" to speak of the political domination and abuse of one collective part of a nation by another collective part of that nation. This was a natural extension of the use of the term to mean the mistreatment of the ruled by the ruler, since what was meant was the mistreatment of the minority by the majority in a democracy. I take this to be a kind of transitional document in the discussion of oppression, as it retains the link between ruler vs. ruled and still uses "oppression" sometimes to refer specifically to illegitimate taxation, but also opens the possibility for oppression to refer to a conflict between social groups.

In a related (though limited) sense, Edmund Burke's *Reflections on the Revolution in France* of 1790 also is surprisingly progressive. He speaks of the state being oppressed by commoners if they are allowed to rule, as well as of the problem of the majority oppressing the minority. However, Burke also expressed a startlingly familiar threat-*cum*-warning for those of us who look to recognize, name, and eradicate oppressions:

> The atheistic libellers, who act as trumpeters to animate the populace to plunder . . . find themselves obliged to rake into the histories of former ages (which they have ransacked with a malignant and profligate industry) for every instance of oppression and persecution which has been made by that body or in its favour, in order to justify, upon very iniquitous, because very illogical principles of retaliation, their own persecutions, and their own cruelties. (Burke 2001, para. 240)

Burke's warning reminds us that not everything that has been or will be called oppression really is oppression. In order to avoid using the term incorrectly, we need to have a good account of what oppression is, and here Burke moves us toward a different conception of the harm of oppression:

> After destroying all other genealogies and family distinctions, they invent a sort of pedigree of crimes. It is not very just to chastise men for the offences of their natural ancestors; but to take the fiction of ancestry in a corporate succession, as a ground for punishing men who have no relation to guilty acts, except in names and general descriptions, is a sort of refinement in injustice belonging to the philosophy of this enlightened age. (Burke 2001, para. 240)

While I will disagree sharply with Burke's view, since I think that there are conditions under which we should "chastise men for the offences of their natural ancestors,"[1] this passage is worth looking at closely. It suggests a new sense of the harm of oppression, a "refinement in injustice," as Burke calls it: what we might term "cultural domination," a kind of psychological harm that distorts and destroys the traditional culture. Burke was arguing that it is oppressive to have one's history reinterpreted and "genealogy and family distinctions" destroyed by a hostile social group, and then to be blamed for acts that have now been reinterpreted as crimes, even though one could not have committed them because one was not then alive. As we shall see, Burke's reference to enforced cultural reinterpretation as oppression will be mirrored by contemporary social theorists.

A second conceptual shift in understanding oppression in the nineteenth century came with the idea that social mores or conventions, and not just the formal dictates of the political ruler, could be oppressive to certain groups. Anticipating this shift near the turn of the (eighteenth to nineteenth) century, Mary Wollstonecraft, in *A Vindication of the Rights of Women* (1792), uses the term "oppression" to refer to the denial of equal education and equal freedoms to women. Wollstonecraft examines how not only laws, but also traditions, unconsidered but widely shared prejudices, and social expectations led to these inequalities.[2] Later, in the nineteenth century, John Stuart Mill in *On Liberty* (1859) similarly writes of oppression of the minority by the dominant social mores of society.

> Society can and does execute its own mandates: and if it issues wrong mandates instead of right, or any mandates at all in things with which it ought not to meddle, it practises a social tyranny more formidable than many kinds of political oppression, since, though not usually upheld by such extreme penalties, it leaves fewer means of escape, penetrating much more deeply into the details of life, and enslaving the soul itself. (Mill 1978, 219)

In *The Subjection of Women*, Mill writes at length on the "oppression" of women by men, that is, of a social group by another social group that is not necessarily a political minority vs. majority issue. Sometimes this oppression seems to have a particularly legal and economic cast to it, other times it refers to general mistreatment or brutality.

The third conceptual shift of the nineteenth century in the understanding of oppression was brought about by Hegel and consists in seeing oppression as a failure to recognize the equal moral worth and dignity of another. Although Hegel himself did not focus on oppression as such, in attempting to explain the possibility of human slavery for beings capable of absolute freedom, he introduced the idea of psychological domination for future thinkers. In chapter 3 I will return to a fuller discussion of Hegel's influence on ideas about psychological domination.

Marx made the fourth conceptual shift in the nineteenth-century understanding of oppression: to see oppression as causally based in the economic system. Marx wrote about how capitalism systematically and materially disadvantages the working class. The oppression of the working class is not political oppression, since they may well have equal legal rights, including the abstract right to own property, even though they do not have political power. In seeing oppression as fundamentally caused by economics rather than psychology, Marx turns Hegel on his head, or, if you will, puts the theory of oppression back on his feet where it belongs. For Marx, oppression begins with division of labor, and thus with the ability of one group of people to coercively appropriate the product of another's labor. This coercive appropriation was not limited to economic class conflict, though. In *The German Ideology* he writes that "the first division of labor was originally nothing but the division of labor in the sexual act" (Marx and Engels 1978, 158). Engels, in his 1877 essay, "The Origin of Family, Private Property, and the State," adds that "the first class antagonism which appears in history coincides with the development of the antagonism between man and woman in monogamian marriage, and the first class oppression with that of the female sex by the male" (Marx and Engels 1978, 739). Thus, Marx and Engels, at least at times, saw the oppression of women as the earliest and longest lasting form of oppression.

To summarize this section, we have seen four conceptual shifts that were made in the nineteenth century in the conception of oppression: first, to see oppression as pervading the social world beyond the strictly political or governmental sphere;

second and closely related to the first, to see oppression as a condition imposed not only by political rulers but also by social convention and tradition; third, to see psychological domination, in addition to physical and political domination, as one of the important causes and effects of oppression; and fourth, to see that an entire economic system of production can be the ultimate origin of oppression. Although the third and fourth conflict to the extent that they propose an ultimate or primary cause of oppression, we can see all four shifts to be represented in most current discussions of oppression.

1.3. Recognition, Distribution, and Three Seminal / ovarian Nineteenth-Century Theories of Oppression

Three of these theories from the nineteenth century have proved seminal for twentieth-century discussions of oppression, namely those of Hegel, Marx, and Mill. Their particularly contemporary influence has been to reveal the systematic nature of oppression, by showing how oppression that begins in one sphere, such as the political, economic, or legal sphere, can then come to permeate the consciousness of people, both oppressed and oppressors.

Nancy Fraser (1995) draws a useful distinction in theories of injustice, which illuminates the differences among those theories of oppression that are most influential for us today. She distinguishes between two kinds of theories of justice according to their demands for solutions to injustice: the demand for recognition and the demand for redistribution. According to those who primarily demand recognition, injustice is rooted in culture and manifested in a lack of respect for or recognition of minority or subjugated cultures. Those who primarily demand redistribution argue that injustice is rooted in economic structures and manifested as inequality in economic goods, either commodities or capabilities (Sen 1999), and I would also add inequalities in the distribution of legal rights. While Hegel founded the recognition theory, Marx and Mill are the seminal distribution theorists. Since these three theories have been so influential in contemporary thought about oppression, I shall briefly critically discuss each in turn before offering my own account. My purpose here is not, of course, to offer a definitive interpretation of these thinkers, and there will no doubt be points at which my interpretations seem lacking in depth or nuance to scholars of these theorists. My purpose is rather to carve out a role for a contemporary theory of oppression informed by contemporary social science from a broad brush description of what I see as the major achievements and failures of these classic theories.

1.3.1. HEGEL'S MASTER/SLAVE DIALECTIC

Although it does not specifically discuss "oppression," many contemporary social theorists regard the master/slave dialectic that paragraphs 178–196 of Hegel's *Phenomenology of Spirit* (entitled "Of Lordship and Bondage") outlines as the canonical classical reading on oppression because it implies an explanation for oppression that appeals to alleged human psychological needs that resonate with some contemporary social movements (Willett 1995; Gauthier 1997). Hegel's idealist view of human motivation differs markedly from that of the liberals I have alluded to in discussing the use of the term "oppression" in the modern period. Hegel's view is that the highest good is not happiness but freedom of a particularly ideal sort. Humans, who are uniquely capable of self-consciousness, attain freedom by mutual recognition of and with other self-conscious beings. But humans do not realize their need for mutual recognition all at once. Rather, we must move dialectically from our primitive origins as a barely conscious being to our ultimate destiny as fully self-conscious beings in mutual recognition of our humanity. In the dialectical historical moment that he writes of in paragraphs 178–196, humans are at the stage where they understand their own need for recognition from others, but fail to understand that such recognition is unsatisfying without their recognizing the other as well. Thus, humans at this stage are led to engage in a life and death struggle for recognition by the other. When one party to the struggle is vanquished he gives up his struggle, trades his (one-way) recognition of the victor for his life, and becomes the victor's slave. But this proves ultimately unsatisfying to the master, since the one who recognizes him is no longer his equal, a fully self-conscious being. At the same time, the slave learns self-discipline and to set aside bodily or material desires, and this frees him from external needs. In the end it is the slave who is freer than the master, though neither can come to complete freedom until they come to see their need for mutual recognition of each other as abstractly equal, self-conscious beings.

For some contemporary social theorists, Hegel's master/slave dialectic describes the conditions of oppression and of its solution. They interpret many contemporary social movements as a struggle for recognition, and the hegemony of the Western, the white, the male as attempts to deny recognition to others and to subjugate them. Consider the image of the sanitation workers marching in Memphis in 1968 holding signs "I AM A MAN," that demand recognition of their equality with white men from the society. Yet, these social theorists see in the social movements of oppressed peoples a hypersensitive slave consciousness that understands the true needs and abilities of both the oppressors and the oppressed. The social condition of oppression is but a dialectical moment in human history, to be overcome by mutual recognition. Hegel thus adds an important psychological account of the causes and effects of oppression, and his methodological contributions are psychological and dialectical analyses.

Useful as this theory may be as a psychological explanation scheme (and I will question that usefulness in chapter 3), Hegel does not provide us with a systematic or unambiguous account of oppression. First, it is not clear what recognition consists in, or how it is related to the basic necessities of life, such as food and shelter. Nor does it seem particularly plausible that persons are more highly motivated by their need for recognition, than for the satisfaction of their basic physical needs. Second, the idea of a life and death struggle is either metaphorical, and so rather vague, or it does not describe some clear cases of oppression. Oppression often seems to flourish when it is kept in place not by armed struggle but by willing, or at least grudging, compliance by the oppressed, including individuals who have never engaged in any kind of life and death struggle, a point that Rousseau appreciated, as we have seen. Hegel might be interpreted as suggesting that we look to the collective struggle and recapitulation of the group. But what such collective struggle or collective recapitulation amounts to is unclear. Furthermore, Hegel provides no plausible answer to the question: Why does the slave capitulate completely and forever? If it is merely to save her life, then why does she not escape when the master turns his back? Third, mutual recognition is also vague. It may seem that contemporary Western democracies epitomize the formal mutual recognition required by Hegel to overcome the master/slave dialectic, yet oppression still exists in them.

More importantly, however, the Hegelian account of oppression is too ideal and not firmly rooted in the material facts of everyday existence. Yet, this is where we live everyday. Most instances of oppression are not merely cases of psychological harms, as significant as those may also be. Torture, beatings, killings, malnourishment, unemployment, enforced servitude—these are the material effects of oppression that must first be addressed. And for this reason, in addition to the theoretical problems of vagueness and ambiguity, I think we cannot be content to rest on Hegelian theories.

1.3.2. MARX'S THEORY OF ECONOMIC ALIENATION

Marx accepted the idea of the historical dialectic from Hegel but insisted on a materialist revision that begins to correct the overly abstract and ideal conception of Hegel. As I noted above, Marx introduced into the discussion of oppression the idea that oppression was fundamentally located in class struggles. In "Manifesto of the Communist Party" (1872) Marx and Engels claimed that economic class delimits social interaction, and the struggles between and within economic classes determine the future of the society. "The history of all hitherto existing society is the history of class struggles" (Marx and Engels 1978, 473). They then explained in this mainly polemical work how all class struggle can be overcome with the communist revolution. Marx's insistence on the systematic material, particularly economic, origin of oppression constitutes his fundamental insight into the nature of oppression.

In "Estranged Labor" (1844) Marx outlines his theory of alienation (which I take to be his theory of oppression) under capitalism. Alienation is, in the first instance, a material harm for Marx and becomes a psychological harm only as a consequence of the material one.[3] The workers are alienated, or separated, from something essential to them in four ways. First, they are alienated from the product of labor, in the sense that their labor product is literally taken away from them. Although the worker exchanges her labor power for wages, she does so under coercion, having death as the only other option. In "Wage Labor and Capital" (1847), Marx explained how the wages of the working class must fall to mere subsistence, which means that some of them will starve. Surplus value is created by labor and then turned into capital, which enriches the capitalist and further strengthens him in his struggle against the worker. In this way there is a double alienation of the worker from her product. As Marx put it, the product confronts the worker "as an alien object exercising power over h[er]" (Marx 1964, 111), and by enriching the capitalist it strengthens his ability to coerce her into laboring for him. Second, they are alienated from the labor process, in the sense that they do not choose how or when to work, or what to produce. Again, because the capitalist sets the terms for the worker's survival, the worker cannot assure that the hours and conditions are physically tolerable or that the product is beneficial to her. These two forms of alienation, which might in themselves be acceptable were the exchanges equitable or uncoerced, lead inevitably under capitalism to two other forms of alienation. The third form of alienation is that workers especially, but also capitalists, are alienated from their species being. "Species being" is Marx's term for the essential nature of a species, which in the case of humans is to be socially cooperative and creative producers. Uniquely, humans are capable of subjecting their "life activity" to their will or consciousness. But when the worker is alienated from the labor process, her life activity becomes a mere means to her existence, as the life activity for an animal is merely a means to its existence. Thus alienation from species being constitutes a kind of psychic harm. Finally, the alienation of the worker from the product, under capitalism, causes poverty and intense competition within and between classes. Since profit and wages are inversely related, the worker and capitalist must be antagonists. Marx explained how progress throws businesses out of existence, and "compels capital to intensify the productive forces of labor" (Marx and Engels 1978, 213). This causes the working class to be much larger than the number of workers that capitalism can support, so the workers are constantly competing with each other for jobs, that is, for their survival. Thus, Marx derived the fourth form of alienation: Under capitalism the workers (and the capitalists) are alienated "man from man," in the sense that they come to see each other as rivals for their individual survival rather than as fellow human beings engaged in mutual cooperation for their collective human fulfillment.

Both Marx and Hegel raised an important question about who, if anyone, benefits from oppression. Hegel's answer seems to be that while the master initially benefits materially, the slave ultimately benefits psychologically, in that the slave comes closer to attaining absolute freedom. Marx's answer is somewhat different. The capitalist benefits materially, and since the alternative is to be a worker and face a continual struggle for survival that is sometimes unsuccessful, this is an enormous benefit. But both the workers and the capitalists suffer psychologically from social conditions of continual competition rather than social cooperation, and fear of starvation and death should the competition be lost.

Marx's great methodological contribution to the study of oppression was to apply economic analysis to reveal the sources and extent of exploitation. However, Marx was handicapped by the state of economic analysis at his time. His economic theory was classical economic theory, in which the labor theory of value plays the central role in the determination of production and exchange. The labor theory of value allowed Marx to highlight the role of labor power in the production process, and this cohered with his philosophical view of the moral primacy of labor in production. Marx also attempts to link his micro analysis of the determination of wages and prices with a macro theory of class struggles and economic crises. However, the labor theory of value has been shown to be empirically untenable (Elster 1985, 127–141), and the twentieth-century economic and political struggles of capitalist and communist economies have not corroborated his macro theories either.

For Marx, the state of technological and economic development of a society determines the nature and extent of all oppression. However, Marx's understanding of oppression is not entirely material. First, alienation from species being is a kind of psychic harm, as I argued. Second, in "On the Jewish Question" (1843) he wrote of how bourgeois civil society, that is, a society economically structured by capitalism, alienates human beings from their true human interests. In that essay Marx argued that arguments for the religious emancipation of the Jews in Germany miss the point that no one in Germany is emancipated, in the sense of being free from alienation or oppression by the structure of bourgeois society itself. He argued that there are two contradictions to religious freedom in the German state. First, there is the matter of divided loyalties: either one is a citizen or a Jew (or Christian, or whatever) first; since religion claims a deeper loyalty, there may come a time when one has to oppose one's citizenly duties to fulfill one's religious ones; hence one cannot have religious freedom within a modern civil state. The second contradiction is that civil society of the modern state requires a separation between political or public interest and private interest (e.g., private property ownership). But the two interests can also motivate individuals in opposing ways. Hence one cannot be a free citizen, since carrying out one's duties as citizens will sometimes require one to violate one's private rights. Once religion is placed in the sphere of the private, the first contradiction folds into the second (Marx 1978, 35). Although this early essay is rather vague about what real emancipation is supposed to be, the communitarian vision of the later Marx suggested a melting of the public/private distinction, combined with overcoming all religion.

A third psychological harm of oppression that Marx highlighted is false consciousness. Although false consciousness has come to connote the general phenomenon of mistaking the contingent, social construction of oppressive conditions for objectively necessary, natural (and so justifiable) conditions, Marx's most detailed discussion of the phenomenon centers on the case of "commodity fetishism." Under capitalism, according to Marx, people are confused about the nature of commodities and commodity exchange, and they come to see the commodity as a fetish, or an object of unreasonable attraction. First, people miss the social and coercive aspect of the production relationship in capitalism, seeing it as an objective fact about the human condition. The market is supposed to be free from government intervention, and hence what happens within it, including the formation of an underclass, is the result of unfettered competition, in which the most able win out. Second, people come to confuse the social relations among them as residing in the commodities themselves. Under capitalism commodities are produced by independent producers whose actions are coordinated by the market, that is, the exchange of commodities. The value of one's labor power, and hence one's social position in capitalism, is determined by the value of the commodities one produces. Thus, social relations between persons are determined by the commodities, or by the invisible hand of the market. As Marx put it, capitalism makes for "material relations between persons and social relations between things" (Marx 1978, 321), which is backwards.

Our understanding of commodities constitutes a *fetish* because the commodity itself appears to be a being apart from its producers. This mistake arises from the use value/exchange value separation: "whenever, by an exchange, we equate as values our different products, by that very act, we also equate, as human labor, the different kinds of labor expended on them" (Marx and Engels 1978, 322). So the only value of one's labor is what it can fetch in the market, and this is determined by the almighty commodity, or rather the "money-form."

False consciousness under capitalism masks the oppressive exploitation in capitalist production relations. Previous forms of economic organization, for example, slavery and serfdom, laid bare their exploitative relations. If you were a slave you were a thing exchanged, you understood very well that you were being exploited. Under serfdom, the basic economic relationship was bondage of the serf to the feudal lord. You gave him some of your labor hours, or else you paid him in kind. Under capitalism, however, everyone is free to dispose of their property and labor power as they see fit. All markets are supposed to be free. However, Marx showed that in reality the labor market is a source of exploitation. Workers produce surplus value that they cannot realize, since they do not own the means of production. Because they do not own the means, they must go to the capitalist and sell their labor, and this fact perpetuates the class system of capitalism. But in fact the freedom of the market is not complete. There must also be an element of coercion in order to explain why surplus value does not disappear as more firms enter the market and bid for the workers to realize some of their surplus value. Certain kinds of coercion are permitted, and other kinds prohibited. For example, the governmental control of unions and strikes, and restriction of credit, what counts as theft, anti-trust, insider information, all are rigged to maintain the capitalist class system.

Under capitalism, what are actually contingent bourgeois economic categories such as price, supply and demand, free market, and private property appear to be necessary elements of any economy. Furthermore, rationality, to a bourgeois economist, has only to do with maximizing expected utility subject to one's budget constraints. But rationality might easily be thought to include morality, community, or something other than the race for more commodity consumption. Thus, under capitalism we are confused about what is necessary and what is contingent, and about what constitutes valuable ways to consider the world and its possibilities for us as rational, social beings. Marx thus recognized several psychological harms perpetrated by the capitalist economic system. As Marx wrote about them, they are mainly cognitive harms, or confusions, rather than affective ones, or emotional agitations. However, it is not too much of a stretch to argue that to confuse social problems for one's own personal failings leads to low self-esteem, hopelessness, and despair.

Although Marx moves us in the right direction from Hegel toward seeing material oppression as fundamental to oppression, his theory of alienation is also limited. First, it addresses only economic class issues. Although subsequent Marxists have attempted to argue that other forms of oppression, such as racial and gender oppression, are reducible to class oppression, these reductions are unpersuasive (Hartmann 1979). Marx and Engels themselves, as we noted above, at times recognized that the oppression of women pre-dated class oppression.[4] Second, Marx's theory has been shown in practical application to be insufficiently appreciative of the need for liberal human rights. Although it is surely unfair to judge much of Marx's theory by the failures of the Communist states of the twentieth century, it is I think right to suggest that his inattention to liberal rights, such as freedom of expression and assembly and the need for democratic government, is partly responsible for the horrible abuses of those failed systems.

At root the problem with both the Hegelian and Marxist approaches to op-pression is that they fail to take individuals seriously. This flaw is both a moral and a theoretical one. Theoretically both are concerned with the collective struggles and movements of social groups, but they fail to show how individuals are motivated to make the small motions that add up to the collective ones. This might be an ac-ceptable kind of social theory if it we did not take individuals to be morally primary, and so consider the outcomes for groups to be of greater moral significance than outcomes for individuals. I can see no good argument for such a claim. Rather, the fact that it is individuals who feel pain and pleasure, who triumph and suffer, who die and give birth gives us reason to hold them primary to the groups of which they are members. This claim, that individuals are morally primary, is the liberal view.

1.3.3. MILL'S LIBERAL THEORY OF THE OPPRESSION OF WOMEN

While Marx founded the economic inequality strain of distributive theories of op-pression, Mill's analysis of oppression founded the legal and social inequality strain of the distributive theory of oppression. While Marx took oppression to follow on unequal distribution of the means of production, Mill took unequal distribution of legal rights to be the root cause of oppression. Mill's theory of oppression is naturally closely related to his theory of freedom or liberty, and in turn, his theory of the good. Oppression is fundamentally a denial of equal liberty, which for Mill is the denial of the opportunity to develop one's higher capacities for progressive thought and ac-tion. In Mill's view, we are all naturally motivated to seek our own happiness, but happiness is best sought by seeking to cultivate higher pleasures, the pleasures of the intellect. If we were fully informed, then we would want to do those things that cultivate the intellect, no matter what we may think we want or appear to want. Hence, for Mill, oppression cannot be truly voluntarily submitted to. If it appears that someone is voluntarily submitting to oppression, then either the coercion is not apparent to the observer, or the victim voluntarily submits out of enforced ignorance to the harmfulness or the wrongness of her treatment, or she is not truly being wronged, but is seeking to fulfill herself in the best way she can. Distinguishing which case we have in any particular situation is, of course, very difficult. In the case of slavery, Mill argued that the state ought to prevent individuals from voluntarily submitting. The case of women's inequality is less clear, however. Although he argues for equal political rights, Mill believed that the maintenance of separate spheres for women and men, where women run the household and men the public world, are appropriate and, we can infer, not oppressive. I shall argue in chapter 5 that this is not the case—such separate spheres are inevitably unequal.

Mill, in *The Subjection of Women* ([1869] 1988), provided the first contemporary liberal account of a case of oppression. He concentrated on answering the question, why do women appear to voluntarily submit to oppression? First, Mill showed how oppressors create (actual and alleged) shortcomings and faults in their victims through a combination of force, terror, and unequal opportunity to develop their talents (Mill 1988, esp. ch. 2). Then he discussed how oppressors manufacture and use these perceived faults or shortcomings of the oppressed to justify inequalities

(Mill 1988, esp. ch. 3). Their inferiority makes their subsequent unequal treatment appear justified, even protective. Second, he showed how law creates social conditions of inequality that belie their origin in the law.

> Laws and systems of polity always begin by recognizing the relations they find already existing between individuals. They convert what was a mere physical fact into a legal right, give it the sanction of society, and principally aim at the substitution of public and organized means of asserting and protecting these rights, instead of the irregular and lawless conflict of physical strength. (Mill 1988, 5)

Mill focuses on marriage and property laws that reduce women's abilities to leave or to negotiate greater freedom. He then shows how women and men have adapted to these conditions in ways that seem to justify the laws: Women become specialists in private domestic affairs and cultivate a moral sensibility appropriate to that realm, while men learn to compete in public life and to cultivate their sense of justice. Then, because men's moral sensibilities are more appropriately suited to guiding public political affairs, laws restricting women's participation in public affairs appear to be justified.

> all the education which women receive from society inculcates on them the feeling that the individuals connected with them are the only ones to whom they owe any duty—the only ones whose interest they are called upon to care for; while, as far as education is concerned, they are left strangers even to the elementary ideas which are presupposed in any intelligent regard for the larger interests or higher moral objects. The complaint against them resolves itself merely into this, that they fulfil only too faithfully the sole duty which they are taught, and almost the only one which they are permitted to practise. (Mill 1988, 83)

Third, Mill showed how the attitudes and desires of the oppressed are manipulated by the conditions of their oppression so that they appear voluntarily to accept their own oppression. People raise their daughters to be as content as possible with the given conditions. They believe in the naturalness of the inferiority and consequent subordination of women to men. Thus, like Marx, Mill explained how false consciousness (though this is not his term) can take hold on the oppressed. While for Marx the naturalness of the economic system convinces (most) workers that their oppression is also natural (and so justified), for Mill the naturalness of the gender system likewise convinces (most) women to acquiesce in their (apparent) fate.

Mill's theory of oppression as presented in the *Subjection of Women* makes a powerful case for the claim that women have suffered systematic injustice. However, as a general theory of oppression, it has some limitations. First, and most obviously, it is limited to the case of women. There are several reasons for thinking that this limitation is not simply nominal. Mill himself claimed that the case of women is different from all other cases of political oppression because of its universality and because it is exercised over intimates. His work focuses on family relations, divorce and inheritance laws, and gender norms, and these are specifically relevant to women's oppression. A general theory of oppression will have to explain how institutions more generally create unjust harms for groups of people. Second, Mill placed the emphasis on legal inequality and its consequences, not fully recognizing less subtle barriers to liberation. Mill upholds the traditional division of sex roles in the family, believing that women will freely choose the domestic life of housewife and mother. Although he argues that women should have the right to own property, he fails to see that the separation of public and private spheres and women's confinement to the private, even if freely chosen, will inevitably lead to great economic inequality between men and women. Again because his case is the case of women, he underplayed (although he did not entirely ignore) the explicit use of force for a general theory of oppression. But even in the case of women, Mill also failed to appreciate the degree to which social norms are entrenched outside the legal structure.[5] In the succeeding century we have had the opportunity to observe how difficult it is to end women's oppression through mainly legal means. A general theory of oppression will need to address the extra-legal material and social psychological forces that reinforce and maintain oppression.

1.3.4. FREUD'S INFLUENCE ON CONTEMPORARY THEORIES OF OPPRESSION

As a final note on the influences of nineteenth-century theories on twentieth-century theories of oppression, Freud's psychoanalytic theory must be mentioned. Psychoanalysis has been used to attempt to explain the origin and nature of oppression as a psychological phenomenon. However, Freud himself cannot be seen as offering a theory of oppression because in his view the psychosexual developments that lead to the kinds of harms that we might term "oppression" are biologically determined. This is especially true in the case of women. Hence, they are not unjust but at worst unfortunate facts of nature. Women's inequality simply reflects their psychological and physical inferiority. Nonetheless, as we shall see, Freud's psychoanalytic approach and the idea of the unconscious have been enormously influential for twentieth-century social theorists.

Let us summarize the contributions of nineteenth-century thinkers on the conceptualization of oppression. To the description of oppression, the idea of psychological harms was added. Among the most important of these are disrespect (Hegel) and false consciousness (Marx and Mill). Additional possible victims were identified, especially genders and economic classes. New questions were explored: Who benefits from oppression? How do institutional structures of oppression form? And new methodologies for examining oppression were employed, including classical economic theory, psychoanalysis, and utilitarian moral theory.

1.4. Further Conceptual Developments in the Twentieth Century

In the twentieth century we see the concept of oppression further broadened in terms of the specification of its victims and its effects. Following Marx's emphasis on the economic system and Mill's emphasis on unequal rights for men and women, Charlotte Perkins Gilman, in *Women and Economics*, echoing Mary Wollstonecraft, wrote of the "sexuo-economic" system that oppresses women by constraining their economic options to the sexual servitude of men and thereby over-exaggerating and over-exciting their sexual natures (Gilman 1966). Simone de Beauvoir, in *The Second Sex*, offered the most comprehensive analysis of a single case of oppression. She analyzed the oppression of women as a comprehensive economic, political, psychological, and sexual domination of women by men, through an examination of possible explanations of its origins, and its manifestations and effects through history. Frantz Fanon applied psychoanalytic theory to his analysis of colonial imperialism, which he considered the paradigmatic form of oppression. Oppression, he argued, always involves violence, either direct or indirect, where by indirect violence he meant severe material deprivation, such as controlling the economy and paying only subsistence wages. Because of the psychological consequences of that violence, Fanon argued, only violent response can free the victims from their psychological oppression.

Since the 1970s social theorists and political philosophers have focused on a number of cases of oppression and have provided limited accounts of those phenomena. The women's movement and the rise of feminist theory have resulted in theories of women's oppression that trace their methodological and conceptual roots to Hegel, Marx, and Mill, as well as psychoanalytic explanations. In the Hegelian tradition of oppression as a failure of recognition, there are Cynthia Willett, Iris Marion Young, Sandra Bartky, and Nancy Fraser. In the Marxist tradition of oppression as a failure of economic equality, we find Ann Ferguson, Heidi Hartmann, and Nancy Hartsock. More recently, Susan Moller Okin and Martha Nussbaum follow the Millian tradition of seeing oppression as primarily a failure of legal equality, but with a more nuanced understanding of how the entrenchment of social norms prevents women from attaining real, material equality. And finally, Nancy Chodorow and Dorothy Dinnerstein offer psychoanalytic theories of women's oppression.

Several other cases of oppression are the focus of contemporary social concern. Oppression of racial and ethnic minorities has inspired a large literature, particularly the treatment of African slaves and their descendants, dating back to the nineteenth century. The Holocaust made the oppression of Jews highly salient. Oppression of sexual minorities, including gays, lesbians, bisexuals, and transsexuals, is now a topic of broad concern. Finally, the treatment of the disabled by the able-bodied, the elderly by the middle-aged, and children by adults have each been called cases of oppression.

Following Hegel, this century has developed and emphasized the notion that oppression can have significant psychological effects both on individuals and on the oppressed groups to which they belong. Antonio Gramsci developed the concept of hegemony to analyze the domination of the consciousness of others. And numerous contemporary thinkers theorize oppression as a problem of misrecognition, dehumanization, or a failure of cultural respect (Friere 1970; Clatterbaugh 1996; Willett 1995; Young 1990). Other radical theories are more concerned about the economic distributive aspects of oppression. Catharine MacKinnon's theory of women's oppression likewise is a distributive theory that follows on both Marx and Mill. Oppression in these theories is both an economic constraint and a psychologically degrading and distorting force on women as a group. Finally, liberal political theorists, insofar as they treat aspects of oppression at all, tend to give distributive accounts.

The concept of oppression thus began its life denoting the arbitrary and unjust material harms by a ruler on his or her subjects. As liberalism and democracy advanced to enfranchise more social categories of persons, the concept came to connote a wider range of harms by a wider range of persons. In the nineteenth century, oppression was used more often to refer to harms of one social group by another, including psychological harms, such as failures to recognize or respect persons, and material harms consequent on unequal distribution of social resources and legal rights. As political philosophers began to take note of the injustices of sexism, colonialism, and capitalism, and the oppressed to demand their rights, oppression took on the connotation of cultural domination. By the late twentieth century, we had come to use "oppression" to refer to unjust violence, and economic, social, political, and psychological injustices suffered by a wide variety of social groups. These cases include: colonial natives, racial and ethnic minorities, religious minorities, gays and lesbians, and the disabled. To the questions posed by previous thinkers, the twentieth-century work adds this: Who really is oppressed? Are we all oppressed? Is cultural domination a kind of oppression? And to the methodologies employed, it adds deconstruction or cultural analysis, psychoanalysis, and neo-classical economic theory.

Amidst the competing theories, examples, and explanations of oppression, a consensus has been forged on the idea that oppression comes out of unjust social and political institutions.[6] "Institution" refers to formal and informal social structures and constraints, such as law, convention, norms, practices, and the like. As we saw, in the early period of liberal thought, illegitimate or unauthorized government was seen as the primary vehicle of oppression. Later, in the nineteenth century, other cultural institutions such as religion, economic structures, and social mores were also seen as potential (or even inevitable) causes of oppression. In this century we have seen how social groups, with the explicit purpose of imposing their cultural values or expectations on minority cultures, oppress the members of those minority cultures through domination of such social institutions as the media and popular or high culture. In each case, these are seen by social theorists who write about oppression as injustices that act through our social institutions. The basic flaw in oppressive institutions is that they fail to treat individuals as moral equals; they harm some by allowing others systematic, unfair power and advantage. While social institutions may have other flaws, such as inefficiency or instability, and some may even be matters of injustice, oppression overshadows these in moral terms. Furthermore, it is often the oppressiveness of an institution that causes either its instability or its inefficiency, making oppression also causally primary. Oppression, we can now say, is the fundamental injustice of social institutions.

2. Analyzing Oppression

The task of this book is to provide a comprehensive analysis of oppression conceived as the fundamental injustice of social institutions. In order to begin a systematic analysis of any concept, the theorist must consider the criteria of adequacy that any such an analysis ought to meet. First, an adequate analysis of oppression provides a clear and coherent definition of oppression and conditions to pick out the right cases of oppression. Second, a general analysis of oppression has to answer the general questions and give some guidance for answering questions about specific cases. The main questions that a comprehensive, general theory of oppression must answer are these:

- Who really is oppressed? Who benefits from oppression, if anyone?
- How does oppression originate?
- How does oppression endure over time (in spite of human's rough natural equality)?
- How do institutional structures of oppression form?
- Is oppression an inevitable feature of civil society?
- How can oppression be overcome?

Of these, I take the most difficult and interesting of these questions to be what I will call the endurance question: *How does oppression endure over time in spite of human's rough natural equality?* Our answer to this question will inform our answers to the others. To answer this question theorists have always had to show how the oppressed are induced to participate in their own oppression rather than resist it. So, for instance, Rousseau claimed that vanity perverts persons' desires, so that they prefer material goods to freedom. Hegel claimed that it is capitulation in the face of death. Marx wrote about how the oppressed come under the sway of "false consciousness" and are motivated to participate in the economy out of fear of starvation. And Mill claimed that it is the force of social mores that indoctrinate us into our society's traditions from childhood. I believe that none of these are adequate answers, though each contains a grain of truth.

The third criterion of adequacy for a theory of oppression is that it must point in the direction of a resolution or a reduction of oppression. I take this to be a necessary criterion because oppression is, by my definition, an injustice caused by (at least in part) social institutions. If the theory cannot provide a means by which oppression can be reduced, then either the theory must deny that it is unjust (perhaps locating the harm in a natural and inevitable feature of humans) or fail to give an adequate causal account of its maintenance. Such a theory would be pointless to pursue.[7]

These classical theories of oppression fail to provide theoretically sound or practically useful theories. Both Marx and Hegel make the classic mistakes of collectivist and functionalist theories. Hegel, as I have argued, posits a vague and ambiguous "collective Spirit," which is not only ontologically weird, but fails to provide us with a practical direction for resolving oppression. What, exactly, are we supposed to do to move in the direction of absolute Spirit? What practical steps can we take to advance mutual recognition? Both Hegel and Marx claim that some future, less oppressive social form is inevitable. But what can the individual do to help bring it about? Rousseau and Mill, on the other hand, make classic individualist mistakes. Their individualist theories fail to explain at a social level what has gone wrong and tend to lay blame too much on the individual. But it is implausible to suppose that oppression can be overcome by an act of will on the part of a few individuals.[8] What is needed is an explanatory framework that can explain the social phenomenon of oppression and yet posits mechanisms through which the social phenomena work at the individual level. We need a theory that seeks to explain how the social supervenes on the individual, without reducing the social to the individual. This would give us a theory that is both more theoretically plausible and satisfying, and more politically useful.

In the remainder of this book I aim to present a theory of oppression that explains how it can be fundamentally a social phenomenon, yet does not deny that the social forces that create oppression work through individual persons. In particular, I shall argue that the oppressed are co-opted through their own short-run rational choices to reinforce the long-run oppression of their social group. I will present what I call a social force analysis of oppression, wherein the forces are the motivational factors leading the oppressed to acquiesce to their condition. I will argue that there are two main kinds of forces: material, acting through violence and economic need, and psychological, acting through cognitive and affective mechanisms.

Some questions, such as, what is the origin of oppression, may not admit of general answers. But an adequate analysis of oppression will suggest some natural places to look for an explanation in particular cases. Yet this question is less crucial to answer than the question of how it is currently maintained, if what we are after is a theory that helps us to eradicate current oppression.

As oppression is a social phenomenon, an adequate, scientific analysis of oppression appeals to the best social science available, and not to intuitive or empirically inadequate methods. Because of this criterion, many of the twentieth-century theories of oppression have to be discarded. As I shall argue in chapter 3, psychoanalytic theory and the Hegelian recognition theory are inadequate psychological theories for explaining anything, and there exists an empirically adequate and theoretically coherent alternative explanatory methodology, namely social cognition theory. In employing this psychological theory, my account of oppression is, I think, unique. Likewise, this criterion tells against classical or Marxist economic theories, except as the latter have been reinterpreted and remodeled on the basis of modern economic and game theory. My analysis of the material forces of oppression in chapter 5 will employ game theory, especially bargaining theory, and other concepts from neoclassical economic theory and institutional economics.

The psychological and economic theories must be fully consistent with each other, and they have to be able to explain all the psychological and economic manifestations of various cases of oppression. In this context I shall distinguish between psychological and material forces of oppression, where the psychological forces primarily affect the cognitive and affective functioning of individuals, and only secondarily through these affect the material well-being of individuals, while material forces affect primarily material well-being and only secondarily psychological well-being.

Finally, the psychological and economic theories must provide both a macro analysis at the social level, and a micro analysis at the individual level that shows how the aggregate individual effects cause the macro phenomena. This criterion requires the theory to pay attention to the way that the causal chain links up at different levels. If it appeals to a social force, then how does that force come about? The theory must tell us how individual thoughts and actions come together to create those forces, though, and it does not require that the individuals must intend to cooperate to form those forces.

3. Toward a Definition: Conceptual Distinctions

As I will use the term, "oppression" names a harm through which groups of persons are systematically and unfairly or unjustly constrained, burdened, or reduced by any of several forces. Oppression is a normative concept that names a social *injustice*. Oppression is always wrong; one cannot coherently speak of justified oppression, though some forces that characteristically comprise oppression may in some instances be justifiable. For instance, one might be degraded and humiliated by one's own actions while on a drinking binge, but such harms would be entirely consequent on one's own actions and hence not in any sense unjustified. In this way, oppression is different from some of the harms I named at the outset, such as punishing or exploiting, which are not always wrong. Further, oppression cannot be just any denial of freedom (Bay 1981), since some constraints on one's freedom are natural or social but not unjust. Thus, to make a claim of oppression is to show that the harms involved are unjustified, or correlatively, to show that some harms are justified is to show that they are not oppressive.

To say that oppression is a *social* injustice is to say that it is perpetrated through social institutions, practices, and norms on social groups by social groups. In this way oppression differs from many kinds of injustices that can be done to individuals as well as to social groups. One can be enslaved as an individual or as a member of a social group, as one can be unjustly exploited as an individual or as a member of a social group. Since oppression is a kind of social injustice, an injustice suffered by whole groups of persons, it often wrongs widely and deeply.

Although oppression afflicts whole groups of persons, it is fundamentally the individuals in those groups who suffer. I do not claim that groups are suprapersonal entities that can suffer harm, although that would be a natural misinterpretation of what I have said so far. In chapter 2 I present my theory of social groups, and there it will be clear that social groups are aggregates of individuals, though of a special, non-accidental, sort. Thus, I will argue that it is individuals who suffer the injustices of oppression, though they can do so only as members of social groups. It is because humans sort themselves into social groups and find it nearly impossible as well as undesirable to extract themselves from social groups that they can oppress each other.

To avoid another misunderstanding, I must next distinguish between subjective and objective oppression. Subjective oppression concerns the judgment or feeling by a person or persons that he or she or they are oppressed, that is, systematically and unjustly harmed as a member of a group. To feel oppressed one need not even be able to name the source of suffering as "oppression"; one could simply feel a burden and feel it as unjust. Objective oppression concerns the *fact* of oppression. Objective and subjective oppression are analytically separable: One can be objectively oppressed and not know it or feel it (thus not be subjectively oppressed), and one can judge wrongly or misperceive that one is oppressed, thus being subjectively but not objectively oppressed. In this book I am concerned mainly with objective oppression, and with subjective oppression only as it follows upon objective oppression. Thus, when I refer to oppression *simpliciter* I will mean objective oppression that may or may not be accompanied by subjective oppression for the victims.

Another distinction that I will draw that should not be confused for the subjective/objective one is the distinction between psychological oppression and material oppression. Psychological oppression occurs when one is oppressed through one's mental states, emotionally or by manipulation of one's belief states, so that one is psychologically stressed, reduced in one's own self-image, or otherwise psychically harmed. Material oppression occurs when one's physical being is harmed by oppression, or one's material resources, including wealth, income, access to health care, or rights to inhabit physical space, are reduced by oppression. Either form of oppression may be subjectively recognized or not by its victims. And, as I shall argue in this book, psychological and material oppression mutually cause and exacerbate the effects of each other.

Contemporary accounts of oppression sometimes attempt to define oppression by the harms that the oppressed suffer. Kenneth Clatterbaugh (1996) usefully distinguishes among four kinds of theories of oppression according to the harm suffered by the oppressed. Psychological theories postulate that oppression is mainly an internal state or feeling. Clatterbaugh rightly rejects this theory because it suggests that the proper solution to the problem is individual therapy rather than social revolution. I would add that it does not allow us to distinguish subjective from objective oppression, or the mere feeling of being oppressed from actual oppression. Inequality theories hold that oppression consists in a group's being denied access to some scarce and valued resources. Clatterbaugh rejects this kind of theory on the ground that it does not allow us to distinguish legitimate from illegitimate inequalities. Similarly, limitation theories hold that oppression consists in some limitation of opportunities, and it suffers from the similar drawback that some limitations are justifiable. Finally Clatterbaugh defends a dehumanization theory of oppression. According to this kind of theory, "oppression is the systematic dehumanization of an identifiable target human group. To dehumanize a group is to deny that the members of that group possess the complete range of human abilities, needs, and wants that are valued at that time as important to a human being" (Clatterbaugh 1996, 295). However, he goes on to qualify "a group is not oppressed if there are qualities included in being a human being that are denied them and that they in fact lack" (Clatterbaugh 1996, 295). This qualification is necessary in order to avoid the analogous problem to the ones he identified in the limitation and inequality theories: Some kinds of "dehumanization" may in fact be justified. But the qualification contains an admission that leaves this theory vulnerable to another kind of criticism. Many abilities that we consider important human abilities, a sense of justice or of compassion, an ability to reason, for instance, are socially learned. But if they are socially learned, then the social teaching can be denied. If an ability is considered an essential one to full human status, then it is likely to be denied to the oppressed. Thus, the oppressed might in fact lack some ability, the lack of which objectively degrades them. It was widely held in Mill's time, and he admitted as much, that women lacked a sense of public justice, and thus were not well suited for public life. But Mill was also quick to point out that women were denied the opportunity to develop their sense of public justice, and this denial constituted their oppression (Mill 1988, 83, 90).

What we can learn from Clatterbaugh's work is that oppression cannot be characterized by the harms consequent on it alone. These harms must also be unjustly inflicted. But to see whether harms are unjust, one needs to examine the causal mechanisms by which the oppressed come to suffer them. A comprehensive account of oppression has to characterize not only the harms of oppression, but also the causes of those harms. Thus, my account of oppression will concentrate on how the oppressed come to suffer inequality, limitation, and dehumanization, among many other harms.

In the view of oppression that I will present, for every social group that is oppressed there are correlative social groups whose members benefit, materially or psychologically, from this oppression. I will call the groups whose members gain from the increased prestige and social privileges that their membership confers on them "privileged groups," but this is not to assert that a majority of persons in those groups perpetrate oppression intending to gain unjustly from their actions (or omissions). Even if one is a member of a privileged group, one need not oneself be an oppressor, in my view. One could, for instance, struggle against the social system from which one gains through one's group membership, even if one is powerless to renounce that membership. When John Stuart Mill married Harriet Taylor, for example, he asserted that he renounced his privileges as husband, but in fact he could not do so legally. Were their marriage to have broken down, his legal rights including those he had attempted to renounce would have been upheld by the society. To be an oppressor, according to the view that I will elaborate and defend in chapter 7, one needs to be a member of a privileged group, to gain from oppression of another social group, to intend to so gain, and to act to realize that intention by contributing to the oppression of the oppressed group from whose oppression one gains.

Summarizing these remarks gives us the following definition. Oppression names a circumstance in which four conditions are satisfied:

1. *The harm condition:* There is a harm that comes out of an institutional practice.
2. *The social group condition:* The harm is perpetrated through a social institution or practice on a social group whose identity exists apart from the oppressive harm in (1).
3. *The privilege condition:* There is another social group that benefits from the institutional practice in (1).
4. *The coercion condition:* There is unjustified coercion or force that brings about the harm.

These conditions, I claim, are jointly necessary and sufficient for oppression. My definition resembles Marilyn Frye's (1983) analysis in her classic piece "Oppression" in several respects. In particular, Frye recognizes the first three conditions. The fourth condition, however, is left implicit in her analysis. Rather than looking for coercion, she asks us to investigate who benefits from the social limiting practice. To avoid the objections to Clatterbaugh's limitation theory, we must look not for harm but for unjustly inflicted harm, and it is important, therefore, to make this condition explicit.

Iris Marion Young (1990) has argued that "oppression" cannot be seen as a single, unified phenomenon because attempting to do so inevitably leads to either a reduction of all cases to oppression to a single kind of oppression (e.g., the Marxist reduction of oppression of women to class oppression) or exclusion of some cases that ought to be termed oppression. I intend to do neither: I want to maintain that there are irreducible forms of oppression, and I want to provide criteria that pick out all and only the oppressed groups. Can oppression be treated as a univocal concept? Is the oppression of women the same kind of phenomenon as the oppression of blacks or the oppression of Jews or the oppression of homosexuals? I will argue there is a univocal concept: Although there are great differences in the origins of oppression of and its effects on different groups, each of these oppressions shares a set of features. Such an account will allow us to judge in new cases whether oppression is going on, or some other sort of injustice or justifiable harm. In addition to that theoretical reason, a reason for pursuing a univocal theory of oppression is to provide a common ground for persons of many different oppressed groups.[9]

The main thesis of the book is that oppression is an institutionally structured harm perpetrated on groups by other groups using direct and indirect material and psychological forces that violate justice. I shall argue that material forces, by which I mean physical violence and economic domination, initiate a vicious cycle of harm that subjugates the oppressed to one or more privileged groups. These forces work in part by coercing the oppressed to act in ways that further their own oppression. Direct forces externally affect the choices of individuals, while indirect forces shape the background social beliefs and desires with which we perceive and behave toward others. The most important and insidious of these indirect forces is an economic force that acts by means of the oppressed persons' own preferences and rational choices. Psychological forces, both direct and indirect, reinforce and secure oppressive institutions.

Just as important as the content of my theory is the argumentative methodology that it employs and tradition of political philosophy from which it derives. While current philosophical analyses of oppression use psychoanalytic, Marxist, and Hegelian arguments and traditions, this book uses current social science, in the form of cognitive psychology and modern economic theory, and situates itself in the Anglo-American tradition of liberal political philosophy. The book attempts to demonstrate that liberal political philosophy and social scientific methodologies that have been assumed to be purely individualistic can not only countenance oppression but can give us the tools to understand it and to combat it.

4. Plan of the Book

Since in my view oppression is the fundamental injustice of social institutions, in chapter 2 I present my account of social institutions. The central challenge of this chapter is to set out a conception of social groups that takes both individuals, their moral rights as well as their epistemic and axiological primacy, and social groups, especially their profound influence on individuals' beliefs and actions, seriously. Chapter 3 presents the cognitive psychological theory that explains how humans form and maintain social groups. Part II of the book discusses the three social forces of oppression. I argue that there are two main types of material forces of oppression, violence and economic deprivation, and that oppression cannot survive without being enforced by at least one of these material ways of harming persons. I then separate violence from economic deprivation in order to illustrate how different cases of oppression involve different kinds of reinforcements and argue that they will require different strategies of resistance. Chapter 4 develops a definition of violence and examines cases in the world of oppression enforced by violence. Chapter 5 argues that economic oppression is central to all forms of oppression and to the answer to the fundamental questions I have set out in this introductory chapter. I discuss both direct and indirect forms of economic oppression and argue that indirect economic oppression helps explain how the oppressed can be co-opted into participating in their own oppression. In chapter 6 I discuss and illustrate the psychological harms and consequent reinforcement of oppression. Part III takes up the challenge of overcoming oppression. In chapter 7 I discuss resistance strategies that have been or might be employed by the oppressed and argue that while the main responsibility for fighting oppression rests with the privileged, there is some moral obligation on the part of the oppressed to resist oppression. I also discuss how legal theory might take a greater account of oppression within a liberal legal system. In chapter 8 I argue that overcoming oppression in many cases, especially in the cases that are long-standing and reinforced mainly through the actions of the oppressed—what I will call the indirect forces of oppression—requires re-envisioning social groups and the nature of freedom and equality. I end the book with my own vision of how securing freedom from oppression for women would change the social world.

2

Social Groups and Institutional Constraints

The previous chapter sharpened the concept of oppression. Oppression, I claimed, is an institutionally structured, unjust harm perpetrated on groups by other groups through direct and indirect material and psychological forces. This chapter sets the stage for the explanation of oppression that will come in the following chapters, which use economic and psychological models, by analyzing the notion of a social group that can be an oppressed or an oppressor group, and the notion of an institutionally structured constraint on action. These two theoretical entities, social groups and institutionally structured constraints, play essential roles in my analysis of oppression. Yet positing their existence may seem to some, particularly to adherents of methodological individualism, to be a fatal flaw in any theory of human behavior. Liberals may also view my apparent appeal to collectivism as a betrayal of individual morality. In this chapter I characterize social groups and institutions in a way that meets the plausible objections of individualists, yet allows me to give a social explanation of oppression.

1. Explaining Human Behavior

Social science or social theory aims to make sense of human behavior. The first requirement of a scientific theory is that it be able coherently to fit the facts to the theory, in other words, that it be empirically adequate. But what that means for a particular theory depends on the question it is supposed to help us answer, the bit of behavior it is supposed to help us understand. In analyzing oppression, we begin with the understanding, developed in chapter 1, that we want to explain a social rather than a purely individual, biological, or physical phenomenon. That is, we want an explanation that helps us understand unjust group-based hierarchies. What we want to understand can be captured, as I argued in the previous chapter, by the following set of questions: How does oppression originate? How does oppression endure over time (in spite of human's rough natural equality)? How do institutional structures of oppression form? And how can oppression be overcome? That is, we want to know why some forms of social organization give rise to and then maintain oppression, and what would make that oppression end.

The framing of these questions and the purpose for which information is sought are important elements in judging the adequacy of the explanations offered. This point has been made by many philosophers of science in the past thirty years.[1] It can be made clear by comparing a few ways that the question of the origin of oppression could be answered. We could answer it by constructing a story of the evolution of a species capable of formulating concepts of justice and of violating them. Or we could answer it by constructing a story of how a particular society's forms of social organization give rise to an unjust domination of one group by another, where those particular forms of social organization do not exist in a different society in which the same pattern of unjust domination does not exist. The first of these proposed explanations does not meet our purposes, but might be otherwise scientifically adequate and true. That is, it might explain something, but not what we seek to explain. The point is that the explanation has to be relevant.

We want to answer these questions in ways that are not only relevant but also useful to us, in that the answers provide workable solutions to current social problems. The questions and the kinds of answers that I seek concerning oppression lead me to seek particular kinds of explanations. Not only must those explanations accord with observation (better than competing theories), and be relevant, they must also offer practical solutions. To draw an analogy with studying the physical world, suppose that what I want to understand is how this system of pilings, towers, wires, and roadway supports the traffic over this bridge span. This question might be answered at many levels of analysis, but if I want answers that help me make a better bridge, it is unlikely that answers that refer to quarks or gravitational forces exerted by distant stars will help me much.[2] Rather, I would need to refer to the forces exerted by cars, wind, and cable tension. Similarly, if I want to solve the problem of oppression, then theories that postulate as the fundamental units of analysis social groups, social institutions, and the relations among individuals that result from them are likely to be the right level to explore. As in engineering, however, it is often the case that going one level below the phenomenon that one is primarily interested in is an effective way to understand and manipulate it. Although engineers want to build good bridges and roadways, they often need to appeal to theories about the chemical and mechanical properties of asphalt, cement, steel, and so on to do so. So in a social theory of oppression, it is likely that appeal to a level of analysis just under that for which social groups and their members are the primary units will be useful.[3]

Social science or social theory offers three kinds of explanatory strategies: intentional explanations, subintentional explanations (including sociobiological or genetic explanations, subconscious cognitive, and psychoanalytic explanations), and supraintentional explanations.[4] I shall argue for an intentional explanation of oppression and supporting subintentional and supraintentional explanations that explain how the relevant intentions are formed and how persons' intentional actions collectively constrain the formation of subsequent intentions.

A supraintentional explanation posits forces working at the level of groups or collectives of persons that determine the course of human history. Dialectical theories such as Marx's or Hegel's theories of history are the prime examples of supraintentional social theories, but contemporary social sciences often make some appeals to some supraintentional forces as well.[5] I reject this as my explanatory strategy for a theory of oppression, given my purposes here, because it will not help us to understand human behavior in a way that is practical or useful. On a dialectical theory, historical events are inevitable in spite of individual action. Hence, it will be difficult to prescribe individual actions that might be useful in eradicating oppression. Furthermore, if we want to be able to assign moral responsibility for actions, we need an intentional account. However, I shall argue that we cannot come to any understanding of oppression as a socially structured phenomenon without making appeal to supraintentional social forces, either. Some philosophers argue that there are good ontological reasons to reject such forces (Elster 1983a). But recent debates in metaphysics and philosophy of science convince me that one's ontological beliefs should follow from the explanatory theories one accepts rather than the reverse (Quine 1969; Churchland 1982). If the best explanatory theory appeals to some theoretical entity, that gives us the best reasons we can have for positing the existence of that entity. Nonetheless, I think that there are good explanatory reasons to reject supraintentional explanations.

I shall not pursue a sociobiological or genetic explanation of human behavior, though I think that there is a place for them in the explanation of the origin of oppression. My reason for declining to pursue a sociobiological account of oppression is that I doubt that sociobiology can give us precise enough explanations of any contemporary case of a social hierarchy for those explanations to point to a cure.[6] Sociobiology attempts to explain social regularities by showing that they are genetically adaptive. Cases of oppression are, for the most part, relative to a social context. One society condemns homosexuality, another does not. In one society persons with dark skin are oppressed, in another they are not. For such cases, the most that sociobiology could offer us is an explanation of the tendency to form of social hierarchies, not of any particular social hierarchy. While such an explanation could be interesting and useful for certain contexts, it would not offer us any assistance in either deciding whether a social hierarchy is unjust or eradicating it.

There are two plausible exceptions to the cultural relativity of social hierarchies, namely the subordinate status of women and disabled persons. Is it likely that sociobiology would give us useful explanations of (contemporary) oppression in either case? Since the theory cannot be expected to make normative judgments about justice, we can only ask that it explain the differential and objectively more onerous conditions for women or the disabled. First take the case of the arguably ubiquitous lower status and lesser life conditions of women.[7] Let us assume that the lower status and lesser life conditions are a result of or consist in the greater investment that women almost universally make in caring and other altruistic activities. A sociobiologist cannot explain this based on the male/female sex differentiation generally, since there are plenty of animal species in which the females devote less of their time to altruistic species duties such as rearing the young. Sociobiology or evolutionary psychology explains sex differences by the differential investment in gamete (egg and sperm) production in females and males. But this cannot explain differences in rearing practices if in some species males rear young, in some females do, and in some both do. So the explanation will have to refer to features that are unique to the human species, or at least shared only by species whose female members live (on average) similarly lesser individual lives. First, the sociobiologist must determine the actual biological differences between human males and females, separating out the culturally imposed ones. Then, given these presumed facts, the sociobiologist has to show why it is adaptive for humans to organize in such a way that males dominate over females. Sociobiologists cannot appeal to some merely average biological difference between men and women, if there is a great overlap in that attribute in the two sexes, since that would predict a hierarchy that cuts across sex. If the swiftest are needed for hunting, for example, then it should be the swiftest, not the men, who hunt. While men are on average swifter than women, plenty of women are swifter than plenty of men. Furthermore, since the domination of human males over human females is most immediately caused by the sharp division of labor by sex found in every society, the sociobiologist must show that division of labor by sex is adaptive. Suppose that this can be shown (which, given the efficiency of some sort of division of labor, is not unlikely). This is still not sufficient to explain the constancy of the hierarchy, since it then has to explain why the male sex roles always receive higher status, no matter what the role is. Sociobiologists cannot appeal to some objective value of the work done by each sex, since what counts as women's work or men's work differs greatly from society to society. In sum, sociobiology might (or might not) be able to explain the existence of a sexual division of labor, but it is unlikely that it can explain the constancy of the hierarchy of men over women. Yet it is precisely the hierarchy, that is, the existence of domination relations between the groups, which a theory of oppression has to account for.

Now consider the case of the disabled. The first problem to note is that what counts as disabled varies across societies. Dyslexia, for example, is not a disability in a culture without a written language. However, we could come up with a core set of disabilities that are universally counted as disability, such as mental retardation or limb paralysis. Some disabilities cut across the whole range of genetic endowments, since disability can as easily come from non-genetic causes (e.g., accident, non-heritable disease) as from genetic factors. Given this, it seems to me that the best explanation for their disadvantage relative to others in their society is economic—it costs more to care for or even accommodate them than to let them linger on the fringe or die. Of course, once a society has scruples about letting people with disabilities languish or die, then it often costs less to accommodate them. Either way, the best explanation of the treatment of the disabled is surely economic and moral, not sociobiological.

I also reject psychoanalytic explanations of human action, but I shall leave the argument for that rejection to chapter 3, where I compare it to the subintentional level explanatory theory that I accept, namely cognitive psychology. My main explanatory strategy is intentional, via rational choice theory. For my purposes, if an intentional explanation is theoretically and empirically satisfactory, then it is to be preferred to any other explanatory strategy on practical grounds. Intentional explanations follow roughly this form: A person (P) has a set of desires (D) and beliefs (B), which included the belief that an action (A) was the best (or a good enough) means to achieve all or some of D. Hence, P did A in order to bring about D. For the intentional explanation to be the right explanation there cannot be any intervening cause of the action, such as an involuntary twitch or unconscious desire that gives rise to the same behavior.[8] We are rarely able to look into the workings of the minds of agents to see if there are such intervening causes, however. Rational choice explanations add the assumption that the beliefs are substantively rational, that the desire set is not inconsistent, and that the action was optimal for achieving the agent's desires. These assumptions are clearly stronger than what is required for intentional explanation (Elster 1984, ch. 3).

Intentional explanations are commonplace in everyday life. Indeed, understanding each other in this way might even be said to be required in order to engage in everyday human conversation (Davidson 1984; Pettit and Smith 1996). We have lots of practice examining our own and each others' beliefs and desires; we have no trouble at all accepting that we are moved by them. And if we are convinced that we have our beliefs or desires wrong, we will, for the most part, attempt to change them.

One reason, then, to prefer intentional explanations of behavior is because they are relatively straightforward and simple. They are the stuff of everyday folk psychological explanations. The reason for preferring intentional explanations of oppressive behavior in particular is this. Suppose that we explain some aspect of social life as oppression that comes about as a result of actions $m_1, \ldots, m_n$. Now we see that $m_1, \ldots, m_n$ are in fact the means to some state s_1. But suppose that we can show with our moral and political theories that s_1 is unjust, and thus undesirable. So we have an argument for not doing $m_1, \ldots, m_n$. Of course, I do not believe that this will immediately result in our not doing $m_1, \ldots, m_n$, for there may be many who are unpersuaded by the claim of injustice, or on the whole not motivated to relieve the injustices, since the cost of doing so would be, in their judgment, too high. Furthermore, while the sequence $m_1, \ldots, m_n$ results in oppression, that does not entail that each of $m_1, \ldots, m_n$ are separately oppressive. But the point is that an intentional explanation gives us a place to start to resolve oppression. The same cannot be said for subintentional or supraintentional explanations, as they do not explain oppression by reference to individual human actions. But this is what we can most readily consciously manipulate (with some exceptions that I note later in this chapter in the section on institutional constraints on action). In order to resolve oppression that has been explained by either of these means, we must first translate the explanations somehow into individual action sequences to pursue. Then we still face the problem of motivating individuals to actually pursue these actions sequences, as in the intentional case. Hence the most immediate route to resolving oppression would be through an intentional explanation of it, if a valid one is available.

Although intentional explanations are most appealing for these theoretical and practical reasons, it is also crucial that our explanatory theory recognize the constraints within which individuals act. We act within constraints set by and respond to consequences of biological, psychological, and collectively socially generated (some intentionally and some unintentionally) facts about us and our future options. Contingent biological facts about us, features of our environment and our past histories, social norms for beliefs and desires that are common in our society and that we are taught to share from childhood, combine to form collective social facts within which we must act. But these constraints do not disable intentional explanations. They determine much of the content of our beliefs and desires within more or less narrow boundaries.

Biological facts, for instance, place only very broad constraints on beliefs and desires. For example, humans need about 2,000 calories per day, but there are indefinitely many different ways to achieve that. And the biological facts become less constraining as we make technological progress in manipulating our environment and our bodies, or social progress in conceiving a greater range of solutions.

Social factors place much more narrow constraints on our actions generally. Consider the diet example again. Although one way to achieve 2,000 calories would be to include pork in the diet, there are many cultures in which that is socially forbidden. Since social facts constrain actions so narrowly, social facts will be crucial variables in our explanatory theory of oppression. Among these constraining social facts are social institutions and social groups. But to a much greater degree than biological constraints, social constraints change over time. This suggests that our theory of oppression has to incorporate social facts as both endogenous and exogenous variables in the theory. Such a requirement may sound difficult if not impossible to satisfy. However, economic theory provides us with a model to follow in this regard. For it models short-run and long-run markets differently in just this way. While the number and productive technologies of firms are held to be exogenous in the short run, they are endogenous in the long-run model.

An objection to my proposal to include social groups among the variables in my explanatory theory comes from methodological individualists, who argue that since social groups are "nothing more" than groups of individuals, we ought not to construct theories that explain using social groups. I have two responses to this claim, the second of which I shall elaborate later in the chapter, once the concept of social group I am using is clear. First I want to point out that though I agree with the individualist who claims that social groups are nothing more than individuals and their interactions, the claim that we therefore must not posit social groups in our social theory does not follow. Even if we accept the possibility of ontological reduction of social groups to individuals and their actions, this does not imply that there can be no useful explanations at higher levels. To see this, consider an analogy from macroeconomics. There are many unreduced aggregate social facts that the economist makes use of in explaining and predicting the overall behavior of the economy, such as gross national product, inflation, unemployment, and the like. These quantities are clearly aggregates of individual goods bought and sold, prices for individual goods, persons employed and seeking jobs, etc. Yet, with them economists explain behavior such as the actions of the Federal Reserve Board chairman, the actions of individual investors in the stock market, or presidential election outcomes. What is more, these things cannot be explained by referring to the individual actions, prices, and so on because of the referential opacity, or intensionality, of those facts. That is, the Federal Reserve Board chairman and individual investors, and probably many voters as well, consider the inflation rate, GNP, and the unemployment rate, in deciding what to do, they do not consider the actions of individual buyers, sellers, employers, and job seekers. It would take a professional economist who is privy to some specialized government accounting procedures as well as an incredible amount of data to reconstruct the aggregate numbers from data on individuals. Macroeconomics cannot explain without making use of unreduced aggregate social facts, despite their ontological reducibility. Second, I will argue that without positing social groups as causally efficacious entities, we cannot explain oppression or many other aspects of human behavior. That I hold this view is already apparent from my definition of oppression as a fundamentally group-based phenomenon. The conception of social group that I offer here will make that aspect of the definition clearer. However, my argument does not rest merely on a definition. Rather I shall show that certain behaviors that most would classify as oppressive can be explained only if we use the concept of a social group in the explanation. As I have argued, and will further clarify, social groups play an essential role in oppression, in the sense that individuals are oppressed only as members of social groups. Therefore, in order to understand oppression we need to acknowledge and theorize social groups. To this task I now turn.

2. Social Groups

We are individuals who belong to social groups, some of which we choose to belong to and some of which we belong to whether or not we would choose to belong if we could. Yet social scientists, philosophers, and theorists have often clouded this picture of social life by ignoring, reducing, or denying one or both kinds of social groups. A wide array of literatures with varying approaches and interests use the concept of the social group, sometimes to deny that there is any real extension to the concept, sometimes to try to explain social groups in individualistic terms, sometimes to demonstrate the irreducible causal role of social groups, and sometimes to argue for the political significance of a particular social group. Among those theorists who think that "social group" is a useful concept, there is wide disagreement about what the conditions are for a collection of objects to constitute a social group and what its attributes may be. My strategy in this chapter will be to set out a conception of social groups that is plausible, ontologically conservative, and that preserves the possibility of individual human choice. Most importantly for the project of this book, though, my conception must sustain the analysis of oppression that I will give in subsequent chapters. I shall argue here that competing conceptions of social groups cannot sustain a group-based account of oppression.

There are three ways that collections of socially significant objects might be formed: naturally (as in sets of humans of the same sex or age), socially (as in the set of all corporations in the United States, or all persons who are of the same tribe or ethnicity), or accidentally (as in the set of persons in either Los Angeles or Sydney at 8 A.M. GMT on August 25, 2004). I am interested mainly in social groups because these are the groups that humans have some control over and because they matter greatly to individual human beings. Of course, sometimes a collection that originally arises naturally or accidentally comes to be a social group, so my account of social groups will include these as well. Accidental groups are groups of persons whose connection (other than sharing the property of personhood itself) to all of the other members of the group is fully specified by the terms of group membership. For example, the passengers of TWA flight 800 form an accidental group because they have no more in common with all of the others than that they were passengers on that ill-fated flight. Social groups, broadly speaking, are non-accidental groups that are formed by or maintained by some social fact or action, either intentionally or as an unintended consequence of some social fact or action. What makes a fact or action social for humans is that some intentional human action played an essential role in bringing it about. In stating things this way I am committing myself to the view that intentions are themselves social, which aligns me with one side of a controversy,[9] though I am comforted there by the company of the likes of such philosophers as Wittgenstein (1953), Sellars (1963), Dummett (1978), Burge (1986), Hurley (1989), and Pettit (1993) whose arguments for this claim I refer to and endorse, broadly speaking, but will not here rehearse.

Among those who take social groups to be real, and this is itself a large and widely divergent group, there is disagreement about a fundamental point about what social groups are and how they are formed and maintained. Historically, there are two broad categories of approaches. One approach, the intentionalist approach, claims that social groups are formed and maintained by individuals who intentionally enter into them and maintain them through rules and norms, explicit or implicit. The paradigm kinds of social groups for the intentionalists are the social club, the modern state, or the conversational pair. With this approach we can associate names such as Max Weber, Jean-Paul Sartre, Raimo Tuomela, and Margaret Gilbert. The other approach, the structuralist approach, claims that social groups are structural features of the social environment, formed by rules, norms, and practices, explicit and implicit, and include individuals who may never consider or even see that they are a part of them, even though membership in the group has some effect on their lives. The kinds of groups that structuralists focus on include social classes, races, genders, and cultures. Among the important structuralists we would include: Karl Marx, Émile Durkheim, and Nancy Folbre.

The intentionalists generally attempt to occupy the ontological high ground to deny the existence of social groups of the structuralist sort, while the structuralists defend the political high ground, claiming that the intentionalists focus on the weak force of interpersonal relations while forces of history move with structural social groups. Both camps claim that they have found the uniquely "basic" social group. I believe that there is something to be said for each side. These two approaches highlight two ends of the spectrum of social groups. On one end there are social groups that consist of persons who have voluntarily entered into them, the other of primarily non-voluntarily socially determined members. Ignoring or denying one and focusing entirely on the other leads us to make bad normative prescriptions or insignificant social theory. Given a particular interest, for example, questions concerning rights of assembly and speech or questions concerning technological change, one might be wise to focus on one or the other kind of social groups.

Intentionalists and structuralists see their positions as diametrically opposed because they share the mistaken notion that intentionalist psychology is incompatible with the existence of irreducible social forces. I shall be arguing here for a compatibilist position, holding that while all action is intentionally guided, many of the constraints within which we act are socially determined and beyond the control of the currently acting individual; to put a slogan on it, intentions dynamically interact within social structures. On my view, individuals, whose actions are intentionally guided, though perhaps not toward the ends they achieve, exercise social control of the social constraints. But at the same time individuals act within socially determined constraints that guide and shape their intentions, and so on. The intentionalist is correct to see that action begins with the beliefs, desires, and capacities (both psychological and material) of the individual acting agent, but wrong to suppose that that rules out social forces beyond the control of that agent, forces that affect her beliefs, desires, and capacities. The structuralist is correct to see that from the point of view of the acting individual, there are groups to which she can choose to belong and those unchosen groups to which she either belongs or does not, but which she cannot choose to enter or leave. But the structuralist mistakenly attributes these to immutable forces of history located beyond the influence and responsibility of individual human beings. Thus, I will argue for a theory of social groups that is intentionalist in method and ontology, but preserves some of the structuralist content. My theory recognizes social groups postulated by both camps; to avoid the confusion that would be generated by calling them intentional and structural groups, I shall adopt the terms "voluntary" and "nonvoluntary" social groups, which more aptly capture the distinction.[10]

Other compatibilist positions have been proposed by Carol Gould (1978, 31–39; 1988, ch. 2), Richard DeGeorge (1983), and Larry May (1987). On their (separate and somewhat different) views, social groups are constituted by "individuals-in-relations," where the relations are socially enabled or constructed but then adopted by the individuals as their own. For example, two persons married to each other constitute a social group by virtue of the relation of marriage, a relation that is in the first instance socially constructed, in that it depends for its existence on laws and customs that define the relation, but that comes to be constitutive of their identity as persons in that they begin to think of themselves as a social unit who take on joint projects and actions. This is a compatibilist view in the sense that it preserves the intentionalist notion that individual intentions are primary in the explanation of action, yet it also preserves the structuralist notion that social structures cannot be reduced to individual actions alone. It differs from my view, though, because it is an internalist account of social groups, in that the social relations in part constitute the self-identity of the persons related through them. While I find this internalist view appealing for some purposes, it cannot account for what I am calling nonvoluntary social groups precisely because those groups, assuming they exist, consist of persons who do not necessarily self-identify with the group.[11]

The theory of social groups I offer is an externalist account: What makes a person a member of a social group is not determined by any internal states of that person, but rather by objective facts about the world, including how others perceive and behave toward that person.[12] This is not to deny that such facts tend to cause particular patterns of thoughts, feelings, and actions on the part of the persons who are subject to them, or that these thoughts, feelings, and actions can give rise to objective facts that reinforce group membership. The externalist account of social groups asserts that externally imposed constraints are necessary, and can be sufficient, for social group membership. The externalist account denies that all groups are voluntary, while allowing that voluntary actions by the members themselves can create the external constraints that compose social groups.

My theory of nonvoluntary social groups fits the description of what Philip Pettit calls "holistic individualism," which means that the social regularities associated with nonvoluntary social groups supervene on intentional states, and at the same time, group membership in these and voluntary social groups partly constitutes the intentional states of individuals. The theory I will offer is designed to fit what has been called a structural rational choice theory by Debra Satz and John Ferejohn (1994), which means that I will model human action as (basically instrumentally rational) individual choice constrained within socially structured payoffs. These socially structured payoffs are themselves the products of intentional states, of individuals making choices constrained by socially structured payoffs, which are the products of intentional states, and so on.

Because we are individuals with separate plans, intentions, and reasons, whose plans, intentions, and reasons are constrained by social facts about us that we did not choose, a comprehensive theory of social groups must account for both voluntary and nonvoluntary social groups. To argue for this claim, I will examine what I take to be the best theory of voluntary social groups available and show that the phenomena that it accounts for are significant features of social life that neither encompass nor are encompassed by the nonvoluntary social groups. The theory of voluntary social groups that would best fit with a rational choice theory has recently been proposed by Margaret Gilbert in her book *On Social Facts*. This section has three parts. In the first part I set out Gilbert's theory of (voluntary) social groups. In the second I show that her theory cannot account for nonvoluntary social groups. In the third I give an account of nonvoluntary social groups, which I argue is complementary to, but cannot completely replace, Gilbert's theory.

2.1. Voluntary Social Groups: Common Commitments

In *On Social Facts*, Gilbert presents an intentionalist account of social groups that is inspired by Georg Simmel's view that to be a social unit is just to be conscious of constituting a social unity. Gilbert presents a subtle technical account of the semantics of "we" as used in the "full-blooded" sense of standing for and including oneself in a plural subject. On her account, appropriately using "we" requires that the persons who are included by the demonstrative are "jointly ready" to share in some action in the relevant circumstances, and that they all recognize this fact. Appropriate uses of "we" in this full-blooded sense indicate that the referent of the demonstrative is a plural subject, and being a plural subject, is both necessary and sufficient for constituting a social group. Gilbert's account makes heavy epistemic demands on the individuals in a social group. They must share some goal or belief, they must be ready to act together on this belief or for this goal, and they must express this to each other and recognize their expression so that there is common knowledge of their joint readiness. By the term "common knowledge," Gilbert

•

generally refers to what she also calls "a paradigm case of common knowledge," which implies conditions that go farther than the account found in David Lewis's (1969) seminal work on common knowledge. Lewis's definition of common knowledge is the following: F is common knowledge in a population P iff everyone in P knows that f and everyone in P knows that everyone in P knows that f, and so on, for all the infinite levels of mutual knowledge. Additionally, Gilbert requires for her definition of a paradigm case of common knowledge that the persons in P recognize that they are in a situation of common knowledge of f (that is, f is "open*") and they have common knowledge of what it is to recognize this openness*.[13] For Gilbert, then, only small collections of individuals who are close to each other in proximity and understanding can constitute social groups. Indeed the primary social group for her is the conversational pair, two persons out for a walk together, or a couple making love or dancing.

Gilbert's analysis of the semantics of "we" rests on an analysis of cases in which it is or is not appropriate to use "we." In her restaurant example, Bernard and Sylvia, who have no previous social connection, are having lunch with an engaged couple when the man says to his fiancée "Shall we share dessert?" Bernard then turns to Sylvia and says, "Shall we share dessert?" Sylvia finds this use of "we" inappropriate, not Gilbert says, because she thinks that it is inappropriate to share a dessert with a near-stranger, nor because it suggests romantic intent after the engaged couple has agreed to share a dessert, nor does Gilbert think that "we" always connotes intimacy. Rather, Gilbert claims that Sylvia should find this use of "we" inappropriate because Sylvia has never in the past indicated to Bernard a willingness to do things of the relevant sort with him and this use of "we" implies that she has or that in some way she has made it plain to him that she would be so willing, that is, Sylvia finds this use of "we" to be "semantically irresponsible." A proper use of "we" never surprises a member of a plural subject because using "we" properly implies that the members of the plural subject are ready to share together in the action, and this fact is public.

The condition on plural subjects that readiness to share something be public is as important as the readiness itself for avoiding surprise. The publicity of the readiness makes the joint readiness of all common knowledge among them, and so makes it unsurprising when anyone then uses "we," assuming the readiness of the others as well, to express the joint readiness. How do we go, then, from the condition of each of us being ready to share in a joint project to actual joint readiness? The answer is that the readiness of each has to be made public, for example, by being expressed by each one in turn, or by being tentatively suggested by someone and not rejected by anyone, and in either case it has to be in a situation where all can gain common knowledge of the expression or of the fact that no one has rejected the suggestion. That is, the public expression of readiness has to be a paradigm situation of common knowledge. When readiness is so jointly expressed and that expression becomes common knowledge, Gilbert argues that there arises a "presupposition-licensing or surprise-avoiding"(Gilbert 1989, 194) normative situation, that is, a situation in which none of the group may be surprised by anyone's use of "we" or reference to the jointly shared project. From the fact of readiness together with the expression of it under the proper circumstances, a set of norms arises governing the group members' uses of the fact.

Gilbert's (1989, 222–223) account of social groups may be summarized as follows. A social group is a set of individuals who meet the following three conditions:

1. Willed-unity condition: Each person must volunteer to share in some action, belief, or attitude.
2. Expression condition: Each person must express his willingness for unity in a situation that they each recognize will lead to common knowledge of that willingness.
3. Common knowledge condition: The fulfillment of the expression condition must be a paradigm case of common knowledge.

The expression condition guarantees that members of social groups not only recognize but also will their unity, that is, their willingness to share a belief, action, or attitude. And the common knowledge condition guarantees that they recognize that each so wills the unity. Thus, to be a social group the members must know that they are a social group, they must pool their wills toward some belief, action, or attitude, and it must be commonly known that they know of this pooling. Now each may refer to a common project or belief, or make a proposal to the group that they share some new project or belief, without anyone being rightfully surprised by their inclusion in the proposal.

Gilbert's concept of social group describes a common and important kind of phenomenon. Not only do many social groups meet these conditions, as she illustrates, but the social groups that do are clearly important in our lives: school groups, teams, clubs, religious communities, friendships, conversational groups, and many, many more. Most of the time we act as a part of one or another of these groups. These groups are governed by tacit norms, which constrain and guide our actions. In deciding how to act or think we are constantly considering the right or appropriate or acceptable way to act or think. In some situations we are guided by natural facts and scientific laws, or even moral facts and moral laws, but much of our lives concerns social issues of rightness or appropriateness. Gilbert's account of social groups explains the origin and force of these tacit norms (Gilbert, 1996).

Gilbert's social groups are not reducible to any set of facts about the individuals alone. Persons in social groups of this sort cannot by themselves become members of social groups, act as part of the group, or share a group belief. This can be seen most clearly by considering the willed-unity condition. It requires the group to be willing to jointly share in some activity, belief, or attitude. To jointly share is more than for each to have the end as a goal. Each must also will that they jointly share it. The test that such joint sharing is going on is that if anyone fails to do their part, or attempts to withdraw their endorsement, that person may appropriately be blamed for doing so. To use Gilbert's paradigmatic example, if you and I are going for a walk together and thus constitute a social group, we will jointly share the goal of walking together, and if I suddenly start walking faster than you can readily walk, you could appropriately rebuke me, and we will both see that you are within your (social) rights to do so. The social fact that there are now norms governing our behavior by virtue of our so joining our wills is irreducible to non-normative facts about each of us as individuals, our beliefs, or our intentions.

The social groups that Gilbert describes all have in common that they recognize themselves as a social group. Gilbert calls this fact the "recognition corollary: all the members will recognize that the group exists, when it does" (Gilbert 1989, 223). In addition, Gilbert's groups contain only voluntary members, for in order to meet the willed-unity condition one has to, minimally, will that one become part of the unity. Thus, if there exist nonvoluntary social groups, groups whose members do not will themselves to be joined with each other, they are not Gilbert groups.[14]

2.2. *The Existence of Non-voluntary Social Groups*

Of course Gilbert recognizes that there are some other entities that people call social groups that do not count as such on her account. The counterexample she discusses at some length is economic classes. She gives four reasons to think that economic classes are not social groups. First, most social scientists that Gilbert has read (except Marxist social scientists) do not count classes as social groups. But this does not show that Marxists are wrong to count classes as social groups, so we may ignore this response. Further, I think that economic classes, while not a straw man exactly, are surely not the strongest or most common counterexample among social theorists now—what about race or gender? Second, she notes that in the *Communist Manifesto* Marx was calling for the proletariat to become conscious of itself and adopt a joint commitment, that is, to become a social group in Gilbert's sense. While this shows that Marx thought that there are important differences between a *Klasse für sich* and a *Klasse an sich*, it does not show that he thought that one would constitute a social group and the other would not. Besides, what Marx thought constituted the set of social groups is of little more importance to the argument that there are non-voluntary social groups than what Gilbert's social scientists think form social groups. Third, Gilbert lists four other conceptions of social groups that she thinks are inadequate to pick out the set of social groups, including "population credited with importance by some major social theorist," and "population of a kind with an important effect on societies" (Tuomela 1995, 228). But these, she argues, "clearly run the risk of not cutting nature at the joints, of lumping together phenomena which are quite significantly different, and not very significantly the same" (Tuomela 1995, 228). This list does not, however, include viable alternatives such as the one I present below.[15] Finally, Gilbert argues that her use of the term "social group" for the phenomena she describes is particularly apt given the Latin root of *socius* or ally. Allies share a common purpose and act on a joint commitment. But equally one might argue that they share merely a common interest and not necessarily a common goal or purpose, or even that the common interest is more common than the common purpose, and that this can be seen by the fact that many of the groups that we normally call social—including some allies—do not always act cooperatively or coordinately. Gilbert has not given us reason enough to think that economic classes are not social groups. More to the point, though, she has not given us reason to think that she has picked out the only things that could be social groups. It is now my task to propose a set of groups that we ought to take to be social and give an account of them.

2.3. Nonvoluntary Social Groups: Common Social Constraints

Social theorists (especially non-liberal ones) commonly talk about collections of persons who suffer various forms of oppression. A short list of such collections in the context of contemporary U.S. culture would include women, African Americans, Native Americans, Asian Americans, the poor, the working class, Jews, gays and lesbians, and the disabled. Likewise there are their correlatives, the dominant collections: men, white Americans, Christians, the middle class, straight people, able-bodied persons. There can be no doubt that we *can* cut the world up this way, since we do so all the time; the question I want to pursue is whether it is an explanatorily useful way to do so, and whether these categories are forced on us by the social facts of our world. I take it that if the answers to these questions are affirmative, then we will have reason to call such collections social groups. But they are clearly not social groups in the sense of Gilbert's social groups; these are large and anonymous collections of persons, for whom neither the willed-unity condition nor the common knowledge condition could be satisfied except under rare circumstances (perhaps during revolution, for example). So if these collections are social groups, then there is a second kind of social group to recognize.

Social groups, whether voluntary or nonvoluntary, are collections of persons who share something that is socially significant. As Gilbert shows, members of voluntary social groups share joint commitments or joint projects. The members of a nonvoluntary social group share social penalties and rewards consequent on their being so grouped. They need not intend to share this, but it is in some sense inescapable; other agents and the social structures agents put in place assign them these penalties and rewards because they are seen as belonging to these social groups. This fact may not lead to group consciousness or even self-consciousness. But it has serious consequences for social justice.

There are many social constraints on individual actions. By constraints I mean facts that one does or ought to rationally consider in deciding how to act or how to plan one's life, or facts that shape beliefs and attitudes about other persons. They are the factors that must be modeled in rational choice explanations of actions, as the preferences, choices, common beliefs, strategies, and payoffs that agents consider in making decisions or as the default assumptions that agents use when they act on intentions that are not fully or rationally considered. Not all constraints on action are social in origin, some are biological (humans are mortal; I am slower than Marion Jones) or psychological (humans have limited cognitive capacities; I am less mathematically gifted than Andrew Wiles), some are physical (humans cannot survive a free fall from space). Constraints are social when they come about as a result of social actions. These constraints include: legal rights, obligations and burdens, stereotypical expectations, wealth, income, social status, conventions, norms, and practices. As with other kinds of constraints, some social constraints affect the entire species (all human societies need some method of preparing food for consumption), some affect smaller groups than that (Muslims do not eat pork), and some affect me individually (I am a vegetarian by moral conviction). Many of these constraints are the result of intended collective action, such as laws that prohibit social funding of abortions, judicial practices that normally assign child custody to mothers, tax structures that favor the middle class. But many of them are the unintended consequences of other intentional actions: stereotypes of Jews as overly concerned with money, of women as overly emotional, or of Asians as especially good at mathematics; the relatively high incidence of single African American mothers; and the conventional marriage proposal that has men doing the asking and women the responding. Some social constraints might be partly intentionally and partly unintentionally caused: Racial segregation in the cities comes about not because all the people want to live in segregated cities, but because a few want total racial segregation, some others want to be in the racial majority, others want not to be the only ones of their race on their blocks, and still others want to sell before their property values are completely depleted.[16] Some social constraints might also have partly natural causes: deaf persons are rarely born in a culture where they can share the native language. Social constraints are not unchangeable facts; they are purely exogenous variables in a social theory only in the short run. But as John Maynard Keynes pointed out, we all live in the short run; social constraints are among the facts we have to face in planning our lives.

Social constraints affect actions through the penalties and rewards that one can reasonably expect from them. Individuals are motivated to act in their interest and the interest of others whom they care about. If it is a social fact that in a certain area of town women are likely to be harassed or assaulted, then individual women will be motivated to avoid it. That does not mean that all women will avoid going there (indeed, some feisty women might even take it as an inviting challenge to do so), but just that for any woman there will be a cost to going there that she ought (rationally) consider in making a decision about where to go and by what route. Social constraints help to explain individual actions by revealing the incentives that individuals have by virtue of their membership in nonvoluntary social groups.[17]

It may be objected that rewards or incentives cannot be said to constrain actions; constraints must narrow the range of possibilities of action, while rewards or incentives merely guide rational persons in choosing.[18] First, I do not mean to suggest that all constraints are negative. I intend the word "constraint" to be normatively neutrally, more in the sense of "frame" or "guide." Whether a constraint is negative or positive, just or unjust are separate judgments that depend on factors that I will discuss at greater length in chapter 7. Second, rewards can reframe a situation in a way that is negative for an individual actor. An example of Larry May's illustrates: Suppose a professor offers a marginal graduate student a fellowship on condition that the graduate student sleep with the professor.[19] The offer is a new opportunity that the graduate student could not have expected, and thus one might object that because the offer constitutes an additional choice not a restriction of choices, it must be advantageous. However, as May argues, the offer changes the situation for the student in a way that she might well not have chosen: She must now live in an academic environment in which she knows that her professor considers her as a sexual object and not simply as a student, and in which her sexuality makes a difference to her academic success. Thus, the reward offered has changed the situation arguably for the worse for this student. Likewise, examples can be concocted in which a social penalty reframes a situation positively for an individual; consider the constraint on men not to cry in public (Frye 1983, 14).

Some social constraints form default assumptions that affect individuals' beliefs and attitudes. According to cognitive scientists, we make implicit assumptions all the time in our thinking about what holds true in normal circumstances, and apply these assumptions until and unless some feature of our situation forces us to reassess things. These implicit assumptions are called "default assumptions" (Hofstadter 1985). Without the ability to make lots of assumptions without thinking about them first, we would be hopelessly mired in the frame problem, unable to find the relevance of any situation for our own needs and desires in time to act effectively. Of course, sometimes these assumptions are false, but given our finite cognitive capacities, the complexity of facts we would need to think everything through, and the need to act relatively quickly in many situations, default assumptions are an evolutionary advantage.

Among the kinds of default assumptions we make are stereotypes about individuals based on visible features that they share with others: Women are relatively small and weak, Asians are good mathematicians, African Americans are from the South or the inner city, gay men are effeminate, women and minority professors got their jobs to fill affirmative action quotas. Stereotypes originate in naturally, socially, and accidentally formed collections of persons, and they become social facts when they become the default assumptions that we make when we first meet someone or when we hear someone described to us or see someone on the street. Stereotypes guide us to form beliefs about an individual before we have the kind of evidence for those beliefs that we would require if that individual did not share some other attribute with the collection to which that stereotype attaches. We see a black man and assume that he is from a city, even if in the same context we would not make that assumption about a white. We have an Asian student in our class and ask her to do the class report on game theory rather than the one on hermeneutics. Default assumptions not only make false beliefs easier to form when they do not hold, but they make it more difficult to form the correct belief that would otherwise be quite plain to see. We see a woman and assume that she could not lift the box in front of her, even if, were it a man of approximately the same build and size, we would think that he could. And we make that assumption even when we see that she is wearing the brown uniform of a UPS driver.[20] Finally, stereotypical default assumptions cause us to have attitudes towards the groups to which we attach stereotypes. Assuming that women are weak and small, many men form a superior and protective attitude toward women in contexts where there are physical challenges. Assuming that Asians are good at mathematics, many whites form a resentful attitude toward Asians in math and science classes. Other conceivable collections of persons may have no stereotypes attached to them: Is there any belief or image you form upon hearing that some otherwise anonymous individual has attached ear lobes?

Social rewards and penalties are often distributed to individuals based on the default assumptions that others make about them. This means that individuals themselves have no control over those rewards and penalties unless they can make it clear in the relevant situations that the default assumption is false. Of course, if one is getting a reward that one does not merit, it is tempting to try to look like an average normal member of the collection to which the stereotype attaches and to make it look like the stereotype is true in a great percentage of cases of members of that collection. Where one wants to show that a stereotype does not apply to one, it can be difficult. Counterexamples are often honestly construed as misperceptions rather than as true counterexamples in social life as well as in science.[21]

The account of social groups I propose, then, is this: A *social group is a collection of persons who share (or would share under similar circumstances) a set of social constraints on action.* The account fits both voluntary and nonvoluntary social groups, since it does not refer to the cause or reason for the existence of similar social constraints on the persons who share them. This definition is similar in some respects to the concept of group as a seriality, a concept that Iris Marion Young borrows from Sartre to understand groups. Like my own view of groups, she understands groups as structural conditions on persons, but conditions that "condition the dispositions and affinities of people without constituting their identities" (Young 2000, 101).[22] No group membership constitutes one's identity, since identity is individual and determined by how one negotiates the many group-based constraints on one's actions, in addition to other, more individually determined constraints. While Young is concerned to show that groups do not determine identities, it seems worth pointing out that one could embrace some group membership (particularly voluntary ones) as identity creating, and many persons in fact do so (Copp 2002).

Membership in a nonvoluntary social group is socially and not individually determined. The patterns of distribution of social rewards and penalties according to stereotypes generate and help to define social groups. Social groups are formed not by the intentions of the individuals in them to join together and share in a particular project, but by the actions, beliefs, and attitudes of others, both in the group and out, that constrain their choices in patterned and socially significant ways. Members of nonvoluntary social groups share the same social constraints as a result of others' decisions, while voluntary group members share constraints that result from their decisions and actions to join together, against a background of social constraints consequent on others' decisions. The voluntariness of social groups admits of degrees: A social group defined by a common religion, for example, is more voluntary if there are more choices (with decent expected outcomes) for people to leave and join other religions or reject religion entirely. Members of nonvoluntary social groups experience constrained or enhanced choices by comparison with others who are similarly situated in every respect except membership in that group. One implication of this theory is that blacks and whites form two separate social groups. To see why, consider how a black middle-class man in America compared with a white middle-class man in America faces different constraints on their choices due to their respective races. The black person can expect to be treated differently and judged differently because of his blackness even when outwardly behaving in the same way as the white man who appears to be of the same social class. In stores the middle-class black is likely to be followed by store workers, he is likely to be harassed by police in white neighborhoods or if seen driving an expensive car, women cross the street when they see him coming down the sidewalk, people expect that he likes sports and plays them well. Equally, though he may not notice his privileges, the middle-class white man is treated differently from the black—he is not followed, he is given the benefit of the doubt by police, he is approached by colleagues as an expert on things other than sports, and so on. These social constraints affect the actions one considers and the choices one makes in clear and predictable ways: The black man does not expect to be left alone, so he acts as one would when being watched; he expects police harassment in certain situations, so he either avoids those situations or adopts an attitude of innocence, deference, or defiance to cope, and so on.

One of the important differences between voluntary and nonvoluntary social groups is that one need not recognize that one is a member of a particular nonvoluntary social group to be a member. One simply needs objectively to face the constraints that other members face, whether or not one recognizes them as patterned constraints that one shares.[23] I take this to be a good feature of my account because it is common for people in oppressed groups not to recognize their oppression, not because they do not recognize that they face constraints, but because they tend to see the constraints as their own individual problems or idiosyncrasies.[24] My account of nonvoluntary social groups includes groups whose members are conscious of themselves as forming a social group, groups whose members are not so conscious, as well as nonvoluntary social groups with members who mistakenly think that they are not members. Nonvoluntary social groups come in and go out of existence when beliefs, attitudes, and actions change. Sometimes nonvoluntary social groups lose their nonvoluntary character but some members choose to form voluntary social groups. For example, Irish Americans used to be a significant social group—being labeled an Irish American would have many consequences for one's possible actions. But now there are not very many such consequences, unless one chooses to name oneself Irish and participates in voluntary activities with other Irish Americans, making it difficult to argue that it is a nonvoluntary social group.[25]

Although one need not be conscious of oneself as a member of a nonvoluntary social group, social awareness of a particular social group has significant consequences for the group members. Membership in some nonvoluntary social groups may give one a sense of identity, group solidarity, or self-worth. These psychological benefits come only when one becomes aware of oneself as a member of this social group. (Likewise, there can be psychological costs to becoming aware of oneself as a member of a social group: I painfully remember the day that I realized that I could not hope to be a football player because I was a girl.) Awareness of oneself as a member of a social group does not make the group into a voluntary group, though, as that requires also that there be some shared project and the common knowledge of that sharing. Still, groups that have become self-conscious are closer on the continuum to voluntary social groups.

How does one come to be grouped into a nonvoluntary social group? There are different signs for group membership depending on the social group, but in each case membership is assigned by others through default assumptions that go into effect when they recognize or think they recognize some typical trait or behavior that is very salient in the culture for grouping. So, for instance, skin color, hair length, dress, voice pitch, word choice, size, walking or sitting style are all well known signals of race, gender, class, and sexual orientation. Some of these are more or less matters of choice up to the individual doing the choosing, and nearly all them are, given enough (sometimes drastic) intervention, somewhat changeable. In that sense one could say that there is a voluntary aspect even to nonvoluntary social groups. But this sense of choice is not the same that is in play with voluntary social groups. These choices are not negotiable or malleable by the individual—in choosing to be in this nonvoluntary social group or that there is no room for a pooling of wills or joint choice. In the marketplace of social group norms, the individual is a norm-taker, not a norm-setter.

Although there certainly exist social groups that meet Gilbert's description and are thus voluntary, and although their voluntariness is significant in many contexts, my externalist account of social groups easily extends to include the entire range of social groups from the most voluntary to the most involuntary. Gilbert's paradigm examples of social groups, the conversational pair, two people out for a walk together, or a couple making love or dancing, form the most voluntary end of the continuum. They are social groups on my account because their actions and expressions create norms that constrain their subsequent actions, as Gilbert described. Somewhere in the middle of the continuum come the nonvoluntary social groups that have become self-conscious and pro-active. They began as groups formed entirely by the intentions and actions of others. As they became aware of themselves as a group able to establish their own, internally recognized norms, their constraints are more internally generated. Close-knit families may lie closer to the voluntary side of the nonvoluntary groups; large diverse, political groups close to the nonvoluntary side of voluntary groups.

2.4. Some Objections

Recall that the individualist objects that since social groups are nothing more than collections of individuals and their interactions, we ought not to employ the concept of social group in our explanations of human behavior. Early in the chapter I argued that the ontological reducibility of social groups to individuals and their interactions does not entail that social groups cannot be an explanatorily useful concept. Now we are in a position to complete the argument against methodological individualism by showing that social groups are explanatorily useful. I claim that in order to explain some features of social life, it is essential to recognize nonvoluntary social groups. If this is so, then methodological individualism is doomed as an explanatory dictum for the social sciences. I take methodological individualism to be the claim that all *explanations* of social phenomena must in principle be reducible to statements about individuals, including their beliefs, desires, goals, and so on. In order to make the point, one traditionally offers an example that the methodological individualists can then try to attack. Traditional structuralists use examples like the well-known check cashing example of Maurice Mandelbaum (1955). This example works, like the macroeconomics example that I gave above, because of the intensionality of the facts that explain the actions of bank tellers and patrons. We cannot replace standard holistic explanations of why the teller cashed the check for the patron that refer to monetary and banking rules and practices with statements that refer only to actions of individuals and their interactions. I argue that another example that the individualist cannot escape would come from examining a social fact that is a consequence of socially constructed default assumptions rather than explicit inferences. For instance, how do we explain the door opening ritual, as it is called by feminists, in a case where a small man with packages rushes to open the door for a large able-bodied woman (Frye 1983, 5)? It does not make sense unless we include in the explanans reference to default assumptions about social groups, namely the stereotype of women as weak and small. For the man cannot infer that the woman actually needs help here, or that he is in a good position to offer it, unless he draws that inference based on social groupings of persons rather than on the visible individual traits in the actual situation. If one objects that it is custom or habit that explains why the man always opens doors for women, then one must explain the origin of the custom or habit, and this explanation will rely on references to social groups. Furthermore, this example involves social groupings that the persons did not voluntarily enter, so that one cannot reduce the group to the kinds of intentional states that Gilbert refers to.[26] It is precisely where the social constraints that compose nonvoluntary social groups are involved that we need to refer to irreducibly social facts to explain human behavior.[27] Thus, we cannot do without the concept of nonvoluntary social groups.

Another kind of objection to my account of nonvoluntary social groups argues that because there are interacting sets of social constraints that each individual faces, there is no way to individuate a set of them that picks out a unique social group. This objection takes two different forms: one to the existence of the social group itself and one to our ability to discern accurately the consequences of belonging to the social group. I take it that the first is the more crucial objection for me to block, since if it is correct, there are no social groups at all. But the second is also important to block, since I claim that my theory is valid only if it is practically useful. So I shall discuss both forms.

An instance of the first form of this objection to social groups comes from work in feminism that claims that there is no way to separate out the "woman part" from a woman, that is, to separate her membership in the group "women" from her other social group memberships, such as race, class, and sexual orientation. Thus, any account of social groups that tries to set aside one of these categories to name a group will be unable to come up with clear identity conditions for group membership. Elizabeth Spelman, who holds this view, writes: "One's gender identity is not related to one's racial identity as the parts of pop-bead necklaces are related, separable and insertable in other 'strands' with different racial and class 'parts'" (Spelman 1988, 15). One way to interpret this objection is to say that what we cannot do is locate in the individual the identities that match up with social groups. First, note that my account is not trying to do that; my account is an externalist account that is trying to locate in the world the social constraints that compose social grouphood. Spelman's objection may be reinterpreted against my account as follows. My account supposes that in the world there are constraints that apply to all women, others to all men, others to all African Americans, and so forth. It is what one might term a "vector force" model to suggest the analogy with mechanics. With mechanics, it is an empirical matter whether objects on earth or in space, moving in a straight line or a curve, in the presence of friction or on a frictionless surface would all behave the same way in the presence of two different sources of inertial force. But they do; the vector force model works. Does the vector force model work, modulo the imprecision of social facts, in the social world as well? As with multiple forces in mechanics, multiple group memberships will affect the direction and intensity of the overall social constraints for an individual. Translated into the language of vector addition, Spelman's objection amounts to the claim that the individual vector forces *change* in the presence of different other forces. For instance, she argues that being a man positively contributes to one's overall life choices if one is white, but negatively if one is black.[28]

On one point we agree: It is an empirical question whether the vector force approach works. However, I disagree with the analysis of this example. Over a wide range of measures of social outcomes, being a man and black leads to more and better choices than being a woman and black. Black men out-earn black women,[29] they have a wider range of professions open to them, black men (like men of all races) are physically dominant over black women, more black women are relegated to the servant jobs of society, and most black political, religious, military, and social leaders are men. Although black men are treated more harshly by police than black women (except for the fact that the latter are subject to rape by police), the same can be said for white men as compared with white women. Objections of the form, "black women face different and more severe problems than white women' or 'white women think of themselves as superior to black men" are red herrings to the question of whether the vector force model works. To compare the constraints that form the social groups of men and women one must compare within race, class, and other significant social groupings (groupings whose significance can be determined only empirically).[30] While it may be difficult to measure with precision the effect of constraints, or worse, to weigh different sources of value like psychological well-being vs. life expectancy, these difficulties do not tell against the existence of the patterns of differences in social constraints, and so the existence of nonvoluntary social groups.

However, as Nancy Folbre (1994, 67–68, 271 n. 4) suggests, it may be that we need a much more complex theory of the interaction of various constraints than the vector force model represents. She suggests that there may be important ways that the constraints interact, causing there to be important interactive terms. For example, although there is a male/female wage gap for both blacks and whites that favors men, the wage gap is larger for whites than for blacks, and although there is a black/white wage gap for men and women, it is larger, though in the same direction, for men than for women.[31] This suggests that with respect to the wage rate constraint, at least, there are interactive effects between race and gender, but these effects do not reverse the direction of the constraint. Since we are unlikely to be able to precisely measure the relative strengths of constraint anyway, direction is all the precision we should require of the model.

The second form of the objection is raised against our ability to accurately locate such nonvoluntary social groups amidst the tangle of social facts that characterize individual lives. One obvious way to locate nonvoluntary social groups is to begin with statistics by looking at various collections of persons to see whether they have different outcomes, for example, levels of income, life expectancies, frequency of imprisonment, from other identifiable collections. It is then necessary to determine whether there is reason to believe that some systematic social constraint is in operation (Thurow 1979). Against statistical identification of social groups, however, Anthony Flew (1985) contends that it is a fallacy to argue:

> that because members of one social set are not represented in some occupation or organization in the same proportion as in the population as a whole, therefore members of that social set must be being, whether intentionally or unintentionally, discriminated against, and cannot have enjoyed equal opportunities to pursue that occupation or to enter that organization. (Flew 1985, 10)

Flew is correct to worry about the indiscriminate use of statistics to infer discrimination, but surely statistics can give us a lead on what collections to investigate. He argues further that the conclusion from statistical differences that there is discrimination "can go through only on the assumption that abilities, inclinations and the senses of actual choices fall into the exactly the same distribution pattern in the social set in question as in the population as a whole" (Flew 1985, 10). But this does not follow, for the "inclinations and the senses of actual choices" are endogenous variables in the equation that relates a social "set's" treatment to the outcomes of its individuals; that is, how one is treated surely helps to determine what one believes one can reasonably choose, and so one's desires as well. To suggest that women do the low- or unpaid work of society because they have some natural, maternal urge is to add insult to injury.

I think that in fact Flew is more concerned about the implication that statistical patterns of discrimination against a "social set" would show that there are non-voluntary social groups at all, that is, the first form of this objection. Flew uses the term "social set" explicitly to avoid having to postulate that there are any social groups. He writes, "we employ the expression "social set," rather than "social class" or "social group," in order to disown any undesired implications that the social sets in question must be either social classes or else other social or racial groups which may either be seen by others, or see themselves, or be organized, as such" (Flew 1985, 10). If it is Flew's concern to suggest that persons do not suffer discrimination as members of social groups, however, showing that statistics about outcomes cannot alone reveal such discrimination does not show that there are no nonvoluntary social groups.

Another kind of objection is that this account of social groups makes our ontology unacceptably large. Again there are two forms of this kind of objection. One form objects that adding social groups to the list of things in the world is unnecessary. I take it that I answered this objection in my discussion of the failure of methodological individualism; social groups are necessary for social explanations. But my conception of social groups is also ontologically rather conservative. I do not postulate anything like a collective mind, or absolute spirit. Social groups are terminological devices to discuss the clusters of constraints that certain collections of persons face. We need some such device since these clusters of constraints and the persons who face them are socially significant. But they are something more than mere terminological devices because they are intensional concepts, concepts that have meaning as such for individuals. That is, being classified (by oneself or others) as a member of a particular social group often has real implications for one's other beliefs and desires, implications that do not arise from merely extensionally equivalent descriptions.

The other form of the objection is that there are indefinitely many trivial nonvoluntary social groups that meet my definition. For example, the group of beautiful women turns out to be a social group because they share certain constraints (or enhanced choices) throughout the world; they are more likely to be courted by rich men, for instance.[32] Then there is the correlative, the non-beautiful women. And what about short people, bald men, and so on? It is indeed a consequence of my view that these groups I have named are social groups. However, I disagree that this list goes on indefinitely, or that the groups are trivial. For the test of social grouphood is exactly whether the constraints that the members face have some social consequences. If they do, then they are not trivial, by definition, though surely some social consequences are not very deep. But not all features that persons share have social consequences; the collection of persons with attached ear lobes does not constitute a social group precisely because there are no constraints with any social consequences that such persons face. Whether a collection of persons comprises a social group is an empirical question that depends on whether they face common social constraints. Not all possible collections do, but any collections that face common social constraints hold some interest for social scientists.

3. Institutionally Structured Constraints

As I defined them above, social constraints are facts that one does or ought to rationally consider in deciding how to act or how to plan one's life, or facts that shape beliefs and attitudes about other persons, that come about as a result of social actions. Among social constraints I include: legal rights, obligations and burdens, stereotypical expectations, wealth, income, social status, conventions, norms, and practices. These particular social constraints all have in common that they are institutionally structured, and they are thus all crucially important in the definition of oppression.

The term "social institution" encompasses a very broad list of social entities. Included among any sociologists' list of social institutions would be government, legal systems, schools, banks, gender rules and norms, rules of etiquette, media outlets, stereotypical beliefs, class, caste systems, racial, or ethnic classification systems. What all of these have in common are that they specify behaviors in specific situations for persons who fit particular roles regardless of their individual characteristics, and the specified behaviors are in some sense required under threat of some penalty for noncompliance. Andrew Schotter defines social institutions as follows: "A social institution is a regularity in social behavior that is agreed to by all members of society, specifies behavior in specific recurrent situations, and is either self-policed or policed by some external authority" (Schotter 1981, 11). While this definition concisely captures much of what I mean by a social institution, it is too voluntaristic; it requires some kind of agreement by all members of society. I disagree with two aspects of this definition: the agreement condition (that there must be some agreement among individuals concerning the behaviors specified) and the inclusivity condition (the requirement that all members of society must so agree).

First, we can weaken the agreement condition to require only tacit knowledge, so that instead of there being a socially recognized agreement there can be merely tacit knowledge on the part of the individuals. Second, we can weaken the inclusivity condition to require only some subset (that includes more than one member) of the population of a society. The amended definition reads as follows: A *social institution sets constraints that specify behavior in specific recurrent situations, that are tacitly known by some nontrivial subset of society, and that are either self-policed or policed by some external authority.*

We can now define social groups in terms of social institutions. Social groups are collections of individuals who face common constraints that are structured by social institutions. It may be objected that the phrase "structured by" is too vague. But I would argue that it is general, not vague. Explicit rewards set by groups whose criteria of eligibility are common knowledge, for example, the starting salary for the typical MBA graduate of Harvard Business School would be one kind of constraint structured by a social institution. Another kind would be the tacitly known consequences of wearing a tongue stud in a job interview. Here the social institution is norms for appropriate dress and jewelry, which change fairly rapidly, but are certainly understood by most persons to whom they apply. In both cases these are consequences to actions based on knowledge or inferences made from social facts, which guide behavior in advance through the reward or punishment those consequences represent.

4. Oppression and Social Groups

Recall the account of oppression we have been developing: an institutionally structured, unjust harm perpetrated on groups by other groups using direct and indirect material and psychological forces. Now that we have a definition of social groups in terms of the social constraints that persons face as a result of them, we can give a more precise definition of oppression. First, however, I need to examine the ways in which social constraints can fall unequally and unjustly on social groups. I shall say that social constraints are unequal when they differentially affect the life outcomes of the individuals subjected to the constraints. Take an example of a social constraint that is different, say, segregated public restrooms. They are unequal if they are on average worse for one group than for the other. If, for example, there is no average difference in cleanliness, waiting time, or convenience for the segregated groups, then there is no inequality. If, on the other hand, the segregation leads to greater waiting times for one group than the other (as gender segregated restrooms typically do) or to lesser cleanliness for one group than the other (as racially segregated restrooms often did), then there is an inequality in the social constraint. To say that social constraints are unjust is to say that in addition to falling unequally on different groups, they are unjustifiedly unequal. Inequalities may be justified in special cases by the behavior or special needs of the social groups at issue. For example, it is often argued that gender segregated restrooms are justified by the need to protect men and women from humiliation. However, such attempts at justifying unequal social constraints can easily be manipulated to rationalize injustice.

We can now define oppression in terms of institutionally structured constraints. Oppression consists in the existence of unequal and unjust institutional constraints. I claim that these injustices harm through direct and indirect material and psychological forces. The next four chapters discuss these forces. Recall that a direct force externally affects the choices of individuals, while indirect forces shape the background social beliefs and desires with which we perceive and behave toward others. Direct forces of oppression include unjust laws that prescribe or proscribe behaviors by members of social groups, unjustified terrorist, police, or military actions by some groups on other groups, or unjust norms that deny equal opportunities to members of some social groups. Indirect forces of oppression work through the choices of the individuals in the social groups. These include choices that oppressed persons make to accommodate their oppression and stereotypical beliefs that allow them and others to rationalize and accept it. While indirect forces of oppression work through the affective and cognitive psychological processes that form beliefs, desires, and ultimately, actions of the individuals, direct forces are necessarily external and concrete.

5. Groups and Group Harms

In order to forestall a certain kind of objection to my account, I need to distinguish between two concepts of group harm. One is a kind of harm that is easily reconciled with individualistic social science or with the concept of harm that Mill and other liberals recognize as legitimate bases for limiting the liberty of individuals, and the other is not so easily reconciled with either. The former include those harms that are suffered by the individual members of a group because of their membership in that group; I shall call this "group harm *qua* individuals harmed" or just "group harm$_1$." The latter is the harm to the group *qua* group itself, not necessarily to any particular member of the group; I will call this "group harm *qua* group" or just "group harm$_2$." Group harm$_2$ is harm done to non-accidental groupings where the harm is a harm to the group itself, not just to the individuals that constitute it.[33] To see that these two senses of group harm are different, consider a group which is obliterated not by any harm done to any of the members but rather by the withering away of shared purpose. We might see this as a kind of group harm$_2$, since the groupness is obliterated, but not a kind of group harm$_1$, since no individuals are harmed. Nonvoluntary groups cannot suffer group harm$_2$ if group harm$_2$ is considered to be something over and above—not reducible to—the harms to individuals consequent on their group membership.

Group harm$_1$ poses no particular problems for an individualist ontology or liberal political theory to recognize and allow remedy for because these group harms can be parsed as the harms of individuals consequent on their group membership. First, note that we have been discussing harm in the moralized, Millian sense that requires a legitimate right not to be harmed in that way. Particularly in the case of nonvoluntary group harms, there is a matter of injustice, as it is clear that the harm is undeserved and unavoidable for the group member. If a voluntary group suffers group harm$_1$, then what needs to be asked is whether the individuals have the right to their voluntary participation in the group. To the degree that the right to voluntarily participate in the group is a justified right, that group harm is an injustice.

Recognition of group harm$_2$ is more difficult to justify on an individualist ontology, since there are not any groups over and above individuals, or on liberal grounds because liberalism rejects the view that groups have the same moral standing as individuals. Liberals hold individual persons to be of ultimate moral value, and this seems to rule out the possibility that groups could also be of this highest moral value. Acknowledging group rights allows the possibility for groups to supersede individuals in disputes. Hence, it would seem that recognition of group harm$_2$ is incompatible with liberalism. Either the harm has to be reconceived as harm of the individual members, that is, group harm$_1$, or it has to be accepted that the harm is not of sufficient moral weight to override individual rights or claims of harm, or the liberal conception of the primacy of the individual has to be given up. On my view the harm of oppression is, in part, of the group harm$_1$ variety; that is, groups can be said to be harmed only in the sense that the individuals of the group are harmed.

6. Conclusion

In this chapter I have argued that any account of oppression that distinguishes it from other harms that can come to individuals and locates it as a social injustice requires an account of social groups. Further, harms that accrue to members of voluntary and nonvoluntary groups must be treated separately in moral arguments. For voluntary social groups, oppression is a harm that comes from choosing to be a member of the group. The question raised for justice by such harm would be: Does the individual have a right to exercise the sort of assembly or speech that membership in this social group entails? The issue for victims of oppression as a result of their nonvoluntary social group membership is somewhat different: Does a just society allow harm to persons who could not choose to avoid their membership? Oppression of either sort of social group may be quite severe and justice may require us urgently to address it. Oppression of nonvoluntary social groups is especially egregious from the point of view of the construction of just social institutions because society at the same time constructs nonvoluntary social groups as objects of oppression.

As I shall argue more fully in chapter 7, the theory of social groups I proposed in this chapter helps us to dissolve the dichotomy of individual and social responsibility. There are social theorists and philosophers who claim that persons should only be held responsible for their intentional actions, and so if some group of individuals is harmed by the unintended consequences of many individuals' actions, there is no responsibility on anyone to correct the harm or to compensate the victims. On the other hand, there are other social theorists and philosophers who suggest that individuals are to be excused for their actions when they are members of oppressed classes, and that to blame them for self-destructive actions is to "blame the victim." The choice between holding only individuals responsible for their intended actions and holding only society responsible for the actions of individuals acting under constraint is a false choice.

As I argued above, the oppression of nonvoluntary social groups is a matter of social injustice that requires rectification by society. The just society should come to see this as a collective responsibility, to be taken on as a plural subject, because it is a consequence of their intentional actions to create social institutions. But not all individuals in society are equally well placed to alleviate such oppression. The oppressed themselves are surely to be held responsible for not acting self-destructively, at least when there is an alternative to self-destruction, but the non-oppressed must be held responsible for loosening the social constraints caused by their actions, even though the harms may have been unintended. For we are to be held responsible for the unintended but foreseeable consequences of our actions. To talk of moral responsibility for the consequences of our actions, however, is to get ahead of ourselves. First, we need a theory of oppression that explains how group-based social oppression of the sort I have been discussing is possible. To this task I now turn.

3

Psychological Mechanisms of Oppression

1. The Need for a (New) Psychological Theory of Oppression

One of the questions a theory of oppression seeks to answer is: Why is this group (rather than that group) oppressed? Why, for instance, are men dominant over women, rather than strong ones over weak ones in others, or intelligent ones over stupid ones in others? However, the explanatorily prior question is why are there men and women at all, rather than simply tall and short persons, lactating and non-lactating ones, and so on, or simply individual persons with their unique combinations of characteristics? Why do long-standing social groups form at all? What is the cause or motivation for humans to segregate themselves and others in groups? I take these questions to require scientific explanation, beginning with our individual human cognitive abilities and propensities.

Once we see how oppressed and oppressor groups form, I shall argue that a material analysis can show how oppression is maintained, and how the economic efforts of the oppressed are often co-opted into maintaining their oppression. Then a second set of psychological questions vex even the casual social observer, namely: why do the groups endure? How do the oppressed come to be psychologically subdued to acquiesce or even participate in their own oppression? Marx, who also concentrated on the material causes and effects of oppression, was likewise afflicted by this puzzle. He answered it, notoriously, by invoking false consciousness, the idea that the oppressed working class comes to believe in the rightness of the social institutions that structure their oppression, which they see as their own personal failings and problems. False consciousness does not adequately answer the questions, however, because it is merely a name for a set of psychological phenomena that themselves require description and explanation. In other words, it is a black box. To get inside this black box we need a psychological analysis.

Of course, I am not the first philosopher to notice the need for a psychological account of oppression. Indeed, there exist many such accounts. Hegel proposed the first one in the form of the Master/Slave dialectic, which so inspired Marx that he focused his life's work on oppression. As Marx found with Hegel's, the existing psychological accounts of oppression are still inadequate, however. As I shall argue, they are all inadequate as social scientific accounts of psychological phenomena, first because they are not *scientific* at all. Some of them have the added flaw that they are not *social* accounts, and hence not suited to explaining the essentially social phenomenon of oppression. Most importantly for my overall account of oppression, the existing psychologies of oppression are not compatible with the best existing account of economic or material oppression. In this chapter, after showing why the existing psychological theories of oppression are inadequate, I draw on the work of social and cognitive psychologists in order to provide an adequate psychological theory of oppression. The idea is to provide a theory that is scientifically grounded and that helps explain social structures of oppression. Additionally, the theory of oppression I propose that takes as explanatory variables the material facts of oppression provided by an adequate economic theory of oppression, and in turn provides explanatory variables, in the form of belief and desire-generating mechanisms, for that theory.

In this chapter I am primarily concerned with explaining how our cognitive psychology equips us for oppression, that is, what psychological mechanisms we have that allow and motivate us to oppress or suffer oppression. Since oppression is fundamentally a social-group–based phenomenon, one part of the question, the part I shall concentrate on in this chapter, is: What psychological mechanisms account for our tendency to form social groups and to invidiously discriminate among those groups? My general thesis in this chapter, then, is this: Originating in the cognitive process of stereotyping, oppression materially and psychologically harms its victims. In the following two chapters I take up the issue of material harms. In chapter 6 I shall attempt to explain how these harms are magnified by psychological harm, and how they strengthen the oppressor and further weaken the oppressed, making escape difficult or impossible.

2. Using Psychological Theory to Explain Oppression

In the literature on the psychology of oppression, two kinds of theories have competed: (1) psychoanalytic theories, deriving from Freud and represented by, among other versions, the object relations theory of Nancy Chodorow; and (2) the recognition theory that is directly derived from the Hegelian master-slave dialectic and most significantly advanced in the twentieth century by Frantz Fanon (also a psychoanalyst himself) and recently propounded by Cynthia Willett. In this section I will illustrate each and show how each is inadequate as a part of a general theory of oppression, or even as an account of all the main features of psychological oppression. I will then offer an alternative psychological theory on which to ground our understanding of oppression in the next section.

2.1. *Psychoanalytic Theories of Oppression*

Psychoanalysis purports to explain behavior by invoking the psychic connections and mechanisms of the unconscious that are inevitably formed through the innately preprogrammed psychosexual development of the young child. All psychoanalytic schools thus attempt to explain the puzzling, apparently irrational, so-called pathological, features of our behavior by showing that repressed unconscious urges are being satisfied or unconscious fantasies are being played out through the behavior in question. Since oppression, if it is not rooted in clear hierarchies of ability, seems to involve social pathology on the part of both oppressed and oppressor, a natural application of psychoanalytic theory is to attempt to explain oppression.

Nancy Chodorow's pioneering work, *The Reproduction of Mothering: Psychoanalysis and the Sociology of Gender*, attempts to explain the pathologies of gender. Why do women mother and men do not, that is, why (and how) do females (typically) become the mothering, caring, nurturing, intimacy-building gender and males become the gender whose psychology and social style (typically) is more suited to the distant relationships of the market, the court, and the battlefield? Not only was this a surprising question when she asked it, she also had a very surprising answer. Women are *not by nature* mothers, she argued, they are made into mothers by their mothers (and, through physical absence and emotional distance, their fathers). How do they do this? The answer Chodorow gives is psychoanalytic, it has to do with various childhood sexual intrigues and the resulting complexes that have been theorized by psychoanalysts since Freud, but with a special emphasis on the "object-relational experiences" of individuals as they mature. Chodorow's theory is a theory of oppression if one sees gender roles as they are constituted as oppressive. Hence, I view this as a psychological theory of oppression, at least of women in cultures where child-rearing practices are relevantly similar. While Chodorow's general explanation of why women mother seems quite right, we shall see that the explanatory theory adduced is not adequate as a psychological theory of oppression of women, let alone as the foundation for a more general theory of oppression.

Chodorow argues that since women raise children and children identify with the same-sex parent and not with the other-sex parent, girls and boys go through different kinds of phases of the development of their ability to have close, sexual and other intimate, relationships with others. The old Freudian Oedipus complex plays a central role in this theory. There is for each sex an *oedipal goal*, and that is some sort of normal heterosexual orientation and role development.[1] The way that the Oedipus complex is *resolved* for boys makes them distant and unable to closely connect with others, and makes them not want or need the same sort of close, almost internal connection that a mother has with a child. Girls' resolution of their Oedipus complex, though, makes them need this sort of connection, and thus they are led to want the kind of exclusive relationships to children that exclusive mothering involves. There is a continued importance of the girl's internal and external relation to her mother, and this lengthens the pre-oedipal phase. This makes girls more relationally complex, while boys' capacities for relations are cut off by the masculine Oedipus complex.

Girls, since they identify with their mothers and, more importantly perhaps, their mothers with them, go through a longer period of symbiosis. Mothers, on Chodorow's theory, tend to feel the separateness of their daughters less because they were also once girls. Both genders of children tend to "live out their mother's preoccupations or fantasies," but girls do so with more empathy. For the boy it is very important that "the mother is as much in need of a husband as the son is of a father" (Chodorow 1978, 104, quoting Bibring 1953), and since the father is often absent (at work) the mother has a tendency to "turn her affection and interest to the next obvious male—her son—and become particularly seductive toward him" (Chodorow 1978, 104). This gets the Oedipus complex going when the father then threatens the son (or so the son thinks) with castration. The kind of evidence that Chodorow refers to concerns child development milestones. For instance, she claims that evidence suggests that children become aware of their genitals around age two, and boys often get more concerned with them because of the difference between them and mother, though girls can develop penis envy at this time, as well.[2] But the links that Chodorow forges between this evidence and her theory are merely to show consistency; nothing in the child development evidence itself could either verify or falsify psychoanalytic theory.

Chodorow does not question the psychoanalytic perspective, nor does she defend it. In fact it is assumed that the reader will simply accept that there is an Oedipus complex, and that our personalities are determined largely by the age of five through the stimulation of sexual drives in us. Chodorow defends her lack of defense of psychoanalysis as follows: "Psychoanalytic theory remains the most coherent, convincing theory of personality development available for an understanding of fundamental aspects of the psychology of women in our society, in spite of its biases" (Chodorow 1978, 142). But given that she presents no defense of or direct evidence[3] for her brand of psychoanalysis, the critical reader is left to judge this claim by examining the evidence for psychoanalysis more generally. Here the picture is not too good for psychoanalysis. In the most sweeping analysis of the empirical evidence for the theory of psychoanalysis to date, Adolf Grünbaum argues that the only empirical test offered by Freud is clinical, and consists of a two-step process: (1) does the specific theory for a patient tally with what the patient thinks is real; and (2) does it lead to therapeutic success? Grünbaum concludes, "Insofar as the evidence for the major causal hypotheses of the psychoanalytic corpus is held to derive from the productions of patients in analysis, this warrant is remarkably weak" (Grünbaum 1984, 278).

Psychoanalysis has received so little positive empirical corroboration that most philosophical defenders of the theory concede defeat here and now claim that it is a hermeneutic, not a scientific, enterprise. As Jane Flax puts it, the goal of the therapist and patient "is not 'truth' in the empiricist sense of what 'really' happened to the patient, but rather understanding which includes a powerful affective and experiential component" (Flax 1981, 566). But on these grounds the theory is also in trouble. First, as Grünbaum meticulously and convincingly argues (Grünbaum 1984, 1993), Freud himself did not intend the theory to be merely an a priori narrative of meaning but a scientifically grounded psychological theory. Of course, we may simply want to say that Freud was mistaken on this. Second, to take psychoanalysis seriously as a hermeneutic theory, we need to ask what criteria of adequacy it would offer as a defense of the claim that it is the best theory of behavior of its kind. I can see two such criteria being (implicitly) offered: first, the resonance test: Does the story that is offered to the patient resonate with her experience or does the theory offered explain some cultural feature that resonates with those who live in the culture (or its descendant culture)? And second, the *coherence test*: Does the theory cohere with the facts as it describes them, that is, can it weave together the facts in a plausible connected narrative? These tests are certainly necessary tests of the initial plausibility of a theory, but they are hardly sufficient to give us good reason to believe them. The resonance test applied by individuals to their own experience is quite subjective, as it asks one to introspect about intersubjectively non-verifiable aspects of one's personal experience. Hence, it is hardly a reliable scientific test, though possibly a starting point to test for initial plausibility. At the level of social theory, a psychoanalytic narrative seems to be open to intersubjective test, since there are so many persons in the culture who could pass judgment on it. But this turns out not to be the case if the theory is postulating some sort of general psyche of the culture, since in that case no one person is the subject, the culture is the subject. The coherence test is a more reliable test, however. Granting for the sake of argument that the narrative is coherent, that is, that it posits a narrative that plausibly ties the facts of psychological development together, the issue that one must address in assessing the theory is whether it is the best theory. Are there other coherent narratives that plausibly explain the same facts? And if there are, do these theories have anything else going for them that Chodorow's theory does not offer? Are they empirically testable, coherent with well-tested or otherwise more acceptable theories of neighboring phenomena, more fruitful scientifically or for progressive politics? Do they rely on less dubious assumptions?

Chodorow has very interesting things to say about the sociology of gender and of mothering, but the entire psychoanalytic account that forms the core of her theory is to my mind unwarranted because there are better theories that are equally (at least) coherent, and that resonate better with my (admittedly subjective) understanding of my life. Chodorow's theory and psychoanalytic theory fails to resonate for me at all. Since many of the events that are supposed to form us happen before we are five years old, and they are now subject to repression by the unconscious, it is difficult to see how we would gather reliable evidence about them anyway. But granting that we can for the sake of argument, almost nothing that she says seems to resonate with any of my experiences in life, nor those of my family and friends. Indeed one woman friend I asked about this remarked that she had never even seen her father's penis, so how could she have so early envied it, or even been aware of penises when she was so young? This account relies heavily on the seduction of girls by their fathers and boys by their mothers, but it seems totally implausible that there is this cross-generational sexual interest (that is, parents for children *and* children for parents) going on in nearly every family, as would have to be the case for the reproduction of mothering as a general phenomenon to happen in the way that Chodorow supposes. It seems to me that aside from a relatively small proportion of the people I know (all of whom are literary intellectuals with very fertile imaginations), psychoanalytic theory is met with complete and utter disbelief, and even horror. Now I am relying on personal, not statistical data here. But Chodorow gives us no other evidence to appeal to other than our own subjective experiences, and on this test her theory fails miserably.

On the other hand, as I have already mentioned, her conclusion seems entirely right to me. To quote Chodorow:

As a result of having been parented by a woman, women are more likely than men to seek to be mothers, that is, to relocate themselves in a primary mother-child relationship, to get gratification from the mothering relationship, and to have psychological and relational capacities for mothering. (Chodorow 1978, 206)

But a wide variety of psychological theories, from social-learning theory to cognitive development theory would also conclude as much, for all she is really saying, when we abstract from the psychoanalysis, is that women are mothers because they learn to be mothers from their mothers (and men learn not to be mothers from their mothers). Later in this chapter I will argue that one could come to this conclusion without the psychoanalytic account, by means of a theory that offers empirical tests and greater initial plausibility of its assumptions.

Another theoretical problem for Chodorow's theory as a psychological theory of oppression is that it is hard to see how it might be extended to analyze forms of oppression other than gender oppression. Thus, if there is a psychological theory that can account for other forms of oppression as well, it will be superior to this psychoanalytic account on what is sometimes called by philosophers of science the "fruitfulness" criterion.

Aside from these theoretical problems, Chodorow's theory, appealing to such early life experiences as determinative of all future (mothering) behavior, offers us no escape from gender oppression. In the end of the book she suggests that her narrative shows how much both sexes should want to change from women-only mothering. But it seems to me that if her argument were right she would have shown what incentives both men and women have to keep things the same. Men get to remain dominant, and women get to charge themselves up with these intensely personal, symbiotic relationships, and given the way that their early training has determined their desires, they have no desire to change this arrangement. Furthermore, psychoanalytic theories generally locate pathologies, including the social pathology of oppression, in personal failings. This also makes the prospects of a solution bleak, for the solution would have to be psychotherapeutic and thus individual, rather than political and collective, unless we are willing to coerce a generation of men and women to act counter to their deepest desires, a project that would surely generate its own pathologies. Although my objections to psychoanalysis as a foundation for a theory of oppression have focused on Chodorow's theory, the problems I have identified in her theory generalize, I believe, to other psychoanalytic theories. First, they attempt to justify their claims by the same dubious criteria of adequacy. Second, they focus on early psychosexual development as explanatory for all future psychological development. Finally, they all focus on individuals rather than institutional level processes. Thus, I find psychoanalytic theory to be politically paralyzing as well as theoretically and empirically inadequate as a theory of oppression.

2.2. Recognition Theory

The recognition theory of oppression originated in the master–slave dialectic advanced by Hegel in a relatively short but well-known section of *Phenomenology of*

Spirit and was recast by Fanon to fit the situation of European colonial oppression in the twentieth century. The basic assumption of the recognition theory is that all persons most strongly desire recognition from others because only through recognition can one become conscious of oneself, a goal that is taken to be universal and overriding. Hegel puts this in his characteristically abstract way when he writes: "Self-consciousness exists in and for itself when, and by the fact that, it so exists for another; that is, it exists only in being acknowledged" (Hegel 1977, 111). Self-consciousness in and for itself is the logical and developmental goal for humanity, according to Hegel, and thus acknowledgment, specifically in the form of recognition by other self-conscious beings, is humanity's primary motivating force. At the beginning of the master-slave dialectic, each individual is only a bare self-consciousness, not yet "in and for itself," and it must reach out to another being that is self-conscious in order to become objectively real in and for itself, a phrase that might be interpreted as "free and aware of itself as free." Only other self-conscious beings can make one's own self-consciousness public and hence real. However, in the dialectical order, this necessitates a competition for recognition between two beings who are as yet bare self-consciousness, since in Hegel's theory (for logical reasons, which I am going to quickly pass over), there are only two choices at this point of an individual's development toward full and free self-consciousness: either become a being-for-itself and make the other a slave who acts under the direction of one's own will, or give up that quest and accept the other as the one who is the master, the being-for-itself. Thus, being recognized without recognizing in return makes one the master over the other, the one who recognizes but is not recognized, who then becomes the slave. For Hegel (and for Fanon as well but for somewhat different reasons), this struggle is a mortal struggle, in which the vanquished submit only to avoid death. In demanding and winning recognition from the slave, the master gains power over the slave and is able to demand from the slave whatever the master desires. So the slave is made to do the work that the master chooses not to do; the slave is made into a mere tool. The master's humanity initially seems to be reinforced by being able to direct the will of another human being; the master seems to become in and for herself.

In the Hegelian version of the story, though, the slave learns to transform objects into valuable things, and this transforms him into an "objectified" human being, that is, a human being who is no longer merely a tool controlled by the will of the master, but one who consciously manipulates nature and transforms ideas into objectively real objects. Furthermore, the slave must learn to ignore his daily needs and desires in order to serve the master, but this frees him from the dictates of sensuous nature. Meanwhile, as the master becomes dependent on the slave, she loses her ability to objectify nature and becomes dependent on the actions of and recognition by the slave, who has been reduced to an animal, a mere tool. In the end (through a process of stoic adjustment to physical deprivations), the slave becomes self-consciousness in and for itself, while the master never is able to reach the in-itself stage because of her dependence on the slave. The master's stagnation, in turn, sets the stage for the dialectical overcoming of the dependency on the master by the slave.

While he clearly appreciated the logic and the psychology of the theory, Fanon criticized this story for its paternalism; it is after all, a very convenient ideology for the powerful to rationalize their domination over the weak and to teach them to obey. Hegel emphasizes that there are two essential stages on the way to true freedom: absolute fear of death and servitude.[4] It is the story of how the strict father raises the magisterial son, how the tough Marine drill sergeant strips the raw recruit of his dignity to make a tough and obedient soldier, or how the violent colonial power teaches the natives to be civilized Christian workers. Fanon, the radical, Afro-Caribbean psychiatrist working in colonial Algeria, rejected the paternalism and ideology in Hegel's theory of oppression while accepting the basic psychological assumption that all persons are motivated by the desire for recognition.

Like Hegel, Fanon emphasizes the need for recognition, which he claimed is necessary for one's dignity, identity, and self-worth. But Fanon puts a psychoanalytic twist on the Hegelian recognition theory. He also thinks that there are two complexes involved in colonial oppression: Whites have a superiority complex from having killed people to assert their dominance, and blacks develop an inferiority complex from having been slaves. Fanon as psychiatrist documents the psychopathological effects of oppression on the oppressed: Confined by laws and regulations, the oppressed learn to "think, dream, and act as a helpless minority of one." They complain of many somatic and psychosomatic afflictions. Oppressed persons turn on themselves and on each other and so become their own "intropressors."[5]

Like Hegel, Fanon holds that one must risk life for freedom, but unlike in Hegel, there is nothing metaphorical in Fanon's analysis. Violence takes on paramount importance in his last work, *The Wretched of the Earth.* Reflecting the circumstances of colonialism, he sees violence as the primary way that the oppressors maintain oppression and the only means by which the oppressed can regain freedom. Oppression is essentially violence for Fanon, either outright violence or institutionalized or incipient violence, and all forms of oppression are seen as a kind of violence: economic, psychological, and cultural violence. The only recourse is counterviolence—violence in the usual sense—against the oppressor. Counterviolence not only chases away the colonial rulers but it also makes the oppressed into an organized people who are self-conscious of themselves as a people, and of their own dignity and freedom. Fanon writes:

> Violence alone, violence committed by the people, violence organized and educated by its leaders, makes it possible for the masses to understand social truths and gives the key to them. Without that struggle, without that knowledge of the practice of action, there's nothing but a fancy-dress parade and the blare of trumpets.... and down there at bottom an undivided mass, still living in the middle ages, endlessly marking time. (Fanon 1963, 147)

In addition, on a personal psychological level, joining in and practicing organized violence against the oppressor releases oppressed persons from their internalized oppression, the inferiority complexes they suffer.[6]

From Hegel and Fanon I believe there is much to learn about the psychology of oppression. In particular, both convince me that humans desire recognition by others, and that this is not reducible to any purely materialistic desire. In addition, Fanon makes a convincing case that psychology is fundamentally social psychology, that to understand the individual and to understand the causes of psychopathology in human individuals, one must understand the social context in which recognition is given or withheld. Furthermore, Fanon's account of liberation is especially important in cultures in which violence is the pervasive method of preserving dominance relations. However, I also find that their theories are limited by an androcentric vision of freedom, fear, and struggle, an androcentrism that limits the applicability of their psychology of oppression to a majority of oppressed people. First, both Hegel and Fanon emphasize violence and the physical aspects of resistance and staking one's claim to freedom. They do this for different reasons, however. Hegel's idealist goal for humanity is to become pure self-consciousness, to be free by being released from sensuous nature, to become a pure soul. If we stake our lives on the struggle for freedom, then, we stake all of sensuous nature, we express our willingness to sacrifice it for our spiritual freedom. This willingness itself, publicly expressed, shows us that we are free, and that showing, for Hegel, makes us free. But, as many feminists and others have argued, such freedom leaves us without any ability to value our freedom. If we have no particularity, no desires, no bodies, what good is our freedom? Viewing us as unembodied, rational souls is androcentric. This view is mistaken because it takes desire and embodiment to be the obstacles to our freedom, rather than essential elements of our selves.

Fanon, on the other hand, insists on the violent struggle to the death for a very practical reason: It is the only way to show the colonial power that the colonized are serious in their threats, and thus the only way to win physical freedom. As a comprehensive theory of oppression and resistance to oppression, however, this seems again to be very androcentric in view. Such an uncompromising view seems plausible only to one who is accustomed to seeing himself as the only one for whom he is ultimately responsible. But that is not true to the experience of caregivers, who are typically women. A primary parent might, in the face of violence, ask herself: Is freedom worth the life of my child? Many parents feel that they would gladly give their lives for their children, and likewise that they would suffer oppression for the sake of saving their children, or at least, to give them the chance to fight another day. And this does not seem unreasonable; surely life is a necessary condition for a good life. Nor does it seem cowardly or deserving of scorn,[7] for such a person is willing to face death or slavery for the sake of someone else—not one's own freedom, but the life of a child. Since life is a precondition for freedom, one could see this as quite a reasonable objection to engaging in the Hegelian or Fanonian struggle or seeing it as the true expression of human freedom.

Cynthia Willett, in her book *Maternal Ethics and Other Slave Moralities*, presents yet a different Hegelian-inspired conception of freedom and struggle that she derives from "interrogating" Hegel's master-slave dialectic with the slave narrative of Frederick Douglass. While she rejects the Hegelian conception of freedom as gained through the stoic rejection of bodily desires and the acceptance of the liberating power of forced labor, she accepts Hegel's claim that the fundamental motivating force for humans is the desire for recognition and finds evidence for both of these positions in Douglass's writings. Willett turns to Hegel for understanding oppression because she holds that Hegel is able to explain socio-psychological aspects of domination that a materialist analysis cannot.

Willett's interpretation of Hegel emphasizes the "ontogeny recapitulates phylogeny" interpretation of the *Phenomenology*, in other words, she takes it that the book describes the development of both humanity in general and individual humans. As Willett interprets it, the master-slave dialectic posits that freedom requires a test of one will over another will, not just of the will over desire or appetite. This competition of wills leads to the near-death struggle that results in the capitulation and enslavement of one of the wills. But as we have seen, the master is ironically prevented from achieving the freedom he seeks, while the slave transcends his unfreedom, in the end, and becomes in and for itself by going through a stoic phase that causes him to separate from his bodily desires. As Willett points out, Hegel thus recognized that it is slave cultures not master cultures that progressively create new and transformative cultures, but he failed to recognize the Eurocentrism of the stoic move. Hegel's narrative of freedom replaces the warrior's concept of freedom with the worker's as humanity progresses toward absolute spirit, and this too proves to be Eurocentric upon Willett's interrogation.

Willett rejects Hegel's narrative of freedom, pointing out the ways that it is a "masculinized" (i.e., androcentric) story because it privileges reason, literacy, and public life. As she explains it, freedom for Hegel, and hence his concept of the moral person, requires a radical break from nature, women, and African men. But in addition to the diagnoses of Eurocentrism and androcentrism, she argues that it conflicts with the phenomenological evidence of the struggle from slavery to freedom that we have from the slave narratives of Frederick Douglass.

Still, Willett finds Hegel to have made an advance over the "classical conception of the slave as akin to the tool or other property" (Willett 1995, 123). I find her argument for the claim that desire for recognition is at the root of slavery unconvincing, however. She argues that Hegel shows how "the master needs the slave not only for rituals of deference but also to play out the fantasies of his own repressed self" (Willett 1995, 127), as opposed to seeing slaves as primarily desired for economic wealth and income. Willett finds supporting evidence for her psychological interpretation in slave narratives, which report that impudence, not destruction of property, was the worst crime that a slave could commit. She reasons: "impudence would threaten the master *only if* the master depends on the oppression of the slave not simply as property but for a sense of self" (Willett 1995, 123). But surely this is not the case. Impudence, or in more neutral terms, disobedience, threatens the master if he wants continued obedience, that is, if he wants to continue the master-slave relationship for any reason. This holds true just as much if slavery is primarily motivated by economic reasons as for any other motivation. Good evidence for this claim can be gleaned from training manuals for animals, where it is stressed that training is upset or derailed if disobedience is not met with swift punishment.[8] Calling disobedience "impudence" allows the master to rationalize to himself the punishment of the slave. Furthermore, to say that honor is being sought from animals as well would contradict the claim that honor cannot be gotten from deference shown by animals, one of the recognition theory's central claims. But perhaps there is more evidence for the claim of the centrality of recognition from Douglass's writings.

As Douglass portrays his experience of slavery and freedom, Hegel seems correct in his understanding of the irony of slavery. While masters did seem to have a social and psychological dependence on slaves, slaves did not feel freed or fulfilled by work, and work was not an essential component of subjective freedom for African-Americans. In her reading of Douglass, Willett focuses on a passage in which Douglass recounts having first resisted when he was threatened with a whipping for an offense he had not committed. In this instant he suddenly saw the injustice and arbitrariness of what the master called "punishment" and reclaimed what he describes as his sense of manhood and of freedom. In seeing the arbitrariness of the punishment and reacting to it violently, Douglass reveals both the master's need for recognition and his own, according to Willett. Where the master's need for recognition is revealed is in the fact that Douglass was to be punished despite the fact that he had not committed a wrong that needed to be corrected; thus, "punishment" of the slave cannot be only for training or correction, but must be to satisfy some other deep-seated psychological need of the master. But this does not follow, either. In the story Douglass relates, Covey, the slavebreaker, threatens to whip Douglass, who then appeals for justice from the master. The master refuses to intervene. This refusal can be seen as simply a management policy on the part of the master that is reasonable on the (of course, unreasonable and immoral) assumption that the slave is a mere tool. Again, we can see the motivation to enforce arbitrary punishment as supporting a purely instrumental attitude toward the slave, and not necessarily as revealing some deep-seated need for recognition from the slave.

Willett offers two other pieces of evidence for the claim that the desire for recognition, and not for material wealth, is the driving force of slavery. First, she claims that it can explain at least in part a point of political history: "the South refused offers from President Lincoln for compensated emancipation and the colonization of blacks" (Willett 1995, 123). The South's refusal on this point, though, was plausibly a demand for recognition from Northern politicians and the Federal Government, not from black slaves. The point shows that the South wanted to maintain slavery rather than sell out. Does it show that recognition was their primary aim in the institution of slavery? It is important first to note that ending slavery would require the South to entirely remake their economy, a proposal that had deep long-term costs, and second that the economic winners and losers in this compensation scheme might well not have been the same as the winners and losers from slavery. Thus, the economic winners from slavery might have had an economic incentive to maintaining slavery, even if overall the compensation would have been adequate. In any case, this evidence does not show the "socio-psychological dependence of white master on black slave" (Willett 1995, 123). At best it would show the psychological dependence of Southern politicians on the institution of slavery.

Finally, and most importantly for Willett's overall project, her theory of the self posits the desire for recognition at the very core. To evaluate this we need to examine whether her theory of the self, which also depends on earlier sections of the book, independently supports and necessitates the desire for recognition as a universal and overriding desire. Willett's project is not primarily to show that recognition is the driving motivation of humanity; that is for her an assumption that she minimally defends. Her defense is mainly indirect: She claims to show that her interpretation of the development of the self leads to interesting, non-masculinist, anti-colonial interpretations of freedom. I shall not argue against this notion of freedom, but rather show that her evidence can be interpreted consistently with alternative understandings of human motivation.

Willett presents a theory of the self that is essentially embodied, and she sees Douglass's views of freedom as consistent with her view. Although Douglass embodies his struggle as his "manhood," unlike Hegel, Douglass does not see freedom as requiring the alienation of the body or of the victory of reason over embodied desire. Willett finds evidence in Douglass of a more embodied and, despite his references to "manhood," gender-inclusive conception of freedom. She argues that Douglass had something like her notion of "tactile sociality" in his discussion of "the veriest freedom." I am less interested here in whether this is an accurate reading of Douglass than whether this idea of freedom and its corresponding notion of the self implicates recognition as a universal and overriding desire. By "tactile sociality" Willett refers to her view that "sociality begins in the caress" (Willett 1995, 41), that is, humans are made into beings who can interact socially through, initially, the tactile interchange between mother and fetus, and later between caregiver and infant. She cites evidence from child development literature that children's affective development, and the ability to socialize successfully with others, is crucially shaped by these early social exchanges of touch, that happen before linguistic interchange is possible.[9] In addition, the caregiver is transformed by these experiences (Willett 1995, 40). Thus, this tactile sociality forms a crucial ethical moment in human lives (one that has been omitted from the dominant ethical theories of the West). The crucial move in the argument from this point for recognition theory, then, is to identify this ethical moment as an exchange of recognition. Thus, recognition becomes the first ethical moment and the defining motivation for humanity. Douglass suggests to Willett that he has something of tactile sociality in mind when he recalls the touch of his grandmother, who raised him, and his mother, whom he saw only at night as she came in from the fields, in speaking of what true freedom would be like. Willett cites Douglass as saying that these experiences, not the struggle with the slavebreaker, provided for him the positive notion of "the veriest freedom" (Willett 1995, 170). Thus, she interprets Douglass's notion of freedom as involving maternal virtues: connection, not separation, and recognition, not negation of sociality. From the child development literature, Willett cites facts such as the need that infants have for human skin-to-skin contact for full affective development, the demands of the infant for attention over and above food, warmth, and cleaning, and the pre-verbal interchanges between child and caregiver that resemble dance more than conversation.

These facts do not contradict Willett's interpretation, but neither do they lend strong support to her theory if there are interpretations of them that do not require recognition as the universal human motivation. For instance, if we interpret skin-to-skin contact and stimulating interchanges as simply pleasurable stimuli, desired by other animals as well who would not require "recognition," then we can fit these observations into any of many other psychological theories. In other words, these observations do not rule out other psychological theories. The issue then is whether it fits into the best theory. I will argue shortly that there is a good theory of the psychology of oppression that does not rely on recognition as the fundamental driving force and fits with our materialist account of oppression better.

Recognition theory purports to be a descriptive theory, yet offers no clear criterion of adequacy for determining if it is correct or not. Although a desire for recognition seems vaguely plausible, none of these authors offer empirical tests of the theory. Like hermeneutic psychoanalysts, they rely on the reader feeling that there is some resonance with the story that they weave. They offer as little in the way of empirical evidence, and for both it is merely coherence with the facts and not evidence for the psychological mechanisms proposed. Hegel spins a story that is supposed to correspond to both human ontogenesis and phylogenesis, but he never considers competing stories (nor does he offer concrete tests of any hypotheses, though surely it would be anachronistic to look for them in Hegel). Fanon also fails to offer competing stories, though he does discuss clinical cases. Yet these clinical cases are only very vaguely tied to the Hegelian-inspired narrative of freedom and oppression.

Willett provides more extensive evidence for her recognition theory, though not enough to convince me that recognition is the fundamental driving motivation for humans. I have argued that her evidence is ambiguous: the narrative of Douglass, a few scattered remarks from other slave narratives, and one fact from political history that is supposed to support the claim that recognition, not economic gain, drove the slave trade. Each of these can be explained by an economic theory that takes slaves to be instrumentally valuable. The child development evidence is ambiguous in that it is about children's desires for touch, play, and other tactile social interchange with the mother and other adults—interactions that could as well be described as simply pleasant stimuli rather than exchanges of recognition.

To take recognition theory seriously as a competing psychological theory, one would need to subject it to serious experimental tests in a variety of test situations, from surveys to artificial experiments to clinical tests of different therapies some of which are based on recognition theory. Yet this evidence is almost entirely lacking. Instead of being a well-worked out and thoroughly tested theory of psychology, it seems to be a fantasy of philosophy. It is not entirely implausible to this philosopher, but it remains to be tested, and thus is hardly the psychological theory on which to rest a general theory of oppression—especially not if there is a viable competitor.

In addition to these empirical shortcomings, there is a common theoretical critique of recognition theory, as well. The recognition theorists share the Hegelian view that, as Bulhan puts it, "the question of oppression is primarily a problem of psyches confronting each other in society" (Bulhan 1985, 118). This quote summarizes what is fundamentally wrong with the recognition theory of oppression. Recognition theorists hold that some groups in society have collective psyches that are locked in a mortal combat with each other that mirrors the struggles of individuals. But this view is ontologically strange, and ultimately psychologically incoherent. It requires that there exist concrete collectives with psychologies, that there are minds writ large, like some sort of Wizard of Oz, and the collectives act as individual beings in response to the actions of other such collectives, as if they had internal sensory and psychological mechanisms like human individuals. Yet collectives do not appear to have those organs or mechanisms, and so psychological theory, which purports to explain the behavior of individuals based on either instinctual, biological, or otherwise constructed cognitive and affective mechanisms, can have nothing to say, except metaphorically, about such entities.

While I am persuaded that humans desire recognition, I am not convinced that the desire for recognition is more fundamental than all other desires, much less that it is the psychological motor driving oppression.[10] Nor does recognition theory even attempt to answer the first question that we set before us in the introduction to this chapter: Why does this group (rather than that collection of humans) come to be a group and to have this or that position in a hierarchy of social dominance relations? For an answer to that question without the drawbacks of the psychological theories of oppression that we have examined, we shall have to look at social cognitive theory.

2.3. *Social Cognitive Theories of Stereotype Formation*

If we want to understand the psychology of oppression, I believe that we need to begin at a point prior to the motivation question, that is, to understand how individuals think about, feel about, and decide to act toward others. By this I mean that we need to understand why individual humans form groups and come to identify with their group membership, when they do. On my view, oppression is fundamentally a group phenomenon. To study the psychology of oppression as a matter of individual motivations to oppress, as psychoanalysis and recognition theory do, is to approach oppression in the wrong way. Social psychology has always studied the right sorts of phenomena to build an understanding of the psychology of oppression. In particular, social psychologists have long been concerned with the formation of stereotypes and attitudes about individuals and the groups that they belong to, and ultimately, the causal efficacy of those stereotypes and attitudes in behavior. Since its origins as an independent discipline at the turn of the century, social psychology has been concerned with the formation of beliefs and attitudes toward other persons and how these are manifested in behavior. In its early days, however, social psychology was limited by some of the same theoretical and methodological defects that we found with psychoanalytic theories and the recognition theories, namely, there was little understanding of the causal mechanisms that underlay these thoughts and feelings and actions. Social psychology, where it was useful or more than mere speculation at all, was largely a descriptive enterprise; beautiful theory could be spun, but justification for the theory was remote and basically limited to the resonance and coherence tests.

The key development in making stereotype research a scientifically viable endeavor was the cognitive revolution of the 1960s. The cognitive revolution has enabled psychology to go beyond the level of description to empirically testable causal explanations of psychological processes by examining the cognitive structures in the brain that cause us to perceive data and draw inferences as we do. Psychologists began to see thought as a string of information-processing and information-generating processes, which could be experimentally studied in isolation and then recombined in order to have a clearer analysis of the whole. Social cognitive theory combines the interests in persons, their social interactions, and their formation of self-concepts with the methods of cognitive psychology; it applies the theories from cognitive psychology regarding general cognitive functions such as perception, attribution, and categorization to understand persons and their interaction. The combination provides a scientific, causal theory of the social psychology of humans. What the theory has to say about how we form groups and beliefs about them is, therefore, crucial to an investigation of the psychology of oppression.

From its earliest days, social psychology has been keenly interested in the formation and function of stereotypes in our thoughts about and actions toward each other. Stereotypes are generalizations that we make about persons based on characteristics that we believe they share with some identifiable group. Stereotypes group us by, typically, visible characteristics and then carry with them a whole host of inferences about us that go well beyond the immediately visible and, often, the truth. For example, a white, middle-class, middle-age female perceiver from a rural state sees a brown-skinned, short-haired, taller than average person walking across campus and judges that it is a black man, then her stereotypes of black man cause her to form the beliefs that he is heading toward the gym to play basketball, probably listening to gangsta rap on the headphones he is wearing, and likely to be from a large city. If it is dark out and there is no one else around, she might entertain a more sinister belief about him, as well, and steer away from him. This example illustrates the two levels involved in stereotyping: from the visible characteristics (brown skin, short hair, tall) to the group (black man), and then from the group to characteristics about individuals in the group (basketball, rap, etc.). Stereotypes have, as this example shows, only a tenuous connection to the truth about individuals; they require minimal evidence for the wide range of inferences that they set in motion in our minds—from skin color, hair length, and height she inferred musical tastes! Because these inferences are to characteristics that we believe set groups of persons apart from other groups, stereotypes form the very foundation of our beliefs about groups. But how do we formulate these beliefs, and how good are they for our purposes?

There has long been a debate in social psychology research about the evidential basis for stereotypical beliefs and about the functions that stereotypes serve. On the one hand, it appears that stereotyping is a pervasive and unavoidable activity of humans, and so the processes underlying it must be adaptive, or at least not maladaptive. On the other hand, much injustice can be done to the individual who is grouped by a stereotype and whose choices or opportunities are limited by that grouping, especially when the stereotype does not hold in the particular case. So stereotyping seems very possibly to be an immoral activity. An early, precognitive theory about stereotyping held that stereotypes harbor a "kernel of truth" in them about individuals, that stereotypes come out of observations of individuals who belong to groups, and that inferences are made about the groups' characteristics, and these characteristics in turn are applied to other individuals who share the feature that causes others to group the members together. But it is just in the application of the stereotype to a new individual member of the group that the hypothesis may fail; the kernel of truth might be missing entirely in this individual case—this black man might be listening to Bach on his way to orchestra practice.

The cognitive revolution brought with it the idea that stereotype formation is a kind of categorization, like our categorization of all our perceptual data. Cognitive psychologists hold that categorization is a fundamental process of thought that is essential to efficient information processing.[11] Individual thinkers are seen as cognitive misers, whose goal is to simplify experience and frame it according to what is relevant to our needs and interests. Since we often need split-second decisions to act smoothly and efficiently in our environment, human cognitive processing has evolved to provide quick and dirty generalizations that, in a great enough proportion of our encounters, suffice to allow enough of us to survive and propagate. Greater precision, it is theorized, would require more time and attention, and would too often have cost the thinker its life in the primitive survival of the fittest. The cognitive miser, thus, is an efficient but often wrong generalizer, who cannot be blamed for the overgeneralizations that he sometimes develops that do not apply, though he could, perhaps, be trained to generalize more carefully in crucial situations.[12]

The cognitive model of categorization, of which stereotyping is one type, holds that a category is represented by a prototype, from which there is extensive variation within the same category, and where the distance from the prototype determines the fit of the individual within the category. Categories are formed by accentuation of the similarities within categories and of the differences between categories. Stereotypes, as categories, are thus biased by this accentuation process. In what direction are they biased? A pair of important concepts in this connection is the in-group and the out-group. This distinction in social psychology pre-dates the cognitive revolution (Allport 1979), and is roughly this: the in-group refers to the group to which the perceiver belongs and the out-group refers to any groups to which she does not belong.[13] Stereotypes typically favor the in-groups and disfavor the out-groups of the person holding the stereotype. There are cognitive consequences of in- and out-group membership well-documented in the psychology literature, in particular, in-group heterogeneity (the belief that members of the in-group have varied and individual characteristics), out-group homogeneity (the belief that members of the out-group are essentially all the same), and out-group polarization (evaluation of "good" out-groupers more positive than warranted by evidence, while evaluations of "bad" ones more negative than warranted) (Fiske and Taylor 1991). But typically also there are common stereotypes that favor majority populations and disfavor minority ones. One theory closely associated with the cognitive miser model holds that stereotypes form in response to salient or novel information, and this novel information is then accentuated to make a group of persons who display this characteristic even more different from other groups (Fiske and Taylor 1991). Such a theory explains how stereotypes of minorities as very different from majority groups would form from evidence of small but novel differences.

The cognitive miser model fails to explain some crucial data about stereotype formation, however. First, it fails to explain the variety of stereotypes applied to the same persons by the same thinker but in different circumstances. And second, it fails to explain why the accentuation of differences leads to beliefs that tend to benefit (materially and psychologically) dominant populations and disfavor dominated ones; if this were a neutral cognitive process one would expect some stereotypes of each group to be positive and some negative. That is, the cognitive miser model fails to account for motivations that determine which stereotype will apply under what circumstances.

In some experiments, called "the minimal group" experiments (Oakes et al. 1994), in the early 1970s, Henri Tajfel tried to determine the minimal conditions for formation of in-group and out-group solidarity. In these experiments Tajfel and his colleagues randomly assigned schoolboys into two groups, but led them to believe that the grouping was based on real (though rather meaningless and trivial) criteria (e.g., their estimation of number of dots on a screen, their preference for Klee or Kandinsky paintings). The subjects were allowed no social interaction and they were not allowed to know even the identities of the others in the group. Nevertheless, the subjects treated their group membership as an important and salient fact. When asked to assign money to individuals they tended to assign more to those in their "own group" even though they were making no assignment of money to themselves and they knew this. These experiments were taken to show several things. First, that it takes very little information or basis for identification for people to establish an in-group/out-group distinction. Second, that discrimination behavior can be motivated by this minimal in-group/out-group distinction. Third, the experiments show that no actual facts about the groups (to be accentuated) have to be involved for positive evaluations of in-groups. Tajfel argued that two processes are at work here: first, group formation or categorization by social group, and second, the distinction between in-group and out-group according to one's assignment. The first of these is explained by categorization theory applied to the group. But the second was unique to social psychology, that is, cognitive psychology could not suggest a process that applied outside the social realm, as well. In order to explain these results, Tajfel came, over the course of the next decade, to develop a theory now known as social identity theory (Tajfel 1981).

Categorization theory suggests that people categorize their perceptual data to bring order to it, to give it meaning by relating it to other information and one's interests so that they can efficiently use it. Social categorization into in-group and out-group is likewise an attempt to order information about other persons, by connecting it to one's prior information and one's interests. How do we characterize our own interests? Here Tajfel suggested that we categorize ourselves by the in-groups and out-groups to which we belong, and so put a social ordering on our world, including our place in it. Thus, he linked the notion of the self with social categorization in the concept of a social identity, which he defined as "that part of an individual's self-concept which derives from his [sic] knowledge of his [sic] membership of a social group (or groups) together with the value and emotional significance attached to that membership" (Oakes et al. 1994, 82, quoting Tajfel).

Social identity theory postulates that individuals are motivated to develop a positive social identity, and that this is done by establishing the "positive distinctiveness" of one's own in-group. People want to believe that they have positive attributes, and because they identify themselves in part by the social groups that they consider their in-groups, people want to see their own groups in a positive light. Since not all groups can easily be seen positively when compared to other groups, people sometimes have to manipulate their beliefs in order to maintain a positive self-image. Even members of dominant groups can have self-image problems when they consider their advantages unwarranted. Several studies have shown how humans create or alter social stereotypes in order to manage their self-image; here I will discuss two such studies. An influential study by Curt Hoffman and Nancy Hurst suggests that stereotypes can be manipulated to rationalize social injustices. In particular, their research shows that gender stereotypes could arise simply as "explanatory fictions that rationalize and make sense of the sexual division of labor" (Hoffman and Hurst 1990, 199). The experiments involved telling subjects stories about a fictional planet where there were two categories of beings, Orinthians and Ackmians, and where there were two kinds of social roles, homemakers and city workers. The authors described each of the beings with personality traits, occupations, and species. They made it so that there was no correlation whatsoever between the personalities, social roles, and category. In one experiment they made the Orinthians and Ackmians the same species and in another they made them different species. The authors then asked the subjects a set of questions, which the authors manipulated as follows: they always asked about role and category distribution, they sometimes asked for an explanation of why the Orinthians and Ackmians occupied the social roles that they did, and they asked for traits specific to each category. Finally, they interviewed the subjects to see if the subjects could detect the purpose of the experiment. (They could not.) The authors found that a strikingly large number (72 percent) of the subjects in the explanation condition attributed the roles to personality differences and stereotyped the categories by personality differences that reflected stereotypes of gender differences in personality. (Remember, there were no personality differences.) In the no explanation condition the subjects were much less likely to stereotype the categories. They interpret these results as showing that "objective sex differences in personality are not necessary to the formation of gender stereotypes; the fact of an unequal role distribution is sufficient" (Hoffman and Hurst 1990, 206). Further, the studies show that stereotype formation is at least partly mediated by the attempt to explain or rationalize the category-role correlation. Hence, stereotyping cannot be seen as an unbiased information-processing phenomenon, but one that is creatively manipulated by persons to serve their interest in a coherent rationalization of the social roles and the social groups that perform them.

A pair of studies conducted by Nyla Branscombe and her colleagues suggests that persons think differently about their social group-related privileges and disadvantages in order to bolster their social identity or to avoid group-effacing facts, and that this use of "social creativity strategies" is common to both advantaged and disadvantaged social groups (Branscombe 1999; Branscombe 1998). In one study Branscombe asked gender-segregated groups of men and women to write down ways that they had been privileged, for one set of groups (she calls this "the privilege condition"), or disadvantaged, for another set ("the disadvantage condition"). Their responses were coded for degree of severity by independent coders. The subjects then were assessed by a standard self-esteem scale, and by questions that assessed their emotional attachment to their gender group, their feeling that membership in that group was a positive experience, their general satisfaction with their lives, and their current mood. Branscombe found first that men tended to identify trivial ways that they were disadvantaged (e.g., having to pay for drinks) and serious ways that they were privileged (e.g., having higher incomes), while the reverse was true for women (e.g., having limited freedom of movement because of the threat of sexual assault vs. having doors opened for them). She also found that thinking about privilege or disadvantage had significantly different consequences for men and women.

On all of the well-being measures, thinking about privilege in men resulted in lower scores than when disadvantage was focused on. Different effects emerged for the gender comparisons in the two conditions on the personal and group relevant measures. Thinking about privilege resulted in less pride in and attachment to their gender group in men compared to women. However, on the personal measures, thinking about disadvantage resulted in higher personal self-esteem in men compared to women. (Branscombe 1998, 173)

Tajfel recognized the phenomenon of social creativity in interpretation of stereotypes on the part of disadvantaged groups: they tend to think about disadvantage mainly as a way of creating positive distinctiveness for their social group and increasing their identity with it (Tajfel 1978). Branscombe's experiment points to a correlative social creativity on the part of the advantaged. Her explanation of men's lowered mood when thinking of their privilege is that it is a result of the well-recognized "attribution error" that persons make by explaining their negative outcomes by pointing to external causes and their positive outcomes by attributing them to internal causes. So by focusing on only trivial disadvantages they can see women and men as both having disadvantages and also protect the notion that any success they have is due to their own personal capacities. If women were to also equate such privileges with those accorded men, and men's disadvantages with women's, then this might represent the development of a false consciousness.[14] In another study, Branscombe and her colleagues found a similar pattern of social creativity in accounting the advantages and disadvantages from race (Branscombe et al. 1996).

Stereotypes thus serve not only to group the social world, and then to place oneself in the social order, but also to do so in a way that bolsters the valuation of one's self-identity, insofar as that is possible within the given social realities. By determining alliances and oppositions among in-groups and out-groups, categorization provides the basis of social orientation toward others. Returning now to the discussion of the desire for recognition, the social cognitive description of this desire would be that we have the desire to categorize ourselves as members of in-groups and then to make those groups distinctive, and insofar as possible, positive. Thus, this psychological theory can explain the desire for recognition as a part of our cognitive functioning in a social world.

These theories, social categorization theory and self-identity theory, show how and why persons want to be members of in-groups and formulate stereotypes to structure the social psychological world in which they interact. We have, thus, provided an answer to the "why groups?" question. But we have still not answered the question, "why *these* groups?" There are actually three questions here: Why did these groups (as opposed to other groupings) first get started? Why do they continue as they do? And why do they change when they do? To answer this we must first note that individuals are not creating these in-group/out-group distinctions in a social cognitive vacuum, and (unless we subscribe to a creation *ex nihilo* theory) they never were. There is no first moment that there were human social groups. Humans have always been social groupers, if only by tribe or clan. So if we can answer the other two questions we should be able to theorize how humans came to sort themselves by the groups that we now find. There are two apparently competing accounts of the constraints imposed by existing social stereotypes in the social cognitive literature. One theory is that we learn generalized patterns, called schemas, that are then virtually fixed, causing counter-instances to be misperceived as conforming instances of the schema. The other, propounded by Oakes et al. following Tajfel, is that our categories reflect the reality of social groups, and so, as social groups change, our stereotypes would change as well. It seems to me that to answer both the continuity and change questions involves a combination of these theories.

There are a wide variety of stereotypes that individuals learn from their social environment among which they are normally constrained to choose. One cannot choose to stereotype women as large, aggressive, socially abrasive persons: First, one would never think of that (except to come up with an outlandish example for an academic paper), and second, one would have too hard a time communicating with others if one made this highly unconventional assumption. Schema theory postulates that we have cognitive structures, called "schemas," that are representations of concepts, that guide our perception, memory, inferential reasoning, and association, and in turn our behavior (Bem 1981). Schemas are networks of associations that organize our perceptions by assimilating them to relevant networks of ideas. We have schemas for persons (our folk psychology), for events (called "scripts"), and of most relevance to stereotypes, role schemas that code our perceptions and associations for social roles. Role schemas are, thus, one way of cognitively accounting for social stereotypes. Schema research differs from categorization research in that the latter is more concerned with the classification of instances and the former with the application of organized, generic, prior knowledge to the understanding of new information (Fiske and Taylor 1991). The difference here is that schemas generalize from specific instances, and so are represented as lists of attributes or associations, while categories are webs of prototypical and varying instances. As I see it, then, there is nothing inconsistent about accepting both theories as compatible, but serving slightly different functions in modeling the cognition of stereotypes. In particular, role schemas account for the stability of stereotypes and the categorization process for the plasticity and capacity for change in stereotypes.

Schemas frame our perceptions and then code our memories. Recalling the example of the black man on campus, the perceiver took in a few perceptual details and the schema for black man was engaged and several inferences were drawn about the man. In numerous studies it has been shown that were the perceiver to then learn something directly about the person, say by asking him what he was listening to, that fact would be much more likely to be remembered if it were consistent with the schema, that is, if in the example he were listening to gangsta rap (Fiske and Taylor 1991). Thus schemas code our memories and we have a difficult time with memories that do not fit the schema. Schemas also carry emotional responses with them; in the example the perceiver was apprehensive upon judging the object to be a black man. Although schemas are readily engaged by initial perceptions and are important to our cognitive and affective functioning, people are clearly able to disengage their schemas upon the presentation of sufficient counterevidence, under circumstances in which their decisions matter to them.[15]

Sandra Bem has provided the most well-developed account of role schemas in her theory of gender schemas. On her view, girls and boys learn gender roles as they grow up and code these as role schemas for gender. Gender, she claims, is the most ubiquitous schema we have: "No other dichotomy in human experience appears to have as many entities linked to it as does the distinction between female and male" (Bem 1987, 304). Children learn that there are gender appropriate and inappropriate attributes, then they apply these to themselves, that is, they identify themselves with one gender and take on the appropriate role for that gender. Through this identification and assimilation the gender schema becomes a self-fulfilling prophesy for cultural myths about sexual difference. Role schemas are thus learned through the social environment by assimilation of the self to the existing role schemas, and reinforced, reified, and justified in the assimilation. Social learning and reinforcement of role schemas account for the continuity and preservation of stereotypes over time, and thus account for the fact that women mother and men do not, for example.

There is a great deal of evidence supporting the idea that gender stereotypes are socially learned and that they are self-perpetuating. Gender stereotypes are learned especially early from one's parents. In an analysis of 172 different studies of parents' differential socialization of girls and boys, Hugh Lytton and David Romney (1991) found that parents' differentially reinforced gender behavior to conform to traditional stereotypes of female and male behavior, even though there was no other systematic way in which they differentially socialized their sons and daughters. There is a large literature about the self-fulfilling nature of social stereotypes, that is, about how stereotypical expectations by perceivers and common knowledge of these expectations cause persons to behave stereotypically. In an experiment by Berna Skrypnek and Mark Snyder (1982) anonymous male-female pairs bargained over three tasks, one stereotypically male, one female, and one neutral. In a third of the pairs the male partner (called "the perceiver") was told that his partner was male, in another third female, and in another third the male was not told the sex of the partner. The female (called "the target") partner knew the sex of the perceiver and what he had been told her sex was. The experimenters found that the behavior both of choosing and bargaining was affected by both the perceiver's perception and the target's knowledge of what the perceiver thought she was. "Targets believed by perceivers to be male chose tasks relatively feminine in nature [sic], and targets believed by perceivers to be female chose tasks relatively feminine in nature [sic]" (Skrypnek and Snyder 1982, 288). Another experiment by Snyder, Elizabeth Tanke, and Ellen Berscheid (1977) showed how the stereotype-generated attributions by a perceiver can cause the target to conform her behavior to the stereotype even if she does not know what stereotype he holds about her. In this experiment the (again male) perceivers were given controlled but specious information about their (again female) targets, with whom they then had a ten-minute phone conversation. The targets got no information about their partners, including no information about what information the males had, but the male perceivers were given snapshots that were purportedly of their partners, but which the experimenters had actually carefully chosen to be of either an attractive or unattractive woman (as perceived by independent coders) independently of the actual attractiveness or unattractiveness of the target subjects. The hypothesis was that the stereotypes of attractive women (that they are more sociable, sexually warm, kind, poised, outgoing) would affect the behavior of both the perceivers and the targets, in particular, that the behavior of both would tend to confirm the stereotypes. The data was coded by independent raters of the conversations, who rated the warmth and enthusiasm of each side of the conversations independently, with no information about the experiment or the men and women in them, and it convincingly corroborated the hypothesis. The authors explained the results by saying, "the differences in the level of sociability manifested and expressed by the male perceivers may have been a key factor in bringing out the reciprocating patterns of expression in the target women" (Snyder et al. 1977, 662).

To summarize the results surveyed here, then, people learn stereotypes from their social environment independently of their fit with the individual attributes grouped by the stereotypes, people's behavior induced by stereotypical attributions, whether true or false in the individual case, guide the behavior of their partners in interactions to conform to the stereotypes, and individuals' expectations of others' stereotypes guide their behavior to conform to stereotypes. Schema theory explains and predicts these experimental results because it postulates that schemas are learned in the environment, and individuals identify with them then assimilate their own behavior to accord with them.

Schema theory can thus account for the stability of stereotypes, but given their rigid entrenchment and self-fulfilling nature, it is difficult to see how stereotypes would ever change. Yet clearly they do; we do not stereotype Polish Americans as we used to, and now there are stereotypes for teenagers who wear baggy pants. Furthermore, the question of origin of particular groupings still has not been answered. To explain stereotype origin and change we need to look carefully at the kinds of things that motivate us to engage particular stereotypes when we do. We have seen how self-identity theory can explain how a particular stereotype from among a set of available ones can be contextually motivated, namely, the particular stereotype that is attended to is the one that makes one's self-identity most valuable to one under the circumstances. There are other sources of motivation that have been overlooked by the psychologists, namely economic incentives to conform to stereotypes or to cause others to do so. For the economically dominant group in society, there is a clear motivation to behave according to the stereotypes for that group, since by doing so one is most likely to reap the financial rewards that go with status in that group.

There is also, as I shall argue in chapter 5, an economic incentive for members of subordinated groups to behave according to the stereotypes for their groups, unless they can successfully pass as a member of a more dominant group. Social groups consist partly in incentive structures for persons to behave in particular ways. Take women in our culture, for instance. There are clear financial incentives for them to marry, since they then have access to a man's wealth and income, which, regardless of race, is on average higher than that of women (Idson and Price 1992), and which, therefore, they could rationally expect in the individual instance to be higher. Then if they have children, there are financial incentives for families for women to subordinate their careers so that their husbands can continue on the fast track in their higher earning potential career. Racial minorities also have some financial incentives to do what is stereotypical for them. Consider a poor black single woman with children. The social stereotype that applies is the "welfare mom." Given her situation, there is a financial incentive for her to receive welfare, especially when one takes into account the cost of alternative and equivalent-quality childcare, and not to marry, since statistically she is likely to find someone who is unemployed or underemployed and she would no longer be eligible for welfare. The point is that social stereotypes reflect the social incentive structures that people ought, rationally, to react to. Therefore, there is often a material incentive to comply with the behavior that stereotypes prescribe.

If the material incentives change, then it is only reasonable to assume that the stereotypes will change to reflect new incentives, though there may be some lag time. When Irish American men were no longer discriminated against in employment so that they had greater options than police work, the stereotypes of policemen as Irish faded. Just as there is a material incentive for persons to conform to their group stereotypes (unless they can pass for a member of a group with higher status), there are material incentives for persons to apply stereotypes to others strategically, when they can do it successfully. Consider the firm interviewing applicants for a position, some of whom are men and some women. Since it is statistically more likely that women will take reduced hours, maternity leave, and so on than a man, there is an incentive for firms, at least when hiring workers who are in their early middle age and who are likely not to stay over an entire career, to stereotype women and discriminate against them, either by not hiring them or by offering them lower salaries for equal work. Likewise, there is an incentive for employers who are hiring in segregated job classifications in which women or racial minorities predominate, to maintain the segregation and with it the lower wages. For dominant groups, it is in the workers' interest to maintain job segregation by maintaining ugly images of subordinate groups and by engaging in discriminatory and threatening behavior. Again, these stereotypes begin to change when material incentives change. As racial minorities entered professional baseball, the stereotype of the ballplayer changed considerably. Thus, economic theory can be combined with self-identity theory to explain how stereotypes are strategically employed and change over time in response to social incentives, both material and psychological.

3. Objections

One objection to any psychological theory that claims to explain all forms of oppression is that it does not apply cross-culturally.[16] We saw this, for example, in Chodorow's objections to Freudian psychoanalytic theory or Fanon's and Willett's objections to Hegel's recognition theory as Eurocentric or androcentric. Might social cognitive theory be likewise criticized? Just as Chodorow and Willett each tried to argue that there are psychological universals in their psychological theory that made it universal, so I want to claim that there are universal cognitive mechanisms that cut across cultures, and that are enacted in culturally specific ways. Consider human linguistic ability. All human neonates who are not seriously brain damaged possess it, yet the particular language they learn to use is culturally determined. Social cognitive theory, as I have presented it, proposes three such mechanisms: categorization (the tendency to organize information under categories), in-group out-group formation and accentuation of difference between those groups, and self-identification with the in-group. In addition, I have argued that people respond to material incentives and tend to give more weight to short-term gains than to long-term ones. What evidence is there that these are universal psychological mechanisms (as opposed to Western or androcentric or modern constructs)? First, even confining the idea of categorization to social categories, there exist numerous studies that show that categorization is a cultural universal, and I could find none that throw doubt on that hypothesis (Troadec 1995; Pinto 1992; Dhawan et al. 1995; Oddou and Mendenhall 1984; Miller 1984; Vassiliou and Vassiliou 1974). Second, a great deal of evidence also exists in the social cognitive literature on the tendency to form in-groups and out-groups (Han and Park 1995; Tzeng and Jackson 1994; Smith, Whitehead, and Sussman 1990; Boski 1988; Ward 1985; Oddou and Mendenhall 1984; Vassiliou and Vassiliou 1974). The very existence and wide acceptance of the concept of the Other in the phenomenological literature also testifies to this. Third, there is also evidence for the hypothesis that persons tend to self-identify with their in-group (Dhawan et al. 1995; Han and Park 1995; de Leon 1993; Turner, Gervai, and Hinde 1993; Boski 1988; Oddou and Mendenhall 1984; Vassiliou and Vassiliou 1974) and somewhat more mixed evidence of the positive attribution bias toward the in-group (Smith et al. 1990; Boski 1988) Finally, there is also some evidence for the claim that cross-culturally, people respond to material incentives and tend to give more weight to short-term gains than to long-term ones (Felson and Tedeschi, 1993; Ostaszewski and Green 1995; Wilson et al. 1995). Although what in-groups and out-groups form and how much persons respond to material incentives or weigh short-term gains over long ones differs by culture, it is clear from the data that these are universal human cognitive mechanisms.

Some remarks about the accuracy of stereotypes and the concept of a social group are in order at this point. Oakes et al. (1994) argue that social groups are real, and our stereotypes reflect the reality of groups: "a group of individuals might be stereotyped in terms of a particular social categorization (as Irish, say) not because this is cognitively economical but because groups are real" (Oakes et al. 1994, 127). Although I think that they are right to assert that social groups are real, I think that they are wrong in their understanding of what social groups are. The process of stereotyping from individual goes like this: We infer from the individual to the group and then project back to the individual. The data we take in is about the individual. The group information stored in schemas is then added to that data, and we project that back to the individual. This is a highly inaccurate process, as my black man on campus example suggests, as do many studies showing the inaccuracy of stereotypes in individual cases.[17] Oakes et al. (1994) argue that stereotypes are accurate because they represent real differences in the statistical facts about the sets of individuals grouped by the stereotype. But these stereotypes often attribute properties to individuals shared by only a minuscule proportion of the group (though it may indeed be greater than the proportion of individuals in another group who share that attribute). While it is then true that there is a real difference in the two sets that does not make the stereotype accurate as a property of the group, much less as projected onto individuals. To put the point concretely, if 1 percent of white women are named Ann, and a much smaller number of women of any other race are, then it is true that there is a real difference here between white women and women of other races, but that does not mean that the group of white women is legitimately stereotyped as a bunch of Anns nor is it a good bet that any particular white woman is an Ann.

I do not deny that there are social groups, however. As I argued in chapter 2, social groups are determined by the set of stereotypes by which we categorize and separate or assimilate those categories to our own, by the social reinforcement of these stereotypes by the self-fulfilling nature of role schemas, and just as important, by the socially structured material incentives that reinforce stereotype fulfilling behavior. Groups are not sets of persons, they are cognitive processes (stereotypes) and socially structured material incentives. Thus, we are not seeing directly the group, but our seeing sets in motion a grouping, and this grouping is objectively real in its effects. This grouping causes us to have prejudices and discriminate against (or for) persons because of how we have grouped them, and regardless of the fit between the stereotypical character-istics of the group and their personal characteristics. Groups are real as constraints on thought, feeling, and behavior. But stereotypical group attributes often are not true, not even a kernel of truth, when applied to individuals.

4. The Cyclical Nature of Oppression

It is a common theme in writings on various oppressions that oppression is self-maintaining: It is characterized as a vicious cycle (Okin 1989), a cage (Frye 1983), a self-fulfilling prophesy (Snyder et al. 1977), a Nash equilibrium (chapter 5 of this book), a convention (chapter 6). To make this point clearer in the context of psychology, let me summarize the ways in which the psychological forces of op-pression are created by and in turn reinforce the psychology of oppression.

There are three ways in which stereotypes are self-fulfilling, one cognitive, one behavioral, and one a combination of cognition and behavior that is best charac-terized as "rational." I have characterized stereotyping as the fundamental cognitive process of oppression. Stereotyping is a kind of categorizing applied to the social realm that is reified in role schemas that are then applied to new data. Stereotyping is the process of taking data, assimilating it to role schemas by which one codes that kind of data, shaping it by accentuation of group difference, manipulating the differences in ways that make the in-group look as good as possible and as different from the out-group as possible. Given the social reality of existing groups, that is, existing attributions to persons based on visual characteristics that they share, new data is more likely to be assimilated to the schemas that currently exist, rather than creating new ones. This means that stereotypes are very stable cognitive structures. So stereotypes that bias some groups positively and others negatively will tend to remain that way even in the face of contrary data.

The second way in which the stereotypes are self-fulfilling is through the psy-chological harm caused by psychological forces of oppression that affect the behavior and performance of the oppressed. This means that persons are victimized, degraded, humiliated, and discriminated against because of the stereotypes that characterize the social group in which they are categorized. Victims of the forces of psychological oppression may suffer from feelings of inferiority, shame, hopelessness, and the like, making them less well-equipped to compete equally with their oppressors and in turn confirming the stereotypes of them as vulnerable, weak, lazy, incompetent, or alternatively, savage, violent, and so on. An even more important, though perhaps more subtle, way that stereotypes harm oppressed groups is through stereotype threat. In his seminal work on this phenomenon, Claude Steele characterizes stereotype threat as "a social psychological threat that arises when one is in a situation or doing something for which a negative stereotype about one's group applies" (Steele 1997, 614). Members of oppressed groups often find themselves in such situations when they are in a position to compete for social goods, such as in schooling, job interviews, or in competitive occupations. In these situations, they fear being reduced to that negative stereotype—even if they believe that it does not apply to them. The fear is stronger the more the person cares about or identifies with the situation, that is, the more the person wishes to perform well in those situations. Steele has shown in many different settings and experimental conditions that persons who face stereotype threat will perform below persons of the same ability level who do not face the stereotype threat (Spencer, Steele, and Quinn 1999). Furthermore, he has shown that persons who are initially identified with the situation, such as schooling, or a particular subject matter or occupation, will tend to disidentify as they become frustrated by their performance under stereotype threat. This explains, for example, why girls who initially like and are talented at math often begin to perform worse and eventually decide they no longer like math, or why African Americans on average perform less well than whites in school and are more disaffected by it. When many of the more talented members of the groups underperform because of stereotype threat and subsequently turn away from the field entirely, the stereotype of the group as not as good in that field is reinforced and the threat becomes self-fulfilling.

The third way that stereotypes are self-fulfilling is through motivating the oppressed themselves to accept negative stereotypes and to choose to act in accordance with them. First, persons are motivated to attach stereotypes to themselves in order to create a sense of being a part of an in-group, and to view this in a positive light. In some cases, though, it is accepting the grouping that is wrong; I would argue that this is the case with gender, for instance. This is what Marx thought was wrong with the class system as a whole. Accepting the grouping, which plays this psychologically fulfilling role of creating a self-identity even when the group is negatively affected by it, is the phenomenon of false consciousness, which we can now understand as a kind of cognitive processing. Second, stigma itself can create a self-protective strategy because the stigmatized can blame their failures on the stereotypes and prejudices of the dominant group (Crocker and Major 1989). Finally, once these groupings exist, social psychological incentives arise for persons to act in accordance with the stereotypes of the group that others assign them to, for the alternative may well be social isolation.

These three processes together help us to formulate at least the cognitive piece of the psychological answer to the question that Hobbes's equality thesis raised for us. *Oppressed persons often acquiesce to and accept their oppression because they come to believe in the stereotypes that represent their own inferiority, are weakened by those stereotypes, and even motivated to fulfill them.*

5. Conclusion

This chapter has attempted to provide a foundation in our psychological makeup for oppression to explain why there are social groups, why particular groups endure, and how groups change over time. I have argued that oppression is fundamentally driven by the cognitive process of stereotyping. Stereotyping makes possible the phenomena of social grouping. It is the cognitive process of categorizing applied to the social world combined with self-identity formation in the individual, whereby the individual orders the social world in a way that best suits her material and psychological interests within the given constraints. Individuals do not create their stereotypes *ex nihilo*. Individuals are constrained in their categorizing by the social groups and stereotypes that they find in their environment and the role schemas that they learn and into which they are trained. Finally I have argued that oppressed groups are motivated to acquiesce in and assimilate these oppressive stereotypes by three kinds of processes that make oppression a self-maintaining system: cognitive, behavioral, and rational.

In the following chapters I will argue that oppression originates in material forces, that is, violence and economic deprivation, but endures by a combination of material forces and psychological forces, acting on individuals and creating common knowledge conditions that reinforce stereotypic social groupings and the material incentive structures in the world. The psychological forces, which I term "psychological forces of oppression," are primarily affective forces that hurt and weaken individuals, making them more susceptible to further oppressive harm. But there are also additional cognitive forces, which create apparently willing victims of oppression, and which make the breaking of the vicious cycle of oppression that much more difficult.

PART II

FORCES OF OPPRESSION

4

Violence as a Force
of Oppression

Forces of oppression harm group members directly and indirectly by reducing social group members' options relative to otherwise similarly situated members of society. Violence is the most forceful and direct way to affect persons' options. In this chapter I will argue that violence is and has always been a crucial component in the origin and maintenance of oppression. In the previous chapter we saw how humans are cognitively wired and motivated to form groupings of persons. One of the key ways that these group boundaries are enforced and differences are maintained is through violence. Oppressor or privileged groups construct and then maintain their advantages and privileges in part through violence or the threat of violence. Violence directed against oppressed groups disables and impoverishes them, while enriching or empowering the oppressor or the indirectly privileged. Although oppression has serious psychological effects and can be effected in part psychologically, oppression does not occur or continue without some ongoing material forces, by which I mean three kinds of things: violence, economic deprivation, or the credible threat of either of these. In this chapter I explore how violence and the threat of violence constrain the actions of groups, harming the victims and benefiting the correlative privileged social groups.

One of the motivating puzzles of this study is what I have called the endurance question: why or how does oppression endure through generations. This is a particularly vexing issue when it comes to the mainly one-sided violence that is a part of oppressive situations. It may seem that violence can always be answered by violence, and if there is enough violent reaction on the part of the oppressed, the oppressor will finally give in for the sake of peace. Their oppressive privileges, after all, come over and above what they could gain themselves in a situation in which they are either at peace with or living apart from the opposing group. Thus, violence in one way may seem to be an obvious way for one group to dominate another, and yet it is puzzling how dominance can be maintained through violence on a long-term basis. Let us call this the puzzle of enduring violence: how can largely one-sided violence continue for generations?

This puzzle is related to a second puzzle that will be explored in this chapter. Sometimes the open show of violence is itself a powerful tool of oppression, while in other cases violence has to be hidden under an ideological cloak. Surprising though it may sound, violence can also be quite invisible in the wider world, as it often is in the case of violence against women. In the case of women, in particular, violence often happens surreptitiously. It is diffuse, and often literally hidden enough to appear unsystematic, and yet it is widespread and recognizable enough to discipline women to stay within what is normatively termed their natural place. I will call this the puzzle of hidden violence: how can violence be invisible?

Some might argue against my thesis of the necessity of material force that (middle class, white, first world, able-bodied) women are oppressed only psychologically, for example. In this chapter I will take pains to dispute this claim concerning women because it stands as the most difficult test of my thesis of the necessity of material force. I will argue first that women as a group are oppressed materially through violence. Second, and more importantly, I will argue that there is a credible, psychologically effective threat of greater harm that is transmitted by the obvious material harm that they do suffer. Women are perhaps the original victims of oppressive violence, and suffer ongoing violence as a part of their ongoing oppression. Violence or the threat of violence work to maintain an effective prison around the oppressed. In some cases that violence is quite openly practiced, while in others it is covert. And this pattern, I shall argue in the following chapters, is typical in other cases of oppression: economic deprivation and fear of violence combine to create and maintain the psychological harms of oppression.

1. Defining Violence

By "violence" I mean to denote actions intended to physically harm a person or persons through application of physical force. This use of the term is more restrictive than some have argued for. I restrict the term because I think it is important to have a separate term for the harm inflicted by forceful, physical violence as opposed to what I shall term "nonviolent" economic deprivation (e.g., through wage slavery), or the "nonviolent" infliction of psychological harm (e.g., through degrading images of one's social group members), for two reasons. First, we need to separate these categories of harm if we are to have a nuanced account of oppression that covers the many different cases we have discovered and might yet uncover. For example, when poorly paid working men toil for subsistence wages all day, then come home and beat their wives, there are two separable kinds of oppressive forces at work on two groups: the working men and the women. It does no social good nor does it reveal more reality to conflate the economic with the violent. Second, violence harms in unique ways and requires unique means of resistance to counteract it. I do not mean to argue or imply that economic deprivation or psychological torture is less harmful than violence in my more restricted sense of the term. Whether it is legitimate to separate these forms of harm depends not on some metaphysical truth of the matter of whether "homelessness is violence," or some similar issue, but rather on whether the kinds of harms require different causal analyses, and whether they require different strategies of resistance and confrontation. The definition of violence I shall offer is primarily descriptive, not normative. It aims to say what violence is, and not to assume a normative analysis of violence or any particular type of action.

Violence connotes first a particularly egregious and immediate harm, damage, or abuse. Second, it connotes harm that comes about in a particular way, namely forcefully, quickly, intensely. One of the Latin roots of the term is *violentus*, meaning forcible or vehement (Wade 1971). Although violence is sometimes used to talk about very forceful, physical events in which humans are not involved, as in "the storm lashed the shore with great violence," I consider these to be metaphorical or peripheral uses of the term. Third, to say that someone inflicts "violence" is to say that there was an intention to inflict some forceful harm. A car accident, while sometimes said to be violent in effect, does not usually lead to the responsible party being called "violent." In those cases where the responsible party is accused of violence it is because she or he used the car as a weapon intentionally to apply force; that is to say, it was neither an accident nor a case of culpable negligence. I define violence, then, as *the intentional, forceful infliction of physical harm or abuse on one or more persons or their material or animal possessions.*

There are several additional objections that might be proposed to this definition. First, one might object that it does not include enough. What about non-forceful inflictions of physical harm or abuse? Imagine a case of poisoning without the use of any force to get the victim to consume it. Suppose Mary puts a completely tasteless but inevitably fatal poison in Sam's drink, causing Sam's death. With most poisons there is an application of force at some point in the process of the poison's deadly work. If the poison acts by destroying the victim's guts, causing pain and agony, then this case would be a case of intentional, forceful infliction of harm. Would we then have to say that forced starvation should be termed "violence," since starvation is such a painful, forceful harm? I admit that starvation is a hard case; in some cases I would say yes, but in others, no. While the force criterion is met, what about the intent criterion? It depends on the scope of the intent of the agent imposing the starvation and the method by which it is imposed. Suppose one person causes another to starve by forcefully preventing the starving person from obtaining food. In that case there is an intentional, forceful infliction of harm and my definition would classify it as violence. Someone may be starved through neglect, though. In that case, if there is an intent to impose starvation, a forceful kind of harm, then it is only if someone is starved with the intent to starve that it would be termed violence. If the starvation occurs through neglect, no matter how culpable, but without intent to starve, then such a starving, however tragic or horrible, is not violence. Returning to the poison case, suppose it works quietly, putting the victim into a gentle dreamy sleep before stopping the heart and bringing death. Then calling this a case of nonviolent poisoning seems warranted, and my definition would so classify it.

The second objection is that this definition includes too much by allowing cases of forceful abuse or damage of property to be counted as violence. Again, I would claim that this accords well with our common use of the term. To say that "she reacted violently" would be a good description of someone smashing up some dishes or throwing a hammer at the television set, even if this did no harm to any person's body. However, the legal use of "violent crime" includes only crimes against people's bodies and not their property (Dobrin 1996). This usage is primarily normative, though, and I am giving a descriptive account of the term. The purpose of defining the term this way in a legal context is to distinguish crimes against persons from crimes against property. While in a legal context this may be warranted, in the context of analyzing oppression I think it is not. The descriptive account concerns how something is done, rather than the disapprobation that accrues to the action. More importantly, it makes sense to include forceful abuse of property as a kind of violence because forceful abuse of one's property, especially of animals, portends or threatens forceful abuse of one's person. It threatens the victim through the show of force, and if aimed at members of a particular social group because of their membership, it transmits that threat to the other members of the group. Furthermore, forceful abuse of property escalates the cost of resistance techniques that potential victims must apply. One must either respond with violence or risk injury in responding nonviolently. While I do not want to argue that such intuitions about the term are definitive for how "violence" must be used, I do maintain that they are reasonable; intuitions about its use do not undermine my case for a restrictive use of the term "violence."

One consequence of my definition is that violence is not necessarily unjustified. Thus, it makes sense to ask if the use of violence was justified in any particular case, which I take to be a good aspect of the definition. It also allows us to speak of state-sponsored use of force as violence without first asking whether the state is a legitimate authority and whether, in the particular case at hand, the use of force was legal and justified. Further, of all the cases of unjustified violence, not all of them are oppressive. Oppression, recall, is a socially systematic, undeserved harm suffered by individuals, consequent on their social group membership. For violence to be a force of *oppression*, then, it has to be a part of the cause of the systematic, undeserved harm of some social group, from which another social group benefits, and which is transmitted through the systematic constraints that make up the social groups.

There are varying kinds and levels of violence that differ with respect to the degree and manner in which they reinforce oppression. First, we must distinguish random violence from systematic violence. Truly random violence is violence aimed at no particular social group and is therefore not a force of oppression. It is important, though, to note that calling an act of violence a "random" act is a theoretical move that might be challenged in particular cases. Domestic violence, for instance, has always been treated in the law, and until recently, by society, as a kind of random violence, though through feminist analyses we are coming to see it as systematic violence against women. Violence is systematic when its victims are a social group, or in other words, grouped by an institutionally structured set of incentives. Thus, systematic violence is part of a pattern of harms that disproportionately affect a particular social group. To say that some violence is systematic, or is part of a pattern of harms disproportionately affecting a particular social group, is not to say that the pattern itself is intentional on any person's part, though it may be. It is important to consider the effect and not the intention here because what matters in considering how violence constructs oppression is how it constrains social groups. Constraints are transmitted through the perceptions of the people who would make up the putative group. Thus, it is the perceptions of the affected, not

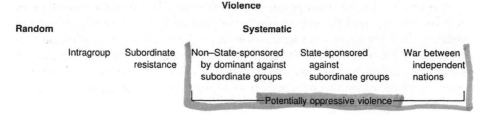

FIGURE 4.1

the intentions of the violent persons, that matter for determining whether the violence is systematic.

Systematic violence itself has to be divided into five different kinds: war between independent, sovereign nations, state-sponsored violence against subordinate groups in society, non–state-sponsored violence by dominant groups against subordinate groups, violence by subordinate groups aimed at dominant groups, and intragroup violence[1] (see fig. 4.1).

The last two of these do not result in harms that can be classified as oppression (though they may be caused by oppression),[2] so I leave them out of this discussion. War between sovereign nations may be oppressive or not, depending on whether the war is to prevent gross injustice in the attacked nation or for some oppressive advantage of the aggressor nation. Two national groups constitute two social groups, and one can, for its own benefit, harm the other. Clearly war is a systematic way of harming another social group. If, for instance, a larger or more powerful nation wages an unjustified war of aggression to subjugate, annex, or colonize a smaller or demonstrably weaker nation, then the war is oppressive, since it would then satisfy the coercion condition.[3] An example of this kind of war would be the many wars waged in the struggles of European states to install colonial rule in Africa—the wars against the Zulus in South Africa waged by British and Dutch-Afrikaner forces, for example. State-sponsored violence against subordinate groups describes political repression of various kinds, be it the maintenance of colonial rule by an imperial power over an indigenous people (such as the reign of the French over the Algerians), terror-enforced rule of a military dictatorship over their own people (such as Pinochet's rule in Chile), or operations by the state internal security forces to quell dissent within a nominally democratic regime (such as law enforcement's violent actions against the Freedom Movement during the Civil Rights era in the United States). These are cases of oppression, where the state is an oppressor group and the victims of the violence are the oppressed. These cases tend to be clear and obvious cases of oppression. They are taken by many to be the typical cases of oppression. They are also typically (but not always) relatively short-lived. For such blatant, violent oppression requires great energy and commitment to sustain, yet at the same time energizes the forces of resistance against it.

The final category of systematic violence, that aimed at a subordinate group's members by members of a dominant group, is the one that most often leads to long-standing, ongoing oppression. This includes violence against women, against gays and lesbians, and racial violence. The reason that this tends to be long-standing, I shall maintain, is that it is more easily hidden under an ideological cloak that appears to justify the violence. One ambiguity of this category's description concerns the word "aimed"—what is the intent behind the violence in this case of systematic violence? As I have argued, there need not be a conscious intent to maintain oppression, so long as it serves that function. To assess blame, of course, we would want to assess the conscious intent of oppressors. But the question of blame is secondary to the questions of whether and how oppression is maintained. Although for an event to count as violence it must involve *intentional* physical force, it only need be intended to be forceful and harmful to be a kind of violence. For it to be part of *systematic* violence, on the other hand, the violent event must be part of a pattern of harms against a particular social group. But that only requires the effect to be part of the pattern. To say that some violence is systematic is to say, then, that the effects of the violence are part of a pattern of violence against members of that group.

One of the insidious aspects of systematic violence is that it affects more than the immediate victim(s) of the force. Who exactly are the victims of violence? The key to fully understanding how powerful yet invisible violence can be as a force of oppression is to see that not only are those who are directly injured victims but also those who see themselves as sharing, or know that others see themselves as sharing, the characteristics that motivated the violence. In other words, all members of social groups are harmed when some of their members suffer violence motivated by their group membership. For, as I shall argue, they suffer from the threat of violence.

2. Threats and Being Threatened

One effect of violence is that it portends future violence. That is, it implies for both the victim and the perpetrator a dangerous situation in which more violence can be expected. The victim fears further attack, and the perpetrator fears retaliation or becoming a victim of some further perpetrator. The fear is more palpable in the presence of an explicit threat. To *threaten* is a four-place relation that relates two subjects, a and b, a set of conditions, $c_1, \ldots, c_n$ and a state of affairs, S. To say that a *threatens b with S under $c_1, \ldots, c_n$* means that a implies that a will see to it that x happens if conditions $c_1, \ldots, c_n$ come about, and b understands the implication. An *explicit* threat exists when a makes his threat to see to it that S under conditions $c_1, \ldots, c_n$ verbally or through a well-understood conventional sign: "if you don't give me your money, I will shoot you." Threats may also be *implicit*, when a signals in a less clear-cut or veiled way: a bully says to another child on the playground, "got any money?"

A *social threat situation* is a common belief that members of group A frequently threaten violence or perpetrate violence on members of group B. In such a case we can say that members of A *pose a threat* to members of B. Oppression usually involves a social threat situation in which members of the dominant group pose a threat to the oppressed group. Sometimes threat situations go both ways, either in reality or in fantasy. Although individual women may threaten individual men, between women and men as groups, it goes only one way. Men (as a group) pose a threat to women (as a group).[4] Social threat situations can be explicit or tacit. An example of an explicit social threat situation is colonial oppression, where the colonial power is an invading force that keeps its power by force of arms, though with an outward appearance of order and peace when there is no open resistance. Social threat situations keep their victims on edge and prevent them from being able to forget that violence is imminent. Hobbes names situations in which there is no security against violence "war": "For as the nature of foul weather lieth not in a shower or two of rain, but in an inclination thereto of many days together: so the nature of war consisteth not in actual fighting, but in the known disposition thereto during all the time there is not assurance to the contrary" (Hobbes 1985, ch.13). A social threat situation is *tacit* when there is a social threat situation that is never spoken about as such, but nevertheless is real in the sense that persons plan and act based on the assumption that that social threat situation exists. Since tacit threats so constrain persons' behaviors, whether a threat is tacit or explicit does not matter for deciding whether it is a force of oppression. But discovering or presenting evidence of tacit threats is clearly more difficult than doing so for explicit ones. One type of evidence of a tacit threat is statistical evidence that a group acts in a more constrained or less beneficial way. Such evidence is not unimpeachable, as it might be claimed that the group contains members who happen to prefer acting that way regardless of any outside force or threat. It might be claimed that women like to stay indoors because they are timid, because they do not like uncomfortable weather, or because they feel it is impious to go outdoors rather than that they stay indoors because they face a tacit threat of violence if they go out. Such excuses deny my basic assumption of equality that, absent oppression, persons' preferences and character traits would be widely and roughly randomly spread across society, rather than clustered in (nonvoluntary) social groups. The second, that differing religious standards of behavior would apply to different groups, is more likely the effect of oppression rather than a sincere understanding of God's will. Both types of responses are countered by the claim that these preferences and behavior standards are endogenously caused by oppression. That is, the tacit threat of violence may have caused women to prefer to behave as if they do not like to go out or to believe that going out is impious. Another type of evidence for a social threat situation comes from direct expressions of fear. This evidence can also be challenged on the grounds that the group that expressed the fear is seeking some unwarranted strategic advantage by doing so. While it is no doubt true that persons will seek advantages from whatever situation they find themselves in, the existence of statistical evidence of systematic suboptimal behavior should be considered prima facie evidence that a social threat situation exists in fact.

There are two more important pairs of distinctions to draw between kinds of threats and threat situations. Threats may be objective or subjective. A threat is objective when there is good objective reason to believe that a will follow through on the threat under the specified conditions, and it is subjective when it is believed by b that a will follow through. A social threat situation is objective when it is objectively true that members of A often threaten members of B, and subjective when members of B believe that members of A often threaten them. Finally, threats may be credible, incredible, or ineffective. A threat is credible when it is both objective and subjective, incredible if not objective, and ineffective if not subjective.

I shall argue that the social threat situation of violence by men against women is tacit but credible. Tacit social threat situations are difficult to recognize precisely because they are not explicitly acknowledged by the community. It is this combination of tacitness and credibility that makes the oppression of women through threat of violence by men so difficult to see. To see why it is effective, though, we need first to look briefly at the effects of violence.

3. Effects of Violence: Trauma and Material Loss

The understanding of the psychological effects of violence has undergone a paradigm change in the past two decades with the acceptance and theorization of the concept of trauma and the inclusion of post-traumatic stress disorder (PTSD) in the *Diagnostic and Statistical Manual of Mental Disorders*. According to the psychological account of trauma, PTSD is consequent on an event that involves "death or serious injury, or threat to one's physical integrity," or witnessing such an event, or learning that a family member or close friend has experienced such an event.[5] Trauma is a psychological state involving a more or less constant feeling of powerlessness and fear for personal, familial, or community security (Brison 2002). Violence is the paradigm case of a traumatic event. PTSD is understood primarily as a disorder that is consequent on a traumatic event. Unfortunately, this definition is only partially helpful for an understanding of the psychological sufferings of persons subjected to systematic violence. Systematic violence is ever-present and when consequent on an involuntary attribute, inescapable. The fact that it is not random maintains the ever-present credible threat of further violence (Becker 1995).[6] *— Gift of Fear*

PTSD exhibits a variety of possible symptoms including depression, amnesia, insomnia, irritability, difficulty concentrating, hypervigilance, or an exaggerated startle response. There are also less dramatic, but still seriously damaging, psychological effects of systematic violence. Persons who are subjected to violence suffer shame and loss of self-esteem. And these losses often make persons unable to cope effectively in society. In effect, they are victimized thrice: once by the violence, then again by the loss of self-worth that one feels when one has been dominated, humiliated, and violated, and then again by the loss of social ties and the ability to cope that these psychological states often bring about. Systematic violence creates even worse problems in these latter two regards, and particularly if the violence is consequent on some involuntary, permanent attribute, such as race or gender or sexual orientation.[7]

Material losses consequent on systematic violence may seem even more evident than psychological ones. When persons are traumatized, injured, or killed, they cannot work,[8] and so cannot acquire the property that they otherwise could. Caring for their injuries or conducting their funerals are costs that the community must bear. Property is sometimes directly damaged and lost by violence. But these losses are not just individual losses when the victim is a member of an oppressed social group. More insidious, systematic losses accumulate disadvantage to the social group over long periods of time. One important aspect of oppression is that the oppressed social group members typically lack wealth relative to members of more advantaged groups. Wealth opens many opportunities and choices for persons. It allows one to own a home, send a child to college, start a business, run for political office, survive the loss of a job, and leave something for the next generation to build on. The major source of wealth is inheritance (Darity 2000, B18).[9] Hence, victims of violence are less likely to be able to pass on wealth to the next generation. If a social group is subject to systematic violence, then their descendants are likely to be less wealthy than and disadvantaged compared to the descendants of groups not subject to such violence.[10] Lack of collective wealth is a key feature of the maintenance of the oppression of African Americans, and this fact is directly related to the systematic violence—from Ku Klux Klan terror that destroyed and uprooted families and communities to inner city riots that destroy buildings and businesses—that they have faced in American society.

I have argued that violence is a force of oppression through its immediate damage and psychological harm, its negative consequences for income and long-term wealth of its victims, and through its terrorizing and income and wealth effects on other members of the social group. Violence thus increases the differences between oppressed and privileged social groups by making the victims of trauma less able to cope with everyday challenges and less able to compete for social resources. In the next section I examine how violence and the threat of violence are pervasive forces of oppression of women. Through a detailed analysis of this case of violent oppressive force, I show how violence can more generally be seen as a powerful force of oppression, closely interconnected with the other two kinds of forces, namely economic and psychological forces.

4. Violence against Women

That human males are on average larger, stronger, and faster than human females is neither controversial nor contrived. What those facts should or must mean for our social institutions, however, is both constructed and actively contested. I shall argue that through the systematic application of violent force against their nearest female relatives, human males have forged institutions that make them dominant over the females. Violence by men against women has expanded to violence against women who are strangers. In the process of dominating and responding to this violent domination, males have become men and females women. Violence, in other words, is the foundation on which gender, the hierarchical organization of human males over females, rests.

4.1. *Sexual Assault and Domestic Violence*

I connect these two forms of violence against women together because they are perhaps the most powerful forces of the oppression of women. Yet in the case of women, the puzzle of hidden violence is particularly pressing. Despite the fact that sexual assault and domestic violence are clear instances of violence, women in our society are not seen as oppressed violently. One might wonder whether rape and domestic violence should be separated because rape can be committed by a stranger while domestic violence, by definition, is committed by intimates. But I have argued that what makes a force of oppression *forceful* and *oppressive* is its impact on the victims, the social group that is oppressed by it. Thus, sexual assault and domestic violence, which are both kinds of violent assault on women because they are women (so I shall argue), belong together in this analysis of oppression. In this section I will concentrate on the incidence of sexual assault and rape in the United States, though this is not to deny that sexual assault and rape are equally or more prevalent in other societies.[11]

Domestic violence against women is a prevalent phenomenon. By the most conservative estimate, each year one million women in the United States suffer nonfatal violence by an intimate, but other studies estimate up to four million, and one in three adult women suffer at least one physical assault by their partner at some point in their lives. Female homicide victims are more than twice as likely to have been killed by an intimate partner than are male homicide victims. While 28 percent of the violence against women is perpetrated by intimates, only 5 percent of that against men is perpetrated by intimates.[12] Much of the violence by women against men is in self-defense or after the man has initiated violence, although in many communities defensive actions by battered women are now considered arrestable offenses. Rape and sexual assault are even more predominately crimes by men against women. In 2001 over 226,000 rapes and sexual assaults were reported committed in the United States, and 92.8 percent of these were committed by men. According to the U.S. Department of Justice statistics, though, that vastly underestimates the actual number of rapes and sexual assaults, since they estimate that women report only 38 percent of their rape and sexual assault victimizations.[13] Thus, a corrected figure for the rapes and sexual assaults in 2001 in the United States would be around 590,000. To put this in perspective, this is just under half as many as the number of young women who graduate from high school each year in the United States, and it is well over twice the number of yearly American casualties (killed and wounded) in the Vietnam War.[14]

Violence against women is pervasive, and thus the question of why it is so long-standing arises. Why does it not generate the sympathy from outsiders needed to end it, as happens with genocide or wars? Why does it not generate the violent reaction from the victims themselves as has happened in other cases that we have examined? Part of the explanation is that violence against women is covert, neither recognized as a systematic war against women by the victims nor by those who would be sympathetic. There are four reasons that violence against women is particularly covert. First, women are often not seen as constituting a social group, and if that were true they could not constitute the victims of *systematic* violence. It is often pointed out that women are not a culture but cut across all cultures, and that they suffer sexual assault and domestic violence mainly at the hands of others in their own cultures. As I argued in chapter 2, women do constitute a social group. The statistics about rape are evidence of this, for women face a serious threat of rape, and men do not. Thus, there is a systematic difference in the consequences of their being recognized as women. Yet, and this is the second reason, this difference is not taken to be a social one but rather a natural one, and so their vulnerability to rape is taken to be a result of natural forces, not systematic violent ones. This appeal to the naturalness of violence against women sets the case of women's oppression apart from violence against religious, sexual, and even racial minorities. Third, women belong to different groups that suffer from many different forms of the types of violence I have discussed, while most other groups suffer from one or just a few very blatant examples on which media, governments, and researchers tend to focus. So it is sometimes forgotten that while female Afghanis (but not female Chinese) suffered under the oppressive and violent rule of the Taliban, and female Palestinians (but not female Americans) suffer from the violent destruction of their homes by Israelis, and lesbians (but not heterosexual females) are subject to gay bashing assaults, all women suffer under the threat of sexual assault and domestic violence. That is to say, they are targeted for these types of violence because they are women. Fourth, the situation of women is, in many countries of the world, and to a greater extent than most other groups, one of terror under the threat of violence. That is, the threat of violence keeps women within the place that is deemed socially acceptable and natural by their communities. Thus, women stay indoors, they appease their would-be attackers, they submit to indignities or demands to avoid overt violence.

The threat of these kinds of violence limits women's mobility. Women, as I noted in chapter 3, think of this as a serious disadvantage to being women, even if they do not generally think of themselves as oppressed. They feel fear, however subtly it affects their behavior, in any place where they might be victims of this, that is, anywhere where there might be men. Furthermore, they feel vulnerable, physically weaker than and so inferior to, men. This further reinforces stereotypes about women's weakness and vulnerability, and, ironically, their need for protection by men. And this stereotype, once assimilated to the self-concept of individual women as a positive distinctive sign of feminine grace, actually makes women weaker than men. Because stereotypes are normative prescriptions for behavior, men assimilate their stereotypes for aggression and violence and women for passivity and weakness. Although many men are not violent, they nonetheless benefit from the systematic subordination of women. Even if they do not use violence, it is impossible for them to refuse their male privileges in every situation. They are able to exploit women economically and sexually, and they gain materially from these abilities vis-à-vis otherwise similarly situated women. All women act under the shadow of a social threat situation, which is, statistically, credible yet tacit. It changes our behavior; it makes us acquiesce to limitations on our liberty that men do not have; it alters our sense of what is possible.

Men's violence against women has a variety of motivations and causes. Sometimes it may not seem like part of a systematic application of force, although it is by the effect on the victim group, not the motivation of the perpetrators, that this must be judged. It is clear, however, that there are many cases of violence against women motivated by the intention to dominate women. These attacks may be most furious in areas where men have traditionally held a monopoly on the use of force. One example of this is the sexual harassment and rape of women soldiers by male soldiers. Recent reports show that at least sixty-three U.S. women soldiers were raped by their fellow soldiers in Iraq in the first year of the war (Hardy and Moffeit 2004). This is despite the fact that women soldiers are armed and at least theoretically have access to military courts. Since prostitutes would surely involve far less risk to the soldiers, there must be some nonsexual incentive to target women soldiers. The infamous Tailhook scandal, in which at least twenty-six women, four-teen of them officers, were sexually assaulted at a convention of naval aviators revealed that not only women were not were not welcome among the ranks, but the men of the navy would go to great lengths to protect their fellow male officers, even when they had personal and professional relationships with the assaulted women (Salholz and Waller 1991, 40). In another nearly male only preserve, the first woman to score points in a Division I (the most competitive) NCAA football game, Katie Hnida, quit her first Division I team, the University of Colorado, after she was raped by a teammate ("Female Kicker" 2004, D6). Examples like these show that men as a group become particularly protective of their superior capacity and pro-pensity to use violence. Were women to become equally adept at violence, the enforcement of women's subordinate status would be in jeopardy.

The argument that sexual assault and domestic violence are systematic vio-lence against women can be summarized as follows: First, these acts are prevalent, not rare. Second, they are almost always by men against women. Third, men and women form social groups that are in positions of dominance and subordination,[15] and these relations are strengthened by acts of sexual assault and domestic violence. Sexual assault and domestic violence reinforce the stereotype of women as weak and vulnerable, making it a self-fulfilling prophecy. Fourth, laws and enforcement practices concerning these acts are systematically different from analogous acts, which do not almost always involve men as perpetrators and women as victims. Sexual assault and domestic violence are not considered just two other forms of assault like beating someone with a bottle or with a fist are just two different ways of assaulting someone. Sexual assault and domestic violence are treated by police and prosecutors quite differently from other crimes in that the "provocation" of the crime by the victim determines the degree to which they pursue prosecution, and this systematically differentiates them from other violent crimes. What is significant about this is that the systematic difference is determined by the gender of the victim. Fifth, because they put women in a social threat situation, sexual assault and domestic violence harm all women. Violence against women, in its many forms, is thus a large part of the explanation of how women are oppressed, and why we have not succeeded in ending the longest standing case of oppression on the planet.

4.2. Sexual Slavery and Prostitution

Another important form of violence against women is the violence applied in the trafficking of women, either as unpaid sexual slaves or as prostitutes. A special case of illegal slavery is the case of slaves held for sexual exploitation. It is a special case in several senses. First, for the fact that nearly all such slaves are females. Second, for the fact that it is perhaps especially harmful to its victims, violating them at such a basic physical and psychic level, and often beginning when they are only children. The harms of sexual slavery are also distributed broadly throughout society through the transmission of HIV/AIDS and other sexually transmitted diseases. Third, for the worldwide nature of the phenomenon—where most other forms of slavery are special cases for one or another industry here and there, throughout the entire world there are female sexual slaves. When it comes to sexual slavery, it is not only an economic benefit for the owners of the brothels who hold them and the participants in the travel industry who supply the customers, but it is also a part of the domination of women by men throughout the world.

The extent of the trafficking in women today is utterly shocking to most people who are not directly connected to it. As we shall see with nonsexual slavery, the slaves tend to come from the ranks of the desperately poor, and as national fortunes change, so do the numbers of women who are trafficked into and out of those countries. Since the breakup of the Soviet Union, the poorest of the former socialist republics have become prime locations for gangsters posing as legitimate businessmen to lure and kidnap women to be sent abroad to brothels. Once out of their country their passports are stolen and they are without money or support by which to return home. In similar ways women from Nigeria are trafficked in Italy and other parts of southern Europe. Japan is a major importer of women from all over Asia, and the list goes on. There are sexual slaves in nearly every country of the world, nearly all of them are female, and most of them are young.

Perhaps no situation is more desperate than the girls who are sold into debt bondage by their families to brothels in Thailand. Girls in Thailand are added baggage to families there, where in a highly sexist society they will not be able to earn much wealth or status, and just marrying them off constitutes a major expense to their families. Because of the highly sexist attitude toward females, in addition to their low economic value, families find it acceptable to sell their daughters to brokers for the brothels. There are other means for filling the brothels with sexual slaves. Sometimes the agents of the brothels lure girls with promises of factory or domestic work. Some girls who are forced into prostitution are simply kidnapped. They are then initiated into sex work violently so that they will do anything, even accept having sex with 15 clients a night, for fear of being beaten or killed. Kevin Bales writes of children sold to brothels in Thailand,

> Violence—their enslavement enforced through rape, beatings, or threats—is always present. It is a girl's typical introduction to her new status as a sex slave. Virtually every girl interviewed repeated the same story: after she was taken to the brothel or to her first client as a virgin, any resistance or refusal was met with beatings and rape.... The immediate and forceful application of terror is the first step in successful enslavement. Within hours of being brought to the brothel, the girls are in pain and shock. Like other victims of torture, they often go numb, paralyzed in their minds if not in their bodies. (Bales 1999, 58)

After their violent initiation has taken root, the girls are relatively easy to control, but they are also unlikely ever to recover, even if they do manage to leave the brothel without a fatal HIV infection.

Sexual slavery harms the slaves by robbing them of choice, subjecting them to the most demeaning possible conditions of work in addition to psychological and physical torture, and finally it leaves most of those who survive the initial brutality with a terminal illness. Although these are the most immediate and horrible of the harms, sexual slavery is also a part of the oppressive economic domination of women by men. The existence of prostitution in all its forms lowers the value of wifely sexual services, and when the prostitutes can be had for a much lower price because they are slaves, the value of sexual services is lowered even further. In a world where most women's market services are also devalued because of oppressive forces, they are further oppressed when their nonmarket services are undercut, as well. Sexual slavery is a small but the most violent and brutal part of the global domination of women by men. The oppression of women cannot be described or explained by reference to a single aspect or force. In the next chapter I will examine these economic forces further. Not only are women harmed economically, they are also harmed psychologically by the existence of the sex trade, and particularly violently imposed sex trafficking. In chapter 6 I discuss how the objectification of women through the sex trade harms women. In the context of this chapter it is sufficient to point out that all women are harmed by sexual slavery, although the slaves themselves are the violently harmed ones. The beneficiaries of sexual slavery are not only the brothel owners who make outrageous profits, but also all men, even those who oppose sexual slavery, because of their continued domination of women.

Violence against women is a force of oppression of women because it harms women as a group, in addition to its immediate victims, while it preserves the privileges of men as the dominant gender. This dominance is bought at a price, however, as men's propensity to use violence to protect their advantages generally also leads them to harm, oppress, and kill each other. Where the violence waged by men against men is typically overt, that against women has been covered by a veil of tradition and ideology. Yet violence by groups of men against other men is still often not seen as a part of the oppression of some groups of men. By studying a list of examples of systematic violence, we can see that there are many cases of oppression that may appear to be natural or justifiable, but are in fact part of a larger set of interlocking forces of oppression, just as violence against women is a part of the global oppression of women.

5. Other Examples of Oppressive Violent Force

Within each of the categories of systematic oppressive violence, there are several important subcategories to consider. In this section I discuss illustrative examples of oppressive violence. These examples allow us to see how violence can divide persons into involuntary groups and initiate oppression as well as enforce it. The explicitness and severity of violence differs in response to differing intentions of oppressors and reactions by the oppressed. The examples allow us to see the extent and variety of oppressive institutions and regimes in the world, answering the question: Who is oppressed? Recall that in order to argue that a situation is one of oppression, we must show that there is unjust harm to a social group, definable apart from the oppressive harm, a benefiting social group, and an institutional structure through which the oppressive harm is transmitted. With this reminder in place, let us examine some additional cases of oppressive violence.

5.1. War between Nations

In the following categorization of oppressive violence, I use the terms *nations* and *states*, following Will Kymlicka (1995), as two distinct concepts. By *state* I intend those political entities that are recognized at the time as the ruling federal governments of some territory. For now anyway, states can be operationally recognized as those governmental bodies allowed seats in the General Council of the United Nations. Not all states recognize the existence of all the other states, but for each of them, many others do recognize them. By *nation* I intend those separate ethnic groups with some prima facie right to self-determination (although I will not try to be more precise here about what constitutes such a prima facie right) (see Wellman 2003). States are all either nations or multinational units, and there exist nations within states that are sometimes denied their right to self-government. This contradiction causes some important cases of oppression.

Many instances of oppression begin when one nation aggresses against another. The existence of nation states or national peoples sets the stage for differentiation, and an aggressive war produces the inequality that benefits the winners and harms the losers. When the aggression is unjustified and effectively institutes domination, it becomes a new (or renewed) case of oppression.[16]

5.1.1. IDEOLOGICAL WARS OF AGGRESSION _Iraq, Iran..._

Ideology connotes an illegitimate insinuation of one person's or group's ideas on another. Thus, the term "ideological" is a heavily normatively loaded one. This normativity cannot be avoided, though, as what is wrong or oppressive about these wars is not only that the ideas are forced on another, but that they are the ideas of the aggressor, not shared by the people of the society on whom they are being forced, and they are ideas that are morally optional. While it must be insisted that all decent societies treat their people with dignity and respect, there are ways that reasonable and moral societies can differ on what that entails (Rawls 1993). Ideologues insist on one of the options to the exclusion of all other (or all) reasonable ones. Ideological wars of aggression are fought to insinuate that option on unwilling people. Although there may well be disagreement on whether the conditions are met for a war to be an ideological war of aggression, once we have identified a war as such, these wars are clearly cases of oppression. The harm of war is immediate and deep, involving loss of life, liberty, and property, sometimes in immense proportions. The social group harmed is the nation aggressed against, the one benefited is the aggressor nation, or perhaps only its elites, and the institutional structure is the aggressor nation's military force and whatever political and economic infrastructure is required to support the military. Although these are cases of oppression, they are typically not long lasting, unless the oppression transforms into another sort of oppression, such as colonialism. Ideological war is an acute form of oppression.

Under the category of ideological wars of aggression I include wars such as the Crusades, which aimed at converting peoples to other religious views, and more contemporary examples of ideological conversion such as the Vietnam War that aimed at curtailing communism. In these cases the aggressor state uses force to coerce another nation to officially sanction either a different religious view or economic or legal structure. It differs from the case of colonialism in that the main object of the aggressor state is not economic but ideological, at least in the first instance. To charge an aggressor state with waging an ideological war, though, is often met with opposition. Since the breakup of the Soviet Union, the United States has wielded far and away the greatest military power in the world and is often charged with waging "imperialist" war, by which the accuser often means that the military action is an ideological war. Since that description would not be acceptable to a majority of the U.S. population, though, the U.S. government tries to justify these actions by saying that either they are self-defense or that they are in the interest of liberating the people from a government that is oppressive. What about cases of wars where the intention of the aggressor is to liberate the people of a state from a dictator or a totalitarian or otherwise oppressive state, that is, to liberate the people from oppression by their own government? Should we say that such a war is oppressive? Some argue that the U.S. war in Vietnam could be considered in this category. But the resistance of the great majority of the people of Vietnam to the U.S. invasion tells against this interpretation. There are cases where one of the superpowers of the Cold War assisted an uprising by a portion of a society against their government, but in these cases it was never only the superpower that is waging the war. So we could consider the Soviet invasion of Afghanistan or the U.S.-backed war against the Sandinistas in Nicaragua. Both cases count as instances of oppression, since they were aimed not at bringing about democracy or some oppression-free conditions, but rather at installing a government that would align itself politically with the supporting country. As I write this, the United States is waging war on Iraq, a war that began to oust the brutal dictator Saddam Hussein from power, but now continues against a seemingly widespread, popular insurgency. Many countries and peoples of the world regard this as an ideological war of aggression by the United States, but many others see this as a case of legitimate intervention against a regime in gross violation of human rights and international arms treaties. We need not decide this issue here, but the example stands as a case where it can be difficult to distinguish oppressive ideological war from violent liberation.

5.1.2. COLONIALISM

Colonialism can also be classified as a state of war between nations if we take nation in Kymlicka's sense. Colonialism occurs when a nation or set of national or ethnic groups in a territory is forcibly occupied by a more powerful nation, with the intent of annexing or occupying the territory and its people for economic gain. Colonial powers seek to magnify the already existing economic inequality between them and the colonized nation. While the colonial power is clearly a sovereign nation, the colonized territory is often unified only by the colonizers' imaginations at first, and possibly later by the colonized in their organized acts of resistance. Thus, the United States came from a set of formerly unconnected territories that joined together to resist the colonizing efforts of Great Britain.

There are many examples of colonial oppression in history. Perhaps none is more brutal than Belgium's colonial occupation and oppression of the Congo in the late nineteenth and early twentieth centuries. King Leopold II of Belgium discovered that vast sums could be made by using the native people of the Congo as slave labor to harvest the rubber from their trees. The loss of life was of genocidal proportions. In his book, *King Leopold's Ghost*, Adam Hochschild estimated that between 1880 and 1920, which includes but goes somewhat beyond the period of King Leopold's rule, the population of Congo fell by half—that is, by approximately 10 million people (Hochschild 1998). Much of this can be attributed to murder, but also to starvation, disease, and to a plummeting birth rate that resulted from women being unable or unwilling to bear children under the appalling conditions. Leopold's Congo became infamous for one of its methods of brutality inflicted by the soldiers and by the natives that they had threatened and coerced into cooperating: chopping off the hands of its victims, living and dead.

> If a village refused to submit to the rubber regime, state or company troops or their allies sometimes shot everyone in sight, so that nearby villages would get the message. But on such occasions some European officers were mistrustful. For each cartridge issued to their soldiers they demanded proof that the bullet had been used to kill someone, not "wasted" in hunting, or worse yet, saved for possible use in a mutiny. The standard proof was the right hand from a corpse. Or occasionally not from a corpse. (Hochschild 1998, 165)

Colonial occupation has typically proceeded by means of appalling brutality, attempting to stun or paralyze the colonized people and thereby keep them from rebelling.

Colonialism is generally practiced for the economic benefits it brings to the colonial power. In the case of the Congo and Belgium, harvesting rubber, which grew naturally in the Congo brought great riches to Leopold and indirectly to Belgians. Other economic benefits that colonial powers have reaped include other natural resources, such as minerals, gold, gems, ores, but also labor of the native people in the extracting of these resources and on the farms and in the factories of the colonists. Colonial oppression typically ends, then, when the economic benefits are outweighed by economic losses. One way that colonized people have resisted is through violent resistance, which costs the colonizers materially both because it disrupts business and because war is expensive to wage. Another way that colonized people have resisted is through work stoppages and slowdowns, which eat away at the profits from colonization.

The issue of benefits raises a couple of interesting questions. First, it is sometimes asserted that the colonized benefit in the long run from some colonial experiences if the colonized are brought to a more industrialized and modern economic infrastructure, and left with a modern democratic political system. This kind of claim is most often made concerning India, which was vastly modernized socially, politically, and economically by the British colonial experience (D'Souza 2002). But the claim could also be made on the part of many other former colonies. Might one then argue that colonialism is not oppressive if it sufficiently benefits the former colony after the colonial power leaves? The second question is the question of whether neocolonialism is also a form of oppression. Neocolonialism is said to occur when the values, religion, political, or economic system of a former colony are still dominated by those of the former colonizer. Does the fact that some of the ideas, values, or social structures of the former colonizer remain itself constitute oppression?

I believe that answers to both questions must be deduced from the basic principle that the human individual is morally primary, which informs my analysis of social groups and oppression in this book. The first question must then be answered no, that colonialism is not to be considered less or unoppressive because of its effects on future generations. The British power in India robbed Indians of fundamental human rights and did so in the name of British imperialism. Many individual Indians thus suffered from the violent repression of the British military might and others from psychological and economic deprivations, which the British had no right to inflict on them. They suffered these things because they were Indians. Thus, they were the victims of oppression, and no future benefits to other Indians will change that; even if one argued that they would have chosen to invest through their suffering in their descendants' fortunes, they were not permitted the dignity to make that decision for themselves and so were seriously harmed.

The second question introduces more complications. On the one hand, it might also be answered in the negative: some aspects of neocolonialism are not forms of oppression for a similar reason. While no one has the right to impose their values or religious views on others, as colonial powers attempt to do, no one has the right to demand that others give up their views simply because of the causal origin of those views either. Now reflection on those origins might give one good reason to suspect their truth or value for one, but freedom of individual conscience is a basic human right and is not to be sacrificed for the sake of some putative social good. Furthermore, to force the victims of colonization to give up their ideals, values, or religion is to victimize them again. Other aspects of neocolonialism might well carry on the oppression of colonialism, though. What about capitalism or democracy—why don't the rulers of a former colony have the right, possibly even the duty, to dismantle those in order to return to a pre-colonial state or simply because they were imposed by the colonial power?

As for democracy, it is simply not plausible to argue that democracy is, in itself, oppressive, if we define it as the rule of the people. Democracy is, of course, subject to the problem of the tyranny of the majority. But then it is this tyranny, not the democracy, which is oppressive. Democracy does not necessarily entail tyranny of the majority. With regard to capitalism, again I want to argue that it is not the system in itself that is oppressive (as it is in the case of slavery or serfdom) but rather the distribution of wealth that often results, which can be rectified by a redistribution of wealth.[17] Capitalism is not in itself oppressive because it permits every individual, regardless of social group membership, to operate as an economic agent in the same way. However, capitalism allows persons to take advantage of and then magnify inequalities that exist independently. Suppose that what is left by the colonial power when it leaves is a capitalist economy with members of the colonial power group, or their co-opted servants from the native group, still owning substantial interests in the economy as a result of the colonial oppression, for example, through theft, coercion, and slavery of the colonized people. Then this is a remnant of the oppression of the colonial power, and it is clearly unjust. It is a basic principle of law that no one should gain from their wrongdoing. Thus, anyone who has gained from theft, coercion, or slavery should be forced to make restitution, to the victims if they are living, or to some suitable descendant if the victims are not living.[18] In the case of stolen natural resources, the victim to be restored would be the people of the nation, who, one may hope, are represented by the postcolonial government. I will expand my argument in the next chapter, where I will discuss the economics of oppression, that the system of capitalism itself is not oppressive, though neither is socialism.

Neocolonialism has also been understood in a more general way to include any domination by a foreign power, even if that foreign power is not a former colonizer. For example, Stephen Shalom defines neocolonialism as "an alliance between the leading class or classes of two independent nations which facilitates their ability to maintain a dominant position over the rest of the population of the weaker of the two nations" (Shalom1981, xiv, xv; quoted in Blanchard 1996, 7). This is a primarily economic alliance, although it may be in part violently maintained by the police force of the neocolonized nation with the assistance of the foreign power, and hence I will take it up in greater detail in the next chapter.

5.1.3. RAPE AS A WEAPON OF WAR

Male soldiers have always considered the raping of women to be part of the spoils of war to which they are entitled. But rape in war is not always only an individual crime or a crime simply of men against women. In some wars the raping of the enemy women has been used by military commanders and civilian leaders as a systematic weapon of war. The purpose of systematically raping enemy women as a way of waging war seems to be twofold: first, to generally terrorize and demoralize the enemy through rape and sexualized torture, and second, to demoralize the combatants by harming, polluting, or possessing "their" women. The first of these purposes can be satisfied by any means of torture and would not have to be aimed specifically at women to carry out its purpose. The latter, however, depends on a background oppression of women, a situation in which women and their sexual activities are considered the property of the men of the country to begin with.

In the infamous rape of Nanking, Japanese soldiers carried out massive rape and torture of Chinese women after the surrender of the city (Chang 2000). There are no good estimates of the number of rapes that occurred, as the shame and humiliation of the victims kept so many from coming forth to allow a full assessment of the scope of the crime. Many women committed suicide rather than live with the aftermath of the rapes. In this case the purpose of or motivation for the rapes is unclear, however. No group of women or girls was spared: Children, young women, middle-aged women, and elderly alike were raped. The commanding officers as well as the enlisted men engaged in multiple rapes. Perhaps the purpose was to terrorize other Chinese to make subduing the entire population easier. This would explain why even elderly women and children, who could hardly be sexually appealing to most young men, would have been targeted.[19] The effect was indeed to terrorize and demoralize the Chinese population.

The more recent case of the rape of Bosnian Muslim women by Serbian soldiers in the Bosnia-Herzegovina War illustrates both purposes of systematic rape as a weapon of war. This was a war in which one national-ethnic group, the Serbian Christians, sought to chase away another, the ethnic Bosnian Muslims, with whom they had shared that part of the former Yugoslavia for generations, through a process that came to be called "ethnic cleansing." As a part of this process, Serb soldiers raped Muslim women to carry out four main purposes: to terrorize the population in order to drive them away from Bosnia and into refugee camps in neighboring countries, to demoralize Muslim men whose female relatives were raped and thereby cause them to quit fighting and flee Bosnia, to impregnate Muslim women in order to create more Serbians and prevent the creation of more Muslims, and to satisfy the soldier's heightened sexual compulsions through organized kidnapping and sexual slavery in "rape camps" (Salzman 2000). The last purpose was satisfied by the kidnapping of women from other areas and ethnic groups, as well. The United Nations has estimated that 20,000 Muslim women were raped and tortured during this conflict.[20]

While it is immediately clear that the threat of mass rape and torture is likely to drive persons from their homes, the second and third purposes require, in part at least, the collusion of the victims' own oppressive gender ideology to satisfy the rapists' purpose. It is commonplace that men are humiliated by the rape of "their women." The reason for this is that the image of masculinity in most cultures requires that men possess women, and in particular their sexuality. Thus, another man taking possession of a man's woman causes the aggrieved man to lose status as a man. Of course, it is also true that men, like women, may simply sympathize with their relative's physical pain and humiliation. But the reaction of women in Bosnia, like those in Nanking, reveals that the pain of their male relatives was not so much grief for the women's pain as humiliation and anger for their loss of masculine pride. The analysis of the third purpose of the rapes, to create more Serbs and prevent the creation of more Muslims, is similarly charged with oppressive gender ideology. It only makes sense if the social identity of the baby is determined by the biological father. Since there are two equal parts to the genetic identity of the baby, there is first a biological objection to this analysis. But secondly, the assumption that there is a noticeable genetic difference between Serbian Christians and Bosnian Muslims is questionable. Finally, the fact that the biological father would have only this minimally differentiating biological influence, and no social influence whatsoever on the baby save that which would come from the foregoing oppressive gender ideology itself, implies that the baby could be completely socially Bosnian Muslim. Only by treating these children as Serbs could they come to be Serbs. Thus, the analysis of oppression in this kind of violence is multilayered and complicated.[21] The Serbs were clearly oppressing the Bosnian Muslims through rape as a weapon of war, but it was the oppressive gender relations within the victim group itself that led to rape being as effective a weapon as it was. Furthermore, the Serbian men were sending "their own" women a message through the rape of the Bosnian women—that women are merely the vessels of men's semen for the purpose of creating more Serbs.

5.1.4. GENOCIDE

The 1948 Convention on the Prevention and Punishment of the Crime of Genocide defines genocide as

> any of the following acts committed with intent to destroy, in whole or in part, a national, ethnic, racial or religious group, as such: (a) Killing members of the group;

(b) Causing serious bodily or mental harm to members of the group; (c) Deliberately inflicting on the group conditions of life calculated to bring about its physical destruction in whole or in part; (d) Imposing measures intended to prevent births within the group; (e) Forcibly transferring children of the group to another group.

Another category that has been recognized especially since the war in Bosnia is the deliberate attempt to impregnate many of the women of a culture through rape. This definition shows that genocide straddles this and the next category of oppressive violence, in that it may be conducted by one national group or state upon another national group, but it may also cut across state or national lines. Since genocide can be considered a war on a particular social group, however, I include it in this first category of oppressive violence.

This definition of genocide must be amended in one respect, however, for our purposes. Why must the acts be *intended* to destroy the group? Is it not enough that the acts have that effect? This definition of genocide is a legal one, designed in part to determine culpability. I have argued that we should define oppression by considering the harm done to the victim rather than the intention of the oppressor or privileged group who cause the harm. That is, the harmful effect on the victim group, provided that it was not deserved harm, as well as the beneficial effects on the privileged social group, determine whether there is oppression. Violence, on my view, does require an intention to inflict harm, and genocide is certainly a species of violence. However, there could be multiple acts of violence which, taken together, result in the destruction or near-destruction of an entire group without there being a conscious intention to destroy the group. The massive killing of Native Americans on this view constitutes genocide without having to decide whether there was an intention to destroy the Native Americans as such.

Genocide clearly counts as a kind of oppressive violence because, first, it is an unjust harm to a social group, definable apart from the oppressive harm, since it must be a national, ethnic, racial, or religious group. Second, the violence of genocide is perpetrated by a social group because it is believed by members of that group that it benefits that group. Now particularly with genocide, one might wish to argue that it cannot possibly benefit someone or even some group to annihilate another group. While I would certainly admit that genocide forever morally stains a perpetrator group, and therefore cannot truly be seen as benefiting them, it still must also be admitted that in the short term at least the perpetrator group gains some satisfaction from the violent purging of their rivals. There may also be longer term gains, such as the just-mentioned European genocide of Native Americans, which resulted in the expansion of European American landholding across the American continents. This case also shows how genocide that is particularly successful from the perpetrator's perspective can be hidden from memory and accountability for many generations, if not forever. As the saying goes, the victor writes the history books, and this is particularly true for a "victorious" campaign of genocide, where the losers are mostly or all dead. Third, genocide occurs through institutional structures in the sense that the victim group, and often the perpetrator group as well, are national or religious groups by which they can be identified. In recent cases of genocide, such as the Rwandan genocide of the Tutsis by the Hutus or the killings of the Bosnian Muslims by the Serbs,[22] the two groups had lived together as neighbors in an integrated community quite peacefully until the genocidal violence began rather suddenly. However, once it began it was quite easy for one group to separate out its victims by telltale institutionalized signals, such as different names, dress, and religious practices.

Genocide is an extreme application of violence as a force of oppression, but most forms of oppression involve violence at a lower level than that. Most oppressor groups would not wish the complete annihilation of the subordinate groups, perhaps because of moral constraints, but mainly because economic exploitation is a common motivation for oppression. Genocide often results in the theft of the land and property of the victims by the oppressors, giving even this form of violence an economic motivation.

Oppressive wars between states or nations, where one nation aggresses against another weaker nation or where one nation's soldiers commit mass rapes against the women of another, are the most obvious, spectacular forms of oppression. Particular cases of oppression may be traced to the outset of such wars, answering the question, in those cases, why is this group oppressed? Such oppression may continue for generations or centuries. But they may also engage world sympathy and concern, often in the form of United Nations resolutions or even military intervention. The next category of oppressive violence brings typically lower levels of worldwide scrutiny because they occur within nominally national borders, or do not concern national groups as a whole.

5.2. State-Sponsored Violence against Subordinate Groups

Some types of oppressive violence are employed on subgroups of society by the state. This happens only when the subgroup is not in power and the oppressor group seeks to maintain power and advantage by the use of force. Thus, this form of violence is typically subsequent to the origin of the formation of the oppressed and oppressor or privileged groups. Rather, it is, at least in part, the way that pre-existing relations of oppression are maintained by those in power.

5.2.1. ETHNIC CLEANSING

Ethnic cleansing is the attempt to annihilate (in which case it is also genocide) or remove an ethnic group from a particular territory. It may be state-sponsored, as in the case of Serbian attempts to remove ethnic Albanians from Kosovo, where it is an organized military action of the government, or state-sanctioned, as in the case of the Hutu's attempts to annihilate the Tutsis in Rwanda in 1994, which is conducted largely by civilians but with the full knowledge of the government and no protection afforded to victims. Ethnic cleansing, even when it is not also a case of genocide, clearly fits the description of oppressive violence. It unjustly harms the group that is removed from their homes for no reason beyond the fact of an ethnic identification, which I presume cannot be a justification for forcible removal. Yet, it seems to the perpetrator group to be to their benefit, and materially at least it must be so, for they are able to seize the property of their victims. Like genocide, ethnic cleansing is a harm that is transmitted through the institutional structures that create and maintain ethnic identities.

5.2.2. VIOLENT ENFORCEMENT OF OPPRESSIVE LAWS

Government claims a monopoly on the use of violence or the threat of violence, but its power can be legitimate. When it is not legitimate, when its laws are unjust, the enforcement of those laws is a case of oppressive, state-sponsored violence. Examples of this are, regrettably, too numerous to count. They exist on every continent in every decade. Amnesty International compiles annual reports on violations of human rights by governments around the world, and few governments are entirely innocent of these charges. One example close to home is, as mentioned previously, the enforcement of segregation laws in the United States up until the mid-1960s, and the violent reactions by law enforcement to the Civil Rights Movement resisters. Another example is the enforcement of Islamic law in Iran under the Islamic Revolution, which began in the late 1970s under the leadership of the Ayatollah Khomeini, but continues even as I write this. In *Reading Lolita in Tehran*, Azar Nafisi (2003) chronicles her life under these laws. Women are forced to cover their bodies from head to foot and not allowed to show anything but their faces. They are not permitted to wear makeup or paint their nails. It is against the law for women to have sex outside of marriage.[23] Morality police roam the streets looking for violators, compelling women to submit to arbitrary and humiliating searches, including "virginity checks." Violators are beaten or even stoned to death. In one story, typical of the treatment of young women, Nafisi's student Sanaz is visiting with friends in a resort town when the morality squads come:

> And then "they" came with their guns, the morality squads, surprising them by jumping over the low walls. They claimed to have received a report of illegal activities, and wanted to search the premises.... Their search for alcoholic beverages, tapes, and CDs had led to nothing, but they already had a search warrant and didn't want it to go to waste. The guards took all of them to a special jail for infractions in matters of morality. There, despite their protests, the girls were kept in a small, dark room, which they shared the first night with several prostitutes and a drug addict.... Apart from brief excursions to the rest room at appointed times, they left the room twice—the first time to be led to a hospital, where they were given virginity tests by a woman gynecologist, who had her students observe the examinations. Not satisfied with her verdict, the guards took them to a private clinic for a second check.... The girls were then given a summary trial, forced to sign a document confessing to sins they had not committed and subjected to twenty-five lashes. (Nafisi 2003, 72–73)

In Iran the women are particularly badly treated by the state. They are constantly aware of the possibility of violent treatment by agents of the state, even if they adhere to the rules set by the state. Women form an oppressed social group, as they are harmed by this violent treatment, their harms are transmitted through institutional norms for what they can do, and where they can go and with whom. While the men in this society are also subjected to strict laws, they are the beneficiaries of the oppression of women in the sense that they may behave in much less restrictive ways and have power over the women with whom they are intimate, even if they choose not to exercise it. Women must ask men to accompany them when they go out, and in many occupations these restrictions make women rare or nonexistent. The motivation for this sort of oppression seems to be religious fundamentalism taken to an extreme, but the motivation need not be shared by all the men in the society for this to be an effective prison around the women. The violence wielded by the government is directed against women and men who appear to be involved in women's violations of their assigned place. In this way the women are kept in check both by the violence against them and by the violence against the men who are sympathetic with them.

5.2.3. LEGAL SLAVERY   *+ prison labor*

Slavery is the economic arrangement in which the worker has no control over any aspect of the work or of his or her life. The legal slave is the property of another and may be compelled to work on pain of corporal punishment. Unlike other economic systems, there is no motivation for the slave to remain a slave, and hence this economic system must be maintained by violence. Slavery is not legally sanctioned anymore in any country of the world, although slavery as a practical institution still exists and is widespread throughout the world. Legal slavery differs from illegal slavery in that under the former, it is the state that (officially, legally) uses violence to enforce the slave owner's claim on the slave's life, while under the illegal version, which I discuss below, the slaveholder is the main perpetrator of violence to protect his claim. Under most legal systems of slavery, the slave had some limited rights, but not the rights of citizenship. As a state-sponsored institution, the United States had one of the most brutally oppressive systems, which enslaved by some estimates over 20 million human beings over a period of over 200 years.[24] Corporal punishment was common and rape of women slaves by their masters was not a crime. In *The Bondwoman's Narrative*, a novel about a slave's life and escape to freedom, author Hannah Crafts (herself an escaped slave) illustrates the brutality of slavery through the voice of a slave trader, who coldly deplores the fact that the brutality often leads to the loss of slaves, and hence, money:

> But these wenches will die. I have sometimes thought that accidents happened to them oftener than to others. I have lost much in that way myself; probably ten thousand dollars wouldn't cover the amount. If the business in general had not been so lucrative such things would have broke me up long ago. You see my trade is altogether in the line of good-looking wenches, and these are a deal sight worse to manage than men—every way more skittish and skeery. Then it don't do to cross them much; or if you do they'll cut up the devil, and like as anyhow break their necks, or pine themselves to skeletons. I lost six in one season. (Crafts 2002, 104)

For some slaves, their treatment was to them worse than death. In the United States, slaves, or former slaves, had no rights of citizenship until the Fourteenth and Fifteenth Amendments were ratified in 1868 and 1870, respectively.[25]

In the American system, nearly all slaves were Africans or the descendants of Africans, although Native Americans were also enslaved in much smaller numbers.

The children of slave women were automatically regarded as slaves, the property of their mothers' owners. This fact meant that all African or African-descended persons were assumed to be slaves until proven otherwise. They formed a social group, treated unjustly and harmfully, through the legal and social institutions that constituted slavery. Slavery, whether the old legal variety or the new illegal one, is motivated by the economic profits to be made from the slave's production. With legal slavery, their reproduction was also profitable, since the offspring of slaves were typically slaves as well. Slave owners and the consumers of slave-made goods and services are the beneficiaries of slavery, and they were typically distinguished racially or ethnically from the slave class, distinctions which allow for easy identification of slaves and rationalization of their brutal treatment.

Slavery was outlawed in the United States at approximately the time it became a less profitable means of production than the sharecropping and wage labor systems that succeeded it, combined with the growing industrialization of the country. There were many beneficiaries of slavery. First among them were the slave owners, but also the nation as a whole whose wealth was built significantly on the backs of this source of unpaid and highly exploited labor. Slavery thus fits the model of violent oppression well: there was a clear social group of harmed persons, a group of beneficiaries, and a violent system of social coercion that kept slavery in place.

5.2.4. POLITICAL IMPRISONMENT, POLICE BRUTALITY, AND TORTURE

Another important and well-recognized form that violent oppression can take is the imprisonment and torture of persons who are actively opposing an illegitimate government. While torture clearly fits the definition of violence as a forceful infliction of injury on a person, imprisonment fits the description of at least the threat of violence, in that a person may not exercise personal freedoms without risking an immediate violent response. Imprisonment may be actual violence, too, if the conditions under which a prisoner is kept are sufficiently injurious, such as deliberate starvation or infliction of illness. Torture may be defined as the deliberate infliction of serious or painful injury or humiliation of a person in order to extract information or confession, or to break the spirit of the prisoner or some group who cares about the tortured person's welfare. While torture is always violent and perhaps always wrong, it is not always a force of oppression, since a violent criminal may be tortured by a legitimate government in a way that does not constitute a systematic treatment of members of some social group.

Again, there are too many cases that fall under this description to name them all. A prominent example is the imprisonment of Nelson Mandela and other members of the African National Congress in the second half of the last century. The South African government for most of the twentieth century was a white, European-descended minority that denied equal rights and freedom to and imposed apartheid on the black African majority. Blacks were subject to arbitrary arrest and police brutality, as well as numerous daily humiliations at the hands of white persons. In the 1950s the African National Congress, which favored a multiracial state with full franchise and civil rights for all, was beginning to become a more powerful force of resistance to white-only rule. They successfully organized strikes and other forms of civil disobedience to apartheid. As it became clear that these nonviolent means of struggle were ineffective and being met with violence by the state, the ANC, under the leadership of Mandela, began to plan for sabotage and property-directed violence by building a military force. Mandela was jailed in 1963 under a sentence of life imprisonment for his actions, and he subsequently spent 27 years in prison, many of those under the brutal conditions of the Robben Island prison, which was reserved for non-white prisoners. During that time he was kept in a nine feet by seven feet cell with few blankets, no bed, and a bucket for a toilet. He was only rarely permitted visits from his family, or even to receive letters from them. He and his fellow prisoners were forced to labor in a quarry and for long stretches of time were not permitted to speak to one another. They were sometimes not permitted reading material, and at all times their reading material was carefully monitored and censored. They were not permitted to receive any political news from the outside; family visits were carefully monitored to ensure that only family matters were discussed. (Although, it is important to recognize that nearly all of these restrictions were in small but meaningful ways circumvented by these incredibly resourceful and determined prisoners.) This is a clear case of oppressive use of violence and the threat of violence because there is a group—black South Africans—who was being harmed unjustly and whose oppression benefits another group—white South Africans.

One might object that the repression of a violent group such as the African National Congress (or any other violent resistance organizations) is a legitimate function of a government, and hence its use of violence in putting down a violent reaction to its policies is justifiable and not in itself oppressive. On the contrary I would argue that, if the government is itself oppressive, violence may be justified. To justify it I appeal to the principle of self-defense, which is that one may justifiably use violence in self-defense of an unjustified attack, provided that the violence used to repel the attack is proportional to the violence suffered. The principle of self-defense can legitimately be extended to defense of one's social group if the group is under systematic attack. Since, I have argued, violence against group members that is inflicted because of their group status harms all group members, violent response on the part of group members is justified (provided that it meets the proportionality condition). Amnesty International is a worldwide organization dedicated to seeking out information about and opposing political repression and violations of human rights of prisoners, particularly political prisoners. Like the imagined objector, they deny the status of "political prisoner" to groups and persons who use violence in their opposition to illegitimate governments. The African National Congress is one example of a group that they denied political prisoner status to because of this. Yet as Mandela claims, "it is always the oppressor, not the oppressed, who dictates the form of the struggle. If the oppressor uses violence, the oppressed have no alternative but to respond violently" (Mandela 1994, 468). A government that is oppressive is by definition a coercive oppressive force with at the very least the threat of violence behind it. When it responds violently to nonviolent protest of its oppressive policies, it opens itself to the legitimate use of violence by the oppressed.

5.3. Non-state Sponsored Violence

Some forms of violence get no sponsorship or sanction from the state, but neither do the victims get complete or even adequate protection. Because these forms of violence are not so sponsored or sanctioned, these are the forms of violence least likely to be classified as systematic. Thus, these forms of oppression are most covert and gain the least sympathy from outsiders. Some current and recent examples worth considering here are illegal slavery, strikebreaking, and violence against women, and racial, religious, and sexual minorities.

5.3.1. LYNCHING

Although mob violence or summary execution without trial has occurred throughout time, in the United States the combination became so frequent as a practice by particularly southern whites against southern blacks that it acquired a name, lynching.[26] Lynchings were particularly violent summary executions by angry mobs, usually of black males, but sometimes also black females or white males, that were horrifyingly gruesome: hangings, mutilations, and burnings at the stake. Typically the person was accused of some offense, sometimes a serious crime such as murder (of a white person) or rape (of a white woman), or perhaps a petty slight, such as talking back to a white person, or, if the lynching victim was white, some kind of racial "treason." A mob, often led by the Ku Klux Klan, who would hide their faces under white hoods, would seize the victim and drag him or her to a tree or a stake. The victim was then brutally and publicly executed.

This practice had the purpose and effect of terrorizing the black populace in order to keep them subservient to whites. At the end of the Civil War, with the emancipation of the slaves, white southerners wished to find a way to continue to exploit blacks economically. A variety of legal means were devised, and they were augmented by the terror imposed by lynching.

> Practically every Southern state passed labour and vagrancy laws; "the former masters, working through state legislatures, restored a kind of servitude by means of apprentice, vagrancy, and poor laws."[27] Other discriminatory laws aimed at the Negro and his suppression appeared as the years passed—disfranchisement laws, "Jim Crow" car laws, statutes to prohibit common assemblage in school and even in church. As the forerunner of such efforts to humiliate, oppress, and re-enslave the freedmen, the lyncher's rope and torch appeared. (White 1969, 99)

In the years 1882–1927, there were 4,950 lynchings, and of these 3,513 (71 percent) were of black persons in the United States, and 74 percent of them were in the ten states of the Deep South (White 1969, 232–233). At the time this practice was accepted among many whites of the South, and ignored by many in the North. After intense and concerted efforts by the National Association for the Advancement of Colored People and particularly the individual efforts of Walter White and Ida Wells-Barnett to publicize the brutality to the wider nation, lynchings ended in the 1930s.

Lynching was a prime example of a non–state-sponsored form of oppression. Since they are by definition extra-legal, lynchings are not state-sponsored. But one might argue that, as we saw with the new forms of illegal slavery, the state has to overlook them in order for them to continue. This was indeed the case in the American South, where mobs would often take their victims out of an unguarded jail cell. The lynchings were a form of oppression because they targeted members of a particular social group: either blacks or whites who were seen as allies of blacks. The social group that benefited by this was the whites who were able to continue their dominance of blacks, economically or at least socially. Although lynchings no longer occur, blacks continue to be terrorized in some parts of the United States by violence conducted by the Ku Klux Klan and other white supremacist groups, though at greatly reduced numbers of incidents and levels of brutality.

5.3.2. HATE CRIMES: VIOLENCE AGAINST RACIAL, RELIGIOUS, ETHNIC, AND SEXUAL MINORITIES

The FBI defines "hate crime" as "a crime against a person or property motivated by bias toward race, religion, ethnicity/national origin, disability, or sexual orientation."[28] The FBI has recently (i.e., in 1991) begun maintaining statistics on such crimes, although they report that they do "not have any federal jurisdiction to investigate hate crimes motivated by a sexual orientation bias." Although they report statistics for hate crimes against sexual minorities, they are apt to undercount. Systematic violence against racial, ethnic, religious, and sexual minorities and the disabled are cases of oppression: they target members of particular social groups because they are members (or perceived to be members) of those groups, and because they cause the members of those groups, even those not directly targeted, to segregate themselves from those who perpetrate the violence and to behave in other ways that make them subordinate to the majority social groups. It may be difficult to see how these forms of violence would benefit any dominant group, but they can be seen to do so by intimidating the subordinate groups not to question too forcefully the dominant group's privileges. For example, gays and lesbians refrain from displaying affection publicly or calling attention to their romantic partners in ways that heterosexuals would never think twice about. Although many heterosexuals would not be affected by viewing the display of homosexual affection, others would be offended and would wish to shield themselves and their children from it. It would be a loss to those offended even if we take it to be an irrational and largely self-inflicted one. Blacks refrain from approaching whites they do not know in places where they may not be safe. This benefits those whites who wish, no matter how unfairly or irrationally, to remain apart from blacks. Jews may protest Christian symbols actually placed in courthouses, but not the fact that their holidays fall on workdays. This benefits Christians who need not negotiate their holidays around the workweek. In these ways the dominant members maintain their privileges of being left alone in the position of the favored group in society, without having to question or negotiate over their own practices or privileges.

For the year 2003 the FBI lists 7,489 reported hate crimes.[29] Although this surely represents an underreporting of such crimes, it does not indicate a high probability for any one member of these social groups that they will be targeted. Hate crimes are often spectacular and terrifying, and create terror in their target populations far beyond the numbers. The 1999 crucifixion-like murder of Matthew Shepard, a gay man, the 1998 dragging murder of James Byrd, Jr., a black man in Texas, cross-burnings, and swastikas send the message that there are some in the dominant populations who will enforce their dominant position at any cost, to themselves or their victims. The message can be effectively sent in large part because of the history of lynching and the Holocaust, where there were many more direct victims of violence. In the case of hate crimes, at this point at least, the threat of violence is a greater oppressive force than the violence itself. Because of their spectacular and terrifying nature, as well as the fact that they are purposefully targeted, hate crimes constitute a violent force of oppression against many subordinate groups in society.

5.3.3. ILLEGAL SLAVERY

One of the most brutal and life-robbing forms of oppression is slavery, and it is deeply disturbing to learn that it is still a widespread phenomenon today. Kevin Bales (1999) defines a slave as a person held by violence or the threat of violence for economic exploitation, and conservatively estimates that there are approximately 27 million slaves worldwide. To put this in historical perspective, this number is greater than all the slaves believed to have been stolen from Africa during the transatlantic slave trade from the sixteenth to the nineteenth centuries. Most of the slaves are in Southeast Asia, northern and western Africa, and parts of South America, but there are slaves in almost every country of the world. Slavery today is not legal in any country of the world, but in countries where it is a thriving economic venture— Brazil, Pakistan, India, Thailand—the police are either powerless to enforce the law, or worse, are the corrupt enforcers of the slave system. Bales's remarkably courageous work shows how slavery operates very differently in different countries. In some places it is a continuation of an age-old form of a caste or feudal class system, while in others slavery has sprung up as a new response to global capitalist opportunities and crises. What they all have in common, however, is violence and economic exploitation. What makes them forms of oppression is that they are group-based, unjust harms that benefit another social group.

In Mauritania Bales found an example of the former kind of slavery, where the slaves and class of slaveholders are distinguished by race and the relations between individual slave and master often go back many generations. While Mauritania made slavery officially illegal in 1980, the country is ruled by the minority "White Moor" slaveholding class and they do not enforce the law, but rather enforce slaveholder's claims. While many slaves, who are black Africans or so-called "Black Moors," do the same kind of domestic and agricultural work that has been done for centuries by their ancestors, there are also new market ventures that slaveholders have developed to earn cash from their slaves, although Mauritanians produce very little for an international market. Some slaves are sent by their masters to do work such as carrying water from city wells to sell to city dwellers, most of whom have no running water. The money they earn is claimed entirely by the master. While this form of slavery is enforced by violence, including beatings and even killing of slaves who try to escape, the long-standing nature of the master-slave relationship, the fact that there can be no appeal to government for relief, and the threat of violence by displeased masters are sufficient forces to keep the system in place.

In many other parts of the world the current conditions of slavery are relatively new. This is true where the market for a good that can be produced by slave labor has recently appeared. Other necessary background conditions for the growth of slavery are that there is a desperately poor population that can be easily lured away from their traditional support systems and a police and judiciary that is ineffective or unwilling to enforce anti-slavery laws. In such situations greedy slaveholders can effectively use violence to force people into slavery and keep them there for as long as their work produces a profit. Such is the case in the charcoal camps of Brazil, where men are enticed by promise of a salary, food, and shelter to leave their urban shantytown homes and families to go to make charcoal from the Brazilian rainforests for sale to the steel mills. Many of the "employers" turn out to be slaveholders. The men find themselves at a camp at the edge of the forest, at least fifty miles from the nearest town, with no transportation, little food or shelter, and they are denied the wages they were promised. This is done under the pretext that they owe the camp man-ager (the "gato") a debt for the transportation they received to the camp and what-ever food they consume, but in many cases this debt cannot be paid off because the owner is unscrupulous in his accounting and there is no further appeal for the worker. Workers rarely try to escape because of the prohibitive distance to the nearest town and by staying they can be fed at least some food. Those who try to escape are often hunted down, beaten, and starved until they work again or die. Bales interviewed one slave who described conditions in the camp as follows:

> When we got here from Minas Gerais he taught us how to do the work by beating us. We were scared to say anything, as it was clear he would do anything he wanted to us. Very soon we realized that he wasn't going to pay us. When we asked for money he would beat us. Some of my friends from Bahia ran away, but the gato chased after them with dogs and caught them. He brought them back at gunpoint and beat them in front of us. He kept the dogs around us at night so that they would bark if anyone tried to leave. (Bales 1999, 139)

Clearly this is a case of oppressive violence, in that there are groups of people (the desperately poor) who are preyed upon by a group of persons who manage the charcoal camps, and the forest from which the charcoal is made. Yet they are not groups distinguished by gender or even by race, since the gatos are often from the same group of people as the slaves. However, the gatos, while they are better off than the slaves, are not the ultimate beneficiaries here, but rather the Brazilians who own the forests and invest in the charcoal camps. These are people who may never see the camps, and are able to keep the brutality of that existence at arm's length. Racial and ethnic distinctions in the past have played a role in determining who are the haves and the have nots in Brazil. Brazil suffers from a highly unequal distribution of income[30] that distinguishes sharply the small landowning class descended mainly from the Portuguese colonizers of previous centuries and the large peasant class of white, mixed race, and Afro-Brazilians. Brazil was the last country to outlaw slavery in the Americas, and although the country is highly racially integrated, in the sense that there are no racial barriers to equal opportunity, the economic distinctions among classes could not be sharper. It is the wealthy who benefit from the existence of the slaves, and the poor who suffer. Not only do the slaves themselves suffer, but the wages of those poor who are paid a wage to work in the charcoal camps are much lower as a result of the existence of slavery. And not only do the owners of the slaveholding camps gain from the existence of slavery but also those who own the camps that pay depressed wages, as well as the steel mills that purchase the charcoal at lower prices, and so on up the supply chain.

The illegal slavery that is a part of global international markets thus benefits a more diffuse, less easily identified group than the typical beneficiaries of oppression. The beneficiaries are those who participate in the global markets as investors and consumers. What determines who is or is not a part of these groups is a morass of historical forces of oppression that cannot be generally defined but can, with due diligence, be traced in particular places and times. That each place and time has its particular story does not detract from the fact that there are stories to be told, but does detract from the salience of the oppression and therefore from the attention and sympathy that it generates.

5.3.4. STRIKEBREAKING

Strikes, or collective refusals to work, are legitimate ways for workers to collectively exercise market power in capitalism in order to raise wages and secure better working conditions. After all, one is always (morally) permitted to refuse to work for wages. As Marx pointed out, the market power of the capitalist far exceeds that of the individual worker. While the worker must earn his daily bread, the capitalist can sacrifice only economic profits, not her means of existence, if she does not run her business for a day. Collective bargaining on the part of the workers, which allows them to pool their meager surpluses to exercise some patience in negotiations, is only rational and fair. However, because it is an effective strategy, and because the material wealth and power of capitalists is much greater, capitalists constantly try to thwart the abilities of workers to organize or effectively to conduct strikes. This conflict has been waged both in politics, where capitalists attempt to use their financial power to secure laws against unions or strikes, and with the sanctioned or unsanctioned use of violence. Thus, violence has been used to coerce and intimidate strikers to work for low wages and in poor working conditions. Consider the case of the coal miners of West Virginia portrayed in the movie *Matewan*, a fictional historical account of the coal mining wars there in the early 1900s. Workers there protested the poor conditions of the mines, which caused many to perish in mine cave ins and which the coal companies did little to prevent. They also protested the poor pay and the corrupt accounting at the company store. When they went on strike, the coal company hired a fictional version of the Pinkerton mercenaries to break the strike through violence. The lone law enforcement agent was powerless to prevent either the mercenaries from attempting to coerce the workers to quit their strike, or to prevent the inevitable armed struggle between the two sides. Although in the movie the workers won the shootout, as the credits roll the audience is told that in fact the Pinkertons returned in greater numbers and were able to force the workers back to work on company terms.

Strikebreaking counts as a form of violent oppressive force, if it can be shown that the workers form a social group. Clearly in the case of striking workers or unions they do, since they are then a voluntary group with explicit and tacit membership rules. Workers also form a social group on my account, though, even if they do not belong to a union or are not part of a striking workforce. The reason for this is basically Marx's reason for calling workers a social group: workers face common social constraints in that they cannot choose to own a business and hire labor, but must sell their labor power at wages that are set by forces beyond their control. The benefited social group is the capitalists, who form a social group for the correlative reason that they need not sell their labor but rather can hire labor and earn a profit on their capital instead. That is, they face similar social constraints with other capitalists, and these constraints are improved when the workers are not able to collectively bargain. The use of violence enforces the economic deprivation of the workers through violence. Although in the United States violent strikebreaking is effectively prohibited by law enforcement, it is still practiced in parts of the world, and helps to maintain the economic domination of U.S. consumers, businesses, and investors.

In this section I have surveyed the major types of oppressive violence, categorizing them by the level of organization of the social groups perpetrating and suffering the violence. The examples show a wide variety of types. In each case violence explains how the oppressed are harmed and kept in a position of subordination, under control of the perpetrators. I argued that in some cases violence originates oppression, while in others it maintains pre-existing dominance relations. But in every case it is a powerful means—perhaps the most powerful means—of maintaining oppression.

6. Violence and Oppression

Fundamentally, systematic violence is oppressive because it alters the sense of the possible of its victims, victims who are not only the direct objects of violence but also those who share group membership with them. Systematic violence circumscribes their choices to their own detriment and for the benefit of others. The cases that we have examined in this chapter involved systematic violence on social groups, where the victims of the violence are not only the directly harmed but also those who share group membership with them. We have seen how persons' fundamental freedoms are curtailed by oppressive violence, ranging from, in the extreme cases of war and genocide, the fundamental right to life or freedom from terror and brutality, to lack of freedom of movement, and in somewhat less extreme cases freedom of choice in occupation, sexual partners, and rights of self-expression.

The differences in brutality and salience of oppressive violence stand in indirect proportion to the long-standing nature of the oppression. Wars, genocide, mass rapes last for a short period of time and are highly salient, yet they also typically end quickly. Victims are often aided by massive international movements, which mobilize forces against the oppressors. Violence against racial, religious and sexual minorities is somewhat longer lasting and less thoroughly brutal. These oppressed groups sometimes find it difficult to mobilize large protests against their treatment, except when there are particularly brutal events that are known to sympathetic outsiders. Slavery offers an interesting pair of contrasting cases in this regard. While the old, legal slavery was brutal, the newer forms are even more so. While legal slavery lasted for centuries, particular cases of the new forms of illegal slavery are beginning to motivate international movements and are likely to either end through pressure on governments to crack down on slaveholders or the closing of world markets for the goods that the slaves produce. Finally the case of violence against women is the most long-lasting of all, yet is often so covert, consisting largely in the tacit social threat of violence, as to be doubted that it constitutes a real phenomenon at all. In the next two chapters I will discuss further the economic and psychological factors that explain this relationship between the level of brutality, the economic motivations of the oppressors, and the long-lasting nature of the oppression for these different cases.

Our examination of the force of violence answers in part some of the questions posed in the introductory chapter. First, it often answers the question of the origin of dominance relations between groups. Second, it can answer in part the endurance question: why do some groups, particularly women, suffer ongoing oppression for generation after generation, and why is it so difficult to recognize as oppression? Violence very severely disadvantages a group in numerous ways, both by harming individuals in the group, and by the secondary harms suffered throughout the group via threats of violence. Systematic violence and social threat situations against group members disadvantage that group materially and psychologically. Materially, they can disadvantage members of the group by disabling them physically, either temporarily or permanently (Neath 1997). Violence can disadvantage them by destroying their goods, or by keeping them from pursuing opportunities for building wealth that are not denied to others. Group members are either forced to react with equal opposing force to throw off the oppression, or they must adopt strategies of indirect resistance that may not succeed in overcoming oppression, passive non-resistance, or even acquiescence, while privileged groups gain in wealth and power. Systematic violence and social threat situations also disadvantage a group psychologically. They cause terror and trauma not only in the immediate victims and their families but also in the other members of the social group, who quite rationally take themselves to be equally at risk for victimization. By traumatizing and paralyzing its victims, the effective, credible threat of violence can effectively cause oppressed groups to harm themselves. Yet the systematicity of violence against women is difficult to recognize, and social threat situations, as I argued earlier, may be tacit yet credible, and so also difficult to recognize.

Systematic violence is not the only form that oppression takes, but it is clearly the most immediately harmful, both materially and psychologically. Its primary effect is to enforce domination, exploitation, and segregation, which give immediate benefits to other social groups, including the perpetrators of the violence. State-sponsored violence is very clear to all concerned and difficult, though not impossible, to rationalize, and thus often brings an effective response. However, systematic violence that is not officially state-sponsored, yet harms subordinate social groups while privileging dominant ones, is more difficult to recognize and name as oppression. Those who are oppressed by such violence often find it hard even to name their own terror and lack of material success as due to oppression, and instead find reasons to blame themselves. In the next chapter we will see how economic forces of oppression work both directly and indirectly to reinforce the violent forces of oppression to form an effective prison around the oppressed, not only through externally imposed constraints, but sometimes also through the choices of the oppressed themselves.

5

Economic Forces
of Oppression

1. Economic Deprivation

In the previous chapter I suggested ways in which violence can cause a social group to be poor, or at least poorer than, the dominant social group. Economic institutions have their own ways of maintaining oppression, making social groups more vulnerable to the material and psychological harms of oppression. Economic deprivation harms, and economic institutions can systematically harm, specific social groups. Social institutions that are not recognized as economic institutions can also enforce economic deprivation, and thereby oppression, on certain social groups. Consider for example the distribution of labor by race, which happens when occupations are racially segregated. If that causes undeserved economic deprivation for one group, then the social institutions that cause this distribution oppress through economic force. Social institutions that transmit economic forces often appear to be or stem from innocuous or idiosyncratic cultural, social, religious, or even biological differences among people. However, I shall argue that such social institutions transmit forces of oppression, often through the apparently free choices of individuals.

By 'economic deprivation' I mean the forces that cause persons to be poor, to be unable adequately to secure material existence through the production of goods and services. Poverty is not an absolute term; what counts as an adequate material existence is relative to time and place. While only a poor person would lack indoor plumbing in contemporary Western societies, in another time or place that would be perfectly acceptable. So, when we say that someone or some group is poor, we already mean that relative to others in that time and place. We do not mean by poverty the same thing as inequality, which is a completely comparative term. No one who has a decent standard of living in some absolute sense (i.e., has adequate food, shelter, and the expectation that they will continue to be materially secure from extreme distress) is poor, even if they lack much of what their neighbors have. The concept of economic oppression, I argue, also extends to those groups who, while not poor in an absolute sense, still have reduced life options compared to dominant social groups as a result of their relatively poor circumstances.

This claim raises two questions about economic oppression. The first is whether *poverty* is equivalent to economic oppression. The second is whether *economic inequality* is equivalent to economic oppression. That is, can we say either that members of a group are economically oppressed if and only if they are poor or if and only if they are economically unequal to members of another social group? I will argue that neither poverty nor inequality is a sufficient condition for economic oppression, but that inequality is a necessary condition. Poverty is not necessary for economic oppression in cases where there is great inequality that reduces the options of one group relative to others in society. In such a situation, the relatively poorer group might be oppressed even if not absolutely poor. Poverty is not sufficient for economic oppression if it is not systematically related to social group membership. This point will be controversial because it suggests that "the poor" are not a social group. The account of social groups that I argued for in chapter 2 is that social groups are constituted by some common constraints that are not equivalent to the group's defining features. If the poor are a social group, then anyone who chooses poverty will be a member of the group. But then poverty cannot be oppressive because it is not undeserved or unfair. This is not to deny that poverty can be, and usually is, oppressive; poverty itself causes further poverty, and so it is an exacerbating feature of the oppression of persons who are poor. Poverty makes it difficult to invest in the kinds of things that make for opportunities and options in life. Like psychological oppression, which I shall argue is self-reinforcing, poverty reinforces economic oppression.[1]

I have described the forces of oppression as harming group members both directly and by reducing social group members' options relative to otherwise similarly situated members of society. Thus, for there to be some economic oppression there must be economic inequality. Economic inequality, when it is consequent on social group membership, causes much other harm. Economic inequality harms psychologically and makes one vulnerable to violence. Economic inequality makes one less able to invest in education and training or in business enterprises, and that further exacerbates economic inequality. This suggests that inequality might be a better candidate for a necessary and sufficient condition of economic oppression, but even here I want to deny such a neat relation. Even if it is systematically related to social group membership, inequality is not *sufficient* for economic oppression if the inequality comes about fairly. Take the Amish communities in parts of the United States. In order to avoid the distractions and temptations of consumer society, they voluntarily keep themselves relatively poor (though perhaps not impoverished by world standards), and thus create inequality between the Amish and non-Amish.[2] Their relative economic deprivation, then, is not an aspect of oppression, but a fair result of a voluntary commitment to a valuable way of life. However, inequality is a *necessary* condition of economic oppression. One might object to this claim that the people of a country might be uniformly poor (though this is not common), and yet we would still want to say they are economically oppressed. The former colonies in Africa give us some examples, although poverty is not completely uniform even in these countries. But we would still want to say that the people of, say, Chad, are economically oppressed ultimately stemming from the colonial rule of France, even if the French are long gone from its borders. The appropriate comparison class would be the French (and other former colonial nations), not groups within Chad. In discussing economic oppression, restriction of the comparison class to "similarly situated members of society" seems to rule out international comparisons, which is unacceptable in this age of the global village, where the economics of one society affect the lives of those in others. Inequality, we can say, is a necessary condition of oppression when considered from a global perspective, although in many cases of oppression we need not even look outside the society to find a relatively wealthy group.

Economic oppression is fundamentally a matter of having reduced economic opportunity, consequent on one's social group membership, compared to a group whose members have relatively more economic opportunities. For it to be a case of oppression on the account I have been developing in this book, the inequality must be unfair or undeserved, it must harm, and it must benefit the members of another social group. The oppressed group need not be absolutely poor, but there must be a privileged group relative to which they are economically deprived.

2. Oppressive Economic Systems

Karl Marx presented the most influential account of economic oppression in his work on the history of class and exploitation. On his view, class systems oppress through economic exploitation, which exists whenever one class is forced to give up the surplus value of their labor to another. In ancient (and some not so ancient) economies, slavery prevailed as the original form of exploitation. The slave's actions were completely determined by the master, and the master owned all the product of the slave's labor. In medieval societies slavery gave way to serfdom, where the lord's relation to the serf became less like that of a master to a slave and more like a hereditary landlord to a poor tenant without an option to leave. The lord exploited the serf's labor by directing the serf to work on the lord's land or by taking in kind or cash rental payments from the serf's products from the land he occupied. The rise of a merchant class in late medieval times and the forcible removal of serfs from their lands brought about the development of capitalism and the exploitation of the working class by the class of owners of capital (Dobb 1947, ch. 2; Marx 1967, ch. 27). Now the exploited class was "free" to contract for employment with other capitalists, but their poor bargaining position vis-à-vis capitalists would leave them, according to Marx, with few real options but to accept mere subsistence wages while creating great wealth for their employers.

Marx's explanation of economic oppression is still useful, but it does not tell the whole story of oppression. Marx reveals how the social production of goods creates surplus value, and that exploitation occurs when this surplus value is unfairly distributed. However, Marx's analysis of what counts as fair distribution is open to dispute. His key insight was to see that economic oppression is crucial to oppression, but he tried to reduce all oppression to economic oppression as a consequence of his commitment to historical materialism. Any other force that shapes history—violence for example—he saw as just another economic power. In *Capital* he writes: "Force is the midwife of every old society pregnant with a new one. It is itself an economic power" (Marx 1967, ch. 31). Yet many feminists and race theorists have argued that such a reduction cannot account for the oppression of women or the oppression of non-whites (Hartmann 1979; Ferguson 1991; Folbre 1994).

Marx divided history into five main epochs: primitive communism (hunting and gathering or agricultural societies), slavery, serfdom, capitalism, and socialism. While his historical facts may be questioned, this is a useful division of the ar-chetypes of economic systems that have been tried in the world, although different political, geographic, and cultural facts in different societies shape the economic system in importantly different ways. Taking the four modern economic systems into account, it is clear that the first two, slavery and serfdom, are oppressive economic systems. For each of them classifies groups as workers whose labor is to be appropriated for the exclusive use by others without compensation and without the consent of the laborer. The work of slaves and serfs was coerced by force or the threat of force. In these systems one is either born into, or forced into, a class. If one is in the laboring classes, that is, a slave or a serf, then one is harmed by being forced to work without compensation. If one is in one of the dominant classes, that is, lords (and their ladies) or slave owners, then one is benefited by the work of the op-pressed class. Thus, all the conditions for oppression—an unfairly harmed and coerced social group and a benefited social group—exist in the case of serfdom and slavery.

Marx also tried to argue that capitalism produces a similarly oppressive eco-nomic relationship between workers and capitalists, and that socialism would be the end of classes and therefore the end of oppression. On the other hand, many have argued that socialism deprives persons of their natural rights to property, or, as Robert Nozick colorfully put it, prevents "capitalist acts between consenting adults" (Nozick 1974). Since capitalism and socialism are the major contending economic systems today, it is important to examine these claims carefully to determine whether either one is oppressive as a system. That is, are capitalism and socialism necessarily oppressive, as slavery and serfdom are?

To begin that investigation, one feature that we should grant to both systems is the property of self-ownership.[3] That is, each person is said to own her- or himself in the sense that she or he cannot be forced to work against her or his will. Without this feature capitalism immediately devolves into a system of slavery, since some persons could be owned and then forced to work. Socialism, likewise, devolves into a kind of serfdom, since without property in their persons, any person or all persons can be made to work for the good of others, through a system of social roles that determine what work one will do and for how long, independently of the individ-ual's wishes. With this clarification in mind, let us examine each system in turn.

2.1. Capitalism

The core defining feature of capitalism is that it is an economic system that allows private ownership of the means of production, that is, of capital inputs to production. In such a system, under very minimal assumptions of differences in preferences and/

or initial distribution of capital inputs, markets will develop, including markets for labor.[4] The definition of capitalism entails that these markets be free of undue government intervention. Some government intervention is necessary, however, to enforce laws against coercion, theft, fraud, and to enforce contracts. Many different economic systems with different consequences for freedom and oppression have been called capitalist, and many of the differences hinge on what counts as undue government intervention. Even the most libertarian defender of capitalism will accept that "neither open nor concealed force" (Hayek 1944, 27–28) should determine prices, wages, or which transactions will take place. Externalities, which are costs (benefits) that are incurred by persons who are not compensated by (do not compensate) the ones who inflicted the costs (benefits), can be seen as a kind of concealed force, or at least an illegitimate way for one person to take advantage of another, and thus laws that redistribute property rights to compensate for externalities would likewise be legitimate under capitalism. Capitalism is also held by most libertarians to be compatible with laws that protect the consumer from hazardous products or the worker from unduly hazardous conditions or long working hours. These might be defended on the grounds that otherwise the consumer or the worker is subject to fraudulent concealment of the actual qualities of the product or the nature of the work. But that defense would not work in cases where the hazards are fully revealed to the consumers or the potential workers, who can then be free to consume or to choose in light of full information. A more promising justification of such laws was provided by Friedrich Hayek, who argued that laws that create the conditions for the proper working of competition, or that encourage competition, are compatible with capitalism (Hayek 1944, 29). Although he is not altogether clear on why this is so, he might reasonably be seen to be appealing to the internal logic of capitalism itself, arguing that since the goal is an efficiently working market, competitive market conditions are to be encouraged within capitalism. Since the temptation to hide information about hazards would always be great, there would be a tendency for competitors to cheat. Laws would give them the proper incentives (in the form of fines or liability for damage) to make safe products and conditions. Nozick rejects the idea that any social system should have any goal other than the protection of a historical system of entitlements, and so would reject Hayek's argument. But many other defenders of capitalism would not, and it would have other advantageous implications. Thus, I shall suppose that any laws which further competition are also allowed as appropriate governmental intervention. Such laws would include those that prevent externalities from affecting others without some compensation, and laws preventing monopoly or monopsony power from dominating the market. Finally, although Hayek did not recognize these, I would argue that capitalism is compatible with laws designed to prevent noneconomic, invidious discrimination among social groups, such as that associated with racism or sexism. Such laws are compatible with the goal of capitalism to further market-based competition, which is based on the relatively anonymous interaction of buyers and sellers. Discrimination for reasons not based on the product of the labor would introduce inefficiencies, and in the context of our argument, would introduce oppression for reasons that are not strictly economic in nature, that is, not related to the structure of capitalism itself.[5]

Capitalism probably cannot be defended as a system that is not necessarily oppressive unless it can be shown that it is compatible with the provision of social services, such as a welfare minimum, provided that these do not stand in the way of furthering competition. As with the above mentioned laws against discrimination, provision of such services is not required, but it is enough for my purposes to show that they are compatible with capitalism. The best way to argue for this claim is to show that the justification of capitalist property rights itself rests on the right to a minimum standard of living. Then, as Jeremy Waldron puts it, "if anyone thinks that property rights may legitimately be enforced, he or she must think the same about welfare rights on the present approach, because their recognition is part and parcel of the justification of property" (Waldron 2003, 47). The standard entitlement theory approach to the justification of private property rights, stemming from Locke, is to begin with the claim that the fruits of the earth are our common legacy, and then to justify individual appropriation from that common legacy, subject to provisos. The point of the provisos is to recognize that each person has a right to draw sustenance from the world in some way or other. Thus, Locke denied that all the natural resources were simply up for grabs and introduced the proviso that there be "enough and as good left for others" (Locke 1980, ch. 7). Since on the entitlement theory view, after the initial appropriation of the natural resources, things come into the world already owned (Nozick 1974, 160), there seems to be no way for the person who has no resources to gain sustenance and so must die. But that would include all (at least infant and toddler) children who are not cared for by others who will charitably share their wealth, and so they must die. Since that contradicts the notion that everyone has a right to gain sustenance from the world, it seems that some welfare minimum, at least for the helpless, is required by the very justification of property. We can extend this argument from the helpless to all those who lack effective resources in their environment to make a living. If the economy effectively prevents them from making a living because they have no marketable skills and no usable capital, then again the right to gain sustenance from the world would entail that they should be guaranteed a social minimum. Thus, a justifiable capitalist society must provide sustenance for all who cannot, for whatever reason, provide it for themselves. Now I grant that this way of speaking is loose. It will take judgment to determine who *cannot* provide sustenance for themselves and who simply *will not*. A capitalist society might decide to provide specified work for the ones who they suspect of being unwilling rather than unable. But it is not necessary for me to make these judgment calls; it suffices for my purposes to show that some guaranteed social minimum is a necessary limit on the right to own property in capital.

Let us say, then, that what counts as clearly acceptable (for the sake of classification as capitalism) governmental intervention includes laws that prohibit force and fraud, or that prevent market inefficiencies such as externalities and monopoly or monopsony power, or that provide a social minimum to the unendowed, or that prevent invidious discrimination against social groups by gender, race/ethnicity, disability, religion, or sexual orientation.[6] Taxation at reasonable levels for the sake of meeting these goals is clearly acceptable, as well. Let us say that what would not count as acceptable intervention would be what would cause the system to be classified as socialist, namely public ownership of the means of production, or a system of taxation so drastic as to amount to the same.

Capitalism faces many allegations of oppressiveness. Although one might argue that a system is oppressive if it is inefficient relative to another system and thereby causes unnecessary misery and suffering, that charge is seldom laid against capitalism. The charges against capitalism are primarily moral: that capitalism exploits workers, that it causes great inequalities in wealth, and that it causes extreme poverty for the worst off members of society or for members of other societies whose workers are exploited by transnational capitalism. John Roemer (1988) has argued that the charge of exploitation is, morally speaking, a red herring. He shows how exploitation can arise in morally neutral ways, and that when there is a case of morally unacceptable exploitation, the cause of the moral objection to the system is not the exploitation of labor or capital, but rather the fact of an inequality in wealth and opportunity arising from an original inequality in the distribution of capital, wealth, talent, or luck. Now if Roemer is correct, then we can dismiss the charge of exploitation for the sake of our argument, since exploitation is not in itself the problem but inequality is. We can also dismiss the charge of extreme poverty at least for the argument regarding the intrinsic and necessary oppressiveness of capitalism, since it would be consistent with capitalism to guarantee a social minimum, as I have argued. The charge of intrinsic or necessary oppressiveness then revolves around this inequality in the distribution of resources, an inequality that capitalism, it must be recognized, appears to exacerbate.

The case for the claim that capitalism is oppressive can be summarized as follows. Capitalism divides society into (roughly) two classes, workers and capitalists, and constrains the workers far more than similarly situated capitalists.[7] It harms the workers by causing them to be poorer, to have less leisure time, less (or no) access to health care, less adequate nutrition, and less access to educational opportunities. Workers live lesser lives than capitalists. These facts must be granted. However, this is not enough to confirm that capitalism is an oppressive economic system, since it must also be shown that the harms to the workers are unfair and undeserved, and this is just the point where the defenders of capitalism will argue that capitalism in itself does not oppress. The fundamental moral defense of capitalism rests on the observation that in capitalism workers are not forced to work; they are free to accept or reject any wage contract. Thus, any wage contract they make is voluntary, and so uncoerced, and so it cannot, by my definition, be oppressive. If wage contracts generally are not oppressive, then capitalism is not oppressive. Call this the choice negates oppression thesis. Let us see if that thesis holds.

2.1.1. CHOICE AND COERCION

Another way of asking this is to see if voluntary wage contracts are *ipso facto* uncoerced. A necessary condition of coercion is that one lacks a choice, but one has to lack choice in the right way to be coerced. Choices may be voluntary or involuntary, freely made or forced. To be coerced to act is still to act, that is, to exercise some choice. Even when you get mugged (a paradigm case of coercion) you have a choice in the sense of two options: give the mugger your money or refuse and risk losing your life. But a coerced choice is different from a voluntary choice psychologically and morally. Psychologically, coerced persons feel that they are compelled to act as they do by the unacceptability of their other options; one says in such circumstances that one had "no choice" but to act as one did. Morally, coercion is a prima facie wrong because it violates justice and the autonomy of its victim.[8]

There are two competing philosophical accounts of coercion, which I shall describe, following Alan Wertheimer, as an empirical account and a moralized account. An empirical account "maintains that the truth of a coercion claim rests, at its core, on ordinary facts: will B be worse off than he now is if he fails to accept A's proposal? Is there great psychic pressure on B? Does B have any 'reasonable' alternative?" (Wertheimer 1987, 7) Empirical accounts ask about the allegedly coerced agent's state of mind, about whether he feels that his choice is voluntary, or made under conditions of duress. They are parallel to psychological theories of freedom and do not require a prior normative theory. A moralized theory "holds that we cannot determine whether A coerces B without answering the following sorts of questions: Does A have the right to make his proposal? Should B resist A's proposal? Is B entitled to recover should he succumb to A's proposal?" (Wertheimer 1987, 7) Moralized theories of coercion claim that the state of mind of the allegedly coerced person is irrelevant to the question of whether she is coerced and that the only relevant matter is whether the agent is denied some choice that she ought morally to have. Thus, moralized theories are embedded within a moral theory, typically a theory of rights or entitlement.

Many Marxist arguments for the claim that workers are coerced in capitalism employ empirical accounts of force and coercion. For example, G. A. Cohen (1988) argues that workers are forced to make contracts that exploit them, or that subject them to hazardous conditions, because they had no "acceptable alternative" to making these contracts. He argues that the proletariat is unfree because they are forced to work for capitalists who exploit them. Their only alternatives to working for the wages proposed by the capitalist are starvation, or begging, or going on the public dole, and these are not acceptable alternatives because they involve death or serious disenfranchisement from society. Hence, workers are forced to make exploitative contracts. This is an empirical account of force, since it simply examines the alternatives open to the persons, not whether the options are deserved.

However, one might argue that a moral theory sneaks into the account in assessing the acceptability of one's alternatives. If an alternative is unacceptable because the agent *feels* that it is (an empirical question), then the theory is not moralized, but it threatens to leave us with the view that all hard (i.e., psychologically difficult) choices are forced. If, on the other hand, an alternative counts as unacceptable because it is undeserved or unusually unfair, then the theory of force is moralized after all. Cohen explains what he means by "unacceptable" as follows. An alternative B is unacceptable compared to A if and only if B is not worse than A or B is not thoroughly bad, where "thoroughly bad" is understood in an absolute sense in expected utility terms (Cohen 1988, 282).[9] He claims that by taking "thoroughly bad" as "absolute *in some sense*" we avoid the conclusion that rational persons are always forced to do what they do, since they always do the utility-maximizing thing.

But Cohen's understanding of unacceptable alternatives leads to the conclusion that all hard choices are forced choices. Perhaps survival is an objective criterion of acceptability, but it is difficult to see what else is objectively unacceptable in the absence of a moral theory, and it is clear that survivability is too weak as a criterion of acceptability. Furthermore, Cohen's understanding does not allow choices to be forced when the options are not so "thoroughly bad," but when they are unfair, unequal, or undeserved. Suppose that a person has a choice between two mediocre and uninspired high schools, but is denied the option of attending a very good high school in her neighborhood because she is black. This is a case where we would want to say that she is forced to choose the school she chooses, even though it is not "thoroughly bad," since it is morally unacceptable that she should be prevented from attending the good school on grounds of race.

Like most Marxists, Cohen argues that force, oppression, and exploitation are *objective* circumstances of workers in capitalism. That claim seems to me to be right when understood as saying that oppression goes deeper than mere feeling of the workers, that oppression involves their physical circumstances. This explains how workers can be oppressed even when they do not feel as though they are: they could be in objectively bad circumstances and believe that they deserve them and so deny that they are oppressed. It would be a mistake to take the claim of objectivity to imply that oppression is therefore non-normative, however. We can make sense of a moralized theory of force as objectively determinable *by an objective moral theory*, where the theory of force is moralized, and we can require that the harms suffered by the forced or coerced persons be objective harms.[10] Thus, we can agree that force, coercion, and oppression are objective, while maintaining that the theory of force, and so on, are moralized theories.

Like Cohen, Jeffrey Reiman (1987) conceptualizes force empirically, but he applies it to situations of *structural force*, where a group of persons together make choices within constraints that only appear statistically, relative to other persons in society. That is, it appears only when one examines the outcomes statistically, comparing groups of persons. This sort of force is built right into the structure of society, through its laws, social practices, and norms. Structural force is difficult to see, since, as Reiman points out, there is some play in the alternatives open to the "forced" persons, some sense in which they can choose how they will comply with or fit within the constraints of the structures. Reiman argues that the working class only appears to be unforced in making employment contracts because they can choose which capitalist to contract with, but their range of options "imposes fates" on them that guarantee that there will always be workers who lack access to the means of production and thus have to make less advantageous contracts with capitalists (Reiman 1987, 12–13). This is the sense of force that we must recognize if we are to make any headway in understanding oppressive economic structures, since oppression is a structural phenomenon.

In contrast to these empirical accounts, Nozick argues that only a moralized account of coercion supports the moral force of a coercion claim. On his view, one cannot claim to be coerced simply because one has bad alternatives, but only if one had the *right* to better ones. "A person's choice among differing degrees of unpalatable alternatives is not rendered nonvoluntary by the fact that others voluntarily chose and acted within their rights in a way that did not provide him with a more palatable alternative" (Nozick 1974, 264). The example he uses to argue this point is choice of marriage partners among (presumably heterosexual) men and women who have the same preference orderings over the members of the other gender as all the other members of their own. Suppose that there are 26 of each, with names A–Z for men and A'–Z' for women, and suppose that they are rank ordered by each member of the opposite gender in alphabetic order, so that A is preferred to B is preferred to C, and so on by women and A' is preferred to B' is preferred to C', and so on by men. Suppose that their preferences are transitive and that they prefer any of the other gender to remaining unmarried. Then if they are perfectly free to accept or reject any other partner, A will marry A', B will marry B', and so forth. In this situation B's options limit him to selecting from among B'–Z', C's options are limited to C'–Z', and so on. Are they coerced into marrying their partners? Nozick argues that clearly they are not, but that on an empirical account of coercion they must be (provided that the agents' first choices are significantly more preferred by them to their other choices). They are not coerced, according to Nozick, since each of the women who they could not marry had the right to choose another partner to marry, and thus limit the men's choices. But to say that this is coercive is to say that these men are owed some remedy, and the only possible remedy would be to violate the women's choices and coerce them into marrying men whom they do not wish to marry. Thus the choices that these people make, even those of Z and Z', who are each getting only their 26th choice of mates, cannot be coercive.

On Nozick's view, coercion claims must be judged against a theory of rights. Cohen denies this, pointing out that Nozick's view "has the absurd upshot" that the criminal who is imprisoned justly is therefore not *forced* to be in prison (Cohen 1988, 256). Clearly there are two senses of "force" being used here: in Cohen's use P is forced to A whenever P finds the alternatives to A unacceptable or physically impossible to resist, while in Nozick's use force arises only when P's rights are being violated by someone's denying her another alternative. The issue concerning the use of "force" would be entirely semantic but for the fact that each is trying to derive a moral conclusion from them. In Nozick's case the conclusion comes immediately: being forced to do A means that one's rights are being violated and thus one is being wronged. In Cohen's case the moral conclusion comes down the road a bit: if P is forced to A then P is unfree, but since the lacked freedom is not a *moral* freedom, the moral implication arises only when one shows that it is unjust for P to be unfree, and that has to do with the fairness of P's situation as compared to that of her fellows. In deciding on the fairness of P's situation, Cohen may not appeal to the fact that P is forced, for no moral conclusion can follow from it, as the marriage case or even the prison case clearly show. "Force" has no normative force unless it appeals to a background moral theory when determining what counts as an acceptable alternative, either a theory of freedom that tells us when it is obstructed immorally, or a theory of justice. Thus, Cohen's account of force is either normatively impotent or it appeals to a background moral theory after all.

David Zimmerman objects to moralized accounts of coercion because they do not appeal to freedom in explaining why coercion is prima facie wrong. On his view, coercion is wrong "because it involves frustration of the victim's desire to remain in the pre-threat situation or involves a use of his preference structure as a mere means" (Zimmerman 1981, 130). Coercion is wrong because it violates *freedom*, not justice as Nozick would have it. And if a threat frustrates one's desires or manipulates one into choosing what one does not want by offering only poor alternatives, then it violates one's freedom. But as was the case with Cohen's non-moral account of force, a lack of this sense of freedom is not itself prima facie wrong. It is, to be sure, against the interests of the agent. But to argue that it is a *wrong* we must make the case that the freedom denied is essential to the dignity or autonomy of the agent, or that the agent had a right to that freedom. That is, we need to ask prior moral questions. So if coercion is to be even prima facie wrong, there is no avoiding the background moral theory. Yet Zimmerman uncovers an important aspect of coercion that Nozick overlooks: to be denied autonomy in a sense that is essential to one's moral agency may count as a way of violating a person's moral rights, but to speak in terms of rights is sometimes to neglect an agent's moral claim to that autonomy. Coercion, then, should be judged against a background moral theory that takes autonomy, as well as property rights, seriously.

I agree with Nozick that coercion claims are to be judged against a background moral theory.[11] Oppression claims themselves are prima facie moral claims for remedy or redress. The point of the coercion requirement in my account of oppression is to transmit the prima facie moral claim, and Nozick shows convincingly that only a moralized account can do this. To accept a moralized account of coercion, however, is not necessarily to accept Nozick's account. First, one may reject Nozick's theory of rights as historically grounded. Moreover, one may argue, as I do, that coercion claims must be judged against a broader moral theory than the theory of property rights. As in Nozick's account of voluntary choice, I take coercion to be a nonvoluntary choice where the voluntariness of the choice is moralized, and where a choice that is involuntary but which could not be altered by human action is also not coerced. But where Nozick discusses only violations of rights as the requirement of involuntariness, I argue that the moral background should be broadened to a theory of justice. Here's why. Rights are formulated within social institutions and norms that are taken for granted. Rex Martin writes that rights "are institutional practices which require an institutional setting" (Martin 1993, 2). Within a set of social practices, which normally appear to be determined prior to moral or legal systems, rights may be justified as fair and just rules for interactions among individuals. The emphasis on rights tends to obscure the contingent nature of the social practices and the way that background social institutions and practices rig the competition for the gains from social cooperation in favor of some and against others. While seeing that rights must be morally justified for a system, political philosophers tend to take their own social practices, or the ancestors of those practices, for granted.[12] For example, consider a Nozickean world where two persons have the same rights but where the parents of one are wealthy and generous to their child and the parents of the other are poor. Clearly they have differential access to the gains from social cooperation. On Nozick's theory there can be no more moral consideration of the situation than whether the line of succession of the property rights is unbroken by force or fraud. But it is arbitrary to restrict moral consideration to property rights as they have been protected and enforced by the state powers in that historical chain. These powers have also denied women and serfs and slaves the rights even to seek to own property, for instance. Almost every person now living has some of these disenfranchised persons in their past, but some have many more than others, and some are more immediately related to and related only to such persons. Even if the men who have owned property had the right to acquire the property and treated no one else unjustly in acquiring it, there were many others who were prevented from competing with them for a claim to it. Since owning property enables one more easily to acquire more property, those who were denied the right to own property were not competing on an equal or fair basis even once they were given those rights. Thus, there have been violations of justice, if not of property rights per se, in the transmission of every claim to property ownership that comes through Nozick's historical account.

The point I am making is more general than this, however. I am claiming that since social institutions define the available options in favor of some groups and to the disadvantage of others, and since this advantage and disadvantage is sometimes unjust but not a violation of (historically or currently specified) rights, we need a broader moral theory as the background moral theory in our account of coercion. Specifically, we need a moral theory that can recognize injustice in social institutions. To illustrate the problem, let us reconsider Nozick's marriage example. Suppose again that the men and the women each have preference rankings of all the members of the opposite gender, and that these rankings are transitive (i.e., if A is preferred to B and B to C, then A is preferred to C) and strict (for any two choices A and B either A is preferred to B or B to A), but suppose that the rankings are not exactly the same for each member of the two groups. Now suppose that there is a quaint social norm such that the men are allowed to propose to their favorite women and the women are allowed only to accept or reject the proposals and not to propose, and again suppose that everyone is free to refuse to marry anyone whom they would rather not marry. In such a situation it can be shown analytically that: (1) a stable set of marriages will form, in the sense that no one will be paired with someone who he(she) likes worse than someone else who likes her(him) better than his(her) partner; (2) the men (the proposers) are systematically advantaged over the women (the group who can only accept or reject), in the sense that all the men are happier or at least as happy with this match as the one that would have arisen from the match made by women acting as proposers and men as the group who could only accept or reject, and all the women like their match less than or at least no better than the alternative match in which they get to propose.[13] That is, the men are benefited as a group by this matchmaking arrangement and have a common interest in maintaining it, even while they compete with each other within it and it gives both men and women *equal rights* to reject any proposed partner. This marriage market shows that the norms that govern transactions can seriously disadvantage one group, even while they are voluntary and equal under the law.

Nozick's model of force is an agent-to-agent model; the marriage market example shows that unfair force can also be applied by institutions on agents, and thus that Nozick's model is too limited.[14] Social practices, institutions, and norms give persons power (or differential access to burdens and benefits) in relationships, and sometimes they do so by differentiating between persons on account of gender or race. In the marriage market example the power to propose enforced the best possible outcome for men within the confines of a stable matchmaking institution that allowed women the right to reject any suitor. Social institutions thus create unequal power in relationships among individuals of different groups. As Reiman also saw, the agent-to-agent model conceals the force relationships between persons with unequal power. What we need, then, is a moralized theory of coercion that reveals these relationships and determines when they are unjust. Thus we need a model of institutional coercion that takes a theory of fairness and justice as its background moral theory. The definition of institutional coercion that I propose is the following:

An institution (economic system, legal system, norm) is coercive if the institution unfairly limits the choices of some group of persons relative to other groups in society.

The account of coercion that will support the claim that oppression is prima facie unjust is a moralized account of coercion, including institutional coercion. Choice negates oppression, then, only when the choice is uncoerced.

2.1.2. FAIRNESS AND CAPITALISM

To be counted as fair, a social institution should, at minimum, distribute the burdens and benefits impartially with respect to nonvoluntary social group membership. If this does not seem to the reader to be an obvious minimal condition on fairness, then the condition might be motivated by asking whether rational persons would agree to this institution behind a veil of ignorance and choose to maintain it once the veil is lifted. On any reasonable account of fairness, there would surely be no social institutions that would arbitrarily benefit certain social groups at the expense of others, for example, men at the expense of women, white persons at the expense of persons of color, straight persons at the expense of gay or lesbian ones, or make any other humiliating discriminations between nonvoluntary social groups. Surely much more needs to be said about the fairness of social institutions, but to return for the moment to the question of whether capitalism is necessarily oppressive, what about the differential rewards to workers and capitalists which cause the inequalities in choice that these two groups enjoy in capitalism—is this a source of coercion? Appealing to the notion of coercion just presented, the question is whether the choices of the workers are limited. Their choices are limited if they would have more choices under similar conditions but a different economic system. This means that what we have to do is to compare the choice situation of workers under capitalism with the choice situation of persons under socialism. If the benefits to capitalists are not at the expense of workers but rather also increase the workers' choices, then there is no coercion.

Consider the two graphic illustrations in figures 5.1 and 5.2.

In each scenario there are two possibilities, either capitalism or socialism. The height of the bars represents the number of choices open to each group of persons and the width represents the number of persons in the respective groups. In the left hand half of the graphs we have the situation of capitalism, where there are two

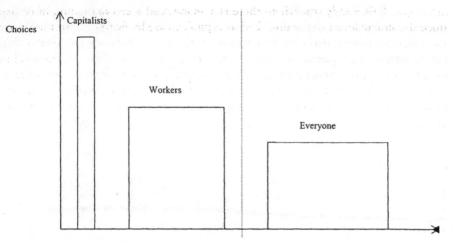

FIGURE 5.1

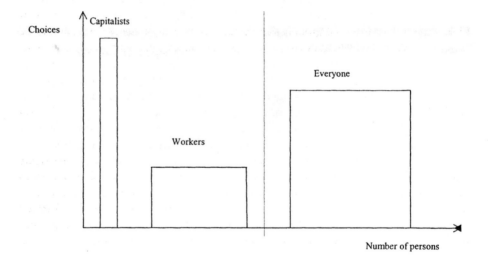

FIGURE 5.2

groups, while in the right hand half of the graphs we have the situation of socialism with no class distinctions. In figure 5.1, the number of choices for the workers is greater in capitalism than the number of choices for everyone in socialism. In figure 5.2, the number of choices for the workers increases when they become part of the classless society of socialism. So the question is whether figure 5.1 or figure 5.2 is a better representation of the tradeoffs between capitalism and socialism. One of the fundamental claims in favor of capitalism is that it increases the wealth of the worst off while enriching the best off. If we take wealth to be a proxy for the number of choices for persons, then figure 5.1 would be more representative of capitalism than

figure 5.2. This is only true where there is a guaranteed social minimum, of course, since the unemployed or the unskilled in capitalism are likely to be extremely poor. But given a generous enough social minimum, the claim that even the worst off are better off under capitalism than they would be under socialism is plausible. Thus, inequality is not necessarily coercive, provided that the worst off are not worse off than they would be in a noncapitalist system. And since it is compatible with capitalism that there be a guaranteed social minimum, capitalism is not intrinsically oppressive.

2.2. Socialism

Socialism is a system in which the means of production are publicly owned. As with capitalism, I will define socialism as entailing self-ownership, in order to distinguish it from a kind of serfdom. Self-ownership requires that no one can be forced to work without their uncoerced consent. Since in socialism it is the state that determines who produces what and how, and then how that will be distributed, there is plenty of room, even with self-ownership, for oppressive forces to develop. In order to show that socialism is not intrinsically oppressive as a system, I will argue that a socialist society can develop mechanisms for production and distribution that are not oppressive.

First we will want to prevent the state from deciding on production or distribution according to social group membership. In a socialist economy it should be possible to allow a meritocracy to determine who will fill what roles in the economy. Of course, there will have to be standards or criteria by which the most talented for each occupation are chosen, and these will have to be implemented by individuals who make judgment calls. As we shall see in the next section, there are many ways that what appears to be a meritocracy can actually be an "old-boys network" reinforcing oppression. But that does not prevent the criteria from being specified without reference to any social group membership and insisting on impartial application of the criteria. It will be objected, though, that the greater problem is in getting persons to apply for the more difficult, dirty, dangerous, or otherwise unpleasant tasks of society. However, it is not contrary to socialism to allow differential reward of occupations in order to inspire a competitive labor force even for these jobs. Indeed, one could argue that under socialism it is easier to ensure that such unpleasant jobs are properly compensated rather than forced upon an oppressed group.

A classic objection to socialism is that since the state controls the means of production, it controls the means that people have to achieve their various ends, and will distribute according to the state's evaluation of those ends, which will inevitably have two bad outcomes for freedom and justice. First, the state can invidiously discriminate against social groups. We have argued that this can be avoided, however. Second, the state can decide that some ends are not worth supporting and so not provide the means to pursue them.[15] Now it is not contrary to socialism to allow persons to use their personal property in any way that such property could be used under capitalism. But what is prohibited is the amassing of the wealth that is needed to undertake production of commodities, that is, goods for sale. There is no reason that the state cannot support artistic or recreational endeavors that are pursued by large numbers of people—symphonies, soccer leagues, and the like. It will be objected that only when the state sees those as valuable will the support be available, and it is inevitable that a small minority preference will not be supported. If this minority preference constitutes a social group, then perhaps this is a place where oppression can occur in socialism. Although this is true, it is no less true in capitalism. The difference between socialism and capitalism in this regard is only in who decides which minority preferences will be pursued. Under capitalism that is decided by the ability of the minority to pay for the activity or good or to convince private foundations to support them; under socialism it is determined by the ability of the minority to convince the majority that the activity or good is valuable enough to be supported. Now one might argue that this opens the possibility once again for discrimination against minority social groups with preferences for activities or goods not shared by the majority. For example, suppose a minority cultural group practice an expensive ritual. How will the state go about deciding on whether to subsidize this activity? Again, invidious discrimination against social groups must be avoided, but not every expensive activity can be supported. But, again, this is not different from the kinds of problems of supporting minorities in capitalism. If it happens that the group itself cannot support the activity and it seeks social support, then the support will only be forthcoming if the state can be convinced that it is important enough to provide the support for it. Although this sort of judgment call by the state leaves open the possibility of oppression, it does not make oppression a necessary result. Hence this objection, while it raises important cautionary notes for socialism, does not show socialism to be necessarily oppressive.

The experience of the twentieth century with so-called Communist regimes has shown that the fundamental problem of a centrally planned economy is that it tends to create a class of government officials who have much greater power and lead much less constrained lives than the rest of the society. Central control of the means of production entails the centralization and accumulation of power in the hands of the decision makers, who can choose to benefit themselves materially. "Planning leads to dictatorship because dictatorship is the most effective instrument of coercion and the enforcement of ideals, and as such essential if central planning on a large scale is to be possible" (Hayek 1944, 52). Those who are not decision makers lack this power and are harmed by their lack of power to control external objects except by permission of the decision makers. In the twentieth-century communist regimes this power imbalance caused great economic stagnation—slow growth, absurd misallocation of resources, lack of innovation, and the like. More horrifically, though, the rise of communist dictatorships led to forced labor and drastic systems of punishment. Thus, we seem to have another case of oppression: oppression of the citizens by the politicians in control of the means of production.

The examples of the USSR and the People's Republic of China bear witness to this claim. However, just as there are oppressive capitalist economies, there are oppressive socialist economies. I am asking whether socialism is necessarily oppressive, though, and as with capitalism, I would deny that even this basic difficulty with socialism shows it to be necessarily oppressive. First, note that capitalism also has the tendency, unless there are controlling countermeasures, to accumulate power in the hands of a few. But while I would agree that capitalism must set up a class system, socialism need not do so, and without one, there is no particular social group to be oppressed in the manner just suggested. Suppose that the socialist system is democratic and carefully builds in mechanisms to encourage participation by the citizens in the democracy. Suppose also that different industries are run by boards containing the many different stakeholders in the industry: workers, consumers, persons affected by the resource use, and so on, and that these boards have revolving membership. In this way power could be dissipated and held by different people at different times. Then there would be no lasting or stable group that could be identified by their greater or lesser constraints to compose a social group that is oppressed or that is privileged by the social system.[16] Thus, socialism need not be oppressive. It may not be economically efficient under this scenario, but a lack of economic efficiency does not entail oppression.[17]

What we have seen in this section is that while both capitalism and socialism can support oppressive regimes and institutions, they need not do so. Both systems need to prevent invidious discrimination against social groups in the economic sphere. While both systems have particular groups that can be vulnerable to oppression, both systems can be combined with political measures to avoid oppression. In capitalism it is important to prevent poverty of working or unemployed classes through a guaranteed social minimum. In socialism it is important to prevent the development of a permanent ruling elite and to develop mechanisms for participatory democratic control of the means of production.

Oppressive economic inequalities can come about in a variety of ways. One is through the economic system itself, as in the case of slavery and serfdom. But economic systems that are not oppressive in themselves can also contain within them mechanisms by which some are deprived economically. This is especially true for capitalism, which encourages and fosters economic inequalities. We have also seen how socialism fosters political inequalities that can become oppressive, and how socialism can harbor some of the same forces of oppression as capitalism. The mechanisms by which oppressive economic inequalities originate and are maintained are what I call the economic forces of oppression.

In the following sections I distinguish two kinds of economic forces: direct and indirect forces. Direct forces cause inequality through the intentional actions of a dominant group on a subordinate one. Indirect forces cause inequality through the choices and decisions of the members of the oppressed group themselves, as they try to live in the face of other inequalities and injustices. It is important to distinguish these two forces for both normative and descriptive reasons. First, once the case has been made that something is a direct force of oppression, the moral case for opposing it has already been made. A direct force is a constraint that is completely external to the victim, and hence there can be no question of the victim's role in the harm that is caused by his or her action under the compulsion of direct oppression. There is also no question that the force should immediately cease. The normative issues of responsibility and remedy are not so immediate for indirect forces. Although any force of oppression indicates an injustice, it is more challenging to show that there is oppression and, further, to oppose indirect forces is to oppose the choices and decisions of the oppressed, and so possibly to victimize them once again. I discuss the difficulties involved in choosing the techniques of resistance to indirect forces of oppression in chapter 7. Second, there is an analytic or descriptive reason to differentiate the two kinds of forces. Indirect forces must work through the psychology of the oppressed to result in choices and decisions that harm. This means that to understand how or why the oppressive force is transmitted requires a look into the victim's psychology, as we saw already in discussing the transmission of violent threats and of choice under coercion. I will discuss the psychology of oppression more fully in the next chapter.

3. Direct Forces of Economic Oppression

Direct forces of economic oppression are means by which members of a dominant social group maintain their wealth and income by intentional actions designed to keep members of subordinate social groups economically inferior and exploitable. Oppression is systematic and group based, and thus crime is not generally a means of oppression, although many direct economic forces of oppression are criminal or illegal. What follows is a catalog of direct forces of economic oppression.

3.1. Enslavement

The most extreme form of direct economic oppression is slavery. I discussed slavery in the last chapter as a kind of violence. Slavery is a clear example of how violence and the threat of violence works to enforce economic oppression. Slavery always requires violence, whether at the beginning or throughout, though it can be maintained through psychological coercion in addition to the threat of violence. Slaves often become dependent on the order and discipline that confines them, and they find the thought of freedom painful and frightening (Bales 2002). Slavery is also an economic system, with clear implications for inequality between slave and slaveholding groups. As we saw in the previous chapter, slavery has changed as an institution over time. While it used to be a legal institution, slavery is now illegal in most countries of the world. The slavery that now exists we would not term an economic system, but rather it has become a part of the global capitalist system. Slavery is the extreme loss of free will and choice about movement, action, production, and social relationships, backed up by the threat of violence, whether by the slave owner or the state. What makes slavery a form of economic oppression is that slaves are forced to produce goods or services for the slaveholder, who exercises complete control over the production and distribution of the goods or services. Slavery impoverishes the slave and enriches the slaveholder.

Although we might like to think of slavery as an economic system that ended with the end of legal slavery, slaves and slaveholders still exist to a shocking degree and this modern slavery flourishes in some economies. As we saw in the previous chapter, modern slavery has become a prevalent social institution within contemporary global capitalism. In India and Pakistan there are whole communities in hereditary debt bondage, and it is not uncommon for free parents to sell their children into bondage in return for a small amount of money or even a loan. The carpet industry of South Asia could not survive without the work of child slave labor. In Eastern Europe and Africa women are lured into going abroad to Western Europe, North America, and other African countries for jobs, which, when they arrive at their destination, turn out to be brothels from which they cannot escape and in which they are forced to perform dangerous and degrading sex work. In Brazil and West Africa, men are lured by the promise of jobs to far off plantations, and then forced to work for no wages and not permitted to leave under the threat of death. In virtually every country of the world there are slaves (in Canada estimates are 10,000–20,000 and in the United States 100,000–150,000), and most countries of the world provide slaves for the world market (Bales 2002).

Modern slavery exists for several reasons. First, gross inequalities of wealth and great poverty among many lead some to be desperate enough to sell their children into slavery or to be lured into slavery by false promises of decent wage work. Second, international markets for cheap goods and services provide demand for the goods produced. In these widely ranging markets, where the shoes are sewn in India and worn in Iowa, it is easy to hide slavery from the view of the consumers of the goods. Third, governmental unwillingness to crack down on slavers and on the sale of goods made from slavery makes laws against slavery impotent. This is another effect of gross worldwide inequality: poor countries are unwilling to risk lowering their overall standard of living, or that of the elites, by ending the economic transactions that involve slavery. Fourth, powerful organized crime groups effectively make governmental interference infeasible and grow more powerful from the profits made from slave labor.

Modern slavery is obviously harmful in the required ways to fit my definition of oppression. It harms physically, psychologically, and severely reduces life options. But it is not so clear that it is a group-based phenomenon. We are only beginning to understand how slavery works, and there are not large social groups threatened by slavery as was true of old style slavery. Modern slavery tends to prey on more local conditions of status and poverty than, say, all West Africans being vulnerable to slavery. Still, we can say something about the groups vulnerable to slavery. In countries where sex trafficking is common, young women are the ones primarily preyed upon, rarely male children and almost never adult men. Children of the poor in very poor countries are often vulnerable to domestic slave work or cottage industry slave work, where women and men are not (Becker and Cudd 2003). In India the low castes are vulnerable to slavery, and not the higher castes. In other words, it is a group-based phenomenon, but as we saw in the previous chapter, different groups are vulnerable to slavery in different places of the world. Even modern slavery is, thus, a group-based phenomenon.

3.2. Segregation

The second type of direct economic force is segregation. Segregation is the enforced clustering of persons by social group status in certain residential areas, educational institutions, and occupations or jobs. It is by definition a group-based phenomenon. There are two distinct types of segregation: de jure segregation, where segregation is legally defined and enforced, and de facto segregation, where segregation is not legally sanctioned, but social groups practice and enforce separation that is not legally required. Many infamous de jure systems of segregation, such as those that involve race, as in the apartheid system of South Africa and the Jim Crow laws of the southern United States, or caste as practiced in India, have ended. It is tempting to think that de jure segregation is now over. But legal sex segregation is still rampant in the Muslim countries of the world, and still defended by many all over the world. This is clearly a form of oppression, and it is being resisted actively by groups of women in those countries. Furthermore, the prohibitions on or obstacles to immigration constitute a kind of legal segregation, which may in some cases be a form of oppression.[18]

De facto racial and gender segregation continues in the United States to a depressingly high degree. Racial segregation is rampant in residence and education, and it is an important component of the wage gap between whites and non-whites. Occupational gender segregation is a major force of women's economic oppression (Jacobsen 1994, ch. 6). Segregation at the job level, that is, at the level of particular job titles within firms, is even more rigid. For example, Donald Tomaskovic-Devey describes two shoe factories in North Carolina, one in which all the assembly workers are men and the other in which all the assembly workers are women. While the occupation, shoe factory worker, is gender integrated, the jobs are completely gender segregated. It is also worth noting that the former firm is unionized and has much higher wages than the latter (Tomaskovic-Devey 1993, 24). Tomaskovic-Devey's study of job-level segregation gathered data from a random sample of households in North Carolina in 1989. He found that only 14 percent of jobs were demographically balanced by gender, meaning that the population in each job reflected the proportion of females (52 percent) in the labor force. Eight percent were mixed but male-dominated (1–29 percent female), 9 percent mixed but female-dominated (71–99 percent female), and 69 percent were either all male or all female. In terms of racial segregation, he found 51 percent are all-white, 5 percent all-black, and only 19 percent are demographically balanced (i.e., 22 percent black). Thus, job segregation by race (taking into account black-white difference) is nearly as pervasive as job segregation by gender.

To show that job segregation is oppressive, it must be shown that it is harmful to the members of some social group, that it benefits another social group, and that it is undeserved or unfair. It has been shown by many social scientists that occupational or job segregation is harmful to women and to racial minorities and that it benefits men and whites. Tomaskovic-Devey, for example, measures the female-male wage gap in his sample at 71 percent (i.e., women earn 71 percent of the hourly wage men earn, on average) and the black-white wage gap at 78 percent. Of this he estimates that 86 percent of the gender wage gap is accounted for by gender composition of the jobs, and 20 percent of the racial wage gap is due to the racial composition of jobs. It is easy to explain using neoclassical economic theory why segregation lowers the wages of those excluded from a certain occupation or job, since the excluded will compete for the available jobs and occupations, which will also have some residual members of the non-excluded class competing for them. Since the supply of workers will be higher in those jobs that are available to all than in jobs and occupations from which they are excluded, the wage rate will be lower for the jobs that the excluded class may compete for. Thus, segregation by job or occupation clearly harms the excluded class by lowering wages. The benefit to men and whites can be measured simply by the converse of the wage gaps. In other words, men earn 141 percent of what women earn and whites earn 128 percent of what blacks earn. Although there are surely women and blacks who are earning the average or even higher than the average wage for white men, the averages reveal that on a wide basis, white men are advantaged by their race and sex. Finally, though, it must be shown that the benefit or penalty is undeserved to show that it is oppressive, and this point is somewhat more controversial.

Indeed, much of the literature on the gender wage gap in economics concerns whether women somehow deserve to be paid less than men. The argument goes something like this. Women choose to be in sex-segregated occupations because they prefer the working conditions available to them there and will accept lower pay to work there—a theory known as "compensating differentials"—and because they prepare for women's occupations rather than occupations which require higher levels of training and skills—differential human capital investments. Women, it is alleged, choose occupations that allow them more work flexibility and lower penalties for temporarily stopping out of the workforce in order to care for their families. Further, women seem not to want to work with men in occupations that are outdoors or require more physical exertion. This crowds them into certain occupations, which accounts in part for their lower pay by the argument given above, as well.

There are many responses that must be made to these allegations, however. First, if women are socialized to do more of the domestic work of society, then they are being treated as means to someone else's or society's ends, and it is unfair to penalize them for doing so. Second, if women can expect less from market work because of the gender wage gap, then market work provides a less good option to them than childbearing and childrearing. So the observation, even if it were a confirmed observation, that women prefer children more than men do, does not explain, let alone justify, the existence of the gender wage gap. Third, gendered preferences over working conditions in the presence of a gender wage gap cannot explain or justify the existence of the wage gap, by the same argument. Given the wage gap, the opportunity cost for taking work with better working conditions is lower. Fourth, there is no good evidence to suggest that women's jobs actually do involve better working conditions. In fact, women's jobs often involve less flexible hours than men's jobs; women's jobs often involve dirty and physically demanding activities (e.g., housecleaning, nursing); and women's jobs often bring less status and respect.

It is not clear that the neoclassical human capital theory explanation provides a good account of job segregation. Sociologists tend to reject human capital theory in favor of what they call social closure theory, which says that a dominant social group creates and preserves its identity and advantages by reserving certain opportunities for members of the group. Social closure strategies include such old boy network strategies as asking friends and acquaintances (of the same social group) for recommendations for employees to hire or put in firm training programs and refusing to find members of different social groups qualified for jobs. Sexual harassment is a blatant social closure strategy. Such processes are sexist and as such clearly unjustified.

Racial job segregation is due to a combination of human capital differences and racist social closure processes. It is clear in the case of race, as in the case of gender, that the human capital differences between whites and blacks are unjustified reasons for lower status, although for different reasons. While it is not alleged that blacks have different preferences for kinds of work or would accept compensating differentials, it is rather claimed that blacks have lower levels of education than whites. Although this is true, it is no doubt a function of the historical racial discrimination and lowered opportunities blacks have been allowed as a result. Thus, although the black–white wage gap is in a greater part due to human capital differences, those differences are themselves largely the result of oppression. Black–white segregation may be less the result of currently active social closure processes than of historical ones, but it is no more justified for that fact, yet it does indicate that different means must be pursued to integration.

De jure segregation is clearly unfair, based as it is on an involuntary group membership of persons, but de facto segregation can often be shown also to result from undeserved and unfair inequalities between social groups. De jure segregation harms psychologically by sending the message of inferiority that is socially endorsed, but de facto segregation can make group members also question their right to equal treatment. Both de jure and de facto segregation harm economically by reducing wages of the excluded subordinate group, while benefiting the dominant group with higher than normal wages and all the social advantages that accrue to greater wealth and income (Jacobsen 1994, 241–245).

3.3. Employment Discrimination

The third type of economic oppression is (invidious) employment discrimination, which can be divided into two types of discrimination: occupational or job discrimination, which is discrimination in the types of jobs offered, and wage discrimination, which is discrimination in the wages offered. According to economists' definitions, employment discrimination occurs when "two persons who have equal productivity and tastes for work conditions, but who are members of different groups, receive different outcomes in the workplace in terms of the wages they are paid and/or of their access to jobs" (Jacobsen 1994, 310). Again, discrimination is by definition group-based. With occupational discrimination, individuals are not offered jobs because of their social group status, which is irrelevant to their qualifications for the job. It can happen at the occupation level (construction jobs are male, secretary jobs are female) or at the job level (in this shoe factory all the line workers are male, in that one female). It is not synonymous with prejudice, since there can be reasons for discrimination other than prejudice against the social group, such as the ability to exploit a monopsony, imperfect information on the part of the employers, or what Adrian Piper calls "higher order discrimination" (Piper 1990), which occurs when an employer discriminates against an employee because of the customers' or co-workers' prejudices. Both types of discrimination are harmful. Wage discrimination harms in straightforward ways—by reducing income and wealth. Occupation discrimination harms by enforcing segregation, which we have already seen to be harmful. Since discrimination is based on nonvoluntary social group status, it is unfair.

According to standard neoclassical economic theory, discrimination cannot occur in a perfectly competitive market in the long run, except as it caters to the prejudices of customers. Any firm that discriminates against a group for reasons unrelated to qualifications will end up paying a premium to those workers it hires and/or hiring workers who are less productive for the same wage as the more productive workers from the excluded group. In the long run such firms cannot compete and will be driven out of the market. Nonetheless, employment discrimination appears to be thriving. However, to argue this using the dominant economic theory and its statistics is not a trivial task. Begin with the uncontroversial claim that wage disparities by group exist in the United States and virtually every economy. In every country in the world, women earn less than men, though it approaches parity in Scandinavia. In the United States and many other countries, there are great wage disparities by race and ethnicity. Economists begin from these disparities and then try to find what they consider purely "economic reasons" to explain the disparities. Whatever is left when the explained disparities are taken away is the measure of discrimination. The economic reasons that are taken into account are of two basic types: preferences on the part of employees for certain types of jobs (working conditions, etc., as mentioned above) and human capital investments (which is taken to represent productivity) of the employees. Both kinds of reasons are typically considered to be the voluntary choices of the individuals involved, and therefore it is tempting to conclude that any differences in wages due to those factors are morally acceptable. There are problems with the measurement of preferences, though, since they are measured by the expressed preferences of persons, which does not allow one to consider the degree to which the choices are made under coercive circumstances, nor does it allow us a noncircular measurement of the premium placed on more pleasant job conditions, since those are measured by the degree to which persons will take lower pay for jobs.[19] There is a further, and to my mind quite revealing, problem with this methodology of measuring discrimination. Even if the individuals of some groups do have preferences that lead to lower wages, and they invest in human capital at lower rates and thus earn lower wages, we cannot infer from those facts that those are the expressions of voluntary choices of individuals and so not aspects of oppression. For the preferences are formed under existing conditions of oppression, and the human capital investment decisions are made under conditions of discriminatory wages and workplace segregation. I will expand on these two points in section 4 of this chapter when I talk about indirect forces of economic oppression. However, for understanding the employment discrimination component of economic oppression, it is important to note that the "unexplained wage differentials" method of measuring discrimination does not in any way amount to a complete assessment of unfair or undeserved group-based restriction of opportunity, that is, oppression.

The only methodology for discovering discrimination directly is to send out resumes or job candidates who differ only by race or sex to see if they are offered employment or wages at different rates. The use of job candidates has obvious control problems that can be alleviated by the use of resumes, which can provide double-blind experiments. One recent study showed that resumes with African American-sounding names received 50% lower callbacks for interviews than those with white-sounding names. Furthermore, the study showed that having better qualifications benefited the white applications more than the African American applications (Bertrand and Mullainathan, 2004). This strengthens my argument that the existence of discrimination is itself a deterrent to human capital formation, since if group members are rewarded less for developing human capital, they will be less motivated to do so.

3.4. Group-based Harassment

A fourth force of economic oppression is sexual, racial, and ethnic harassment in the workplace. I would define group-based harassment as the singling out of a minority group member for disrespectful, degrading, or humiliating behavior, which maintains or tends to maintain segregation. Harassment may even go as far as battery or assault. Thus, this force of oppression can be violent, but what makes it also economic is its enforcement of segregation. Group-based harassment is often an explicit technique used by the dominant group members to maintain their monopoly on better paid jobs or over better housing or to keep disliked groups out of their neighborhood. An important documented case of sexual harassment is revealed in the legal case known as *Robinson v. Jacksonville Shipyards, Inc.*,[20] which became the basis for hostile environment sexual harassment law. Lois Robinson was one of only a few female welders in the shipyards, and she was subjected to continual degrading treatment, including pinups displayed in a way that she could not avoid seeing them, and being seen to be forced to view them by her male co-workers, sexual innuendo and jokes, and various sexual and demeaning remarks and gestures toward her. She was regularly told, directly and through such treatment, that she did not belong in the workplace because of her gender. Robinson successfully sued on grounds that her fellow workers created a hostile environment. Some argue that this behavior is normal male behavior, and that it is not necessarily directed at the women. But, again, whether or not economic domination is the intent of the specific individuals who are doing the harassing, it is a significant constraining factor on subordinated groups in certain occupations and is a major cause of de facto segregation. Furthermore, it cannot be argued that the behavior is not intentionally designed to make the workplace a comfortable place for some and uncomfortable for others, and that the difference is delineated by social group status.

For the same reasons that segregation and discrimination are unfair and harmful, so is harassment. Harassment also causes significant harm because it conveys a threat of violence or is in fact violence.

3.5. Opportunity Inequality

The fifth force of economic oppression is what has been called by some "discrimination before the market," but which I shall call opportunity inequality, which refers to differential access to schooling, healthcare, nutrition, and other necessary investments required for a successful working life (Schiller 1989). As a result of economic deprivation, members of many oppressed social groups suffer from these basic deprivations.

Jonathon Kozol (1991) has written several books on the state of American schools and the inequalities that exist between the schools of the rich and poor in America. In *Savage Inequalities* he compares the schools of many urban, poor, black neighborhoods with those of affluent white ones, such as this comparison of two school systems in New Jersey:

> in an elementary school in Jersey City, seventeenth-poorest city in America, where the schools are 85 percent nonwhite, only 30 of 680 children can participate in instrumental music. The school provides no instruments—the children have to rent them—and the classes take place not in "music suites" but in the lunchroom or the basement of the school. Art instruction is also meager.... Computer classes take place in the storage closet. This may be compared to Princeton, where the high school students work in comfortable computer areas equipped with some 200 IBMs, as well as with a hookup to Dow Jones to study stock transactions. These kind of things are unknown to kids in Jersey City. (Kozol 1991, 158)

These descriptive anecdotal stories of inequality are backed up by clear statistical evidence of the consequences of these differences:

> the high school dropout rate of Jersey City, 52 percent, translates to failure for some 2,500 children every four years. The corresponding rate in Princeton, less than 6 percent, translates to only 40 children. Behind the good statistics of the richest districts lies the triumph of a few. Behind the saddening statistics of the poorest cities lies the misery of many. (Kozol 1991, 158)

Opportunity inequalities are not only harmful in themselves but also because they make victims less able to compete for economic and social goods. This is a group-based phenomenon because oppressed groups often are economically deprived and so lack the means to satisfy these basic needs. This begins a vicious cycle for oppressed groups in which they lack opportunities and thus cannot make human capital investments, which leads to lower earnings and ability to create wealth, which in turn leads to lesser opportunities for themselves and their children, and thus the cycle begins again. Kozol describes this process as self-justifying, concealing the causes and interests that led to the initial inequalities:

> One cannot dispute the fact that giving poor black adolescents job skills, if it is self-evident that they do not possess the academic skills to go to college, is a good thing in itself. But the business leaders who put emphasis on filling entry-level job slots are too frequently the people who, by prior lobbying and voting patterns and their impact on social policy, have made it all but certain that few of these urban kids would get the education in their early years that would have made them look like college prospects by their secondary years. First we circumscribe their destinies and then we look at the diminished produce and we say, "Let's be pragmatic and do with them what we can." (Kozol 1991, 75)

As we saw with occupational segregation for blacks in the United States, historical economic oppression leads to a lack of human capital with which to level the playing field of the competitive job market, resulting in lower income. And this in turn results in lower opportunities in a wide range of categories, from health care to education to opportunities to invest in entrepreneurial or capital-building activities.

In many places in the world, women as a group also lack access to education, nutrition, and health care equal to that of men in the same societies. Particularly in Africa females attend school in significantly lower numbers (UNICEF 1997, 98–99). In Asia and North Africa particularly, women are often less well nourished than men. Although women have a longer life expectancy in most of the world, they often are sicker, in part because they are less well nourished and are less likely to have precious healthcare resources expended on them rather than the more valued males in the family.[21]

These inequalities for women also institute vicious cycles of oppression, but in somewhat different ways than for minority social groups. Women have been stigmatized as the inferior sex and therefore less worthy of investment. But the lack of investment in the health and education of women leads to their inability to prove themselves, on a large scale, to be as capable as men are in a wide variety of the valued social activities that men engage in: producing knowledge, marketable goods and services, political organizing and ruling, and so on. To put it in the language of economics, unequal investments in women's human capital leaves them with less human capital and furthers the notion that they are the inferior sex. Since some sexual differences are obvious and obviously significant, and since all societies enforce some gendered division of labor, the claim that one sex is inferior to another in particular tasks is plausible to many and seems to justify differential treatment of the individuals of each sex. These facts entrench gender-based social inequalities to a degree unequaled by any other group-based social inequalities.[22]

3.6. Neocolonialism and Governmental Corruption

The direct forces that I have discussed work within societies to pick out social groups for oppression as compared with other groups in their societies. But the most glaring economic inequalities in health, nutrition, and education exist worldwide between different international groups. In some cases international inequalities do qualify as oppression, but not all. It is important to sort through these cases carefully in order to see where globalization is a source of progress, where it is a continuation of past colonial oppression, and where it may be the vehicle of a new form of colonialism.

Recall that on my account of oppression, there must be a group that is harmed, one that benefits from the oppressive conditions, and the harms must be undeserved or unfair. These conditions hold for those nations that are linked by ties of past colonial oppression wherever the former colonial power continues to benefit from the linkage at the expense of the former colony, say because the rulers of the former colony were put in place by or supported by the former colonial power, and where the people of the former colony are harmed in one of several ways. The people might be harmed by the unfair inequalities that are instituted or maintained in their society by the continuing enrichment of the elites who were empowered by the colonial power. The people might be harmed by having to pay high taxes to support those elites or to pay off loans the elites have borrowed from the IMF or the colonial power and squandered on personal indulgences.

There are also many cases where both the former colony and the former colonial power are benefited by the trade that is done between the countries. In these cases there is no neocolonial oppression. To say whether a group of persons is benefited by trade involves a counterfactual judgment, comparing what is the case in the presence of trade with what would be the case without trade. While neo-classical economic theory suggests that international trade is always good in the sense of raising the overall welfare of a country, it is also clear that trade creates winners and losers. If the country is able to spread the gains from trade in such a way that everyone benefits, or at least no one loses, trade is clearly a benefit and so could not be a force of oppression. In most countries it is not politically feasible to spread the gains so evenly. If the gains from trade create a systematic set of losers, then it is a source of oppression. But it is only *neocolonial* oppression if there is some link between the benefited social group and some previous colonial power. If there is no connection, then the oppression is likely a case of governmental corruption, a case we dealt with in the previous chapter, since government is, by definition, the body claiming a monopoly on violence within the society.

Finally, the argument is even less clear for countries that engage in international trade but have no previous record of colonial exploitation with each other, but there are still possibilities for oppression that would be best described as coming out of global capitalism and that have a resemblance to colonialism. Suppose that an elite arises indigenously, perhaps through organized crime or violent manipulation of the breakdown of legitimate government, as has occurred in Russia in the wake of the breakup of the Soviet Union. Now suppose that this elite is able to internally dom-inate the people coercively but to convince international businesses and govern-ments to make capital investments in the country from which the elites then skim the profits. In this situation we would have a kind of neocolonial oppression, where the new elites are collaborating with the international firms or foreign governments to deprive and defraud the remainder of the people. The people are deprived of the opportunity to seek international investments from which they can gain as well, and if the elites default on any loans taken out in the name of the people, then they will be liable for repaying the loans or for any resulting defaults on the loans. Although this oppression is economic and occurs through the forces of global capital, it would be a mistake to argue that global capitalism is therefore necessarily oppressive. In this case it is governmental corruption: the coercive, illegitimately wielded force of the elites, which is the basic cause of oppression.

Many charge that multinational agencies, particularly the IMF and the World Trade Organization (WTO), oppress poor the peoples of poor nations by imposing structural adjustment policies (SAPs, in the case of the IMF) and unjust terms of trade (in the case of the WTO) on them. While I do agree that oppression may occur through SAPs and unjust trade agreements, these are often wrongly blamed on the IMF or the WTO. SAPs are imposed as conditions on loans from the IMF, and they are intended to make the economy more capable of generating capital for investment, which is the purpose for which the loans are made. SAPs are an attempt at monetary and fiscal reform to make the economy more competitive and better able to grow in terms of its GDP. Growth in GDP, while it ignores the informal economy and home production, almost invariably is correlated with im-proved outcomes for the citizens of a nation in terms of such crucially important values as life expectancy, literacy, and maternal and child mortality (Dollar and

Kraay 2002). Reforms sometimes fail to achieve their objectives, however. Sometimes they are misguided and sometimes they are undermined or ended before they can have their hoped for effects. Politically they are often difficult to maintain because there are always winners and losers, and because the gains inevitably involve fundamental social changes and come after the losses. Reforms are like investments for the future, and sometimes the gains are too vague or uncertain to sustain the will to invest. Gains and losses are also not uniformly distributed and can be manipulated by those in power to benefit themselves and their friends. Similarly multinational trade agreements entered into by trade representatives for countries can be manipulated for the benefit of certain sectors of society rather than the whole of society. The WTO exists to lower overall barriers to trade, in order to avoid the kinds of trade wars that have historically led to serious financial upheavals (such as the Great Depression) and even wars between nations. No nation is forced to accept any agreements brokered by the WTO; the WTO has no army and no police force. It can merely judge that another country is justified in erecting a trade barrier as a response to an existing one by a country, in order to give that country an incentive to remove the barrier.

In sum, I would argue that the multinational financial and trade organizations are not oppressive neocolonial forces. Their loans and rulings can be manipulated, however, by the powerful political forces within a nation to benefit some at the expense of others. Since this institutes a situation in which some group or groups are benefited while anothers are harmed through a systematic policy, it is an instance of economic oppression.

4. Indirect Forces: Oppression by Choice

Many writers have noted that some of the harms of oppression are to some degree self-inflicted wounds. This is also the case with economic oppression. Indirect economic forces cause inequality through the choices and decisions of the members of the oppressed group themselves, as they try to live in the face of other inequalities and injustices. I call this phenomenon "oppression by choice," in order to highlight the twin facts that it is a force of oppression, and yet comes about through oppressed persons' choices. This force of oppression is particularly invidious because the oppressed choose the conditions under which they suffer. Everyone may seem content, and suggesting that there is oppression or victimization is likely to be met with hostility by privileged and oppressed groups alike. So it is deeply entrenched in the functioning social institutions of the society. When indirect forces can be seen to be at work in a case of oppression, we can predict that it is a long-standing one, and that resistance to it will be difficult to motivate or maintain.

Although there are other examples that could be used, women in contemporary Western societies, in the face of certain prejudices and economic forces of oppression, often make decisions that reinforce their oppression. In the next section I illustrate the rational dilemma that women face in trying to live within these oppressive constraints. In the following section I will argue that this indirect force of oppression can be seen to be acting in other cases of oppression as well.

4.1. Women's Choices

There is a loaded query aimed at feminists that goes something like this: Don't (relatively privileged, middle and upper-class) women *choose* to stay home with the kids? The point of the question is simply this: If one chooses her situation, how can anyone call it oppression? The question is rhetorical; it is supposed to absolve society of any guilt for putting women into a disadvantageous position vis-à-vis men. The question presupposes an analysis of oppression that says that a society in which persons may choose their occupations is free (at least in this sphere), and if the society is free then there is no oppression (in that sphere), no matter what results from their choices. If someone freely chooses her situation, she is responsible for its consequences, and if she was rational when making her choice, then she must really want, all things considered, whatever she could foresee as its consequences. That is, choice confers responsibility, which is a corollary of the choice negates oppression thesis we examined earlier. As we saw, this thesis holds only if the choices are uncoerced. A social institution is coercive if it unfairly limits the choices of the members of some social group relative to the members of other social groups.

Contemporary Western society is commonly thought to be free in this sense (among others) of occupational choice. There is anecdotal evidence for this belief: The ranks of the owners of business and leaders of government and education include people who raised themselves from the bottom of the socio-economic ladder to near the top, and their stories, appealing as they are, become well known.[23] Since there are those who do succeed in climbing the ladder in their chosen field, many infer that it is possible for all to do so. And they further infer that this implies free choice of occupation, subject only to the constraints of native talent. There is also an a priori argument that economists give for the claim that there is no discrimination on the part of business against any particular racial group or gender. Since businesses are out to maximize profits, and indeed (so the argument goes) cannot survive if they do not, they must seek to hire the most talented individuals regardless of race or gender. Thus, they do not discriminate on the basis of race or gender, since those who would discriminate would tend to go out of business.[24]

At the same time, women who are employed in the outside labor force in the United States continue to earn about 77 percent of what men earn (Institute for Women's Policy Research 2003). How can we explain this wage gap? As we saw in the section on direct forces of economic oppression, there are two general kinds of sources of wage differentials between genders: (1) outright discrimination against women; (2) gender differences in human capital investments that give rise to the gap. Although the first item—the discrimination explanation—can be shown to have considerable support (Institute for Women's Policy Research 2003), it is unlikely that it completely explains the gender wage gap. First, segregated workplaces are common, and it is common to hear women claim that they prefer to work with women. Second, since employers in the United States are also at least as prejudiced against blacks in this society, one would expect that the black–white wage gap would be as severe as the female–male wage gap. But the black–white wage gap (comparing only men) is less than half (15 percent) of the female–male wage gap (40 percent) (comparing only whites).[25] (I do not mean to imply that black men are less oppressed than white women, but these statistics suggest that the discrimination against each group leads to different kinds of bad consequences for them.) In the United States, well-established Civil Rights law states that employers must pay equally for equal work.[26] But while this law seems to have decreased the wage effects of racial discrimination, the wage gap among men and women has decreased to a lesser degree. This lends evidence to both explanations, so that it is not necessary to choose between them.[27] Thus, at least some of the wage gap results from different occupational choices of women and men.

Why would women choose different occupations if that causes them to have lower wages? In this section I argue that there is a vicious cycle that is instituted by several existing gender inequalities that causes women rationally to choose such occupations. The wage gap sets women up for this vicious cycle. What makes it particularly insidious is that the cycle is the result of apparently rational choices of individual women themselves. In her book *Justice, Gender, and the Family*, Susan Moller Okin explains how women are caught in "a cycle of socially caused and distinctly asymmetric vulnerability" (Okin 1989, 138). By "asymmetric vulnerability" Okin is referring to constraints on women's choices relative to men's. If these constraints are unfair, then the social institutions that cause the asymmetry are coercive, and hence oppressive. To show that these choices are both rational and coercive, I need a model of how such decisions are made, and for this I shall borrow heavily from Okin's illustrations. The explanation I shall give of why the wage gap persists is an example of an *invisible foot explanation*: The individually rational choices, taken by large numbers of individuals, lead to socially suboptimal outcomes. To show this I build a simple rational choice model of a man and a woman of the same age (say around 25) with exactly equal talents, education, and work experience (i.e., equal marginal productivity of labor). Let us suppose that these two, call them Larry and Lisa, have decided to marry and to have children together. In the beginning they have equal power in the relationship to enforce their individual intentions for collective action. Suppose that they harbor no prejudices about "men's" or "women's" work, and that with exception of the specific tasks of impregnation, conception, childbearing, and lactation, they are equally capable, and believe they are equally capable, of all childrearing and domestic tasks. Suppose that they also believe that one parent ought to take primary care of the children, in other words, that neither socialized childcare nor equally shared care by both parents is as good as care by one parent who specializes in the children's care. Then if there is a wage gap between men and women, and Larry and Lisa have rational expectations about their relative earning potential, and if they consider only family income in making their decision, they will decide that Lisa should specialize in childcare and Larry in wage work.

This decision has enormous implications for their future and the relative share of power in the family. In staying home, it will be rational for Lisa to take on the burden of the greater share of other domestic work as well and will come to have greater skill for it. Her skills for outside employment will become less valuable, and especially relative to Larry she will become even less valuable as a wage worker for the family. Lisa will become the domestic specialist and Larry the specialist in wage work. Even later, when the children are grown to the point where both parents feel they can work outside the home, her value as a domestic worker will be on the whole greater than Larry's, and his greater value as a wage worker will guarantee that he need never take on a large share of domestic tasks.

This division of labor could be neutral with respect to power in some societies, but not in societies such as our own in which wealth determines power, domestic work is unpaid, and divorce laws do not evenly divide wealth (Arendell 1986). In a relationship the relative power of the partners is determined largely by the opportunities available to each if the relationship should end.[28] While Lisa's value as a domestic worker does not increase much since it is unpaid work, Larry's value increases with experience. He builds what economists call "human capital." If their relationship ends, then Larry has the human capital to guarantee that his income will continue the same, while Lisa, whose skills and value as a wage worker have atrophied since she took on the domestic work, will see her income fall appreciably. Even if divorce laws evenly divide the accumulated wealth between them, the difference in their future incomes as a result of their uneven human capital will be greater the longer the marriage (and hence her domestic specialization) has lasted. Furthermore, Lisa still faces the wage gap, which was the reason that she specialized in domestic work to begin with. Thus, Lisa's prospects are considerably dimmer than Larry's if the relationship ends. And this means that she has less power in the ongoing relationship.

Her lack of power might be manifested in many ways in the marriage. He can demand that she work more hours than he does, that she continue to serve him after each has put in a day of work. He may demand that, if she gets a job outside the home, she sacrifice her job to meet family needs and emergencies, she take time from work to care for sick children or household repairs. He may demand more leisure time or refuse to share his wages with her. He may beat or rape her with much less risk of punishment than if they held power equally, since she will turn him in only when the loss of utility from her lower income (and whatever else she thinks she loses) without him is outweighed by the loss of utility of being beaten or raped.[29]

If Larry and Lisa represent typical men and women in society, then there are serious consequences for all men and women arising from the typical individually rational choices about work and family. If it is the case that women typically make the decision to subordinate career and work to family and domestic tasks, then women will be seen as the domestic workers of the society and as unreliable wage workers. There is evidence, statistical and anecdotal, showing that this is indeed a significant obstacle to equality of opportunity for women in the workforce (Fuchs 1989). Employers tend not to trust that women will stay with their careers, or that if they do, they will devote the kind of time and energy to them that men will.[30] Women, on average, are poorer risks, and so employers will not invest in specialized training for them as easily as for men, and women will not be promoted as quickly as men. The supposed unreliability of women, on average, counteracts the a priori argument that purports to show that employers ought not to discriminate against women. If women are less reliable workers, then it makes sense for employers to do whatever they can to skirt the laws that demand equal treatment for men and women, for statistically speaking women are poor risks for jobs that require mobility, independence, and devotion. But these are, typically, the more highly paid and otherwise more attractive positions. This means that women will on average earn less for the same skill level as men. But it was this fact, the wage gap, that forced women (and men) to make the choices that led to this outcome. Thus, the cycle is complete. It is a vicious cycle because the opportunities for women are lowered, or at best remain stagnant, as a result of each revolution.

If the outcome for Lisa looks so bleak, then why does she agree to the original division of labor? Is it really a rational choice for women themselves? Rational choice theory, combining cooperative and noncooperative game theory, suggests that it is rational under the right conditions (see the appendix). Begin with the assumption that Larry and Lisa can unproblematically come to a joint decision. The choices that they face are for each to work for wages or to do domestic work. They cannot both choose domestic work in their society and still make a living. If they choose to both do wage work, then because of the wage gap Lisa will still have less power in the relationship, since her income is lower, and their children are less well cared for (in their view, by hypothesis). If they choose to have Larry do domestic work and Lisa do wage work, then their children are properly cared for but they have a lower income than before. The share of power is indeterminate in this case; it depends on how much she gains in human capital and how much he loses by not working, and whether the wage gap is offset by her gain and his loss. Under some conditions it will be optimal for Larry and Lisa to divide the domestic and wage work as I hypothesized; the frequency of this division in our society suggests that the conditions necessary are normal conditions. Now relax the assumption that they can unproblematically come to a joint decision over the division of labor, and let them bargain over it. Larry is bound to get what he wants in the negotiation, since his no-agreement outcome is better than hers. Even if they break up he will gain more by virtue of the wage gap. She will resist his demands only if her break up outcome is better than his demand, that is, if she expects that her life with him as the domestic worker will be worse than her life without him and working for wages or as a domestic worker married to someone else.[31]

The fact that individual women's choices make the situation worse for all women does not play a role in the rationally self-interested calculation in a sufficiently large society. If there are many women facing the same kinds of options, then what any one woman chooses does not affect the overall position of women. One marginal woman cannot change the stereotype of women for better or worse. This situation is analogous to a market where there are many buyers: One buyer influences the market price by a very small amount and so acts as a price taker. Similarly, Lisa must take the stereotypes of men and women and the resulting wage gap as, for all practical purposes, given. Where the result in the market is an invisible hand that allocates goods efficiently, the result of individual rational choice in a vicious cycle is an invisible foot that grinds down the social position of women.

The Larry and Lisa model shows how a vicious cycle can result from simply an initial social inequality and subsequent rational, apparently voluntary, choices. Even the maintenance of the social inequality is the rational result of the choices made by individuals, given an initial social inequality.[32] The vicious cycle in the Larry and Lisa example is an example of an oppressive vicious cycle. A cycle is oppressively vicious only if it is harmful. In the Larry and Lisa example I argued that women's employment opportunities are continually degraded both for the individuals and for women as a group, and this is clearly a harm. My example is one in which only women suffer from the cycle, but one might argue that one can escape the cycle if one does not share Larry and Lisa's beliefs about child care. So they should be held responsible for their beliefs and their consequences; we should not indict the social institutions for allowing oppression to arise from such pathological beliefs. Yet the fact that Larry can have those beliefs and still not get mired in the cycle indicates that the cycle picks out women specifically for worse treatment. Furthermore, the current structure of work and the lack of adequate day care for many parents makes stay-at-home parenthood a necessity for many families.[33] And it is, after all, possibly true that children ought to be cared for primarily by one parent. Some people, namely the Larrys of the world, benefit from the vicious cycle that the Lisas face. This is true even for those Larrys who regret the cycle, since their wages are relatively better than the wages of the Lisas. Furthermore, this economically oppressive cycle reveals one of the strong motivations for women to remain in violent relationships with men. Thus, the cycle is harmful for one social group and benefits another social group.

We come then to the coercion criterion. The vicious cycle phenomenon we examined has the character of coercion because it leads to fewer and worse life choices for women than they would have were it not for the vicious cycle, both on the individual level and at the level of the wage gap for all women. This lack of choice has no redeeming aspect that leads to greater freedom either. One just cannot argue that women have more freedom as a result of the wage gap, or their lack of social power, or the ever-deepening hole that women retrench for each other by choosing traditional domestic roles. The option for Lisa in the model is to eschew traditional domestic roles, either by not marrying, not having children, not raising children as they would have them raised, or by getting Larry to do the domestic work. Each of these thwarts Lisa's desires except the last one. That option, though, requires agreement by Larry and results in lower living standards for the family as a whole, because of the original wage gap. Relative to the choices men face, relative to what the situation would be if there were no original wage gap, these are bad options. More importantly, they are unfair. Women's freedom of choice here is like that of the marriage market illustration of section 2: women's freedom is complete only within an unjust framework of options. Any acceptable background moral theory would regard this fundamental asymmetry in the available life choices and power as unfair. Thus, women are coerced in making the choice to eschew economic power and status for domestic servitude. So I conclude that the vicious cycle is coercive. This implies that women are oppressed by the vicious cycle phenomenon, and thus, by means of their own individually rational choices.

There are other groups of women who also face vicious cycles of indirect economic oppression. Young women who choose to be prostitutes in the face of grinding poverty find that through that choice they not only make themselves vulnerable to violence and disease, but they also strengthen the economic forces that oppress them. In countries that suffer under enormous debts to the IMF, tourism is often encouraged by the international community as a way of raising foreign revenue to pay off their debts (Judd and Fainstein 1999; Sassen 2002, 254–274). When the women then participate in the tourism industry as prostitutes, they build that industry, which then sucks in more women, and crowds out other possible avenues of employment. Why would someone invest his capital in a marginally profitable manufacturing firm when he could own a very profitable brothel, after all? While it is true that many women are forced into prostitution through violent coercion, the majority are enticed by the promise of a wage. That is, like Lisa choosing to opt out of the market, these women are making individually rational choices to become prostitutes. Now prostitution is surely an occupation that has negative compensating differentials; there can be few, if any, occupations that are more dirty, risky, and undignified than that. But in countries such as Thailand where sex tourism is so profitable, there is little chance for women to earn a living in any other way, and the treatment of women generally in society is very poor. Yet, in joining the sex workforce these women are strengthening an industry that crowds out other opportunities. Furthermore, as sex tourism becomes a wider part of the economy, prostitution comes to be seen as a legitimate way for women to have to earn a living. So, through their own rational choices to become prostitutes (or to sell their daughters to brothels), Thai women are reinforcing their own oppression.

Women who choose to do domestic labor abroad in order to support their families may be making a rational choice under the circumstances, but once they are abroad they find that they have little or no bargaining power in their relationships with employers and immigration authorities, and can be forced to take low wages and acquiesce to poor working conditions. In working abroad they are not building industries in their own countries that could help to provide opportunities for themselves and other women to earn a living in their homeland. And this lack of opportunity is precisely what lowers their bargaining power vis-à-vis their foreign employers. Of course, any one poor woman would face insurmountable obstacles in attempting to build a viable industry herself. Thus, in making their individually rational choice to work abroad, they are reinforcing the forces of economic oppression that presented them with such poor options.

4.2. Choices of the Oppressed

Oppressed groups, particularly those who suffer economic oppression, generally face similar structural constraints that cause them to structure their own preferences and make decisions that then come to perpetuate their oppression. Persons sometimes do this in the name of group identification or the tendency to form and exaggerate ingroup-outgroup differences. Racial segregation in the United States offers a case in point. Blacks and whites tend to live in different, segregated neighborhoods. The direct economic forces of oppression (occupational segregation and opportunity inequality) have caused the lives of blacks and whites to differ considerably, and for blacks to live in significantly poorer circumstances, on average, than whites. Since Blacks tend to get information about job opportunities and form preferences about life outcomes among other blacks, whose opportunities themselves have been (unfairly) limited, they tend to form preferences for the kinds of lives that those opportunities allow. Thus, in black ghettos in the inner city a proportion of male children dream of becoming star athletes or rap stars far beyond their actual probability of succeeding in those occupations, and failing that, figure that they will become drug dealers or gangsters. Many female children choose to have children early (or perhaps they simply do not choose not to have children early), giving them the illusion of independence early in life, but also effectively limiting their future opportunities to invest in human capital that will reap significant financial and status returns. Although it may be a rational calculation of their chances for middle-class success, the choice to prepare for these lives often forecloses any opportunity to join the middle class and reveals that their preferences have adapted to the opportunities available.

A Marxist analysis of the plight of the working class reveals another form of the vicious cycle phenomenon. On the Marxist analysis, to put it in the language of neoclassical economic theory, workers are induced to work for wages that allow the owners of firms to make an economic profit because workers must work for wages to survive while mere survival is not at stake for firm owners. But this increases the bargaining power of the owners of capital to a greater degree than the workers, and hence in future bargains the workers are no less able to capture some of that profit. Now on the neoclassical theory, there is a problem with this analysis. If there is economic profit to be made, then neoclassical theory says that new firms will enter the field until there is no more profit. But that is only in the long run, and in the meantime owners of capital are enriched, while workers remain roughly at subsistence level. If workers were to act collectively, to pool what resources they have and organize a strike, they could increase their bargaining power. Indeed this has been a successful strategy for workers in the past. But that raises a collective action problem, and as in the Larry-Lisa model, they would have to lower the total payoff (to workers and firms) to implement this strategy. Furthermore, strikes are difficult on the individual workers' families and have to be undertaken in the face of an uncertain future. This causes, as is typical with collective action, a tendency for some to free ride on the efforts of others.

The vicious cycle phenomena that we have examined each involve a characteristic set of problems. First, there is an initial inequality that shapes the rational decisions of the oppressed. Second, under some circumstances, the oppressed seem to shape their preferences to embrace the feasible set of options they are faced with, while under others, they seem to constrict their outlook about the possible alternatives, while under still others, they are faced with an insurmountable collective action problem. That is, either they declare the grapes that they cannot reach to be sour, or they decide that the grapes' being out of reach is a fact that cannot be changed and must be worked around. While it is clear that the first problem is a case of injustice, it is not enough to point to it only once the second problem arises. For the second problem is the crux of the indirect force of oppression: The oppressed are co-opted to help keep themselves in their oppressed state. Resisting this second problem requires either changing the preferences of the oppressed or changing their belief in their power to change the situation, a power that could only come through collective action. In chapter 7 I will take up the problem of resistance to indirect forces of oppression in some detail.

5. Conclusion

In this chapter I have discussed three main forms of economic oppression. First, I discussed the notion that an economic system can be, in itself, oppressive. I argued that while slavery and serfdom are intrinsically oppressive, capitalism and socialism are not. However, both systems lend themselves to oppression in characteristic ways, and therefore each sort of system must take certain steps to guard against their respective characteristic oppressions. While capitalism characteristically leads to economic inequality, it can prevent poverty, or oppressive inequalities, of working or unemployed classes through a guaranteed social minimum. While socialism characteristically leads to domination by a permanent ruling elite, it can prevent oppression by developing mechanisms for participatory democratic control of the means of production. Furthermore, both systems will be economically oppressive if they allow invidious discrimination in housing, employment, or education, and so laws against such discrimination must be avoided.

The second form of economic oppression is what I called the direct forces of economic oppression, including enslavement, segregation, employment discrimination, group-based harassment, and opportunity inequality. Direct forces are restrictions on opportunities that are applied from the outside on the oppressed. They may not always be clearly visible, either because they happen far from the reach of legal authorities or from the view of consumers, or because they are diffused in a large society, and only apparent from a statistical analysis and comparison among social groups. But direct forces, once seen, are to be opposed immediately. The third form of economic oppression is what I called the indirect force of economic oppression, or oppression by choice, where the oppressed are co-opted into making individual choices that add to their own oppression. When this force is at work the oppressed are faced with options that rationally induce them to choose against the collective good of their social group, and in the long run, against their own good as well. But choosing otherwise requires choosing against their own immediate interests, and changing their beliefs or preferences in ways that they may resent. Economic forces of oppression are particularly long-lasting when they involve this combination of belief in the stability of and preference for the status quo by the oppressed themselves. For in these cases it is not immediately clear that the status quo is to be opposed directly by nonmembers of the oppressed groups, since that heaps more harm on the oppressed. The indirect economic force of oppression is a central cause of enduring oppression.

6

Psychological Harms of Oppression

1. Psychological Harm as a Force of Oppression

If oppression is a group phenomenon, and groups are constructed in part by stereotypes, then it follows that stereotyping is a fundamental psychological mechanism of oppression. Stereotypes, and the in-group/out-group formation processes that they are a part of, form the groundwork for the possibility of oppression as a group phenomenon. Stereotypes would be toothless, however, were it not for the objective individual actions and social forces that align with and are directed by them. Being excluded from a group that one wants to belong to or included in one that one does not want to be included in is not, by itself, seriously harmful. Serious harms arise when one is thereby made the object of violence, degradation, exploitation, discrimination, social exclusion, or another force that makes one suffer psychologically or materially. In this chapter I turn to the many nonviolent and noneconomic forces of oppression. Human activity involves a great deal of symbolic activity, in the many forms of language and image production, distribution, and consumption. Because our psychological makeup is such that we are symbol-using beings, we have many ways of harming each other with these symbolic activities. It turns out that the saying "sticks and stones may break my bones but words will never harm me" is at best only partially right: if the words make people think I (and my kind) deserve the sticks and stones and so urge people to harm me, if they make me think that I am not worthy of equal concern and respect, if they make others shun or exclude me, then the words harm me too. In this chapter I discuss the symbolic ways that stereotyping gets its teeth to become oppression of groups, rather than some fairly innocuous social distinguishing that appropriately would be called "mere words."

There are three important distinctions to clarify as I begin my discussion of psychological harms of oppression. Psychological harm can be group-based or individual. Individual psychological harm happens when one individual is abused by another person or persons not because of and not by means of their social group membership. The abuse may be violent or it may be psychological—words or actions that denigrate, humiliate, disrespect, or terrorize. Group-based psychological harm happens when an individual is so harmed because of her or his group membership. In this case there are additional words that can do the psychological harm, namely, racial epithets, gender slurs, and humiliating or degrading descriptions and images of one's social group. Oppressive psychological harm is group-based, by definition. As with the distinction between random and group-based violence, the distinction between individual and group-based psychological harm may be difficult to make in practice. One difficulty arises when both parties are members of the same oppressed group. I maintain that this is a case of individual and not group-based harm, even if the words expressed by the perpetrator are the same words as words which, when expressed by a member of a privileged group relative to the victim, would create group-based psychological harm. For example, one woman calls another woman (of the same race and class) a "crazy bitch." Plainly this indicates hostility, anger, perhaps hatred. But when spoken by a woman these words cannot carry with them the same message or meanings as when spoken by a man, which indicate in addition a threat to exercise masculine domination by violence or other systems of power (legal, mental health, etc.) that accord automatically higher status and authority to men than to women.

Another apparent difficulty for the distinction arises when the perpetrator of psychological harm is from a group that is privileged relative to the victim's social group, but the perpetrator did not intend to commit a group-based harm or did not use any of the conventional signs of the victim's subordinate group status to transmit the harm. As I have argued before in this book, the crucial factor in assessing group status and harm is the effect on the victim, not the intention of the perpetrator. This is true for two reasons: first because intention is difficult to assess, and second because intentions may not be consciously admitted. Also, members of privileged groups are often quite unaware of their privilege—their prerogative to ignore these group relations is part of what constitutes their privileged status. Thus, in this case again, it is the effect on the victim that matters, and if the harm brings up for the victim and is transmitted through her subordinate status, then it is group-based harm.

A final problem arises for this distinction, then, when the victim herself does not recognize the harm as group-based. Take for instance a relationship between a battering husband and his battered wife, where they both believe that violent and psychologically abusive behavior is due to her failure adequately to perform her "duties," such as cleaning the house, satisfying him sexually, and keeping the children quiet. Even if the wife does not believe that the abuse she suffers is part of group-based oppression, what matters is whether it is in fact a part of the systematic violence against women. That is, does the abuse fit the four criteria of oppression in the same ways as other instances of the oppression of women? Is it harm that is unjust and happens to her because she is a woman? If the answers to these questions are "yes" then this psychological harm is objectively a part of oppression, and so only by including these cases can we maintain an objective account of psychological oppression.

A second important distinction parallels the distinction drawn in chapter five between direct and indirect economic forces of oppression. Direct psychological forces cause inequality through the intentional actions of members of a dominant group on members of a subordinate one. Indirect psychological forces cause inequality through the choices and decisions of the members of the oppressed group themselves, as they try to live in the face of other inequalities and injustices. As I argued in chapter 5 regarding economic forces, it is important to distinguish these two forces for both normative and descriptive reasons. Normatively, once the case has been made that something is a direct force of oppression, the moral case for opposing it has already been made, whereas the issues of responsibility and remedy are not so immediate for indirect forces. The descriptive reason in the case of psychological force is more complex than in the economic case. While all psychological forces must be internal to the victim's psychology in order to harm, indirect forces work through the psychology of the oppressed to mold them and co-opt them to result in choices and decisions that harm the oppressed while benefiting the privileged. As with indirect economic force, I argue that indirect psychological force is the key to understanding how oppression can be so enduring.

A third distinction in psychological forces of oppression has to do with how the force is applied and can be drawn between those that are more directly applied to an individual and those that are diffused throughout the culture. Andrew Kernohan (1998, xi) draws an analogy with pollution to illuminate this distinction in a discussion of what he calls cultural oppression. Pollution develops in two ways, either as a large point-source, where the source can be definitely located, or as a non-point source, where the pollution comes from many small sources that are diffused throughout the environment. When the sources of pollution are small, they are not harmful in themselves, but only become harmful when they become part of the larger set of sources which together make up a polluting mess that cannot be effectively dissipated in the environment. Likewise, some psychological forces of oppression can only be seen when they are taken together as a whole set of small slights or insults against a group. Stereotypes themselves happen in this latter, cultural way. That is, one person's belief that certain sets of persons typically exhibit a particular characteristic does not make a stereotype. It becomes a stereotype of a social group only when this belief is widespread. Following Kernohan, I will call these two kinds of psychological forces "point-source" and "cultural" when it is necessary to distinguish them. This distinction parallels the distinction between violence or a direct threat of violence and the threat of violence suffered by oppressed persons who feel threatened by a heightened degree of violence against members of their group. Violence happens when someone is forcefully, physically injured. Threats of violence can be directly made, or they can simply exist, diffuse in the community, because others with similar social characteristics regularly suffer from violence. Likewise, while individual psychological forces are or stem from face-to-face assertions of differential power and value directed at persons because of their perceived group membership, cultural psychological forces form the background social beliefs and desires within which we perceive ourselves and others and act on those beliefs and desires. Like tacit threats of violence, cultural psychological forces can be invisible and insidious.

Since members of social groups see themselves as sharing some attributes or features (if only the feature of being lumped under similar stereotypes by others and thus treated similarly), they will be threatened with harm upon learning of other members of their group being harmed. Thus, group-based psychological harm spreads

from the immediate victims to others when the harms are publicly or widely recognized. Both direct and indirect forces of oppression work through stereotypes to
create and maintain a social environment in which persons are stereotyped and their
actions thereby constrained. The forces of oppression that I discuss here each have a
large literature in a variety of fields, from social history to philosophy to literature to
psychology and sociology. I cannot hope to do justice to this literature; instead my
purpose here is to show how the psychological forces of oppression tie into the
psychological theory of stereotyping that I have argued for, and the larger social force
account of oppression I am offering in this book.

2. Direct Psychological Forces

Direct psychological harms are intentionally inflicted by dominant on subordinate
groups. These forces can be applied by either large point sources that cause harm in
themselves, or by small and diffuse but frequently encountered cultural sources. I
begin this section by discussing the psychological harms brought on by large point
sources. These include terror and trauma, humiliation and degradation, and objectification. Terror and trauma are caused by violence and the threat of violence.
Violence, almost by definition, originates outside the victim, but threats require the
victim to participate psychologically to generate the threat, if only by processing the information. Humiliation, degradation, and feelings of shame in oppressed persons are
brought on by many direct forces of psychological oppression, including degrading
images of one's social group, hate speech or group defamation, harassment, and social
distancing. These are direct forces because they originate externally through the
direct confrontation by privileged others who intend to generate these feelings in
their victims. Feelings of shame and lowered self worth may also rebound indirectly
through oppressed individuals' psychologies from material forces of oppression, as
well as from the direct psychological forces, and I discuss these indirect forces of
psychological oppression in the following section. The third category of direct psychological oppression is objectification, which happens when persons in social groups
are systematically treated as objects, or as Kant would put it, as means to another's
ends and not as ends in themselves. This force may be applied as a large point source
(such as when men rape women) or in a culturally diffuse way (such as when women
are objectified in a culture that systematically portrays them as objects for men's
sexual pleasure). The final three categories of direct psychological forces are all
clearly non-point, cultural sources. Tradition and convention form, in my view, one
category because together they form the given background of social meaning that
defines the constraints of agency for a culture, even if one rejects or objects to the
given dominant cultural traditions and conventions. Religion is an immensely important source of tradition, with its own self-justifying belief system, so I treat it as its
own category. A third category of non-point sources is ideology, by which I mean the
more or less intentionally created beliefs of a culture. These political, social, and
scientific theories purport to offer rationalizations of mere tradition and convention.
Described this way one might question the distinction between religion and ideology.
I have separated them mainly because religion, or theological belief, tends to be

older, less subject to intentional change, and less subject to critique by evidence or experience than the other sorts of theories, and thus closer to a tradition or habit than to a justificatory theory. Although nothing hangs on this distinction from the perspective of a theory of oppression, the question of how to resist this force of oppression may well be affected by the degree to which religion is more or less like scientific theory. The final category is cultural domination, which refers to the force exerted on minority cultures to assimilate or defer to the majority culture practices.

2.1. Point Sources

2.1.1. TERROR AND PSYCHOLOGICAL TRAUMA

Through violence and the threat of violence, terror reinforces the domination of some groups by other groups in all cases of oppression. The trauma that violence and threats of violence cause often has severe, continuing psychological effects that themselves create further harm long after the perpetrator is gone or the threat has been withdrawn. These effects ramify the material effects of oppression by making their victims less able effectively to cope with the everyday challenges of life. When these effects are concentrated in a social group, the effect is to further the stereotypes of the group as inferior.

According to the psychiatrist Judith Herman, "Psychological trauma is an affliction of the powerless. At the moment of trauma, the victim is rendered helpless by overwhelming force" (Herman 1992, 33). She distinguishes three main categories of symptoms of PTSD: hyperarousal, intrusion, and constriction. Persons with PTSD go into state of alert as if danger might return at any moment, even when danger is past and the alertness is maladaptive. People with PTSD have a variety of other energy-sapping symptoms. They take longer to fall asleep and awaken more frequently; they are often afraid and mistrustful. Secondly, persons with PTSD often suffer from intrusive thoughts about their experience of violence, living through the event as if it were continually recurring in the present. Reliving a traumatic experience carries with it the emotional intensity of the trauma event. However, memories of trauma are fixed, frozen; they do not assimilate into other memories in a linear way, and they lack verbal narrative and context. Thus, they are difficult to process and deflate. PTSD often causes victims to reenact the scene of trauma, whether in play (mainly for children) or through taking dangerous risks. Third, persons with PTSD also suffer from periods of dissociation from reality, either where they are in a state of surrender to the inevitable or an altered state of consciousness. "These detached states of consciousness are similar to hypnotic trance states. They share the same features of surrender of voluntary action, suspension of initiative and critical judgment, subjective detachment or calm, enhanced perception of imagery, altered sensation, including numbness and analgesia, and distortion of reality, including depersonalization, de-realization, and change in the sense of time" (Herman 1992, 43). Thus, there is a typical psychological dialectic of trauma: The contradictory responses of intrusion and constriction alternate, often at the extremes of each. "The instability produced by these periodic alterations further exacerbates the traumatized person's sense of unpredictability and helplessness. The dialectic of trauma is therefore potentially self-perpetuating" (Herman 1992, 47). For most, though, intrusion gives way to constriction, in the form of a more general state of anxiety and fear. But this is also often accompanied by feelings that the victim is just going through the motions of life, a kind of disengagement.

Trauma severely disrupts human relationships and the trust that victims have in other people and in the divine. Trauma thus makes it more difficult for oppressed persons to cooperate in many projects that might ease or erase the material effects of oppression. Another effect of the isolating tendency of trauma is that victims tend to believe that little can be done to make their lives bearable. Estimates of suicides of trauma victims are controversial, but some studies show that a significant minority (19 percent) attempt suicide. Purposive action and social cooperation help the traumatized individuals to recover and to resist oppression. Indeed, clinical studies show the more stress-resistant individuals seem to be those who are highly sociable, with thoughtful and active coping style, and strong perception of ability to control their own destiny (Herman 1992, 58). The last element here explains why privileged persons would be more stress resistant than persons from oppressed groups. This creates its own vicious cycle for the oppressed: they are more vulnerable to the psychological harm of trauma owing to their oppressed status, that is, the fact that they are less able to control their destiny, and once traumatized they are reinforced in their beliefs that they are less able to control their destiny and thus suffer greater harm by the trauma.

Although some persons are more resistant to trauma than others, trauma is nearly inevitable for most persons given severe enough violence or threat. The most powerful determinant of whether there will be psychological harm and how great it will be is the character of the traumatic event, not the individual personality of the victim. There is a typical dose response to trauma: the greater the exposure (in terms of time, number of events, or intensity of event) to traumatic events the higher probability of suffering PTSD and the longer the duration of the affliction. Element of surprise, threat of death, deliberate malice of perpetrators all add to the intensity of an event (Herman 1992, 57).

Herman argues that prolonged, repeated trauma raises further issues for its victims beyond the episodic trauma of the immediate victim of a single violent event. Of particular importance to this study is that prolonged, inescapable trauma co-opts the victim—the captive—into willing acceptance of her circumstances. Prolonged trauma, which happens when victims are trapped in captivity, such as in prisons, concentration camps, religious cults, rape camps, brothels, and (cruel and controlling) families, creates a situation of coercive control, where constant violence is not necessary to maintain the subordination. In these situations there is someone who is clearly in control and not just intentionally using force against the captive, but doing so with the purpose of keeping that person in a certain place and carrying out certain tasks. Creation of a willing victim is the goal of the captor. There are well-known material and psychological techniques for doing so. Initially, violence is used to traumatize the captive. As I described previously, if the violence is intense enough or lasts long enough, this causes most individuals to respond by withdrawing inward and desensitizing themselves to reality, making them less likely to strike back. Threats of further violence against the victim or persons or animals close to the victim are then used by captors to maintain terror and trauma. Typical techniques of captors include inconsistent and unpredictable outbursts, capricious enforcement of petty rules, and destruction of the captive's autonomy by strict rules about dress and diet. The isolation of the captive is further enhanced by disrupting and minimizing their connections with friends and family. This causes victims to forge ties with perpetrators for material and emotional sustenance. It begins often with unwilling compliance for the sake of a reward or just a lessening of torture (Herman 1992, ch. 4). Kevin Bales, whose work on modern slavery has been pathbreaking, writes of the Thai girls forced into sexual slavery:

> In time, confusion and disbelief fade, leaving dread, resignation, and a break in the conscious link between mind and body. Now the girl does whatever it takes to reduce the pain, to adjust mentally to a life that means being used by fifteen men a day. The reaction to this abuse takes many forms: lethargy, aggression, self-loathing, suicide attempts, confusion, self-abuse, depression, full-blown psychoses, and hallucinations. Girls who have been freed and taken into shelters exhibit all of these disorders. Rehabilitation workers report that the girls suffer emotional instability; they are unable to trust or to form relationships, to readjust to the world outside the brothel, or to learn and develop normally. (Bales 1999, 59)

Captives' compliance becomes more automatic and eventually is offered preemptively. At this point it is not necessary to use violence often, and the coercion becomes less obvious to the outsider, as well as to the captive and the captor. Bales notes, "when slaves begin to accept their role and identify with their master, constant physical bondage becomes unnecessary. They come to perceive their situation not as a deliberate action taken to harm them in particular but as a part of the normal, if regrettable, scheme of things" (Bales 2002, 84).

Prolonged endurance of traumatic events and the inability, perceived or actual, to escape from them thus entails additional psychological harms on the victims. Herman calls this further psychological harm from violently enforced captivity "Complex PTSD," claiming that this newly named syndrome better accounts for prolonged trauma. Complex PTSD is properly diagnosed, she claims, when the following factors are present:

1. History of subjection to totalitarian control over a prolonged period;
2. Alterations in affect regulation;
3. Alterations in consciousness;
4. Alterations in self-perception (helplessness, shame, guilt, self-blame);
5. Alterations in perception of perpetrator, including an unrealistic attribution of total power to perpetrator, idealization or paradoxical gratitude, acceptance of belief system or rationalizations of perpetrator;
6. Alterations in relations with others (distrust);
7. Alterations in systems of meaning (loss of sustaining faith; hopelessness and despair). (Herman 1992, 21)

This description fits many individuals who are members of oppressed social groups and who are subject to the most immediate forces of the oppression of those groups. Frantz Fanon, in *The Wretched of the Earth*, chronicled the psychological effects of systematic, state-sponsored violence on its victims in the Algerian resistance to French colonialism. Violence and the credible threat of violence bring about in persons terror, and feelings of inferiority, shame, and hopelessness. They bring about a variety of psychoses and neuroses in some victims and make others resign themselves to being dominated. Fanon describes how the victims of torture suffered from deep sadness, sleeplessness, loss of appetite, motor instability, lack of interest in life, inability to construct moral arguments or justifications, and phobias related directly to the forms of torture inflicted upon them (Fanon 1963, 272–289). He argues that the feelings of resignation were much more widespread, however, reaching out to the Algerians who were subjected only to the everyday insults and deprivations of life under colonial rule. As with the slaves described by Bales, these everyday constraints caused many of the people to passively resign themselves to their lives. "A belief in fatality removes all blame from the oppressor; the cause of misfortunes and of poverty is attributed to God: He is Fate. In this way the individual accepts the disintegration ordained by God, he bows down before the settler and his lot, and by a kind of interior re-stabilization acquires a kind of stony calm" (Fanon 1963, 54–55).

This sense of resignation to fate describes the situation of members of social groups where all the members of the social group are subject to a "history of subjection to totalitarian control over a prolonged period." The oppression of women exemplifies these features of captivity. There are the immediate victims of violence and captivity in the women who are raped, subject to domestic violence, or forced into prostitution. While rape is typically episodic, domestic violence situations and prostitution are often situations of long-term captivity. The typical behavior of abusive men includes isolating the woman from her outside acquaintances, controlling her dress and diet, setting petty rules, arbitrary and violent outbursts for violations of those petty rules, and occasional emotional rewards. The systematic use of coercive techniques to break women in prostitution is so typical that it is known among its practitioners as "seasoning."

I maintain that women as a group suffer from the trauma of subjection to totalitarian control. Of course, not all women suffer from all the symptoms of PTSD or complex PTSD—not all women have flashbacks to traumatic events or suffer from a pervasive sense of hopelessness and despair. Rather, they suffer in two senses from a group-based trauma. First, women as a group suffer from the fact that trauma is a common feature of women's lives. That is, the image of the group is shaped by the image of the victim of trauma. Stereotypes of women as hysterical, not quite rational, given to sudden rage or tears all may well have their roots in the fact that many women are subject to traumatic violence. Worse, the dominance of men over women that creates these traumas is made to seem natural by various social institutions. Pornography eroticizes this sort of control of women by men, making women's sexual submission to men appear natural and normal to both men and women. Domestic relations that are structured by the threat of violence or economic coercion make the dominance of men in even nonviolent families seem natural or at least normal, that is, to be expected. Second, to a milder extent than immediate victims of violence, most women do share some of the effects of complex PTSD. There is a history of subjection to totalitarian control over a prolonged period; women often suffer from a pervasive sense of shame, as I shall discuss below; women often do think of men in completely unrealistic ways, as captor, savior, or ruler, and typically they accept the belief systems or rationalizations of men for their dominance.

2.1.2. HUMILIATION AND DEGRADATION

Persons who are members of oppressed groups often are made to feel humiliated or degraded by their status and by the unappealing stereotypes that are applied to them. To feel degraded is to feel lowered, less worthy of equal dignity and respect than other persons. Degradation that comes to individuals as a result of oppression comes to groups through the stereotypical images that apply to the group. A group is degraded when their image is lowered in worth relative to that of other groups. Because of the negative stereotypes that attach to oppressed groups, nearly all oppressed persons feel degradation and the consequent shame. Privileged groups cannot suffer degradation at the hands of others, though they may (objectively, relative to some moral conceptions of human worth) degrade themselves by being an oppressor group. Various social structures may cause degrading group harms. Stereotypes of blacks as lazy or violent harm all individual blacks. A practice of discrimination against the disabled in employment harms all disabled persons. In both cases the group is in a relatively powerless position. These practices reinforce negative stereotypes about these groups, degrading the social perception of their groups in a downward spiral. Blacks who cannot work because they are seen as lazy appear to be lazy because they do not work. The disabled who cannot work because of discrimination appear to themselves and others to be unable to work.

When persons are subjected to unequal treatment as a result of their social group membership, they feel shame. If the causes of the feeling seem to one to be unjust, it may cause one to feel envious and angry. In her novel *Woman on the Edge of Time*, Marge Piercy writes poignantly of the experience of degradation through the character of Connie:

> How did they stay so young? Did they take pills? Something kept them intact years longer, the women with clean hair smelling of Arpege. The women went on through college and got the clean jobs and married professional men and lived in houses filled with machines and lapped by grass. She had not looked that young since— since before Angelina was born.
>
> Envy, sure, but the sense too of being cheated soured her, and the shame, the shame of being second-class goods. Wore out fast. Shoddy merchandise. "We wear out so early," she said to the mirror, not really sure who the "we" was. Her life was thin in meaningful "we's". Once she had heard a social worker talking about Puerto Ricans, or "them" as they were popularly called in that clinic (as were her people in similar clinics in Texas), saying that "they" got old fast and died young, so the student doing her field work assignment shouldn't be surprised by some of the diseases they had, such as TB. It reminded her of Luis talking about the tropical fish he kept in his living room, marriage after marriage: Oh, they die easily, those neon tetras, you just buy more when your tank runs out. (Piercy 1976, 35–36)

Connie's belief that she and other members of her social group (Puerto Rican women) are objectively, materially degraded leads to both shame and anger, but also a sense of resignation.

As psychologists have amply demonstrated, people like to think well of themselves; we have a deep desire for self-esteem and self-respect. Where self-esteem is valuing oneself highly, self-respect is the belief that one is worthy of a high value. Self-esteem often comes from self-respect. Self-esteem is often taken to be what philosophers call an intrinsic good, a good that is desirable in itself and not only for the sake of what it brings.[1] Self-esteem is also an instrumental good, though; it makes possible the confidence and the will to compete, to resist oppression, to help others, or even to enjoy everyday pursuits. Persons who are humiliated or degraded suffer from a loss of self-esteem. Humiliation and degradation give rise to shame, as well. Shame arises when one feels that one is lacking in some important way, one is not good enough or not as good as others. While shame is episodic for members of dominant classes, arising mainly when individuals transgress moral norms, shame is "a pervasive sense of personal inadequacy" for the oppressed (Bartky 1990, 84). Shame arises from felt inadequacies or shortcomings. Since stereotypes of subordinated groups depict their members as inadequate, shame is an inevitable consequence of oppression, and especially of those forces of oppression that most serve to remind the oppressed of these negative stereotypes.

Oppressed persons are directly humiliated and degraded through hate speech or group defamation, harassment, social distancing, social distrust, and objectification. Hate speech takes the forms of racial, ethnic, and sexual epithets, as well as more subtle forms such as gestures and other expressions of disrespect and disdain aimed at persons because of their group status. Group defamation is the expression of opinions about the attributes of members of a social group that are largely false and serve to incite or justify other forms of psychological and material harm against the members of the group. This includes speculations about the essential biological basis for inferiority of groups and other rationalizations for discrimination against individuals classified as individuals belonging to that group (Matsuda et al. 1993).[2]

Harassment includes but is not limited to hate speech and group defamation, and is directed against nearly all oppressed groups in one form or another. Sexual harassment is the most well known because it is now a part of the law, even if its enforcement is not yet effective. One kind, called quid pro quo sexual harassment, involves coercive threats and offers by employers or educators. Quid pro quo sexual harassment is a kind of direct sexual objectification (which I discuss below) that sends the message to women that they are welcome only as sex objects. The other kind is hostile environment sexual harassment, in which employers, educators, fellow workers, or fellow students[3] create a work or learning environment that not only is hostile to productive work or education but also that cause women and girls, and in some cases gay persons, a variety of psychological and material harms. Gender harassment, which differs from sexual harassment in that it does not involve explicit references to sexual activity but attacks women as members of the dominated group, harms women in much the same way. These send the message to women that they are not welcome in the workplace or the classroom, or that they are only welcome as sex objects or house servants. Harassment against gays and lesbians commonly involves hostility or violence more than coercive offers (though the latter is not unheard of—consider blackmailing closeted gays and lesbians). Racial and ethnic harassment also often begins with hate speech or group defamation, including threats of or intimidating references to slavery or lynching, and then may escalate to vio-lence. Since harassment involves sending a message to individuals that, because of their group status, they are unwanted or inferior, harassment can raise feelings of shame or inferiority only in members of oppressed groups, because such messages could only be harmful or plausible to someone who is a member of such groups. White men cannot be sent the message that they are inferior because of their group status; they can be unwanted because of their group status, but only by those from whose fellowship they could not gain much materially.

Social distancing refers to a well recognized and measured phenomenon among social psychologists, in which persons physically move away from, as if disgusted or affronted by, persons in certain social groups. Nearly all oppressed groups suffer from this form of humiliating treatment (Lott and Maluso 1995). Social distrust consists in taking someone to be less trustworthy or less authoritative than is warranted by clear and direct evidence because of their social grouping. Some examples should suffice to get the reader to recognize the phenomenon.

- An American black man, well dressed and with a sophisticated manner, gets into an elevator in a fancy Jerusalem hotel. The white American woman already in the elevator clutches her purse and shrinks away (Thomas 1990).
- A woman says something relevant and important in a meeting. Her contribution is ignored. A man later says the same thing. He is warmly congratulated (Sadker and Sadker 1994, vii).[4]
- A middle-class black college professor is regularly followed around in stores by clerks in the Midwestern town where he lives and works.[5]

Social distrust makes people feel that they are not wanted or that their contributions are not valued, and it makes it more difficult for people to make the kinds of cooperative agreements that materially benefit them. While social distrust of some groups is manifested as fear or avoidance, for women it is not fear but rather a denial of cognitive authority or physical respect. Women, like children or the disabled, are more likely to suffer from being disregarded or being taken as no threat at all. Their space is more likely to be intruded upon or their bodies touched inappropriately or carelessly. These kinds of affronts further reinforce the stereotypes of weakness, insignificance, vulnerability that afflict women, children, and the disabled.

2.1.3. OBJECTIFICATION

Objectification as a direct force of psychological oppression refers to treating dom-inated persons as mere objects, ignoring their full and equal status as persons. Ob-jectifying treatment involves an epistemic and a pragmatic dimension: first, seeing something as an object for the satisfaction of one's desires, and secondly having the power to force a person to be that object. Sexual objectification has received con-siderable attention as a result of the feminist movement (MacKinnon 1983, 1987; Haslanger 2002), but slaves are clearly objectified, as are workers whose basic hu-man needs are ignored for the sake of squeezing out more profits. Hannah Arendt talks about the treatment of Jews by the Germans during the Holocaust as a literal objectification: the Germans made the Jews into mere tools, *homo faber*, to build their war machine (Bar On 2002, ch. 4).

On the definition given above, objectification is necessarily an unjust harm, since it involves disregarding the deep moral equality of human persons. What is it to disregard the deep moral equality of human persons? Humans have qualities and abilities that other things lack that make us special, and humans ought to be preserved and protected *for these qualities*, not simply because they are genetically human. What makes humans morally special in the animal world is that we have the capacity for a sense of the good and the right, the capacity to desire, to value, and to plan for a future to be lived expressing those desires and values. These abilities are threshold goods; they are fully active once they exist at a certain threshold. Any other things that would prove to have these qualities and abilities at that threshold level would thereby qualify for similarly reverent treatment. On these grounds, humans are morally superior to mere objects, as well as to nonhuman animals (as far as we know). Humans with normally developed human brains all have these capacities; even if some have a greater capacity for deliberation about means or ends than others. Since all such humans rise above the threshold for having these qualities and abilities, they are morally equal, and equally deserving of the right to exercise these capacities.[6] Dehumanizing objectification robs someone of their right to express these unique qualities, and that is what makes it deeply morally wrong. Treating persons this way psychologically harms them because it is humiliating and degrading, and to succeed in treating persons in this way usually requires traumatizing or terrorizing them, or instilling in them the belief that they are unworthy of equal treatment because of their social group status.

Slavery objectifies, not simply by employing a person as a tool, since legitimate and fulfilling work does this as well, but rather by treating the slave as someone who does not have desires and values of her own. Patricia Williams writes of slave laws, "I would characterize the treatment of blacks by whites in their law as defining blacks as those who had no will" (Williams 1991, 219). That is, the legal chattel slavery treated black persons as if they were not capable or worthy of living according to their own desires, values, and plans, and so as if they were less than human. By treating people as if they were less than human by virtue of their group membership, objectification constructs and strengthens stereotypes of those groups as inferior, as less capable of planning and directing their own lives than those from privileged social groups.

The sexual objectification of women involves taking women to have a nature that suits them to be objects for the sexual pleasure of men, that is, to naturally desire to fulfill men's wish that they be subordinate to men, to fulfill men's desires rather than to seek to know and fulfill their own (Haslanger 2002, 228). When women are treated as though they have no sexual desires of their own, or as if their desires can be dismissed because they have no rights to fulfill them, or as if their desires can be manipulated by coercive offers of promotions and the like, they are objectified. Pornography objectifies women by portraying them as willingly complying with the violent sexual desires of men. It eroticizes the objectification of women.

Apart from directly objectifying actions, there is also a sense in which our culture constantly, tacitly sexually objectifies women so commonly as to constitute direct, cultural, psychological oppression. Women are sexually objectified in this indirect sense when as a gender they are taken to be the representatives of sex and sexual passivity, for example, when goods are marketed to men by displaying women as objects of adornment or sexual pleasure, or through beauty pageants and pompon squads. Law objectifies women when it requires them to be the sex that is to be primarily the servant of the unborn, when, for instance, fetal protection laws are enforced against women but drug treatment programs for pregnant women or pre-natal care is not available. This is especially the case when men's actions that risk harm to fetuses, say men's consumption of drug's or alcohol, are not illegal or even considered problematic enough to warrant further research. Abortion laws, which enforce pregnancy in unwilling women, also objectify in this way (Cudd 1990).[7]

2.2. *Cultural Sources*

2.2.1. TRADITION AND CONVENTION

Oppression, as I hope is clear by this point, is not a momentary event but rather a long-term process, consisting of many events against a historical background of still previous events. It exists in the historical facts of systematic social domination of social groups by other social groups, which, like Rome, could not be built in a day. Traditions and conventions are social institutions, which I defined in chapter 2 as constraints that specify behavior in specific recurrent situations, that are tacitly, commonly known by some nontrivial subset of society, and that are either self-policed or policed by some external authority Oppressive conditions are maintained as tra-ditions and conventions that constrain persons' thought and behavior according to the social groups in which they are categorized and categorize themselves. Although communitarians, among others, have helped us to see the many valuable aspects of traditions for persons, tradition and the social conventions that make them up are among the most powerful indirect forces of oppression. Tradition can be defined as the set of beliefs and values, rituals, and practices, formal and informal, explicit and implicit, that are held by and constitute a culture. Traditions are typically followed unquestioningly. They are only questioned when they are in danger of being dis-carded. Like paradigms in periods of normal science, traditions constitute the back-ground social meanings within which persons can act in meaningful ways. Because tradition constitutes social meaning, though, it is the vehicle by which oppressive beliefs and desires are formed. Oppressive beliefs are those according to which some persons are judged to be of lower worth because of their group membership.

Kernohan (1998, ch. 1) explains how traditions can give rise to pervasive oppressive beliefs in his discussion of what he terms "cultural oppression." Our beliefs about value come largely given to us by our culture. That is, we learn them as small children when we are not in a position to question them, from our parents and other significant adults, who in their turn learned them from their parents and others, and so forth. This is not to say that we cannot question those values and beliefs, but only to a degree. Although we can question our values, we cannot question all of them at once, or even all of them eventually taken one by one. Furthermore, we rarely have reason to question the values we have. The background

beliefs we have are the shared meanings of our culture, and they allow us to formulate the beliefs and desires against which some of the beliefs and desires can be
understood and questioned.[8]

People learn values and beliefs not only through explicit tellings but also
through the implicit signs of whom is to be valued, for what and how. One of the
ways that we learn values from our culture is through the distribution of goods in
society. "People will learn the ethical meaning of goods—what their values are and
to whom they are appropriate—on a case-by-case basis from their cultural environment" (Kernohan 1998, 64). Thus, members of economically deprived social
groups will be seen as of lower value. What does economic deprivation have to do
with tradition? Many of the mechanisms of deprivation that we examined in chapter
5 can be seen as policing a traditional division of labor, such as slavery, discrimination, segregation, and harassment. Another way we learn values from our culture
is through the status that is accorded to various occupations. Religious traditions
that keep women out of the priesthood, the clergy, or the rabbinate, and so on, and
thereby keep them from some of the highest status occupations of the culture teach
us that women are less worthy than men. Since cultures transmit values through
tradition that individuals find unavoidable, those values often include unequally
valuing persons according to the social group to which they are seen as belonging.

Convention refers specifically to regularities in behavior that exist to solve a
particular, social interaction problem for a culture, and, because the solutions are
common knowledge, they are stable regularities. In the language of game theory,
conventions solve coordination problems, which are situations in which there are
several possible ways to coordinate peoples' interests, but everyone has to choose the
same solution in order for everyone to be satisfied to some degree.[9] Many traditions
are conventions, but traditions need not be even that rational, in that there may be
no problem that a particular aspect of a tradition solves. The important thing to see
about convention here is that the coordination problem that is solved may be what is
called a "mixed motive" game. That is, it may be that one solution benefits part of
the society more than another solution. When conventions are regularly and typically skewed to advantage one social group and disadvantage another, they are
oppressive. Yet it may seem churlish, not to mention futile because of their stability,
to complain about any one of them. Consider the expectation that when men and
women are in a car together men usually drive, or the traditional marriage proposal
that has men asking women and women only agreeing or refusing. There are many
examples of mixed motive coordination problems solved in favor of men in the
conventional relations of men and women. For instance, the sexual double standard
according to which women are supposed to be "chaste and modest" as Hume put it,
and men can be open about sexual desires and their fulfillment, could be seen as a
convention that solves the problem of determining (genetic) parenthood. But another conventional solution would be for both sexes to be chaste and modest. Still
another would be for there to be a conventional agreement on social parenthood,
and not to be concerned about the genetic contributions. Traditions often involve
conventional aspects, such as traditional clothing of women, which is typically uncomfortable and mobility-reducing. Clothing style is conventional in that many
other styles and forms are possible but one set is adopted in order to solve the

problem of group identification and to serve the purpose of recognizing specific occasions acknowledged by the group as important. Deviations from clothing conventions for both genders are policed by both men and women. In most cultures the conventions for women are more constraining physically and involve either nearly total coverage of the body or are sexually revealing and even enhancing. In either case the clothing conventions of women reinforce sexual objectification by either coding women as already possessed and thus forbidden sexual objects or as available objects for casual consumption of men. Individuals participate in the conventions one at a time against the background of given conventions and traditions upheld by the others. No one wants to risk being the only one to violate it for fear of social ostracism. But the greater the conformity to the convention, the more difficult it is for any one member to break the convention. Persons in subordinate groups fear breaking conventions even more than those in dominant groups, since the subordinates already are close to ostracism. Even oppressive conventions are stable and policed by the oppressed themselves.

Tradition and convention explain the stability of oppressive social institutions. Tradition forms the background against which our actions have meaning and thus can only be questioned at the margins and one at a time. When a culture values a social group higher than another, its traditions often reflect that and code that social group as less worthy. Conventional arrangements are often systematically skewed in favor of one social group and against the interests of another. Since the existence of a convention can be seen as an improvement on there being no convention at all for even the disfavored group, and since conventions are commonly known, they are very difficult to destruct and reconstruct in favor of another group.

2.2.2. RELIGION

Religion is a form of tradition, by far the most pervasive (within individuals and societies) and important for most persons. Religion is consciously self-justifying, for it purports to offer reasons for following its prescribed traditions, either by reference to divine inspiration or maintenance of the "chosen" group identity. Religion not only helps to make oppression acceptable to both the oppressed and the oppressor groups, in some cases it constitutes oppression by aligning one social group with the sacred and another with the profane. It works both subconsciously and consciously to reinforce the material forces of oppression. There are religious groups that do not cooperate with existing forms of oppression, but they are few. Most religions form a substantial bulwark in the oppression of women, by distinguishing sharply between the religious value of men and women and permitting or even requiring their differential roles and treatment. Some religions actively proclaim social inequalities of groups, such as the Hindu caste system. Many religions sustain existing racial or ethnic divides that permit the in-group/out-group distinctions that we discussed in chapter 3. Distinguishing among groups of persons is an internal activity of nearly all religions. Perhaps the most basic of these are the distinctions between the believers and the nonbelievers, the enlightened and the unenlightened, the chosen and the damned.

Thai Buddhism, for example, constructs distinctions through its assertion that everyone must repay the karmic debt accumulated in past lives with suffering in this life. This in turn justifies the mistreatment of some social groups, since it can be said that their members are members of those groups in order to repay their karmic debt. In Thailand this is a convenient way for brothel owners and pimps to keep their prostitutes in line. Such beliefs encourage girls who are sex slaves to turn inward, as they realize that they must have committed terrible sins in a past life to deserve their enslavement and abuse. Their religion urges them to accept this suffering to come to terms with it, and to reconcile themselves to their fate (Bales 1999, 62).

Religion is a powerful source of tradition and meaning, and thus it can serve to keep even very brutal systems of oppression in line, by making those who suffer as well as those who are privileged believe that God has chosen them for their fates. Often, religion is a limited force for good as well as evil. In Mauritania, Kevin Bales argues that "Religion serves both to protect slaves [in Mauritania] and to keep them in bondage" (Bales 1999, 85). On the one hand the Koran requires the slaveholder to show kindness to his slaves, but on the other hand it permits him to rape his female slaves. Although the Koran says that only persons captured in holy wars may be kept as slaves, and then only until they convert to Islam, Mauritania, which is nominally Muslim and uses Sharia as its official legal system, enforces slaveholder's claims on their slaves. So ingrained is slavery in their way of life that "[f]or many older slaves, freedom is a dismal prospect. Deeply believing that God wants and expects them to be loyal to their masters, they reject freedom as wrong, even traitorous. To struggle for liberty, in their view, is to upset God's natural order and puts one's very soul at risk" (Bales 1999, 108).

The support that religion gives to oppression is not limited to slavery. Religion is an important force for constructing and justifying family life and the roles of women and men within the family. Marriage is, in most cultures, a religious event first, and only secondarily a civil status. Marriage vows in Christianity require women to "honor and obey" their husbands, while not requiring obedience of husbands to wives. Muslim rules for women and men are also asymmetric and unequal, giving men the dominant status in public affairs. In Judaism, in all but the Reformed sect, women and men are likewise prescribed separate roles, and women are unable to serve as rabbis. No major religion of the world, in all of its branches, treats men and women equally. Religions typically forbid homosexual unions and the power of religion to enforce this restriction can be seen in the current debate in the United States over gay marriage. Even when termed "civil union" many persons use religious arguments to oppose this legal status, despite the undeniable fact that the Constitution (absent a specific amendment to the contrary) mandates its adoption as a matter of equal treatment under the law demanded by the Fourteenth Amendment.

2.2.3. IDEOLOGY

By ideology I mean to refer to political, social, and scientific theories that purport to offer rationalizations of tradition and convention. To be an objectionable ideology a theory must be either false, exaggerated, or carried beyond its intended domain of application, and it must be widely believed. Ideology is perpetrated by persons who have an interest in maintaining the tradition or convention that the ideology upholds, and they may or may not believe the theory. These theories make traditions and conventions more difficult to change by giving them the force of moral or rational norm. The stereotypes created and maintained by those traditions and conventions are then that much more difficult to overcome. Living in a way that defies the stereotype that is upheld by ideology labels one immoral or irrational. Ideology directly reinforces stereotypes because they are cognitive structures, and hence influenced by the force of persuasion, which is what ideology offers.

One of the most potent ideologies is patriotism, in which persons come to believe that their nation is superior to all others, even if that means reading evidence through rose-colored glasses, or ignoring it altogether. People in the United States may be among the guiltiest of this, believing in what has been called "American exceptionalism," which refers to the common belief that the United States is especially moral, respectful of human rights, and deserving of its place as the only military superpower in the world (Lipset 1996). With this belief it is easy for many American citizens to justify actions against other nations and peoples that would, if undertaken by foreign nations, count as unjustified human rights abuses or violations of international treaties and war crimes. Writers and intellectuals who deny American exceptionalism and try to expose such abuses for what they are often find themselves branded as extremists, as not quite rational, or perhaps even as disloyal. Worse, such ideology rationalizes sending soldiers to carry out these immoral commands. Soldiers have often been, and are today, from the working class or from economically deprived backgrounds, having chosen that occupation from among a small set of options. In believing the ideology, they accept their missions even when the mission is unjust and they are unjustly coerced into undertaking it.

Science is an important source of ideology in the modern world, though of course it would be a wild exaggeration to say that all science is ideology. An example of ideological science comes from the "economics of the family." Even though "economics" comes from the Greek *oikonomikos*, meaning of or pertaining to household management, the family has been much neglected by economic theory in the past. Today we still see textbooks in which the family is overlooked in lists of important social institutions because it is seen as a natural formation rather than a social construct. In the history of the discipline we can see two basic models of the family: the "household as individual (and father as head of it)" model, and recently, under the influence of feminist economics and the women's movement generally, the "competing-but-unequal-agent model." The first of these we can trace at least to Hobbes, but perhaps is best summarized by the words of the early nineteenth-century economist James Mill.

> One thing is pretty clear, that all those individuals whose interests are indisputably included in those of other individuals may be struck off without inconvenience. In this light may be viewed all children, up to a certain age, whose interests are involved in those of their parents. In this light also, women may be regarded, the interests of almost all of whom is involved either in that of their fathers or in that of their husbands. (Folbre and Hartmann 1988, 188)

This model assumes that women are under the protection of sovereign men, either husbands or fathers, and that men would provide this protection without undue selfishness. Men naturally care for their wives and children; there is no need to consider the constraints that structure this care and concern. This model made attention to the family unnecessary theoretically; economic theory could assume that the only individuals there were may or may not come attached with wife and family, but that would be irrelevant data to the theory. Modeling the economy of the household would be like modeling the economy of the individual—uninteresting.

For economics to even consider families as institutions goes against that ideological notion. In the 1960s economic theory began to take a look at the family with what is called the "new home economics." The 1992 Nobel Prize in Economics was awarded to the founder of the new home economics, Gary Becker of the University of Chicago, "for having extended the domain of microeconomic analysis to a wide range of human behavior and interaction, including non-market behavior." Becker's motivation was to try to apply economic theory to all sorts of areas of behavior that had been overlooked by mainstream economics: crime, animal behavior, and drug use, to name some others. Becker (1991) uses the same basic model of the family as Hobbes and Mill, however. He models the family as acting to maximize total utility (i.e., as an individual), with an altruistic head of the family. He first endows each member of the family with an individual utility function that she or he tries to maximize. Then he shows, in what he terms the "Rotten Kid Theorem," that if there is an altruistic family member, by which he means a member whose utility function has other family member's utilities as arguments, then it is rational for the selfish members of the family to act to maximize total family utility as well. Thus, rational families have male heads who lead by example, persuading their naturally selfish charges to do what is in the best interest of the family as a whole.

Well, there is no arguing with mathematics. Somewhat concealed by the mathematics, however, are three other critical assumptions. (1) wealth or control of income is unequally distributed so that the altruist is able to redistribute income to maximize his utility function (I use "his" here because Becker quite explicitly assumes that the altruist is the father); (2) the egoists in the family (including the altruist's wife) have no better option than the one that the altruist gives them, such as leaving the family; (3) the use of the pejorative term "altruist" presumes that his utility function ought to be maximized, without regard to what he wants; the "altruist" might think it in the best interests of the family to move a thousand miles away, and that counts as altruistic simply because it is the aim of the one in control of the wealth and income of the family. Becker thus understands the family as an altruistic institution led by a benevolent dictator. In such a situation, there is no need for the intrusion of law, since there is no competition for resources. The father's paternalistic wishes are to be fulfilled; the legal status quo of the 1960s is justified; inequality within the family is not an issue. Becker speculates, then, that marriage must have evolved as a deal to protect women, a stunning rationalization of that oppressive institution.

The justification is false, however, and a part of an ideology of families. Becker's analysis thus makes the following mistakes. First, like economists before him, he continues in the androcentric view that intra-family economics is uninteresting. There are no separate preferences being considered here, and no outside options that could constitute a strategic threat to the "altruist's" aims. Once the differences in preferences between various members of the family are considered, however, it is possible to reveal the oppressive nature of the institution. Second, he makes the sexist assumption that the "head of the family" is male and altruistic, while the other spouse is female and, like the children, egoistic. Third, he fails to model the full range of options for the spouses by assuming that they cannot leave the family, and this reinforces his sexist assumption that families maximize a single utility function, which reinforces the androcentric idea that what happens within families is devoid of economic interest. We can see how great his errors are in modeling by testing his conclusions against empirical experience. His conclusion that marriage is a deal to protect women is refuted by the empirical evidence that women have been exploited and oppressed by marriage, for instance, by long-standing and even legally sanctioned spousal abuse, the fact that married women were until relatively recently prohibited from owning property, unequal divorce laws, and countless other laws and norms that constitute the double standard for married men and women. If marriage was any kind of protection of women, then it was the kind that organized criminals offer to legitimate businesses.[10]

I do not mean to suggest that all science is ideology. Indeed, science can be used to debunk the ideology of those purported scientific theories that are infected. Stephen Jay Gould's (1996) work on intelligence studies is an excellent example of this. It is enough for my thesis in this section to show that some science is ideology that supports oppressive social institutions. Theories about rocks and lizards are far less likely to be ideological—to be false and useful to maintaining oppressive social dominance relations—than those about persons, cultures, or social interaction. Scientists police themselves to some degree by checking each others' theories and attempting to remain critical about evidence that is presented in favor of theories. But scientists come to their work with preconceived ideas about persons and cultures, and it may not occur to them that these prejudices have infected their theories. Scientific theories can therefore stand for a time, sometimes generations, as the wisdom of the age, yet be mere rationalizations of the oppressive social institutions to which scientists, like others in their cultures, are blind.

2.2.4. CULTURAL DOMINATION

An important source of psychological harm for some oppressed groups in multicultural societies is the fact that they must constantly struggle for the recognition of their cultural uniqueness. As I argued above, culture and tradition make actions meaningful, and provide the social context in which one's values and beliefs are formed. Because they are the essential meaning creating and stabilizing forces in persons' lives, and because each culture creates different meanings that are not easily interchanged, each person's own culture is important to her. In the midst of conflicting cultural norms, values, and beliefs, an individual can find his values and beliefs challenged or contradicted. This becomes problematic when one's own culturally instilled beliefs and values are consistently condemned or sacrificed for a different, perhaps majority, cultural belief and value system. Consider, for instance, the way that the traditional academic schedule in the United States is constructed around the Christian calendar of holidays. Jewish and Muslim students and faculty will find that the days that they find sacred are not recognized as special, although the Christian holidays are given special treatment.[11] This sends a message of lesser social concern for the Jews and Muslims. In some cultures the dominant religion may even be state sanctioned, allowing legal discrimination against minority cultures. Legal discrimination is a very insulting challenge to one's culture and sends a message of inferiority and disdain.

There are three kinds of problems that we can classify as cultural domination, and different cultural minorities may suffer from one or more of them. One is the problem of *recognition*, which occurs when a cultural minority is not seen as a subculture in its own right. The second type of problem is a lack of *accommodation*, which occurs when the minority's legitimate needs are overlooked and unfilled. The third kind of problem is a lack of *respect*, which occurs when the minority is denied some rights allowed to the majority because they are considered less worthy than the majority. In the example of religious minorities just given, the problem of recognition may still be in play for Jews and certainly for Muslims in many places in the United States, and the problems of accommodation and respect are present whenever they are not permitted to set aside their holidays from normal work and school life.

The phenomenon of "compulsory heterosexuality" (Rich 1980), which refers to the fact that the dominant, straight society takes as a default assumption that people will have or seek heterosexual partners, is an important example of all three of these problems of cultural domination. Compulsory heterosexuality is a kind of false universalism, which is taking the characteristics of the majority or the dominant to be true of everyone (DeBruin 1998), or what psychologists refer to as the "false consensus effect" (Fiske and Taylor 1991, ch. 3). Successful false universalizing requires that a group have the social influence necessary to make their false attributions the default assumptions in major social institutions, such as the law, the construction of buildings and public spaces, or the development and marketing of goods. Compulsory heterosexuality results in insults great and small to homosexuals, who find themselves having to explain their "unusual sexual proclivities" to strangers in order to get health care, health insurance (indeed, if they can get it), an apartment or a home, or just a room for the night. It is a lack of recognition when people fail to see a gay couple as a couple, but it is a failure to accommodate if public institutions fail to make available services that gay persons or couples need. Of course they may even be seen as not entitled to equal protection of the law and may be discriminated against in many ways that would not happen if they were not dominated by the heterosexual community. The case of sexual minorities might seem quite different from that of religious minorities, in that some argue that it is a chosen lifestyle that is not worthy of equal respect and concern. But a similar mistake has been made concerning religious minorities over the years: that they believe in false gods and ought to be pressured into changing those beliefs, or at least, that their beliefs are not worthy of equal respect. Sexual minorities have been accused of both false beliefs and unworthy values. While I will not take on the project here of a full defense of sexual freedom, I will assert that freedom of conscience is involved in both issues, and that at root equal respect for persons requires that persons be allowed freedom of conscience (Cornell 1998). Thus in both cases cultural domination is an unjust harm to the minorities.

A final example that will further illuminate the extent of the problem of cultural domination is the situation of the Deaf in hearing society. The Deaf suffer mainly from the problems of accommodation and recognition. Communications technologies have been developed for speaking rather than signing persons, and the need to accommodate the Deaf by facilitating signing persons is often resented or considered to be a kind of charity, rather than a right of persons whose needs were sacrificed to meet the desires of the majority hearing. The recognition problem for the Deaf has been in their being recognized as a competent community in their own right, rather than as a number of unconnected, disabled individuals. The Deaf maintain that their way of life is not a lesser form of human life to that of the hearing, absent discrimination and artificially constructed barriers. They hold that their difference from hearing folks is just a difference, not an inferiority, and they need not be patronized by the hearing. This conflict came to a head in 1988 when a search was held for the presidency of Gallaudet University, the only Deaf university in the United States. Until that time the presidency had always been held by a hearing person, but the students and faculty of the school lobbied for a Deaf president. They argued that it was time that the Deaf community be led by one of its own. When a hearing president was named, they organized protests and sit-ins, and finally prevailed when the just-named president resigned and a Deaf person was installed (Sacks 1989, ch. 3). Although the Deaf won that battle, they continue to struggle for recognition as a community, and living among the hearing their needs and interests are often sacrificed for those of the majority, sometimes in ways that are unjustly harmful.

2.3. Summary

In this section I have explored seven direct psychological forces of oppression: terror and trauma, humiliation and degradation, objectification, tradition and convention, religion, ideology, and cultural domination. Each such force harms individuals who are members of oppressed groups by robbing them of the material and psychological wherewithal to successfully compete in the marketplace and keep themselves safe from further harm. Some of these direct forces that immediately harm individuals with face-to-face discriminatory treatment I have labeled "point sources," in contrast to those I labeled "cultural forces" that form the background of social meaning against which social grouping, stereotyping, and discrimination is possible.

The applications of psychological forces of oppression are social or political problems that require solutions more extensive than mere compensation to individuals who are directly harmed. Since the entire group is harmed, rectification has to be aimed at the entire group. Elimination of terror and trauma requires concerted effort, but can be successfully done by a society with the will to enact and enforce sufficient legal protections. Countering degradation requires that the worth of the group be raised, and though it may not be too difficult to mandate equal protection of the law, it is difficult to change the minds of people who have degraded or been degraded that the judgment of relative worth was wrong. Likewise countering objectification and the cultural forces of psychological oppression is similarly difficult because it requires this change of mind. Since the harm is inflicted by a social practice, it is more deeply entrenched than individual instances of criminal behavior, passionate transgressions, or momentary lapses. The very background of cultural meaning must change to make the despised group acceptable, no longer associated with negative stereotypes, or no longer considered a social group at all. But were the external, intentionally inflicted psychological harms the only ones, it would be possible to directly confront them, countering hate speech and prejudice with positive speech and counter images. However, oppression often causes its victims to conform to the pressures in ways that cannot be so readily confronted. In the next section I examine these indirect psychological forces, which are harder to counter, since they go beyond the wrongdoing by others and consist in the cooperation of the oppressed themselves.

3. Indirect Psychological Forces

Indirect psychological harms occur when the beliefs and values of the privileged or oppressor groups are subconsciously accepted by the subordinate and assimilated into their self-concept or value/belief scheme. Indirect forces thus work through the psychology of the oppressed to mold them and co-opt them to result in choices and decisions that harm the oppressed while benefiting the privileged. In this section I discuss three such forces. The first force is that of shame and low self-esteem, which are the emotive and cognitive forces involved in seeing oneself as of less worth than others. The second is the cognitive process of false consciousness, which is a cognitive process of coming to believe in an ideology that oppresses oneself. The third is deformed desire, which is the combined affective and cognitive process of value formation, in which the oppressed come to desire that which is oppressive to them. They are all self-inflicted wounds, but wounds that have been inflicted with the weapon that society provides the oppressed. They are difficult to avoid and overcome, because once one is under the sway of these forces, one may not recognize that they exist at all. Furthermore, once recognized, they often hold sway over one's beliefs and desires despite one's best efforts to rid oneself of them.

3.1. *Shame and Low Self-esteem*

I discussed above the ways that humiliating and degrading actions can directly oppress through actions intended to shame and lower the self-esteem of oppressed persons. Shame is experienced by persons who feel themselves to be lacking or unworthy. It can be experienced by individuals for reasons entirely due to their individual circumstances, appropriately or inappropriately. Shame is not the same as guilt, which accompanies the belief that one has done something wrong, whereas shame accompanies the belief that one is not good enough in some respect, either in one's own eyes or the eyes of others. Oppressed persons may feel shame for the entirely externally imposed reason that they have less status because of their social group membership. Oppressed persons are frequently harmed precisely by a message of inferiority, even if they do not really believe that they are inferior. But shame and guilt often come together, for one may feel morally responsible for one's shortcomings. Shame can permeate one's psyche, becoming internalized, echoing within the oppressed person's psychology either because of trauma or because the person deeply identifies with their social group status in a way that lowers their sense of self-esteem. When shame and low self-esteem are internalized they can be considered indirect psychological forces.

According to Herman, shame and self-doubt are typical psychological reactions to traumatic events. "Shame is a response to helplessness, the violation of bodily integrity, and the indignity suffered in the eyes of another person. Doubt reflects the inability to maintain one's own separate point of view while remaining in connection with others" (Herman 1992, 53). As we have seen, the traumatized individual continues to relive the experience of trauma and often to judge harshly her reaction to the experience. But the situation is rigged against the individual who was the victim of violence; her choices in the circumstance are coerced, and even though she survived, the fact that she was traumatized means that she was unsuccessful in deterring the violence. "Traumatic events by definition, thwart initiative and overwhelm individual competence. No matter how brave and resourceful the victim may have been, her actions were insufficient to ward off disaster. In the aftermath of traumatic events, as survivors review and judge their own conduct, feelings of guilt and inferiority are practically universal" (Herman 1992, 53). Thus, shame, guilt, and a lower sense of self-esteem typically follow on traumatic events.

Since trauma is a common experience for the oppressed, the shame that is consequent on trauma is common, as well. Oppressed persons who are not the direct victims of trauma also feel shame because of their social group status. Sandra Bartky writes about how shame is a pervasive emotion for women. Women and other oppressed persons, she claims, feel a "pervasive sense of personal inadequacy" (Bartky 1990, 85). To be shamed in front of someone is to recognize that one is as the Other sees one and to identify (to some extent, at least) with the values of the Other. Oppressed persons are sent the message in the myriad ways that they are harmed that they are inferior in the eyes of the privileged. Martin Luther King, Jr., poignantly illustrates this phenomenon in his "Letter from Birmingham Jail":

> When you have seen vicious mobs lynch your mothers and fathers at will and drown your sisters and brothers at whim; when you have seen hate-filled policemen curse, kick and even kill your black brothers and sisters; when you see the vast majority of your twenty million Negro brothers smothering in an airtight cage of poverty in the midst of an affluent society; when you suddenly find your tongue twisted and your speech stammering as you seek to explain to your six-year-old daughter why she can't go to the public amusement park that has just been advertised on television, and see tears welling up in her eyes when she is told that Funtown is closed to colored children, and see ominous clouds of inferiority beginning to form in her little mental sky, and see her beginning to distort her personality by developing an unconscious bitterness toward white people; ... when you are humiliated day in and day out by nagging signs reading "white" and "colored"; ... when you are harried by day and haunted by night by the fact that you are a Negro, living constantly at tiptoe stance, never quite knowing what to expect next, and are plagued with inner fears and outer resentments; when you are forever fighting a degenerating sense of "nobodiness"—then you will understand why we find it difficult to wait. (King, Jr. 1964)

Conditions of material and economic oppression often cause women and cultural minorities to feel shame and lowered self-esteem. Feeling shame and lowered self-esteem then drains one of confidence and assertiveness, which handicaps one in a competitive marketplace. Thus, shame and low self-esteem are harms, and they are caused by unjust conditions, and so constitute oppressive forces. But the material conditions of oppression are not in themselves sufficient causes of these feelings of shame and low self-esteem. In order to generate them, the oppressed must also somehow assimilate the common knowledge conditions of their oppressive cultures, according to which they are inferior or less worthy of equal dignity and respect. The question then arises: can such assimilation be resisted? And if so, how? These questions I take up in the final two chapters of this book. In the next section, we will see how oppressive cultures generate these false beliefs in the individuals of the culture, oppressed and privileged alike.

3.2. False Consciousness

False consciousness is the belief in objectionable ideology and, when it is believed by those who are oppressed by that ideology, it is an indirect force of psychological oppression. "False consciousness" has been used to refer to beliefs held by members of privileged groups that rationalize and support their dominance, beliefs and desires held by members of oppressed groups that support their subordination, and beliefs held generally about the nature of social relations, which support the status quo relations (Meyerson 1991). I shall use the term to discuss the belief formation phenomena, saving the phenomena of desire formation for the following section. False consciousness, as I shall use the term, refers to beliefs that are false and that are formed under conditions of oppression that support the maintenance of the oppression. To label a belief a matter of false consciousness, then, is to challenge it on three grounds: (1) its falsity, (2) its origin, and (3) its implications for oppressive social relations. While a belief's being false must count against it, one might object that neither the origins of a belief nor their implications matter; we must face the truth no matter what the origin of our belief in it or its implications. Indeed, to argue that the origins count against a belief is to commit the genetic fallacy. I will argue, on the contrary, that certain origins for and implications of beliefs give us reason to reject them, even if we cannot conclusively show that they are false, and this holds specifically in the case of the belief formation processes that result in false consciousness.

Consider a list of false beliefs that support oppressive relations of subordination and domination.

- women's place is in the home
- black men are more prone to commit violence than white men
- women are more nurturing than men
- disabled persons are asexual
- Arabs are terrorists
- rich persons deserve their wealth

Notice first that they each support the status quo in the sense that if they are generally believed in a society, they will support undignified or disrespectful treatment of some individuals consequent on their social group status. Second, these are beliefs that are often held by members of both the groups whose dominance and whose subordination they justify. This has led some theorists to argue that at least some members of the dominant group hold these beliefs because they are motivated to do so (Meyerson 1991, ch. 2). The argument goes like this: people are motivated to think well of themselves and to minimize their beliefs that they have done wrong; receiving undeserved privilege at the cost of others' undeserved harm makes one believe that one has done wrong; however, a belief that one's privilege is deserved, or that another's harm is justified, minimizes the belief that one has done wrong. Hence, members of dominant groups are motivated to believe that their privileges are deserved or that the members of subordinate groups deserve their harms.

The question then arises, how do we show that their motivation is the *cause* of the belief rather than just a happy coincidence for them? To answer this question, we first note that the members of the subordinate groups have no such motivation, unless purely for dissonance reduction. Could all the members of the dominant group just coincidentally have these convenient false beliefs? That seems unlikely, and in any case would be no explanation of the origin of the beliefs. Furthermore, one must note that the dominant group of society—at least some of their members—are those who have the most ability to mold common social beliefs. In modern capitalist society they own the media and the companies that employ people, and run the schools that educate people; in socialist societies they are the political elite who have the power over the media, employment, and education; in traditional societies they run the religions and the tribal councils. They have the power to shape opinion. The answer must be, at least in part, that while some members of the dominant group are passive receptors of the beliefs, some have sought to construct and perpetuate these ideological beliefs through their greater ability to shape public opinion.

It may be objected that people are unlikely to believe patently false things, especially if they can see that they are being manipulated into doing so. Furthermore, false beliefs must be easy to counter with evidence. False consciousness is about tendencies, propensities, proclivities of groups of persons, that is, false conscious beliefs are all about constructing stereotypes. But as we have seen, stereotypes may have a root in some reality and still be false as stated. They can be vague claims that bend in the face of counterevidence and snap back into place when the evidence is no longer directly in view. Even more insidious, though, is the fact that dominant groups sometimes have the power to make a vague false stereotype become approximately true by using legal, financial, political, or religious power to coerce a subordinate group into behaving in a way that fits the stereotype. Consider the case of Lisa in chapter 5, who chose to stay home with the kids in the face of the gender wage gap. Or take the false belief cited above that black men are more prone to violence than white men. It flies in the face of the evidence that most wars worldwide are perpetrated by white men. But it is supported by sensational media coverage of inner city street crime, where black men are often perpetrators, in part created by drug laws that have been particularly targeted at black illegal drug use. Because these beliefs are backed only by evidence that has been created by oppression, and not by any clear evidence of about persons' immutable "natures," they are to be rejected and resisted as false consciousness.

We have been over this ground before: in chapter 3 I discussed how stereotypes are formed despite their untruth and how they support out-group formation and thus oppression. In section 2 of this chapter I discussed ideology and how false beliefs can be perpetrated when they support the status quo of oppression. False consciousness has a special place in the maintenance of oppression, however, because when the oppressed themselves believe false things, which support their place in the social hierarchy, they have additional reason not to resist their oppression or not to even recognize it. For, oppression must be *undeserved* harm, and false consciousness causes them to believe that their place is deserved. In the next section we see how undeserved harm can even be transformed into preferred treatment.

3.3. Deformed Desires

Although we (especially we liberals) tend to think that it is good if persons get what they desire, sometimes persons desire what is not good for them. They might do this because they are ill informed of the true nature of what they desire (the liquid in the cup is gasoline, not ginger ale), or because they do not fully understand the consequences of satisfying their desire (as motivates the saying "be careful what you wish for"). People might also wish for things that are bad for them because they are in the grip of an addiction or because they have a momentarily weak will. Finally, people might desire things that they have been somehow duped or beguiled into desiring. What is wrong with such desires is the way in which, or the circumstances under which, they were formed. For example, Macbeth's desire to wash his hands was a neurotic desire that he developed as a consequence of murdering Duncan. Desires are formed in a social context that makes the desired objects or states meaningful to the one who desires them. Sometimes the social context is oppressive and makes things seem desirable when they would not be so under circumstances of social equality. These problematic desires, which I shall call deformed desires, have been recognized by preference theorists, political theorists, and feminist theorists. They are also known as adaptive or deformed preferences.[12]

Deformed desires are problematic for political theories that hold that the goodness or degree of freedom of a society depends to at least some extent on the degree to which persons' desires are satisfied. Deformed desires, when they can be shown to be deformed by the constraints placed on persons by virtue of their social group membership, constitute oppression in my theory because it measures harm by the degree to which person's lives are constrained through their social group membership. Jon Elster (1983b) defines an adaptive preference (another term for deformed desire) as a preference that has been formed without one's control or awareness, by a causal mechanism that is not of one's own choosing. Adaptive preferences have a typical "fox and grapes" structure, that is, if the grapes are out of the agent's reach, the agent's preferences, if they are like the fox's, will turn against the grapes, the agent declaring them sour anyway. The sour grapes phenomenon is familiar to us all: after I found out that eating scallops would make me violently ill, I found that I had no taste for them; my discovery that there was no organized football league that admitted members of my gender, I desired to watch the game less. Not all adaptive preferences are bad for the agent herself, since they do allow the agent to get more welfare from her feasible set of options. There are less innocent examples of this phenomenon, though. Those adaptations that are made to adjust to unjust conditions of material deprivation or psychological harm consequent on social group membership are oppressive. If one's preferences adapt to oppressive circumstances, then one's desires turn away from goods and even needs that, absent those conditions, they would want.[13] Oppressed persons come to see their conditions of oppression as the limits within which they *want* to live.

A closely related form of adaptive preference formation is the habituation of preference (Sunstein 1993; Sen 1995). Not only do persons tend to become content with whatever they see as their lot in life, they also become accustomed to great privilege and are greatly affected for the worse should they be deprived of this privilege, however unfair it might be (Branscombe 1998). In an oppressive situation in which some suffer great deprivation and others enjoy great privilege, states of affairs in which things are more fairly distributed will not be preferred by the oppressed and will be greatly dispreferred by the privileged. Girls and women are encouraged by multiple sources to think of the kind of work that oppresses them as the work that they ought, by nature, by sentiment, and even by God, to do. All of these sources have powerful effects on emotions, making it likely that women's preferences will favor their oppressive condition. It is not that they will prefer oppression to justice, or subordination to equality, rather they will prefer the kinds of social roles that tend to subordinate them, make them less able to choose, or give them fewer choices to make. These sources also suggest to women, and to men, that it is not social oppression at work, but rather nature (or the supernatural) that puts women in their place. As John Stuart Mill noted in *The Subjection of Women*, the oppression of women is the one kind of oppression that is maintained in part by the affections of the oppressed for the privileged class. Many religions, at least the past and current interpretations of them, insist that women's place is in the domestic sphere, and most prohibit them from becoming religious leaders.[14] Religion also powerfully engages the emotions, and so affects preferences. But social decisions made from such habituated preferences compromise autonomy, equality, dignity, and diversity. Thus, we should be wary of individuals' preferences that reinforce oppression, even when they are sincerely expressed by oppressed individuals.

In a recent article, Anita Superson (2005) gives a number of examples of typical ways that women's preferences have been molded under oppressive patriarchal cultures. The first example, which is Thomas Hill's (1991), is the deferential wife, who defers to her husband's preferences and needs, placing his and their children's preferences above her own needs because of a belief that her proper role is to serve him. The second example (Stevens, 1993) is the *marianismo* woman, who is the counterpart of the *machismo* man, who believes women are morally and spiritually superior but that women should be submissive to men and that their superiority lies in their self-denial and self-sacrifice. Thus, *marianismo* women prefer their men to have more of what they want rather than the women's own (first order) preferences to be satisfied. The third example is the right-wing woman, who "adopts traditional lifestyle either because of religious or anti-abortion views, or because she believes she has few or no economic and social options" (Superson

2005, 1). Another example would be African women who force their daughters to undergo genital surgery because they think that it makes them more beautiful and more acceptable to men who might otherwise choose not to marry them. In each of these cases the women have desires that, when satisfied, help maintain the oppressive structures that caused them to have those desires. These desires are therefore self-reinforcing systems of oppression.

In order to show that satisfaction of deformed desires is harmful, we must show what is wrong with deformed desires. I will raise three objections to deformed desires. First, the desires help to maintain oppression because in acting to satisfy these desires, persons act in ways that harm members of their own social group. The deferential wife and the *marianismo* women both fail to accomplish much in their own right, which lends more credence to stereotypes about women's incompetence, and they help to set up expectations in both men and women that other women will behave this way, and thus they must choose either to fail to meet the expectation or to meet it through similarly deferential behavior. Thus, the deformed desires are immoral. Second, these desires are framed by beliefs that are a result of false consciousness. The desirability of the desires depends crucially on false beliefs. The *marianismo*'s desires only make sense against the background beliefs about the moral differences in men's and women's natures, the claim that women are morally superior and more spiritual. But the belief is either false or has been made true by the oppressive treatment of women. If all women are morally or spiritually superior to all men, it must be because women are very seriously constrained in their actions compared to men. Third, deformed desires harm the one who has them and seeks to satisfy them. This objection, unlike the other two, depends on there being an objective good which the owner of deformed desires does not see, at least at the time that the desire is held. If the objection is apt, it shows that deformed desires are self-defeating.

Superson lists five features of deformed desires that show that they are harmful to the one who has them (Superson 2005, 4–5). First, their source contributes to their deformation, that is, the conditions of oppression cause the victims to have these desires. The desire of the deferential wife (DW) to defer to her husband's wishes is caused by her adaptation to or indoctrination by circumstances in which this is the best way for her to get some of what she would desire in a world without male dominance. Since in forming these desires the DW is acting under coercion, she is harmed. Second, satisfaction of the desires of the nonprivileged benefits the oppressive system. This is the point that Marx made about the plight of the working class under capitalism, that workers constantly enrich the capitalist, making their ability to lower wages to subsistence and withstand any resistance by workers that much stronger. Workers desire jobs, but in working for the capitalist they harm themselves. We already argued that this harms others in the group, but as a member of the group, this also harms oneself. Third, deformed desires involve deception in the nonprivileged who believe that when satisfied they and their group will benefit in some way. Again, since deception is a form of coercion, in forming desires based on deception, the owner of deformed desires is harmed. Fourth, deformed desires conflict with what their bearers may believe "deep down" is good for them. Consider the excessive materialism that capitalism inspires in persons. When a person who is poor attempts to satisfy these empty desires by overspending, they may know that deep down their actions are not good for them, and yet be unable to resist the temptation to purchase the cell phone. Although this is not a necessary feature of deformed desires, when it occurs it is a harm much like the self-inflicted harm of weakness of will. Fifth, deformed desires are both the cause and the result of their owner's not seeing herself as equal in worth to others. Consider the African woman who believes that to make a woman beautiful one must cut her genitals in ways that are often extremely harmful to her, or the American woman who desires breast augmentation surgery to make herself acceptable to men. These women do not expect men to make similar sacrifices for beauty. Thus, their desires for surgery stem from the belief that they are unworthy of equal treatment by others. And in desiring these surgical changes they see themselves as ugly prior to the surgery or as needing to have undergone these drastic changes to make themselves acceptable after the surgery.

Deformed desires are thus objectionable on three grounds: they are harmful to others, they are falsely framed, and they are self-defeating. They are formed by processes that are coercive: indoctrination, manipulation, and adaptation to unfair social circumstances. They therefore constitute a force of psychological oppression, and because they originate within the oppressed person, they are indirect forces. All three such indirect forces: shame, false consciousness, and deformed desires occur as effects of oppression, but bring about additional problems for resisting oppression. First, fighting the external, direct forces of oppression is not sufficient. Second, fighting these forces involves denying some beliefs and desires of the oppressed themselves, and that is painful, if not harmful. Third, the existence of shame, false consciousness, and deformed desires among the oppressed makes it more difficult to argue that there is oppression, since to a casual or unmotivated observer, these indirect forces can deceive. Shame may look like personal inadequacies or personality problems in individuals, rather than a pervasive feature of oppression. False consciousness may masquerade as sincerely held true belief or innocent mistake. Deformed desires may look like legitimate expressions of individual differences in taste. The oppressed themselves often deny that they are internalizing oppression, as if it were an additional fault that they are psychologically weak as well as possessing whatever inferiority justifies their inferior treatment. It is only when one can show that there are corresponding external forces of oppression and that these are self-defeating mental states that it can be shown that oppression exists and has been so deeply embedded in the psyches of the oppressed themselves. Making this argument linking external forces with internal ones has taken me the better part of this book, if I have managed to convince at all. Hence I conclude that these indirect forces of oppression, both material and psychological, are the most damaging and enduring, and explain how oppression can be so long-standing despite the rough natural equality of humans.

4. Can We Break the Cycle of Psychological Oppression?

From our analysis of the psychological forces of oppression, particularly the indirect forces, one might conclude that oppression is inescapable for its victims. Yet, oppression is by definition unjust, and so requires the just to attempt to overcome it, or at least to put up some resistance to it. How might this be done? In the next chapter I will address this question in the context of the comprehensive analysis of oppression that I have offered in this book. Preliminary to that, here are some of the lessons to be drawn specifically from the social cognitive account of the psychology of oppression. Direct resistance of the direct forces of oppression would seem clearly to be required by justice, but without attacking the stereotypes that are self-fulfilling and that invidiously distinguish among us, this will be like trying to put out the flames without removing the fuel. From a cognitive standpoint there exist three courses of action to direct at stereotyping and ideology.[15] First, we need to attack existing role schemas and their rationalizations. We might do that, for instance, by showing how sociobiological explanations of the sexual division of labor depend on androcentric assumptions and privilege men. Second, since categorizing seems to be a cognitive requirement for us, let us propose alternative categories for social groupings that depend more on interest than on accidents of birth, on voluntary groupings rather than involuntary groups. For if we group by chosen groups, there may be some possibility to change our grouping should it harm or fail to satisfy us. Third, we can reveal false consciousness and deformed desires where they exist by exposing the ways in which assimilating oneself to involuntary in-groups and accentuating the differences with involuntary out-groups is, in at least some cases, either an assertion of undeserved privilege or a failure to resist one's own oppression.

Some of the psychological forces of oppression we have discussed in this chapter can be directly resisted by external efforts, such as by changing and then strictly enforcing laws and constructing economic incentives to motivate people to behave contrary to their customs and habits. Countering terrorism and the trauma that it imposes is not easily done, but by taking a strong stance against these ways of enforcing oppression, these forces can be reduced. Likewise, the most destructive of the ways of humiliating and degrading people, such as through hate speech, group defamation, and harassment, can be countered by legal means. But here there is the potential for conflict with freedoms of speech and assembly, which must be balanced against the rights of persons not to be psychologically harmed. I will discuss this at greater length in the last chapter. The other forms of humiliating and degrading treatment, objectification, social distancing and social distrust, probably cannot be made illegal for these reasons, and will have to be countered by more subtle social means. However, if the more blatant and clearly unjust forces of oppression were ended, such as violence, threats, and economic deprivation, along with terrorism, and the cultural forces of psychological oppression, these remaining point source forms of direct psychological oppression would be ineffective. The other cultural forces, those that work through tradition, religion, ideology, and cultural domination, can be countered by making clear the ways that they enforce oppression, since that will make clear the injustice they create. But like stereotypes, they cannot be so easily overcome, even if the injustice they create is obvious. To counter these deep-seated sources of cultural meaning will require acts of will by many people throughout the culture working to change them in the direction of freedom and opposing their oppressive force. In the next chapter we will see how oppressed groups and their allies in opposing oppression have, in some cases, been able to resist the forces of oppression to bring about justice.

PART III

WE SHALL OVERCOME

7

Resistance and Responsibility

Cautious, careful people always casting about to preserve their reputations or social standards never can bring about reform. Those who are really in earnest are willing to be anything or nothing in the world's estimation, and publicly and privately, in season and out, avow their sympathies with despised ideas and their advocates, and bear the consequences.

Susan B. Anthony

Resisting oppression is prima facie morally praiseworthy. Even if one is resisting her own oppression and thereby resisting harm to herself, since oppression is a harm to members of her social group, she is resisting harm to others. But not every reaction to or action inspired by oppression is resistance. Furthermore, people sometimes claim that their actions are aimed at resistance when they are really purely self-interested, vengeful, or misguided antisocial actions. A comprehensive theory of oppression needs to show us how to overcome or resist it and to be able to distinguish (and encourage) legitimate resistance from antisocial behavior or special interest politics. In this chapter I construct a theory of resistance that I claim allows us to classify reactions to oppression. I then go on to discuss the moral obligations that persons have to engage in resistance to oppression, given their social standing as oppressed or privileged persons. Finally, I catalog the various types of resistance strategies that have been or might be pursued against the forces of oppression that I discussed in the previous two sections of the book.

A preliminary objection threatens this project of defining resistance from the outset, however. Some will argue that the theory of oppression I have constructed shows that resistance is impossible, while others will claim that (on any theory) it is futile. To those who would claim it is futile, I simply urge them to look at the many examples of successful resistance, some of which I describe in this chapter. The more serious objection is the claim that resistance is impossible in my theory of oppression. A theory of oppression implies that resistance is impossible if persons, both oppressed and privileged, are constituted by the locus of their social group memberships. That is, if they cannot understand the world outside of the ways in which it is given to them externally. The theory of oppression I have presented does not fall prey to this objection. On my view, oppression (and privilege) consists of the inequality of constraints that persons face consequent on social group membership. But social group membership is externally imposed, and not necessarily a part of the self-identity of persons. Even when it becomes a part of one's self-identity, that requires one to take it on through acts that are, at least at times, conscious acts of mimicry. Thus, on my account of social groups, one's self-identification with a social group is something over and above group membership. Furthermore, since every person is a member of a number of social groups, some of which constrain our actions more than others, we can glimpse what the world would look like from different social perspectives. This leaves the space for one to attempt to separate oneself ontologically, epistemically, and morally from one's fellow social group members or from any particular group membership. To put it simply: we are individuals who must act within group-based constraints. Resistance is possible because even though we must take the constraints as given, we can choose to work against them. We need not fall prey to false consciousness or deformed desires, though these are understandable responses to oppression (or privilege). Resistance is possible whenever we think outside our collective boxes and sacrifice our immediate wants for a long-term vision of a better future.

1. A Theory of Resistance to Oppression

I propose three main criteria of adequacy that I claim any theory of resistance to oppression must meet. First, the theory should correctly classify the cases that we have clear intuitions on, and then in turn help us to classify the cases for which we have less clear intuitions. Second, the account of resistance should allow us to distinguish resistance from mere noncompliance, on one hand, and from self-deceptive compliance, on the other. Some cases of noncompliance will, of course, count as resistance, even as paradigm cases of resistance. Imagine, for example, the Nazi soldier who refuses to comply with his superior's order to shoot a group of unarmed civilians because he regards it as a violation of human rights. By "mere noncompliance" I mean to refer to cases where for reasons (or causes) completely unrelated to the morality of the command one fails to comply. Suppose, for instance, the soldier failed to shoot the civilians only because he was distracted by a beautiful sunset. Further, we would not want to count acts of collaboration as acts of resistance. Third, our account of resistance should, in conjunction with a moral theory, allow us to distinguish morally good from morally bad from nonmoral cases of resistance, for we use "resistance" to cover all three sorts of actions, even though there is a connotation of moral praiseworthiness to the term.

An adequate theory of resistance to oppression will allow us to classify the obvious cases of resistance correctly. Resistance can be undertaken by an individual or by a group of individuals, and just as I identified two kinds of groups in chapter 2, there are two corresponding kinds of group resistance. Voluntary group resistance occurs when there is a planned, intentional resistance by a group, such as the Freedom Riders in the Civil Rights Movement in the southern United States in the 1960s. Nonvoluntary group resistance occurs when the resistance is undertaken by many members of an oppressed voluntary group, but without prior planning or intention, although such resistance may lead to voluntary group resistance. Fundamentally, resistance is undertaken by individuals in individual or collective acts of resistance. The aim of the resistance can be either to end oppression of an entire group or to release an individual from the immediate effects of oppression. Resistance will only result in the end of oppression, however, when taken up by a group of resisters.

Let us take as test cases for our analysis the following three examples of these different kinds of resistance to oppression. First, Gandhi's hunger strike aimed at removing the British from colonial India. In this case there was a clear aim, the aim was the end of oppression for an entire group, and a single individual with some hope of success could undertake the resistance.[1] The second case I propose is African American slave escapes. In this case I suppose that commonly the escaping individual intended in the first instance to free himself, and only in the second instance, if at all, to bring about the end of slavery overall. The third case is the Palestinian Intifada. In this case the aim of the individuals participating might be to end legal, social, and economic injustice, or it might be to run the Israelis out of Palestine and the occupied territories altogether, but in any case it is aimed at eliminating oppression at a group level. In this case, unlike the other two, a single individual could not hope to succeed acting alone, but only through a concerted effort of a large percentage of the population. Two cases that we would not want our theory to classify as resistance to oppression are Theodore Kaczynski, the so-called Unabomber, who claimed to be resisting the growth of technology, and the scattered men's movements to resist paying child support, who claim to be resisting the oppression of men by domestic laws biased in favor of women.

Consider the following rough characterization of resistance to oppression, which we will proceed to sharpen through an analysis of cases and objections:

An act of "resistance to oppression" is an act that *issues from* an *actual case* of oppression, *in the right way.*

This seems to be a good start, but the three phrases that are italicized each require clarification. We would not want to classify just any resistance to coercion as resistance to oppression, since not all coercion is oppressive. Resisting a mugger's demand of your wallet is surely not resistance to oppression. In defining resistance to oppression I shall refer to the four criteria of oppression that I have used throughout the book. So by "an actual case of oppression" I mean that the resistance has to be to a case that meets these four criteria (the group, harm, privilege, and coercion criteria) in order to be considered resistance to oppression. Next, the phrase "issues from" in my definition is obviously too vague. What sort of causation is implied? For example, would actions that are only accidentally linked to oppression count? Finally, the phrase, "in the right way," suggests that only certain sorts of actions that issue from oppression count. Would a bank robber's actions issue from oppression if he were a member of a discriminated-against minority (and hence be excused)? Even if the oppression created the conditions under which bank robbery seemed to him to be his only option, we would not want to say that it was a case of resistance to oppression. Rather, it seems more like giving in to oppression. We need an account of causation that allows us to distinguish actions caused by one's experience (as a witness or as a victim) of oppression from actions that are not so caused, and among those actions that are caused by one's experience of oppression we need to be able to distinguish actions that constitute resistance to oppression from those that are either compliance or otherwise nonresistance. Furthermore, the account ought not rule out actions by the non-oppressed as cases of resistance; surely Michael Schwerner was a resister to oppression when he attempted to sign up black voters in the South.[2] So the experience of oppression that causes the action need not be of one's own oppression for it to count as resistance.

What does it mean to say that an experience of oppression *causes* an action? While it is beyond the scope of this book to defend it, the account of causation that seems to me correct and applicable here is John Mackie's (1965) account of causes as INUS conditions. That is, to say that A caused B is to say that A is an insufficient but necessary part of a condition that is unnecessary but sufficient to bring about B. And this is to say that although there may be many combinations of factors that would bring it about that B, among these combinations there is at least one, say the conjunction of A and several other factors, that is such that in the absence of A those other factors could not bring it about that B. For an action of resistance, R, to count as resistance to oppression, then, it must be that although R might have been brought about by many different sets of factors, an experience of oppression is a necessary condition for at least one of these sets, in particular, for the set of factors that did in fact bring it about that R. Thus, the bank robbery in the case above would not be a candidate for resistance if the robber's experience of oppression were not a necessary factor in the set of factors that cause him to rob the bank. On the other hand, if it was, then the robbery might in fact be a case of resistance. That depends now on whether the robbery was a part of a strategy to oppose the oppression or to work within the constraints oppression has set for the person. In other words, it depends on the intention of the agent who acts.

Experience of oppression can cause one to act either through the agent's intentions or subintentionally. In saying that an action can be intentionally caused I am adopting a Davidsonian account of reasons as causes (Davidson 1980). On this account, actions are caused by a combination of beliefs and pro-attitudes (i.e., desires, wishes, preferences). To say that an action A was intentionally caused is to say that the agent has a pro-attitude, P, toward some goal or end state, S, the agent believes that A will bring about S (call this belief B), and this combination of B and P causes A. So in combination with the INUS account of causes, that is to say that the B and P are each necessary factors of a jointly sufficient but unnecessary condition for A. For an experience of oppression to cause an action through the intentions of the agent is for that experience of oppression to have caused A by means of a belief or pro-attitude about oppression, i.e., the content of the belief or pro-attitude must refer to the experience of oppression. For example, the belief might be "that my people are oppressed" or "that oppression is unjust." Likewise, a pro-attitude caused by an experience of oppression might be a wish that oppression end, or a desire that the oppressor be killed.

An action can be subintentionally caused by oppression, too. Oppression can affect the formation of beliefs or pro-attitudes without the contents of those beliefs or pro-attitudes referring to oppression. For example, an experience of oppression might cause someone to kill another by so frustrating the agent that she kills out of a neurotically exaggerated desire for the other's death. To say that an action *issues from* oppression, then, is to say that the action is, either intentionally or sub-intentionally, caused by the oppression. This is to say that a belief about or pro-attitude toward the oppression either refers to or is subconsciously formed by an experience of oppression, and these beliefs and pro-attitudes formed an insufficient but necessary part of a sufficient but unnecessary condition for the act.

Now given this analysis of how oppression can cause actions, what is it for the experience of oppression to cause a resisting action *in the right way*? Must a person intend to resist oppression in order to be said to be resisting oppression? Contrary to the account of Howard McGary (McGary and Lawson 1992), I argue that there has to be an intention to lessen the oppression, and that the intention to lessen the oppression has to be a part of the cause of the action. McGary presents an example of a slave who kills a cruel overseer because the overseer is a rival for a girlfriend's affections and not because of his cruelty. While McGary maintains that this is resistance to oppression, I disagree. In my view, this slave intends murder in order for a personal goal that is not thwarted by the oppression. He does not intend to end or relieve or protest oppression and hence cannot be said to be resisting oppression by killing the overseer. Without requiring that the act be intended as a case of resistance, we cannot judge the morality of the action as an act of resistance. McGary claims that we cannot know what others intend, especially if they are dead, as in the case of African American slaves. But this just means that it will be difficult to judge in actual historical cases; it conflates the ontological and the epistemological. McGary objects further that intent "is not sufficient for others to establish that a person is resisting" (McGary and Lawson 1992, 40). But this just shows that intent is not a sufficient condition for resistance, a point that I agree with; it does not show that intention to resist is not a necessary condition for resistance. To be sure, McGary is more interested in the question of how historians should describe the events than in how we should judge the actions morally. As I see it, such considerations counsel us to use the principle of charity in imputing intentions to victims of oppression, but it does not show that we need not impute intentions at all.

In what sense does the person acting, in the case of an oppressed person, need to know about the oppression he suffers in order to be said to be resisting? One might argue that he needs to know that he suffers from oppression in order for the resistance to be *to* the oppression. But it is too strong to require that he know the theory of oppression that I offer here, or any theory of it for that matter. The case of the African American slaves illustrates my concern, though many others would as well. In their case, oppression had persisted for generations and many individual slaves had the false conscious belief that blacks are inferior to whites, yet still felt that their treatment by their owner was unjust.[3] An adequate account of resistance should include those who have some vague impression that they are suffering some injustice of the sort that oppression is, but need not have a clear conception of any particular theory of oppression or how their case fits it.

Resistance is clearly incompatible with collaboration with the oppressor, and so we should exclude actions that are nothing more than collaboration, even if the actor thinks that he is resisting. Roger Gottlieb (1990) discusses an example of this kind of self-deceptive collaboration that seems to the actor to be resistance in the case of the *Judenrat* in the ghettoes of Europe during the Nazi occupation. The *Judenrat* were the Jewish leaders who organized the ghettoes and the orderly shipment of Jews to the concentration camps, but rationalized their actions by saying that if they did not do this then the Nazis would do it in such a way that even more would be killed. Judgments about whether an act constitutes collaboration require care. Short-term collaboration, though, can be part of a long-term strategy of resistance. Consider the case of Oskar Schindler, who collaborated with the Nazis to the extent of running some factories for them to make it possible for him to save Jews from the gas chambers by employing them as slave laborers. If we want to distinguish resistance from self-deceptive collusion with the oppressor, it has to be possible for the act of resistance to effect the long-term or overall lessening of oppression, or at least to send a message of revolt to the oppressors.[4]

We can see from our test cases that there are two ways that persons can lessen oppression or send a message of revolt, which we might term "personal" and "distributive," where the former attempts to lessen oppression or send a message of revolt for a single person and the latter attempts to lessen the oppression of or send a message of revolt for an entire group. We can further divide each of these two types of resistance into two categories: the resistance can be carried out either by a single person or through the coordinated or spontaneously coincident actions of a number of persons. An act of resistance, then, can fall into one of four categories: by an individual toward the end of lessening oppression or sending a message of revolt for an individual, by an individual toward the end of lessening oppression or sending a message of revolt for a whole group, by a group toward the end of lessening oppression or sending a message of revolt for an individual, or by a group toward the end of lessening oppression or sending a message of revolt for a group. I can see no persuasive reason to exclude the personal cases from the account, even when directed at reducing one's own oppression; if there can be duties to the self, then surely this must be one. Individually undertaken actions that are aimed at lessening the oppression of the person acting will count as resistance to oppression, for example, a slave who commits suicide to end her slavery.

Since much of the harm of oppression is psychological and has to do with creating a false and oppressive image of members of oppressed groups, some acts of resistance will be mainly symbolic or rhetorical. Under these headings I would include building theories and ideas that reveal oppression, proposing and lobbying for laws that relieve oppression, and creating counter-images through art and the public media to counteract oppressive stereotypes and false consciousness. As with physical acts, these symbolic acts might be aimed at relieving an individual's or some small set of individuals' suffering of oppression or at ending the oppression of an entire social group.

A person or group resists only when they act in a way that could result in lessening oppression or sending a message of revolt or outrage to someone. My account does not categorize as resistance cases where the only ones witnessing the action are incapable of receiving a message of revolt and there is no lessening of oppression. Such cases are surely rare. It is possible to send a message to oneself of revolt or outrage and for this message to be illuminating about oneself. So this sort of case would somehow involve even one's own inability to see the action as resistance. Still, one might argue that even if the agent cannot see the action as resistance, it might actually be resistance when viewed in the better vision of hindsight. However, if such cases count as resistance it is difficult to see resistance as an object of moral praise. Since I am ultimately concerned with the moral duties to resist, I do not regard this omission as unfortunate.

Whose judgment is to count concerning what is possibly effective in lessening oppression or sending a message of revolt, however? Because oppression often restricts the education and experience of the oppressed, we do not want to exclude cases where the person attempting to resist or send a message does so in a way that is not possibly effective for reasons she could not have known. McGary proposes a "reasonable person" criterion (though in a slightly different context). The purpose is to rule out cases of self-deception, but not reasonable, or at least understandable, misjudgments about what might be effective. To implement the criterion we imagine a reasonable person in the same situation. What counts as a reasonable person cannot be easily described; persons are always situated in a historical context with social norms of what constitutes reasonableness. The reasonable person criterion has to be sensitive to what persons can be expected to know given their race or gender or class, and perhaps other social groupings as well. Furthermore, what counts as a relief of oppression also will be contextually determined. For a religious person it may be a lessening of oppression just to practice one's religion, even at the cost of death. Since oppression involves harm, the question of whether oppression is lessened turns on whether the harm has been reduced, lessened, or mitigated. Although this involves subjective elements (since the harm is experienced by individual subjects), that is not to say that the issue is a relative one; the oppression either is or is not reduced by the actions. The same can be said for sending a message of revolt: it involves subjective elements, but it is ultimately an objective matter whether a message was sent or received. The reasonable person criterion applies the prevailing social norms for determining harm and the conceivable methods of lessening it in the given situation. Thus, what is needed is a person who is situated similarly in terms of all the relevant social groupings to the person whose actions one is judging. The test can be summarized as follows: Would a reasonable person, who is similarly situated, think the act is not entirely unlikely to bring about a lessening of oppression or send a message of revolt or outrage?

My account of resistance in light of these further considerations may be summarized as follows:

> A person P is said to be resisting the oppressive situation S through action A just in case, given a reasonable person P' who is situated as P is, the following is true:
>
> 1. P' would regard S as oppressive;
> 2. P believes S is unjust for someone;

3. P' would judge that A is not unlikely to effect the lessening of oppression or send a message of revolt or outrage, either for some individual member of or the entire oppressed group;

4. P intends to lessen the oppression or feeling of injustice or send a message of revolt through A;

5. The injustice in (2) and the intention in (4) cause P to perform A.

This account allows us to focus on the moral implications of an action that resists oppression by setting the most stringent requirement on the intentions of the agent. While it requires that the action be something that could reasonably be expected to be effective, it makes this judgment of reasonableness from the perspective of the agent.

On this account the test cases come out right: Gandhi and the escaping slave are both clearly resisting oppression on this account, since both intended to lessen oppression, either of a whole group or her own, and could be reasonably expected to succeed with their chosen course. The Palestinian Intifada is resistance to oppression, since a reasonable person in the Palestinian's situation would think their actions are not unlikely to be expressive of revolt or outrage, even if they are judged unlikely to be effective. The Unabomber's actions are not resistance to oppression because the growth of technology is not oppressive, even if it was annoying to him. Furthermore, the actions he undertook—letter bombs sent to individuals with no real power to stem the growth of technology—could not be expected reasonably to lessen it or even to protest it because of the incoherence and obscurity of the message itself. The men's movements against paying child support are also not resistance to oppression because men are not, as a group, oppressed by their treatment by family law. Any one individual man may be the victim of an unjust decision by a judge but not because men are an oppressed social group. The fact that the law more often requires men to pay child support and women to have custody stems from the different roles men and women play as fathers and mothers and the greater wealth of men as a group. But these differences privilege men and oppress women, even if there are individual men who wish to play greater roles in their children's lives or who have less access to wealth than the default assumptions made by the law. Thus, the men's movements are misaimed. If they aimed to end the oppression of women by sex role differentiation and all that entails (i.e., the gender wage gap and the resulting coercive expectations of women to be caregivers and men to be breadwinners), then it would be resistance to oppression and it might also have the happy result of lessening the harm to individual men who wish for custody of their children.

This account of resistance to oppression, when supplemented with a moral theory, allows us to distinguish the morally good cases of resistance, on the one hand, from the immoral and nonmoral cases on the other. Since oppression is by definition unjustified, resistance to oppression, as lessening the unjustified harm, is at least prima facie justified. A reasonable moral theory would require that the act of resistance has to be proportional to the oppression and aimed at the right persons (i.e., those who cause or continue the oppression). Thus, terrorism, or violence aimed at civilians for the purpose of creating terror in a population, would normally not be justified, all things considered. One might object that since, on my account, oppression is institutional, there may not be any "right persons." But this is where my theory of social groups as fundamentally composed of individual persons is crucial. There may not be any identifiable oppressors, but because institutions are fundamentally constituted of persons and patterns of individual behavior, there must be at least lots of persons who myopically go along with, even if they never really recognize, an oppressive institution. Those who simply go along with oppression are surely less culpable than persons who recognize and intentionally perpetuate oppression for their own benefit, however, so a resister should treat the former less harshly. In the next section I discuss the issues of responsibility for resistance to oppression.

2. Moral Responsibility for Resistance

What are the moral obligations, if any, of persons to resist oppression? This question must be answered differently for persons who are privileged relative to the oppression under consideration and those who are oppressed by it. There are two questions to separate, then. First, what are the moral obligations to resist of the persons who are privileged by a particular case of oppression? Second, what are the moral obligations to resist of the persons who are oppressed? An objection that has been raised to even asking this question is that by focusing on the victims' obligations I am "blaming the victim." This is a serious concern that I will take pains to alleviate by showing how to avoid wrongful victim-blaming. The first and most important way to do so is to recognize that the victims are not the only ones who are obligated to resist.

2.1. *The Obligations of the Privileged Social Group*

Oppression, by definition, implies injustice, and so someone or some entity has at least a prima facie obligation to end the oppression (Calhoun 1989; May 1992). Those who commit injustice or immoral acts are, of course, obligated to desist. But with oppression it is often complicated to discern who is committing the injustice. I have distinguished between the oppressors and the (merely) privileged. Oppressors bear full moral responsibility for their part in oppression. To be an oppressor is to intend to act in order to continue or intensify the oppression of a social group. An oppressor may be unaware that the injustice that is being committed counts as oppression, or that the harm falls on a social group, but must be aware that he or she is acting unjustly and harming someone thereby. To be merely privileged by oppression is simply to gain materially or psychologically from it. Privilege comes to persons because they are members of a social group that benefits from the oppression that another social group suffers. The privileged need not seek, want, or even notice their benefits; the benefits are unavoidable for them. A clear example of this was John Stuart Mill's renunciation of his oppressive male conjugal rights upon his marriage to Harriet Taylor (Mill and Mill 1970, 45–46). Although it was a magnanimous and no doubt sincere gesture, it was impossible for him to give up the privileges marriage bestowed upon him for two reasons. First, he was able to appear magnanimous in giving them up, an ability that she did not have. Second, since the law did not recognize men's renouncing their rights, he could at any time in the future reclaim them, and that right gave him (to use the language of bargaining theory) a threat position better than hers. Thus, even a feminist such as John Stuart Mill was privileged, if unwillingly, by the oppression of women.

Oppressors, on any reasonable moral theory, are morally required to desist and remedy past harm. There are usually several obstacles to motivating oppressors to do so. Sometimes they do not recognize the depth of the harm that they do. Sometimes they are not moved by the harm that they do because they believe that the oppressed persons are not their moral equals. Sometimes the oppressors are simply moral slackers: they recognize the harm and that the persons they are harming are their equals, but they do not act because they are weak of will or simply immoral. The oppressor has to be very clearly and firmly addressed, and I suggest strategies for doing so in the next section of this chapter.

Privileged non-oppressors are in a more ambiguous moral position than oppressors, although their position is less ambiguous than that of the oppressed. Since they are receiving undeserved benefits through institutions that harm others, the privileged non-oppressors are morally obligated to resist and attempt to change those institutions and to renounce privilege when they are capable of doing so. John Stuart Mill, whose renunciations upon marriage I have mentioned, acted morally with respect to his privilege as a man. Not only did he attempt to renounce privilege but he also worked, through his writings and his actions, to end the oppression of women. However, Mill also was somewhat blind to other privileges, such as his race and social class, and could not be seen as acting in an exemplary way with respect to those systems of privilege.[5] But did he act immorally with respect to these other systems of oppression?

To be privileged is to be able to be blind to a system of oppression and the privileges it grants one (Frye 1983; Bailey 1998). Whites are able to think of themselves as raceless, for example. But if one is raceless, then it impossible for one's race to give one privileges. Thus, being privileged and failing to see privilege commonly go together. On most moral theories, one cannot be held responsible for failing to act to end an immoral situation that one does not see. But one might be able to recognize oppression or unjust harm without recognizing one's own role in that as a privileged recipient of benefits. To see what moral obligations the privileged non-oppressor has, we will have to separate the obligations with respect to oppression from those with respect to privilege. A privileged non-oppressor who recognizes that there is a system of oppression or that a person is treated unjustly is obligated to relieve that situation just in the way that anyone who recognizes that there is an injustice or harm is obligated to help to alleviate it if he or she can do so without sacrificing something of equal or greater moral significance. A privileged non-oppressor who also recognizes her privilege is obligated to renounce those privileges, where possible.

Some ignorance of oppression and privilege is morally blameworthy in itself. If a good case has been made that there is oppression, and that case is generally well known throughout society, then one is responsible for the knowledge of oppression, and hence also for doing one's part toward alleviating it. If one also can be held responsible for the knowledge of one's privilege, as would certainly be the case for whites, Americans, men, wealthy, and able-bodied persons with respect to at least some systems of oppression, then one is obligated to resist the oppression and renounce privilege where possible. In this sense, perhaps, John Stuart Mill may be excused somewhat for some of his ignorance of privilege. But I believe that he, of all people, should have been able to recognize more of the oppressions that privileged him, because of his keen sense of gender injustice.

Resistance to oppression is never easy, either for the privileged or for the oppressed. As the quote from Susan B. Anthony that begins this chapter suggests, resistance means going against the prevailing norms of society. This requires courage and commitment and sometimes extracts a serious penalty. Joan Browning, who, as a young woman protested Jim Crow laws by participating in the Freedom Ride, writes of how it utterly changed the course of her life because of the social stigma that her community placed on being seen as a rebel.

> Being part of the Freedom Movement was a life-changing experience. In partici-
> pating, I lost my only real opportunity for a higher education, and I was alienated
> from my church. I experienced a lifelong separation from my large and loving fam-
> ily, and was set apart from the world in ways that affected all my relationships and
> employment options. For me, and for many other women like me, participation
> made us outcasts—women without a home. (Browning et al. 2000, 198)

Browning does not regret her actions, but she writes clearly and honestly about what they cost her. She was doing what she saw as, and what most people would now see as, her moral duty. Doing one's duty in any realm extracts different costs, but it is important to point out in this book that the expected costs of resistance will sys-tematically differ with one's relation to systems of privilege and oppression. The costs were certainly higher for Browning, a poor, rural, Southern woman, than they were for the white male college students from the North who were also part of the Civil Rights Movement but were able to return to their homes after doing their duty having lost perhaps only a summer's wages.

This discussion shows the importance of generating general social knowledge of oppression. For most of the persons who are well-placed and more easily motivated to end oppression are the privileged non-oppressors. Yet they are also motivated, if unconsciously, to avoid knowing about their privileges, as we saw in chapter 3.[6] Thus, it is important that information about oppression be prominently and con-vincingly presented so that it is undeniable and inescapable.

2.2. *The Obligations of the Oppressed Social Group*

It is usually the case that coercion implies no moral responsibility for the coerced actions and omissions. However, this is not always true.[7] Consider the soldier who is ordered by his superior in battle to kill noncombatants. There are times when we hold someone morally responsible for actions that they could have omitted only on pain of death. It is usually the case that when we choose to do something we are held morally responsible for our action. But this judgment is also defeasible; consider the case of the temporarily insane person who kills her child's murderer. In cases of oppression by choice, as we discussed in chapter 4, there is both choice and coercion. The normal and (morally) problematic choice is to participate in the coercive institution. Choosing not to participate is a kind of resistance to a social force that, given the institutional framework, makes the resistance also a sacrifice for the individual. Hence we must ask: *Are the oppressed obligated to engage in resistance?*

Our moral intuitions as exhibited in our everyday talk about such situations give us somewhere to begin. Within a group of workers on strike, those who continue to work at the factory while the others are on strike are "scabs"; to the strikers they are doing something hateful. To those outside the group of strikers there may be more sympathy for those who continue to work, however. In the women's movement there is a mixed reaction to women who fill the traditional role of unpaid domestic worker. The current rhetoric of the women's movement says "allow everyone to choose the way to fulfill her life, whatever that choice might be," without regard to the consequences women's individual choices have for other women or how her preferences might have developed.[8] But there is a distinct undercurrent that homeworking unpaid mothers feel that they are somehow doing something that feminists disapprove of,[9] and it seems to be the implication of the analysis of the Larry and Lisa example of chapter 5. Like all moral intuitions, these require both conceptual and empirical investigation to justify a judgment. The remainder of this section will attempt to account for these moral intuitions, clarify the confusions, and resolve the apparent paradox of obligations on the part of the oppressed to resist oppression.

Is resistance by the oppressed ever morally required? If so, then should we hold blameworthy at least some of those victims of oppression who do not choose resistance? For example, we might agree with the judgment of the strikers who call those who cross picket lines and continue to work "scabs." I shall take these two questions in turn. Whether we actually want to apply social sanctions to persons who fail to resist is another separate moral issue. (Surely those responsible for the initial oppression have no moral authority to do so.)

It is implausible to suggest that resistance to oppression by the oppressed is morally required at all times with respect to all forms of oppression. I say this for two basic reasons. First, the oppressed may well not understand the oppression they suffer, for it is often a part of their oppression that it is hidden from them under the guises of tradition or divine command or the natural order of things. It would therefore be even more difficult for them to judge what actions are required of them to resist their oppression. Second, oppression is such a pervasive condition of one's life that it would be impossible to struggle against all of it at once. The slave could resist by escaping, for instance, only when the timing is right, but nearly always there is some other way that he could resist. He could refuse to work, try to kill his master, refuse to eat, and so on. But these actions are most likely mutually exclusive. Refusing to work or refusing to eat, for example, puts the master on guard with that slave so that he will not have the opportunity to perform the other acts of resistance. Or, in gathering strength to escape or to revolt, the slave might need to eat and appear to acquiesce for a time.

Resistance to oppression does not seem to fit the duty model, for two reasons. First, the situation that would obligate is coercive. That is, the oppressed are unfairly and unavoidably put in their situation, and coercion normally mitigates moral obligation or responsibility. Of course, it is not true that one is never obligated in an unfair or unavoidable situation. For instance, we have duties to our parents in most cases even though their being our parents is unavoidable (for us), and the duties may be somehow unfair (say, one's siblings refuse to take their turns in helping them out when they are incapacitated). The second reason that resistance to oppression does not seem to fit the duty model has to do with the forms of resistance open to oppressed persons. Sometimes the only way to resist is in concerted effort with others, and if the others will not act, then one's own action might fail to constitute resistance at all. If you are the only worker at the plant who is willing to strike, then it cannot be a duty for you to strike, since your action will likely be ineffective even in sending a message of revolt (e.g., if you just look like a shirker). And if striking (when others strike) is the only course of resistance in this case, then it cannot be a duty to resist.

If resistance to oppression is not a duty, perhaps resistance goes beyond duty and is best judged as morally heroic or supererogatory. David Heyd (1982) presents a reasonable model of supererogation that goes as follows.

An action is supererogatory if and only if all of the following conditions hold.

> (1) The action is neither obligatory nor forbidden.
> (2) Its omission is not wrong and does not deserve sanction.
> (3) It is morally good.[10]
> (4) It is done voluntarily for the sake of someone else's good.

One might object that resistance to oppression does not fit this model because it is aimed at reducing one's own suffering. I think that this should cause us to rethink the model to allow for supererogatory actions that are aimed at oneself. But even if we take the model as it is, resistance to oppression by choice is often aimed at the elimination of oppression for the whole group, and we could restrict the heroic actions to those that aim at ending the oppression of a group or some members of an oppressed group other than oneself.

If resistance to oppression is not strictly a duty, then resistance to oppression is not obligatory, and surely it is also not forbidden, so condition (1) is satisfied. Condition (3) is also satisfied, since to count as a case of resistance to oppression it has to be intended to reduce oppression, that is, to lessen undeserved harm. However, resistance to oppression does not meet condition (2) in all kinds of cases, particularly not in those I termed oppression by choice. (Resistance to other kinds of oppression would meet condition (2) and so arguably be supererogatory.[11]) In oppression by choice the alternative to resistance is participation in the oppressive institution. *By participating in an oppressive institution, one lends some strength and stability to it, perhaps even legitimates it to some degree.*[12] This point is crucial and deserves some elaboration. Institutions are coordinated actions of individual people. Part of what makes institutions so effective at coordinating is they embody the common knowledge of what people will do in certain types of situations, and this in turn narrows down the range of choices of actions one is to perform to a manageable number. This common knowledge becomes stronger and more stable the more times that the expected actions are performed. So if an oppressive institution requiring the actions of the oppressed to be of a certain sort (e.g., female house-cleaning, male shirking) is effective in so coordinating actions in a given case, then it becomes an even greater expectation on the part of others that they will perform the required actions, as well. One has only two options in such cases: resist or strengthen the unjust institution. Thus, in cases of oppression by choice *failing to resist harms others.*

We are left with the situation where one must do harm whether one resists or not, and there is no duty other than the general duty to avoid doing (unde-served) harm. The solution is to do the least undeserved harm. That is, one must weigh the harm of resisting against the harm produced by not resisting. In many cases the harm of not resisting is distributive, though the harm of resisting is felt fully by the individual involved. In calculating these harms one has to also consider the self-esteem that is lost by harming others through one's own failure to resist oppression. In some cases one ought only resist with some sort of symbolic resistance or protest, which causes one less harm than another form of resistance (Hill 1991; Harvey 1996). In my view, then, a duty to resist may be uncommon though not inconceivable. Yet, I do not think it is so uncommon. One important way for the oppressed to resist is by not themselves enforcing oppressive norms on others in their group. For example, it is often said that women are each others' harshest critics, harshest enforcers of the prevailing oppressive norms of female fashion, beauty, morality, and sexual double standards. If women were simply to refrain from criticizing other women who resist those oppressive norms, they would themselves play a part in resistance. This is a nearly costless[13] way of resisting, and thus is morally required in my view.

One might object that insisting that the oppressed have a duty to resist their oppression is a case of blaming the victim, in the pejorative sense. J. Harvey (1996) categorizes the ways in which victims can be blamed in morally objectionable ways. There are three categories that Harvey mentions that might be relevant to this analysis of the morality of resistance:

> [Category 4]: There was in fact moral harm, but then *it is claimed that* in accounting for it, we must look at some crucial contribution from the victim involving some moral or nonmoral failing.
> [Category 5]: There was in fact moral harm and the crucial responsibility of the actual agent is acknowledged, but then *it is claimed that* some contribution from the victim makes the harm more serious than it would otherwise have been, and that that contribution involves some moral or nonmoral fault of the victim.
> [Category 6]: There was some harm, and any responsibility for it by an agent is acknowledged (including how serious it is), but once the harm has occurred, then *it is claimed that* something untoward in the victim's response makes the ultimate outcome worse than it would otherwise have been, and that that response involves some moral or nonmoral fault of the victim. (Harvey 1996, 49–51, emphasis mine)

While I admit that I am victim-blaming in these senses, I think that whether it is wrong to "blame the victim" in these senses depends first on whether the "claim" in the italicized phrases in each category is true. That is, Harvey says it is victim-blaming to claim that the victim either made some contribution to the harm or responded in some untoward way that made the outcome worse than it otherwise would have been. If the claim is false, then these kinds of victim-blaming are mere rationalizations of the victimization. But if the claim is true, then the victim may, depending on the relative contributions of the actions to the harm, shoulder some of the blame for the harm that came about. Just because one is a victim one is not thereby absolved of all responsibility for the outcome of the situation. Suppose someone superficially cuts you while carelessly using a sharp scissors in your vicinity. You are a victim. But that does not mean that if you now refuse to wash the cut or take care of it in any way (supposing that you have clean water, band-aids, and neosporin available to you) you can blame the person who cut you when you lose your hand to gangrene. You are to blame for some of the harm, even though you are a victim. If the claim is true, there is another way that one could still objectionably victim-blame: by focusing on the victims' faults out of all proportion to their relative contribution to the harm. I take this to be a serious concern and a caution to be heeded. But we must not therefore shrink from an honest assessment of the full causal and moral situation.

3. Strategies of Resistance

Now that we have an understanding of what resistance to oppression is and who is required to undertake it, we can begin to explore effective strategies for overturning or abolishing oppressive situations. Many of these strategies are treated at great length by others, and as a philosopher, I do not have much to add to those analyses. My main concern is to catalog the forms of resistance to see whether there are effective strategies against each force of oppression that I have discussed in the book. In the last part of this section I offer one original contribution for constructing a legal strategy to resist oppression.

In the previous section I argued that the privileged non-oppressors are most well placed and easily motivated to resist oppression but also the most motivated consciously or unconsciously to ignore it. I also argued that the oppressed are often motivated to cooperate with oppressive institutions, in part because they see it as in their self-interest to do so, and as I argued in chapter 6, they may be under the sway of false consciousness and deformed desires as a result of their oppression. These facts imply that the first essential element in successful resistance is raising consciousness about particular cases of oppression and building a moral case against them. Gloria Steinem, who has done much to raise consciousness about women's oppression, writes that "there can be no [major social change] without words and phrases that first create a dream of change in our heads" (Steinem 1983, 2). This task, I take it, is both theoretical and rhetorical. The case has to be made that there is oppression, and it has to be simply and powerfully expressed. In this book I have made the case for several examples of oppression, but many others have done so as well, and more simply and powerfully than I have. The theoretical task is not finished, however. There remains much to be done theoretically to recognize and interpret particular social interactions and patterns of interactions that reveal social structures as oppressive. In the previous chapter I listed three specific roles for theory in resisting oppression. First, we need to attack existing oppressive role schemas and their rationalizations. We might do that, for instance, by showing how sociobiological explanations of the sexual division of labor depend on androcentric assumptions and privilege men. Second, we need to propose alternative categories for social groupings that depend more on interest than on accidents of birth, on voluntary groupings rather than involuntary groups. Third, I suggested that we can reveal false consciousness and deformed desires where they exist by exposing the ways in which assimilating oneself to involuntary in-groups and accentuating the differences with involuntary out-groups is, in at least some cases, either an assertion of undeserved privilege or a failure to resist one's own oppression. But theory reaches few people and so cannot fight oppression alone.

3.1. *Rhetorical and Symbolic Strategies*

Rhetoric is both a cognitive and affective strategy that challenges stereotypes of oppressed groups and the false consciousness that accompanies oppression, and persuades and motivates change. Rhetorical strategies range widely from purely cool rational uses of persuasive speech to passionate and creative uses of speech, poetry, art, photography, film, and theater. Martin Luther King, Jr.'s "Letter from Birmingham Jail" is a sustained explanation and defense of the nonviolent resistance tactics of the Civil Rights Movement. It contains not only a defense of the actions but also a sustained argument against the injustices of apartheid and black oppression. On the other hand, his famous "I Have a Dream" speech is full of the creative and allegorical imagery that inspired many to recognize oppression and resist it through his passionate oratorical style. This speech is known to every American schoolchild and revered by most Americans, even those who did not recognize then the injustice of apartheid and do not now recognize the continuing legacy of black oppression. Yet it is such a motivating piece of rhetoric that it has won over the hearts and minds of Americans enough for all to recognize the justice of King's cause.

Some of the most effective rhetoric aims to motivate with humor. The Guerilla Girls are a group of activist feminist artists who stage humorous shows and make posters and billboards to spread their feminist messages. They often state a fact, but dress it up in sarcastic language and imagery to catch the attention of the viewer and yet relay the statistic that underlies their resistance to women's oppression. For example, one billboard boldly states that "Even the U.S. Senate is more Progressive than Hollywood" and has a picture of Sen. Trent Lott's head on top of an Oscar trophy. Underneath are two boxes stating: "Female Senators: 14%" and "Female Directors: 4%." This is an arresting image, and relays the facts, both of which clearly, quickly, and inescapably challenge anyone to deny that women are oppressed in this society.

Other effective rhetoric is specifically aimed at informing the oppressed about their unjust condition and motivating them to resist. Paulo Freire's (1970) work on teaching the oppressed to read and through it to be politically active is among the most famous and effective in this regard. The pedagogical strategy stresses dialogue and equality between teacher and student, modeling both equal relations among persons and activism to change persons' lives.

Public recognition of resisters and martyrs (e.g., Martin Luther King, Jr.'s birthday as a national holiday) and public apologies for past oppression communicate the ideas that resistance to oppression is valuable and honorable. They also recognize the harms of the oppression and honor the victims of that oppression. These events can also serve as good occasions on which to reflect on the legacy of privilege and oppression for social groups that are the descendants of the oppressors and oppressed. Several nations of the world owe their existence to the genocide or near genocide of former inhabitants of the same lands. In New Zealand, Australia, and Canada, in particular, activists of different ethnicities call for the remembrance of those victims, apologies from the descendants of the oppressors, and reparations to the people now living who still suffer harm from those acts of oppression.

Apology and reparation movements are less successful in the United States, despite the obvious crimes of genocide, forcible removal from ancestral lands, mass kidnapping, murder, and slavery. In the United States the argument has been that individuals who are now alive bear no moral responsibility for the crimes of their ancestors. While this is surely true, it is beside the point. An apology would serve the rhetorical purpose of resisting the current oppression that is the responsibility of the privileged citizens. American Indians lack wealth and access to their ancestral lands, and they are harmed by this. At the same time, non-Indians are far more likely to own wealth and to have the possibility of owning those very lands because of the actions of the U.S. government to forcibly remove and kill Indians. Americans of any ethnicity cannot decouple the connection with this genocidal past because the wealth and resources of America are the spoils of those actions. Likewise, slavery considerably increased the total wealth and power of America, and therefore implicates all who enjoy that wealth and power today. Granted, the responsibility of a modern American is not for the original oppression—genocide and slavery—itself, but rather his or her duty is to resist the continuing oppression that is a legacy of that original oppression because he or she is benefited by it and others are harmed by it.[14]

The most powerful symbol of protest against oppression remains the protest march with masses of marchers; the more massive the march, the more effective the protest. Simply the fact that so many people get the word that there is a march, then feel moved to show up for the march, taking time out of their daily routines, perhaps also risking violent treatment by police or counter-demonstrators, persuades others that there are serious problems that demand attention. The massing of persons may be effective in part because it threatens less benign future actions if their issues are not attended to. For example, massive work slow downs or boycotts may be next. Or perhaps even violent struggle. Massive demonstrations engage the media in the cause, since they are newsworthy events. This brings more resisters to the cause. Of course, not all mass demonstrations are resistance to oppression. Dictators can demand that people show up so that they can demonstrate that the government has the support of the people. People may also mass together to resist progressive social change, as the yearly protests against the *Roe v. Wade* Supreme Court decision guaranteeing women abortion rights shows. What these mass demonstrations illustrate is that all such massive gatherings demand attention and explanation, which offers the demonstrators the opportunity to make their case to the public.

Rhetorical and symbolic strategies are useful, necessary, and appropriate for every form of oppression that I have discussed in this book. They raise awareness of oppression on the part of privileged and oppressed persons, as well as others who might be allies or whose opposition to resistance might otherwise effectively prevent it. These strategies also motivate resistance and teach people how to resist. They empower the oppressed with a sense that something can be done and that a future free of oppression is possible. They embarrass the oppressor and reveal his shameful conduct to the world. But, as I have argued throughout, there are powerful material motives for oppression, and these may not be nullified by the power of the pen or even mass protest alone. Hence the resister must resort to other means when rhetoric and symbol fail.

3.2. *Economic Strategies*

As we saw in chapter 5, money is one of the major motivations to oppress. If that motivation is removed, much oppression will cease. Some economic strategies of resistance trade on that fact. Workers who are coercively exploited by their employers can organize work stoppages or strikes to bargain for better wages and conditions of work. They can convince others to join them and effectively shut down an industry or even a nation. An important example of the power of a group of workers to bring about change was the Lawrence mill worker strike that coined the phrase "bread and roses."

On January 12, 1912, ten thousand woolen textile workers went on strike in Lawrence, Massachusetts, to protest pay cuts that left them unable to sustain themselves and their families. The strike was precipitated by a pay cut implemented by the American Woolen Company when a state law went into effect that reduced the weekly hours that women could legally work. This law provided an excuse for employers to capture all the benefits of their recent mechanization by reducing the wages for the women workers, who comprised most of the labor force. "For weeks the strikers held out, mobilizing support through rallies and other events that publicized their plight. By February almost thirty thousand strikers had stopped virtually all production in Lawrence. By mid-March all four of the strikers' chief demands were met" (Dublin and Harney n.d.). This strike was a significant event in the struggle for unskilled workers, women, and immigrants to achieve a living wage—a wage that could allow a person to live independently without charity or government assistance. Of course, success is not automatic. In 1981, for example, then U.S. President Ronald Reagan fired all of the nation's air traffic controllers rather than negotiate their demands with them. Strikers always risk the loss of their jobs, and in some cases violent attack, but even strikes that end badly can sometimes serve to raise awareness of oppressive conditions.

Labor unions can pursue other strategies of resistance than simply strikes, though it is the threat of possible strike that gives weight to the bargaining power of the union. Unions collectively bargain for wages, benefits, and working conditions for their workers, which gives them greater power in bargains than each worker could have alone. While the company collects the power of capital to formulate its threat point in the bargain, labor unions allow workers to accumulate their power to refuse to work or to slow work down in order to formulate their threat point. Furthermore, labor unions politically organize to support politicians whose policy proposals will further the ability of the workers to raise their threat points by protecting their ability to strike and to enforce collective bargaining for all workers in an industry.

Consumers can boycott the goods that are produced by firms that oppress their workers or in countries that oppress their people. This strategy is particularly delicate, however; it can easily be misaimed and end up hurting the victims of oppression more than helping them. For example, while it is surely good to boycott goods made by slave labor, it is less clear that it is a good idea to boycott goods made by workers who are poorly paid or made by (poorly paid) children (Becker and Cudd, 2003). The workers may consider the jobs to be the best way out of poverty that is available to them, and without a further plan to help them, consumers who boycott their products could be harming more than helping. Consumers have successfully boycotted the goods of firms that are oppressing people in other countries. The Nestlé boycott of 1974–1984 succeeded for a time in convincing that company not to falsely advertise the value of infant formula in countries where it was clearly better for women economically and for health reasons to breastfeed their children. (However, it appears that Nestlé is, as of this writing, again violating World Health Organization restrictions on marketing their products.) Consumers can also boycott the provision of inferior goods that enforce their oppression, such as the Montgomery bus boycott that protested the requirement that blacks sit in the back of the bus. The city of Montgomery, Alabama, realized that it was too expensive to continue that particular degrading practice and changed its rules rather than give up its bus system.[15]

Other economic strategies try to increase the economic power of those who are resisting oppression, in order to equal that of the oppressor or simply to raise the standard of living of the poor. Collective investment strategies allow persons to pool their limited funds to concentrate them on a solution to a particular oppressive problem. In many communities there are growing grass roots funds that are managed by small boards who distribute them to women in need of abortion services, but unable to get them because they are poor and because state-provided medical funding for the poor cannot be used for abortions. These funds are a form of resistance to the oppression of women through denial of abortion services. In many Third World countries, micro-credit agencies, such as the Grameen Bank, loan money to the poorest women to allow them to start small businesses to raise themselves and their families out of poverty. These agencies seek to become self-sufficient like other banks by recovering the loans with interest and then loaning the money to new poor clients. These banks attempt to eradicate poverty by empowering women to develop and use their own skills.

Other forms of development assistance by first world nations and intergovernmental agencies such as the World Bank, the International Monetary Fund, and the Agency for International Development are more ambiguously resistant to oppression. On the one hand, these agencies claim to aim at the eradication of world poverty, but, on the other hand, they have been spectacularly unsuccessful for the amount of investment, and many scholars and activists accuse them of having neo-colonial aims to keep the Third World relatively poor in order to provide cheap labor for the benefit of the First World. Since I addressed this charge in chapter 5, I will not belabor it here. These agencies can be important agents of resistance to poverty and the oppression of workers by helping people build schools and economic infrastructure in their countries that will enable them to resist being exploited by multinational corporations that seek to bid down the wages of workers to the lowest possible level. If that level is raised throughout the world, then an equalizing of world wages is inevitable. Of course, this will come at the expense of the privileged, who will have to compete for jobs with Third World workers, a fact that is bound to unleash a backlash that must also be resisted.

Economic strategies of resistance are primarily useful for resisting oppression by capitalist firms who seek to exploit workers through their greater bargaining power and the oppressive conditions of poverty. Through collective investment and micro-credit, poor persons can be empowered to resist other forms of oppression that are not directly economic. For example, a woman who is able to feed her children with her own labor can refuse to put up with an abusive husband or refuse to sell her girls into prostitution. She can send her children to school and provide them with tools to resist exploitation and oppression. A person who is able to labor his way out of abject poverty can hope for a better future and come to expect to be treated by others with dignity and respect.

3.3. Armed Struggle

Nonviolent strategies of resistance, such as those just mentioned, have often worked to bring about positive social and political change. Massive nonviolent actions have brought about the end of apartheid in the United States and South Africa, the end of colonial oppression in India, suffrage for women in England, the United States, and many other countries. Recent examples of "people power" have brought down oppressive Communist regimes in East Germany and Czechoslovakia, and overthrown dictators like Marcos in the Philippines and Suharto in Indonesia. However, when oppression is ongoing, massive, and violent, armed struggle is sometimes required to resist it. There exists a large literature on the morality of waging armed struggle or war; in philosophy it has long been known as "just war theory." If we view oppression of social groups as on a par morally with violent aggression by one nation on another—and I see no reason why we should not—then the just war arguments apply straightforwardly. I will not rehearse that literature, which dates back to the very beginnings of philosophy in the East as well as the West, here, but simply sketch the direction that one must go in applying the arguments.

Three basic principles of just war theory apply when deciding whether to apply force or resist nonviolently and how to apply the force. First, the force must be applied against the oppressors and not the innocent. Second, the force must be proportional to the violence that is being resisted. Third, violence should be the last resort and used only when it is likely to be successful. Most just war theorists hold that as long as one is a noncombatant one is among the innocent. The problem with this way of stating things, however, is that oppressors and innocents are not exhaustive categories. The privileged may be noncombatants and yet blameworthy for their participation in oppression. Yet the point of armed struggle as resistance to oppression is not to punish but to bring an end to oppression. One might argue that violence applied to the merely privileged could serve to bring about negotiations to end oppression and thus be an effective strategy. But this line of reasoning is not consistent with the second principle, that the violence of the struggle be proportional to the violence being resisted. Since the merely privileged are not violent, by hypothesis, they cannot be attacked if we are to remain consistent with the second principle. Furthermore, many of the oppressors are not violent either. The employer who discriminates and segregates acts oppressively but does not thereby do violence. Thus, to be consistent with the second principle we have to exclude both the merely privileged and the nonviolent oppressors as targets of armed intervention.

Why should we hope that the oppressed and their allies will accept the two principles stated above if they preclude action against many oppressors? There are two reasons. First, these are moral principles that can be independently justified. Second, because by adhering to them resisters to oppression have the best chance of bringing about a future of peace and justice after the violent oppression has been stopped. If nonviolent oppressors are attacked, they may reason that a violent reply on their part is justified as self-defense. Furthermore, if the nonviolent oppressors are working within the legal system of a state, such as a state that enforces liberal capitalism and allows discrimination, prohibits labor unions, or fails to provide a just social minimum, then they are likely to be defended by the state with force against resistive armed struggle. Unless the resisters apply enough violent force to overcome the state forces, they will likely fail and their use of force be seen as unjustified. Indeed anyone who holds that the second principle of just war is reasonable will agree that use of force against nonviolent oppressors is unjustified. If the resisters are able to overthrow state forces, then they will have the enormous task of nation-building ahead of them, a task that will be made more difficult by the fact that they have come to power through the questionable use of force. Hence, in my view, resisters should, both morally and pragmatically speaking, use nonviolent methods when opposing nonviolent oppressors.

Just war theory justifies violence to oppose violent oppressive force when it can be successful in bringing about positive change. The Algerian resistance to French colonialism that Franz Fanon reported on is among the best examples of successful violent resistance. Clearly violence made the French occupation very costly, and the costs soon outweighed the benefits of maintaining the colonial presence. Fanon argued that the guerilla war waged by the Algerians had other good social and psychological effects on the oppressed. First, it united the people in resistance to the French, making possible the subsequent task of nation-building. Second, since women fought alongside the men, Fanon argued that women's place was elevated in the formerly traditional Muslim society. Sadly we have seen the reintroduction of Muslim-inspired oppression of women in recent years in Algeria. Most importantly, according to Fanon, the people of Algeria regained a sense of self-respect that they did not have under colonial rule. Fighting for their freedom gave them pride and the sense that they could take care of themselves and shape the world as they wished, without the permission or aid of the European power.

Violent resistance may be justified as a response to violent oppression, but it may not always be prudent. If the violence is extremely unlikely to overcome the violent oppressors, it may be better to resist nonviolently raising the consciousness of the privileged and bringing them in as allies in the cause. Violent resistance, when it has little chance to overcome the violent, may be more like a suicide mission. When the violent oppressor is the nominally legitimate state power, unsuccessful violent resistance be seen by the privileged as even justifying the oppressive treatment by those in power. In early twentieth-century America, consciousness raising by people like Walter White and Ida Wells-Barnett to lynching was far more effective than any violent resistance that blacks could have offered. They were significantly outnumbered and less well armed, and to fight back would have confirmed the stereotype of blacks as violent, justifying harsh treatment of blacks in the minds of the privileged whites. The violent riots in the wake of the acquittal in 1993 of police who beat Rodney King was seen by many outside the black community of Los Angeles as justifying the typical treatment of blacks by the Los Angeles Police Department.

An important category of violent resistance to violent oppression is humanitarian intervention by the international community to stop genocide, aggressive wars by states on weaker neighbors, or massive human rights violations. In December 2001 the U.N.–appointed International Commission on Intervention and State Sovereignty (ICISS) issued a report entitled "The Responsibility to Protect," in which it examined the "right of humanitarian intervention" (International Development Research Centre 2001). The term "right" here is a misnomer, since it is rather the duty and responsibility of the international community to intervene when a state is unwilling or unable to avert serious harms to its people. But it is a revealing one, since military incursions undertaken for less savory political reasons are often defended on the grounds of the right of humanitarian intervention. Furthermore, intervention is sometimes not undertaken when it should be because no state sees its political interests promoted by intervening. Nevertheless, humanitarian intervention is sometimes morally required to stop oppression. The report sets out conditions under which intervention is justified and required. First there must be a "just cause," which is the state's inability or unwillingness to protect its people from mass terror, genocide, ethnic cleansing, mass rape, or forced expulsion. Second, the intervening military force must have the right intention, in particular, the intention to prevent those forms of violent oppression. Third, military intervention has to be the last resort, undertaken only after other means have been attempted to prevent catastrophe. Fourth, the force used is to be the minimal force necessary to secure human protection. Fifth, there has to be a reasonable chance of halting the oppression and the expected consequences of the military action have to be less than that of not intervening militarily.

Of who is military intervention required? The report names the United Nations as the only body that can authorize humanitarian intervention and claims that nations have a duty to provide troops when requested by the United Nations. While this sounds like a good solution in theory, in practice the United Nations sometimes cannot act because of the veto power of the members of the Security Council, and it cannot prevent unauthorized actions undertaken in the name of humanitarian intervention by the lone superpower. While the United Nations has the mandate from its member nations, in the abstract at least, to secure international peace, order, and human rights, nations find it difficult to act because of internal politics, and many deny an obligation to do so. Thomas Pogge (2002) has argued that nations and individuals who benefit from the existence of an international order that is stabilized by the United Nations owe their support to the United Nations in carrying out its mandate. This argument parallels my argument that the privileged are morally required to resist oppression. The Universal Declaration of Human Rights Article 22 states: "Everyone, as a member of society, has the right to social security and is entitled to realization, through national effort and international co-operation and in accordance with the organization and resources of each State, of the economic, social and cultural rights indispensable for his dignity and the free development of his personality." As I read this, following Pogge, this implies that indeed there is an obligation of those who live in relatively free, economically secure, human rights respecting nations to act together to secure such freedom, security, and rights for all. But in both the individual case and the international case, there may be too many oppressions for any one individual or one body to resist. This does not show that there is no obligation. It merely shows that the obligation is imperfect, at worst. Both individuals and the United Nations should deliberate about how best to use their resources to relieve as much suffering as possible.

3.4. *Legal Strategies to End Oppression within States*

A legitimate state must maintain a monopoly on the use of violence within that state. When mobs and individuals take the prerogative to use violence, oppression inevitably results. The first step one can take to end oppression is to demand that the state legislate and enforce strict laws against violence. When the state is ineffective in curtailing violent oppression, a group can argue that the state is failing to enforce internationally recognized human rights as set out in the Universal Declaration of Human Rights, or other conventions endorsed by the U.N. High Commission on Human Rights.[16]

The most destructive of the ways of humiliating and degrading people, such as through hate speech, group defamation, and harassment, can be resisted by legal means. However, law in contemporary liberal societies has only gone part way toward remedying the problems of recognized, oppressed groups. These societies have made one-on-one, direct violence and discrimination illegal, but still can be criticized for making the prosecution of some characteristic offenses against oppressed persons too difficult. Women are a prime example of how law fails in this way, and instead makes women who attempt to prosecute vulnerable to victim-blaming questions that compromise their cases. Why don't battered women just leave their spouses? How can they claim that they are acting in self-defense when they kill their sleeping husbands? Laws that restrict abortion rights seem to ask: why didn't the unwillingly pregnant woman use contraception or refrain from intercourse? When a woman charges rape, it is asked why she was where she could be in harm's way, rather than why the streets (or fraternity house) is not safe. Or consider the experience of Anita Hill. Many asked why did she not simply tell Clarence

Thomas to stop harassing her or resign (perhaps while threatening to sue if he did not write her an excellent recommendation) or at least not follow him from one job to another.

The perspective which the law currently takes on interactions between persons is one from which these seem like reasonable questions. Two theses characterize this perspective, which together constitute what I call the *equal individual perspective*. The first, the *individual actor thesis*, claims that crimes are committed by one person against another, and not by social group members against members of other social groups.[17] The second, the *level field thesis*, is the idea that criminal offenses are an upset in the existing balance of power between two people. Individuals are assumed to be equally situated with respect to social or political power, and crimes occur when one uses force or fraud to upset the balance of power between them. A social balance exists when persons are able to interact civilly, and when there are disputes, they are able to come to a resolution of disputes fairly (and privately), to the satisfaction of both parties, through the use of reason. "Social imbalance" happens when one party is able to take advantage of the other without the other's consent. Using economic power, that is, private wealth, to exploit or outbid another is not considered a disruption of the social balance, unless the bidding explicitly involves the political or judicial process (e.g., by selling votes or political influence). What counts as force or fraud changes over time and across societies that share our concept of law.[18] For instance, it may once have been acceptable to engage in a gunfight as long as both persons have guns and are facing each other prepared to fight, while now that is illegal. Furthermore, on the equal individual perspective a crime must directly affect the victim to affect him at all. If one's own person or property is not directly attacked, then one is not legally harmed. In particular, group defamation or group harm do not constitute legal harm.[19]

The equal individual perspective is not explicitly or consciously sexist, racist, ableist, or in any other way biased in favor of a privileged group and against an oppressed one. It does not denigrate women, suggest that they are less worthy of dignity and respect, or forcibly confine them to the domestic sphere. Against the background of social and political inequality of men and women, however, it is androcentric.[20] That is, it takes the physical facts of maleness and the social facts of manhood and puts them at the center of human experience, while confining the physical facts of femaleness and the social facts of womanhood to the periphery, as if they were less central, less important, or deviant.[21] The equal individual perspective ignores two features of the power relations between men and women that feminists recognize and deem highly unjust. First, it ignores the possibility that men as a group and women as a group are not socially and politically equally situated, especially with respect to sexual matters (MacKinnon 1987, ch. 2). Men have physical, economic, and traditional social advantages that they can use to bargain for, coerce, or physically enforce the traditional gender division of labor or even force sex. Second, the equal individual perspective fails to recognize the harms done to women as a group by crimes committed against individual women that further entrench the gender imbalance of social and political power. That is, when men commit crimes against women, such as sexual assault or spousal battery, they demonstrate their dominance not only to their victims, but to other men and women, as well (Cudd 1990). Men as a group thereby establish a reputation as the dominant sex whenever individual crimes are committed by women against men, and men as a group gain by this reputation, whether or not any particular individual man wishes to gain from it (Friedman and May 1985).

Women (and oppressed groups generally) are therefore at a disadvantage before the law when it is interpreted through the equal individual perspective. They are taken to have powers to resist or repel harms by others that, as a group, they lack, and hence individual women are often blamed for the fact that they are victimized. Recognizing gender-based group power inequality allows us to discern a systematic form of victim-blaming that is impossible to recognize from the equal individual perspective. In this form, problems suffered by victims are seen as private and individually remediable, rather than as a function of the social arrangements of the entire community.[22] Because the equal individual perspective conceals gender inequality and sanctions illegitimate victim-blaming, feminist jurisprudence must reject the equal individual perspective in order to transform the law from a victim-blaming platform. The equal individual perspective similarly conceals other forms of inequality that are the result of oppression. For example, so-called "right to work" laws that restrict the ability of unions to organize treat workers as if their choices about whether to join or not join a union were as simple as choosing between vanilla and chocolate ice cream. They ignore the important imbalance of power between nonunionized workers as a group and their capitalist employers.

If the equal individual perspective fails adequately to reveal and resist oppression, what is the proper perspective? The proper perspective must recognize social and political inequalities and how they make some individual persons vulnerable to attack by others, but more specific to the goal of resisting oppression, it must recognize that there exist social and political inequalities that affect whole groups of persons, specifically systematically disempowered groups.

To begin to see what this perspective needs to be, let us ask why the status quo for women and men cannot be considered to be social and political equality. In what sense is there not a level playing field for men and women, and how does the law privilege men when it assumes that there is? Catharine MacKinnon has argued that we cannot neatly separate rape from normal[23] heterosexual sex, since both may involve force and violence (MacKinnon 1983). Force and violence are eroticized in our culture, and as men are on average physically larger and stronger than women, it is to their advantage as a group to be able normally to use force in intimate sexual encounters. Besides, it is men's use of force and violence that is erotic, not women's (at least, not normally). Since force is an ever-present aspect of normal sex, proving rape (i.e., forced sex) requires proving that the lack of consent was in some way extraordinary, and that the rapist knew it, and that that supposed knowledge penetrated his male desires and privileges so that he really, really knew it. Thus, by assuming that women and men are in a position of equal power in sexual relations (i.e., that force and violence are equally available to and desirable by and for both), and therefore that the normality of force by men on women is consensual or natural, the law makes rapes by men of women a crime that is very difficult to prove (Estrich 1987).

As she suggests, MacKinnon's critique of the androcentrism of heterosexual sexuality can be generalized to many other nonsexual aspects of our lives:

Men's physiology defines most sports, their needs define auto and health insurance coverage, their socially designed biographies define workplace expectations and successful career patterns, their perspectives and concerns define quality in scholarship, their experiences and obsessions define merit, their objectification of life defines art, their military service defines citizenship, their presence defines family, their inability to get along with each other—their wars and rulerships—defines history, their image defines god, and their genitals define sex. (MacKinnon 1987, 36)[24]

The concept of work is androcentric, in that what counts as work is what one gets paid for, and women have traditionally been confined to laboring for no wages. So domestic labor goes unrecognized, unless it is paid for,[25] and when it is paid for, since it is done by women who have few outside options, it is paid little.[26] What men do is regarded as more difficult, or more onerous, or more competitive (Bergmann 1986, 88). Since work is androcentrically conceived, the workplace is androcentrically organized. The normal working day runs past the school day, so that primary parents of school age children, most of whom still are women, cannot be fully integrated in the workplace (Folbre 1994). Pregnancy and breast feeding are often treated more like an optional vacation than a normal, if temporary, condition of life.[27] Time taken out of the paid workforce is viewed as a lack of serious commitment to work rather than as time to refresh and rejuvenate one's entire life, including one's work life (Mincer and Polachek 1974). The forms of sexual interaction and sexual banter tolerated in the workplace conform to the desires and concerns of men, not women (Schultz 1991, 137–140). Women who complain about any of these androcentric aspects of the workplace are then held in contempt as wanting special treatment for what are perceived as their weaknesses.

The legal concept of self-defense is androcentric. Self-defense constitutes a legal justification for homicide when the killer has the reasonable belief that she was threatened by the deceased with immediate, unjustified danger to her life, and the force she used was necessary to repel the threat (Dressler 1995, 199). The legal concept of self-defense thus rules out defensive pre-emptive strikes. Hence, it either confers an advantage on the physically stronger, or it takes persons to be roughly equal in their abilities to use force just powerful enough to counteract that of an attacker. But when the attacker is a man who uses his fists or other nonlethal weapons, a woman cannot normally expect that she can fend off an attack unless she has in a premeditated way armed herself with lethal weapons. Yet if she responds with lethal force, she cannot justify it legally, since it could be claimed that he did not attempt to apply lethal force—he may only be using his fists. Thus, the law seems to confer an advantage on the male batterer (Schneider 1986, 589). One might respond that if a woman expects that she will be beaten by a man in the future, she must simply escape. The core of a self-defense claim is that the force used is necessary to repel an *immediate* threat to one's person (Dressler 1995, 199). Yet, in some cases pre-emptive strikes are the only recourse for a battered spouse to defend herself. For example, if her husband traps her, by holding her hostage, by threatening to kill her if she attempts to flee, or to harm or take her children if she leaves. In ruling out defensive pre-emptive strikes by battered women, the legal requirements of self-defense are androcentric. Battered women who kill their batterers are forced to seek an *excuse* rather than a *justification*—and this difference is critical—by appealing to the so-called "battered woman syndrome" defense to explain why they did not escape. Forcing women to seek an excuse when they ought to be entitled to a justification is a form of victim-blaming, since it portrays them as mere victims— indeed, as victims of a syndrome, not of a battering spouse—rather than as legitimate resisters (Maguigan 1991; Downs 1996).

The laws and legal arguments concerning abortion can also be shown to lead to victim-blaming. Contraception does not meet the needs of women to completely control their reproduction. The only form that is completely controlled by women, sterilization, is irreversible. Other forms require more or less tolerance and partic- ipation by male partners.[28] The pill is highly reliable, except when one is taking antibiotics, but many women cannot safely take it because of side effects.[29] Other forms have a higher failure rate, can be seen and felt by her partner, and disrupt the spontaneity of sexual intimacy. Given these facts about contraception, intercourse often runs the risk of pregnancy. Then perhaps women should simply abandon intercourse. But men as a group control sex and demand intercourse. Although women as a group could, conceivably, band together to change norms of sexuality so that men accept contraception, or even abandon sex with men altogether, this raises a free rider problem for women. Individual women who choose to abandon intercourse would lose men for whom they would otherwise compete successfully to other individual women who "give men what they want." Furthermore, most women, whether or not because of a cultural artifact, enjoy intercourse. So the individual solution that many women choose is to run the risk of pregnancy, then use abortion as a backup.

Meanwhile, the abortion debate rages in sexist and androcentric terms. Abortions are often viewed as for the "convenience" of the pregnant woman,[30] as if being unwilling to give up space in one's body and undergo the rigors of pregnancy and labor were matters of mere inconvenience, like having an annoying relative visiting in one's home. Even abortion rights supporters feel forced to defend abortion as a necessary evil. *Roe v. Wade* is attacked because it carves out specifi- cally a *woman's* right to privacy (as opposed to a married couple's right, as *Griswold* does). Philosophical and religious debates often concern only the status of the fetus (though not all of its rights, especially if it should become a female person). Such debates could focus on unwanted pregnancy as a kind of intrusion by a foreign body, thereby making it a universal experience. We all get invaded by bacteria that make us sick, and we all are potential victims of abduction and use of our bodies for purposes that we do not approve. Instead, these debates focus on fetushood in order to make *that* the universal human aspect of the abortion question.[31] Women are thus again on the defensive in their attempts to exercise their legal rights. They are blamed when contraception does not work, and they are responsible primarily for the outcome of unwanted pregnancy. While the law officially endows them with reproductive rights that are parallel to men's by making abortion a legal option that is under their control,[32] exercising that option is made difficult by the scarcity of clinics, a scarcity created by legally endorsed harassment,[33] and legal requirements designed to make it difficult and expensive to obtain an abortion. Finally, when sought, abortion brings social shame and the risk of violence.

How do these androcentric assumptions in the law lead to victim-blaming? Consider how unreasonable victim-blaming is for other crimes. For crimes such as robbery, it is said, it is not normal behavior for one person to give another money or property without explicit consent given within a structured institutional context. But in sexual matters, formal consent is not normally expected or required.[34] That is, normal sex in our society is "spontaneous," and spontaneity conflicts with the open and rational communication that consent requires. Furthermore, men are normally expected to be the aggressors, so their behavior is considered normal until proven otherwise. Women then should rationally expect to meet some sexual aggression in the workplace, at least in the form of suggestions for sexual intimacy, and women should expect sexual aggression more generally. Women are therefore expected take steps to protect themselves against it. Such expectations are rational expectations in the sense that we can and should predict these behaviors under the current social arrangements, but they are not rational in the sense that such behaviors are acceptable or should be accepted in society. The law can make a difference when it comes to this normative point, and by doing so it can transform the descriptive facts of the relationship between men and women. Feminists demand that the law be used to so transform gendered sexual behavior, just as law has been used to curb other violent behaviors to make life better than the "solitary, poor, nasty, brutish and short" life guaranteed to those in the state of nature.

In each of the examples—rape, sexual harassment, spousal abuse, and abortion— the androcentrism of the law lies in its failure to recognize that women as a group are oppressed, and that this biases norms of acceptable behavior in favor of men as a group. The oppression of women in our society is characterized by reduced and inferior options and outcomes for women vis-à-vis men.[35] Other identities and nonvoluntary social groups intersect with the group women, of course, and in some cases add to or relieve the oppression of subgroups of women to some extent. Certain crimes, to which all women and no men are normally vulnerable, contribute to the reduced options and outcomes of women vis-à-vis men. These crimes I shall call "crimes against women." In the rest of the section I shall use this term to refer only to these special crimes to which women as a group are particularly vulnerable, even though women may of course be victims of other crimes, and men can in some instances be victims of superficially similar crimes that I am calling "crimes against women."[36]

Oppression plays two roles in making women as a group more vulnerable to crime than men are. First, women are in a socially and politically weak position vis-à-vis men because of the existence of background oppression. They are more likely to be raped because of the eroticization of male-on-female violence. They are more likely to be the victims of male violence, including rape and spousal violence, because of traditional norms of feminine and wifely submission. And both these facts lead to the difficulty of proving that they did not somehow seek the treatment that they got. Second, each act of violence against women reinforces the oppression of women. When women are victims of male violence they are seen as weaker, more vulnerable. When men get away with such violence they are seen as more invulnerable to women's defenses. This makes male on female violence more expected, and thus makes women's defensiveness against it normative, in the sense of being *required* of women. But being defensive to violence requires individual women either to prepare for violent reaction or to restrict their freedom of movement. Preparing for violent reaction, if pursued by women generally, would raise unacceptably the total level of violence in the culture. Furthermore, it is unlikely that women would generally pursue this strategy, since it contradicts the gender roles into which women are socialized. Thus, women are expected to restrict their own freedom, on pain of being blamed for not doing so when they are victimized.

Since oppression is a general condition of social injustice that is enforced in part by crimes against women, to achieve justice for all the law must recognize that the oppression of women is a significant part of the criminal offense involved in crimes against women. I am suggesting that the law must take the *oppressed group perspective* when it comes to crimes against women.[37] Legal recognition would consist in seeing oppression as an additional, and socially caused, vulnerability of women to crimes against women and an additional harm done by such crimes. Although the details of what counts as crimes against other oppressed groups will differ, this perspective can also be justified with respect to all such groups.

To recall our discussion in chapter 2, what I am suggesting is that the harm done to individuals qua members of groups be legally recognized as a harm over and above any harm done to a particular victim. That is, I am talking about group harm$_1$, not harm done to the groups qua groups themselves (group harm$_2$). What would the criminal law need to do to explicitly recognize oppression as a harm? We can ask this question with respect to four aspects of criminal law: (1) what crimes are to be recognized, (2) enforcement, (3) standards of proof, and (4) punishment.

The women's movement has made considerable progress in making offenses against women into crimes, but a few more crimes should be recognized if the argument here is correct. Sexual harassment ought to be treated by the criminal law as well as civil law because of its parallels with other crimes against women, specifically in causing oppressive harm. Oppression ought to be recognized as a part of crimes against women, but perhaps as a kind of "special circumstance" that sometimes exists, namely when the victim is a woman and the offender is a man who has taken advantage of the gender-based imbalance of power.[38] By seeing it as a special circumstance, like the possession of a gun in the course of a drug crime, say, the law could consistently see crimes against women that happen in a certain circumstance to be committed by a woman or against a man as a lesser crime. For example, when a man sexually assaults another man the offender commits the crime of sexual assault, but not with the special circumstance of oppression, as it would have been had the immediate victim been a woman.

Even feminists, however, are sometimes unclear about the moral necessity and practical utility of enforcement of crimes against women. Kathleen Ferraro argued that the increased enforcement of domestic violence has come through an unholy coalition comprising feminist domestic violence activists and conservatives who are interested in maintaining patriarchy, and that the result has been a devolution of the public discourse of domestic violence (Ferraro 1996). In the 1970s feminist activists explained women's victimization as a result of women's subordinate social position generally but made little legislative headway. The conservative movement of the 1980s may have helped to bring about greater enforcement of domestic violence laws but did so by pathologizing the particular families in which it occurred, making it possible to pretend that women's subordination generally is not a problem; it is just that there are some pathologically violent men and women. Others have argued that focusing on domestic violence or other crimes against women generally creates a culture of victimhood for women (Heberle 1996; Roiphe 1993). Both of these views are partly accurate, but they are also incomplete. It is not the existence or enforcement of crimes against women that is at fault but rather the failure of the law to recognize the further harm of oppression. Were this to be recognized, then conservatives and feminists would be forced to split, for conservatives could not consistently agree that there is something unjust about women's subordination.[39] As for the culture of victimhood, this would be transformed from seeing all women as potential victims of particular crimes to seeing all women as subject to social injustice. What is wrong with seeing oneself as a victim is that one sees oneself as personally inadequate—it is self-degrading. Seeing oneself as part of a *group* that has been subjected to long-standing social injustice takes away the self-degrading aspect of being a victim.[40] And if women can see that the law has consistently strengthened the ability of men (as a group) to oppress women (as a group), as I have argued here, then requiring the law to reverse course and strengthen women's ability to fight oppression will emerge as long overdue justice.

The women's movement and feminist jurisprudence have made progress in altering the standards of proof required to convict defendants of crimes against women (Berger, Searles, and Neumann 1995). More can be done, though. Something like the reasonable woman standard that has been discussed in sexual harassment cases must be generalized to all crimes against women. This standard requires that what is taken to be offensive in hostile environment sexual harassment cases be determined by what is offensive to a reasonable woman (when the victim is a woman). Debra DeBruin (1998) provides an excellent defense against the two main legal arguments courts have made against taking this perspective. The first objection is that taking the reasonable woman perspective takes the perspective of only a portion of the community in a situation where the standards of the entire community ought to apply. DeBruin's response is to show that because of the androcentrism (what she calls "false universalism") of the law and so-called community standards, an ungendered perspective is impossible, and given the background of women's oppression, a masculine standard is unacceptable. The second objection is that taking the reasonable woman perspective further entrenches sexist norms about women's weakness and their need to be protected. To this objection DeBruin responds by arguing that women do need protection from the serious harm of sexual harassment, not because women are weak but because the harm is so great and so commonplace.

While I agree with these responses, much more needs to be said about what a reasonable woman standard entails. Women's perspectives on what they find offensive now have been formed under conditions of oppression and are unlikely to be reasonable in conditions of freedom and equality. As MacKinnon wrote (borrowing from the nineteenth-century feminist Sarah Grimké) concerning her skepticism about listening for a women's "voice" under conditions of oppression: "Take your foot off our necks, then we will hear in what tongue women speak" (MacKinnon 1987, 91). What the law needs to do is remain flexible on the standards of reasonableness, so that as the oppression of women lessens, the standards of reasonableness change. Supposing that we can come up with a standard of reasonableness from the perspective of women, I propose that the law take this into account in all crimes against women where standards of reasonableness are required. For instance, the reasonable woman standard ought to be applied to determine reasonable limits on defense discovery with respect to the victim's background or to determine reasonable grounds for believing a batterer's threat to use deadly force. Each case of taking the reasonable woman perspective can be defended on the same grounds that DeBruin suggests: there is no genderless perspective, and under conditions of oppression of women, the only just perspective is that of women rather than men, at least where crimes against women are concerned.

Finally, then, punishments of crimes against women ought to reflect the additional wrong of oppression in sentencing. This means that more severe sentences are to be handed down when the crime was assisted by the special vulnerability of the oppressed and serves to further reinforce oppression.

Two objections threaten my argument that oppression should be recognized by the law as a group harm against women. First, one might object that the state has no particular interest in protecting women as a group against men as a group. Second, even if the state can be shown to have an interest in ending oppression, one might object that to punish offenders for the additional harm of oppression, which relies on social conditions not of their making, is to treat them as mere means to social ends. I shall take up these objections in turn.

Modern liberalism requires that the state remain neutral among competing conceptions of the good (Rawls 1993). A liberal might argue that ending women's oppression, when this means ending traditional sexual practices and assumptions about the traditional division of labor in the family, interferes illegitimately with individuals' rights to pursue the good.[41] Yet, liberalism need not approve of all conceptions of the good when realizing these conceptions violate liberal human rights. The right to freedom of religion provides a good example. Religious leaders are not permitted to trap their less willing members by force in order to maintain a religious community, even though that community might represent for the other members the highest good. Likewise, liberalism may not sanction the preservation by force of traditional gender roles. Yet, this is what the law does when it maintains, through coercive state power, the gender imbalances that maintain women's oppression. Thus, a state that does not attempt to level the playing field for men and women sides with the traditional conception of good gender relations, forfeiting its neutrality. Neutrality requires the state to provide the background legal environment in which true gender equality can exist. But this requires ending the oppression of women, because as long as there is oppression there can be no equality. At best we could have some individual women who manage to attain equal outcomes through greater efforts than otherwise equally situated individual men expend.

Ending oppression is a legitimate, liberal social goal. Oppression of women, as of many other groups, is long-standing and pre-dates any crime now committed by a man against a woman, however. Thus, one might object that punishing crimes against women more harshly than similar crimes committed against non-oppressed persons violates one's moral right to be treated as an end in oneself (Kant 1969, 52).

I have three responses to this objection. First, I would point out that I have argued that there is an additional harm involved in crimes against women, namely the group harm of oppression. Thus, those who commit crimes with the special circumstance of oppression are thereby committing additional harms. Second, the crimes against women are accomplished when a man takes advantage of the social vulnerability of women that results from their oppression. Thus, the perpetrator is taking advantage of a special kind of vulnerability, one created precisely by the oppression. There is precedent in the law for more harshly treating offenses that take advantage of especially vulnerable classes of persons, such as sexual abuse of children. Third, all of the main justifications of punishment can be shown to allow punishment to achieve social aims (Murphy and Coleman 1990, 118). There is no particular problem with either the deterrence theory or the moral education view of punishment, as neither of them are predicated on any supposed right to be treated as an end. The retributive theory, which is often linked to Kantian moral theory and hence a supposed moral right to be treated as an end, generally requires that punishment be deserved, that is, that punishment be conferred for some moral wrong committed. If oppression is a moral wrong, then a retributivist can countenance punishment for committing that wrong. Admittedly, oppression would have to fit within a consistent theory of what counts as a moral wrong worthy of punishment, that is, of liability. It is beyond the scope of this book to present a complete theory of liability to punishment, but it is enough for my purposes to point out that punishment for the wrong of oppression would be consistent with some leading retributivist theories. Jean Hampton (1991), for instance, claims that punishment is justified to combat harmful messages of inferiority sent by certain sorts of morally offensive behavior. A number of prominent retributivists, including Herbert Morris (1968), Jeffrie Murphy (1979, 221–260), and George Sher (1987), claim that punishment is justified to rectify an unfair advantage obtained through wrongdoing. Oppression would engage either of these liability triggers.

It is often said that changes in the law cannot themselves effect social transformations on the scale that feminists aspire to (Rhode 1989). The kind of evidence that one cites for this is the lack of social progress that has been made in the United States despite the enormous legal changes that the women's movement has brought about in the past thirty years or the existence of de facto racial segregation in schools and housing despite the 1954 *Brown v. Board of Education* decision of the U.S. Supreme Court and the Fair Housing Act of 1968. Scholars and activists should now identify and catalog the important changes these progressive movements have brought about, learn from the ways that practical application defies progressive social change, and build theory that aids in completing the transformation. I have argued here that practical experiences with the law since the first wave of feminist legal progress challenge us now to forge legal theory that recognizes oppression.

3.5. Resistance to Indirect Economic and Psychological Force

I have argued throughout this book that the indirect forces of oppression are the most insidious forces because they are difficult to see and difficult to overturn, and because fighting against them appears to be fighting against the interests of the oppressed themselves. I argued in chapter 6 that we can reveal false consciousness and deformed desires where they exist by exposing the ways in which assimilating oneself to involuntary in-groups and accentuating the differences with involuntary out-groups is either an assertion of undeserved privilege or a failure to resist one's own oppression. Indirect economic force, which I called "oppression by choice," coerces the oppressed to choose (given unfairly limited options) to participate in the situation through which they are oppressed. As I noted in the section on moral responsibility for resistance, cases of oppression by choice are complicated by the fact that the oppressed have some real options. That is, another prima facie consideration comes into play: choice, prima facie, confers responsibility for the chosen action on the chooser. The oppressed have a real option when they can conceive of and choose any one of several courses of action, each of which may lead them to be harmed in some way, differently, but to a comparable degree. Oppressive institutions present the oppressed with a set of choices that all seem bad: opt in (and suffer the oppression consequent to that) or opt out (and suffer from being isolated in social life in some way). I have argued that choosing to opt in and suffer their particular form of oppression in turn feeds back to maintain that situation for themselves and other members of their group. The other real options involve considerable vision or personal sacrifice if they are to choose them over the exploitation situation, and that fact accounts for the choices of those who are oppressed "by choice." To put it another way, the choices that lead them to suffer oppression by choice appear to be, and may in fact be, individually rational in what David Gauthier (1986) has termed the "straightforward maximizing" sense.[42] The other real options in these situations, if chosen by many of the oppressed group, might succeed in bringing about social change so that the group is no longer oppressed, although they require the individuals choosing this option to make sacrifices, at least in the short term.

In chapter 5 my main example of oppression by choice was women's choice between unpaid domestic work in the home and paid work outside the home. Each individual woman who lives with a (male, able-bodied) partner faces a set of real choices: sharing equally with her domestic partner the unpaid domestic work, negotiating with or coercing the partner to do more of the unpaid domestic work, or doing the majority of the unpaid domestic work, any of which may be while either working or not working outside the home. I argued that the traditional lot of women, shouldering the majority of unpaid domestic labor for their patriarchal families, is a case of oppression by choice. Yet, if women acted together to withhold unpaid domestic services, they could conceivably bring an end to at least this economic domination by men, if not oppression of women as a whole. Another example of oppression by choice comes from the neo-Marxist analysis of the situation of the worker (Roemer 1988). Consider an exploitative factory environment, in which workers receive low wages, work long hours in unhealthy conditions, and their employers reap immense profits, have lots of leisure time, and live in lovely suburbs. Suppose that workers consider going on strike to force management to improve conditions. Any one individual worker faces the choice of striking, continuing to work at that factory, or going elsewhere. To continue to work at that factory is to continue to be exploited, to be oppressed as a member of the working class. Yet, some individuals may view going on strike as too costly to themselves and their families, as they risk becoming even poorer. There may or may not be enough workers willing to strike to make it feasible to do so. Those who cross the picket lines are "scabs" in the eyes of those who do not.

Resistance to oppression by choice requires the oppressed themselves to give up their straightforward self-interest, and for others to encourage, perhaps even pressure, them to do so. The case for a duty to strike when others are doing so seems to me rather compelling in many instances. Here the competing harms are the harm that would come to the individual and her family from her lack of income as against the harm of legitimating the company's claim that their treatment of workers is fair and hence undermining the strike. While loss of income is serious, in most cases that harm can be mitigated by the solidarity of strikers and union strike funds, where they exist. The main point is that all the workers are in the strike together and all suffer similar fates. While the loss of income is worse for some than others, it is only a difference in degree of harm, and not a great one at that. So if the strike is a legitimate case of resistance, which means that it has a reasonable chance of success as far as a worker can tell, there is a duty to strike, and other workers are justified in pressuring their fellows to strike or honor the picket lines.

In the kind of domestic case where my analysis applies where there is oppression by choice, paid work outside the home is not the straightforward self-interest maximizing choice for a woman. She would satisfy more of her interests by staying home and doing domestic work of the family and taking primary care of her children, if she has any. But in doing so she also reinforces the traditional stereotype of women as suited best for this kind of work and less well suited for paid work. Refusing to play the role called for by the traditional stereotype will give her more power within the family and in public institutions, although it exacts some psychic and, potentially, material objective costs (one fails to fit in, to do what is expected, and this makes others angry and potentially violent). But it begins to change the image of women for men, women, and children, and hence the social expectations made of the next generation. Failing to refuse strengthens the hold that patriarchal gender relations has on us all. There is a legitimating feature of women staying home that is parallel to the strike case, which would weigh on the side of harm to others in not resisting. That is, doing unpaid domestic work as a woman reinforces gender norms. It sets an example for her children and others. It may even, if · something like Nancy Chodorow's analysis of single-sex mothering is correct, causally effect the psychological differences of gender that perpetuate female subordination. Thus, it harms other women. Since there is a large number of women who do work outside the home, she cannot claim that hers would be a useless effort; on the other hand, since there are so many women now in the paid workforce, it may also be the case that one free-rider makes no marginal difference. However, I would argue that we are not yet to that point, that there are indications that the traditional stereotype is still strong and harmful.[43] In light of the facts, a woman who can find paid work has duty to do so, unless there is some compelling reason why her children need her specific services. There are, in most instances, other ways of resisting oppression of women; nonetheless, there is a duty for women not to reinforce the image of woman as domestic slave, but to change it to that of a full stakeholder in family and social resources, and this will often require women to resist doing unpaid domestic work.

4. Conclusion

This chapter argues that resistance to oppression is possible and morally required, and it demonstrates that for virtually all different forms of oppression there exist potentially successful means of resistance. All resistance begins with the recognition that there are serious injustices that can be addressed, and then must proceed to mitigate or at least protest the material and psychological harms. Material resistance through economic strategies such as collective investment and labor organizing directly empowers the oppressed, while armed struggle, boycotts, and strikes disempower the oppressors. Legal reform is resistance at its most organized, institutional level. I have argued here that the law should come to recognize the harm of oppression explicitly, and that even though this requires recognition of group harm, it is consistent with—indeed required by— liberalism's fundamental commitment to individual rights.

Indirect oppression, as the most insidious forces of oppression, must also be resisted, even though that sometimes requires the oppressed themselves to act in ways that they do not prefer and may even see as harmful. I have argued here that the oppressed have a moral duty to recognize and fight their own oppression because not resisting is harmful to their fellow oppressed group members. Resisting oppression requires courage and extracts social penalties, as I have argued. Oppressors and privileged persons are morally required to desist and then to help in resistance efforts, but their work alone will not reverse the indirect economic and psychological harms of oppression. Whatever the actions of the oppressors, the oppressed must also tug at their own bootstraps, even when that is painful.

It is tempting to think that when an oppressive regime has been successfully resisted and overthrown, the work of resistance is over. However, history reeks of examples of successful resistance to oppression that is replaced by a new oppressive regime. Think of the Castro dictatorship that followed on the overthrow of Battista, Vladimir Putin's authoritarian rule of formerly Communist Russia, or the Taliban that replaced the Soviet occupation of Afghanistan. Think of the abolition of slavery in the United States that was replaced by racism, apartheid, and poverty for blacks. Think of the many failures of African national governments that followed the overthrow of colonial regimes, or the failure the many democratic movements of the early 1990s on that continent. Successful resistance does not guarantee freedom from oppression, even the resurgence of the same oppression. Freedom is not simply the absence of oppression, but a positive condition in its own right. In the final chapter of this book I will examine the notion of freedom that might be resistant to resurgence of oppression.

8

Fashioning Freedom

When I walked out of prison that was my mission, to liberate the oppressed and the oppressor both. Some say that has now been achieved.
But I know that this is not the case. The truth is that we are not yet free;
we have merely achieved the freedom to be free, the right not to be
oppressed. We have not taken the final step of our journey, but the first
step on a longer and even more difficult road. For, to be free is not merely
to cast off one's chains, but to live in a way that respects and enhances
the freedom of others. The true test of our devotion to freedom is just
beginning.

Nelson Mandela, *Long Walk to Freedom*

1. Oppression, Justice, Freedom

Freedom, in addition to justice, requires overcoming oppression. This book has focused on the injustice of oppression, its causes, and our duty to overcome it. I argued
that our psychological propensity to categorize, which together with our social nature,
leads to stereotyping. Invidious discrimination based on these stereotypes sets the
stage for oppression. Oppression is caused initially by direct material forces (violence,
economic deprivation) imposed from outside, and then reinforced by internalized,
indirect, material and psychological forces. In chapter 7 I explored several ways that
particular cases of oppression can be resisted and projected the hope that by strong
resistance any one case of oppression will end. In this concluding chapter I turn from
justice to the question of freedom to consider whether, even if we are able to resist the
injustices of oppression, we may yet not be free. I shall argue, as suggested by the
quote from Nelson Mandela, that freedom requires something more than an end to
any particular case of oppression; full freedom requires that all cases of oppression
end. This claim, whether true or not, raises crucial questions, however. What is the
future of our species with respect to oppression? Are we headed for a state of freedom
in which all cases, not just this case and that case, of oppression will be rare and short-
lived? Or will we forever be plagued by some cases of long-standing oppression?

Some will argue that it is not possible to overcome oppression, given our
psychological makeup, which is largely fixed in its predisposition to categorize and
our strong propensity to form social groups. It seems that overcoming all oppression
requires us to either change our psychological makeup (which I assume is impossible

without ceasing to be us) or to prevent each other from forming close knit social groups. Even if we were able to overcome our sociality, it is not clear that we would want to. Everything of value in human life is bound up with its sociality; we cannot even imagine what life would be like as a solitary species like the bear or the coyote, for it would be language-less and so beyond our understanding. Our propensity to form close social bonds seems as fixed as our propensity to categorize. Thus, we must take the existence of social groups for granted in exploring how oppression is to be overcome, but we may be able to reinvent them or mold them to suit us. If social groups will exist, then perhaps we can change our stereotypes and discourage invidious discrimination. That would require the privileged to give up their privileges, and persons would have to resist the temptation to take advantage of others through the kind of group level processes that we seem to learn as children: bullying, teasing, peer pressure, and the like. What would motivate such changes?

The history of political philosophy offers us a parallel. In his classic *Federalist Paper #10*, James Madison wrote about the danger of factions, by which he meant groups that share a common interest that is opposed to the rights of others or the interest of the whole community (Hamilton, Madison, and Jay 1961, 77–83). He reasoned that either we could prevent such factions from forming, or we could try to find a way to prevent factions from succeeding in their "schemes of oppression." We cannot prevent factions from forming, Madison noted, without sacrificing freedom, since that would either require us to ensure that we all have the same interests (through some sort of brainwashing) or to prevent groups from forming to discuss their common interests. Thus, the only way we can maintain freedom yet avoid the oppressive forces of factions is to find a way to prevent them from succeeding in satisfying their perfidious interests. Madison proposed that a representative democracy of the sort he had outlined in the proposed U.S. Constitution would be the solution because it would encourage discussion of general philosophies of government rather than particular policy interests if the people were to vote not on issues but on representatives. The record must be judged as mixed here. But in any event, we seek to solve a broader social problem. That is, we seek to project not only a government that will not oppress its citizens, but also a collage of unconnected but overlapping social groups that will not oppress each other. Like the people that Madison was trying to lead, the oppressed can reach freedom only by acting with good faith and good will toward others within a social system that does not reward them for doing otherwise, but instead rewards them when others are free, as well. Toward achieving this end, governments may well play a role, but it cannot be the only force for change without reinstituting oppression through the repression of our individual and social natures. We must, in effect, reward each other for our freedom.

In the last chapter I looked at a number of ways that particular cases of oppression can be resisted. Oppression can be resisted at all levels: by legal means backed up by coercive force, by groups who attempt to alleviate poverty and invest in the abilities of the poor, by individuals who refuse their unjust privileges, or oppressed individuals who refuse to help keep the others in their social groups to the norms that advantage the oppressors. In this chapter I take up the question of what a group is to do when the bonds of oppression are loosened. At that point we embark on the journey of which Mandela writes, the "longer and even more difficult road," on which we must learn "to live in a way that respects and enhances the freedom of others," for only by this route can true freedom be found. Our problem, however, is that we do not yet know what that route looks like or where, precisely, it is going. Our only guide is knowledge that it is our duty not to oppress others and to resist oppression where possible, and our enhanced ability to recognize oppression when it occurs.

The oppression of women, as has been noted by many, is the longest standing case of oppression. Women have become accustomed to being the subordinate sex, and to fashioning their lives within the unequal constraints that societies have imposed on them for at least most of human history. In doing so, women have in many ways forfeited their right to freedom. They rarely demand equality with men and often satisfy themselves with doing better than the next woman or the next subordinate of their society. This has been the individual's rational response to her oppression, after all: attempting to do as well as they can for themselves within the constraints they are offered, rather than futilely refusing to comply with sexist norms. Because women have done so well at accommodating themselves to oppression, in ways both rational and emotional, ending the oppression of women and overcoming sexual subordination is the biggest challenge to our hopes for freedom. For this reason, in what follows I will focus on how women can liberate themselves. Perhaps our struggle to liberate women, then, will unveil the path to freedom for all.

There are several reasons why women's path to freedom might be generalizable to that of other social groups. First, in order to free women, we must learn to change some of the most deep-seated norms of power and subordination. For, they are both long-standing and originate in natural inequalities or differences. Second, in order to change the status of women globally, we will have to learn how to see people as members of multiple social groups not of their choosing; those in power (men) will have to allow members of their social groups ("their" women) to claim other groupings as, at least temporarily, their most important or most threatened aspect of their identity, and those subordinated (women) will have to learn how to insist on it. For it is only if women and men see themselves as part of a gender hierarchy that cuts across race, class, ethnicity and other groupings, that we can address the oppression that gender entails. Gender oppression will not go away by ignoring or denying it, by insisting that there are no women or that women do not have common interests. Third, in the process of seeking their own liberation, women will have to forge friendships and alliances across social groups. In coming to see others as allies despite great differences, we will learn how to be sisters in affirming our common humanity. Well-intentioned men from different social groups may first join out of allegiance to their own race or ethnic grouping, but eventually they too will join this humanistic sorority that stretches across those groups. Then it will be a short step to seeing all of humanity as united in a struggle for universal freedom.

2. Two Senses of Freedom

Many theorists of freedom, particularly since the influential paper by Isaiah Berlin (1969), "Two Concepts of Liberty," have recognized two senses of "freedom." Berlin named them "positive" and "negative," but others have more usefully distinguished between "internal" and "external" (Hirschmann 2003). Negative or external free-dom means something like the absence of interference from outside the person, while positive or internal freedom means the capacity to seek and attain, provided that there is no external interference, one's own good. Positive freedom is often under-stood as autonomy, the ability to be a self-lawmaker, and this requires that one is not manipulated by the social structure under which one lives. One's desires are one's own and one's beliefs are rationally generated. Berlin ultimately rejects the idea of positive freedom because he thought that to posit a breach of positive freedom one would have to impose desires on individuals that they do not acknowledge. For governments to attempt to guarantee positive freedom, then, they would have to posit a good for their citizens and entice them to seek it, that is, in Rousseau's famous phrase, to force their citizens to be free. Berlin, as a liberal, argues that freedom requires merely imposing no impediments to individuals' given preferences. Positive freedom, Berlin concludes, insinuates a totalitarian menace.

In this book I have characterized oppression as being caused by social constraints, and I have asserted the liberal conviction that individuals are of primary moral importance. It may appear that my theory of oppression entails only or primarily a problem of negative or external freedom. But this inference would be too quick. I have also characterized psychological forces and harms of oppression that clearly work internally to the person, even while some of them, such as stereotyping, are externally imposed on the individual. Internal and external freedom cannot be easily distin-guished; they are inevitably intertwined, just as the social forces of oppression work together to maintain an effective prison around the oppressed. The distinction that Berlin drew between negative and positive freedom is not neatly drawn, and his rejection of positive freedom involves two confusions. First, he failed to see that a persistent lack of negative freedom for a social group harms the individuals of that group psychologically, causing them to lack positive freedom, as chapters 3 through 6 have demonstrated. Second, even though the idea that a government might posit an individual's good for her raises the specter of totalitarianism, that fact does not vitiate the claim that an individual's freedom can be compromised by a lack of vision of viable alternative options. A person can lack freedom without there being a clear way for the person to attain freedom in the future.

The first of these confusions suggests that the positive/negative distinction drawn by Berlin does not do the philosophical work we need it to do. Violations of negative freedom turn out to result in deeper harms that slide over into the kinds of harms that violations of positive freedom entail. Violence, for example, results in post-traumatic stress disorder, which robs victims of their ability to plan a coherent life. I shall adopt the terms "internal" and "external" freedom, to detach my theory from Berlin's distinction and to suggest a connection to my terms "indirect" and "direct" forces of oppression. As I shall use the terms, internal freedom requires that there be no indirect forces of oppression imposing on a person, and external freedom requires freedom from direct forces of oppression. These are necessary, not suffi-cient, conditions for freedom. Recall that the distinction between these two kinds of oppressive force turns on the contribution of the oppressed individual's internal mental processes of belief and desire formation. Indirect forces come about through the oppressed person's own psychological mechanisms. Direct forces of oppression begin a vicious cycle that may begin mainly depriving its victims of outer freedom, but as it continues to traumatize them and their fellow social group members, those forces cause their victims to relinquish their hopes and dreams for a better future, which in turn atrophies the ability to imagine a future of freedom. This description fits women's lack of freedom under patriarchy, or the global domination of men. Women have accepted their lesser status in much of the world and work within the constraints to achieve what they can without questioning or challenging the starting assumption that sex must impose a hierarchy of status.[1]

Since the two kinds of oppressive forces often work in concert and reinforce each other, internal and external freedom often fail together, though this is not necessarily the case. A person is not free so long as she is the victim of forces of oppression. As I have argued, indirect forces of oppression are in a sense self-imposed, even though ultimately caused by external forces. Resisting internal forces of oppression, as we have seen, requires restraining individuals (in the best case, individuals restraining themselves) from doing what they want, sometimes rationally, to do. The goal of achieving freedom thus imposes both social responsibility and individual responsibility. As I argued in chapter 7, those who are most privileged by oppression are surely the most responsible for resisting it. Yet, they are also often the least motivated, for they have the most to lose. The privileged have even more to lose than their undeserved privileges if oppression is inevitable and by releasing some from oppression they risk bringing it upon themselves. Motivation for ending oppression, then, may only come after the bonds of oppression are loosened by the oppressed themselves, working with the well-intentioned and insightful privileged who work actively to end oppression. For at this point the possibility of backlash against the oppressors is great, yet engaging in that backlash risks a continuing cycle. Thus, it behooves us all to seek a kind of freedom that is freedom for all if only as defense against catastrophe.

Berlin was correct to worry about the totalitarian menace; formulating someone else's desires or beliefs for them is to deny freedom, and even trying to assess others' true desires and beliefs is fraught with dangers. Yet there is, I believe, a greater danger in standing idly by while freedom is actively denied. This poses something of a dilemma, for it seems that because oppression is so intertwined with our existing social institutions, either we must seek freedom or deny it, and if we seek it we must have a vision of what we seek, and this entails devising conditions under which persons will develop autonomous beliefs and desires. In framing those conditions, we risk totalitarianism. But perhaps that last claim is too extreme. If there is a way between these horns, then it is, I shall argue, through a gradual process of resistance to oppression combined with the will and intention not to oppress new or other social groups. In the next section I sketch out how this process could go.

3. Breaking the Vicious Cycle of Oppression

Since oppression acts through social institutions, the starting point for us must be to begin by attacking the self-generating cycles that those institutions support. Oppression runs a typical sequence: it begins when members of one group violently attack individuals in another social group and proceeds as the dominant group wields economic force on the subordinates. The oppressed respond rationally by choosing within the constraints that they are offered by the oppressors, and they gradually accommodate their beliefs and desires to the oppressive conditions that they find through both rational and nonrational psychological processes. It is at this point in the process that all the most puzzling and tenacious features of oppression appear. Direct forces may become less visible as time wears on and generations adopt the coping mechanisms of their parents; the privileged come to believe that their superiority is natural; the oppressed come to believe in their own inferiority, and become dependent on the dominant social groups for material support and moral leadership. At this point, oppression cannot be successfully defeated by ending only the direct forces. Rather, we need to break the link between material deprivation and dependence of the oppressed social group on others. Achieving freedom then will require not only breaking the interlocking links of the chain but also setting the oppressed on a course toward independence.

By independence I do not mean disconnection from others, but rather the material and psychological preconditions for the ability to form one's own beliefs and desires without oppressive constraints. I have argued that the oppressed are cognitively and emotionally constrained in unjust ways to conform their beliefs and desires to benefit the dominant. These constraints impose emotive and cognitive forces of shame and low self-esteem, the cognitive process of false consciousness, and the cognitive/affective process of deformed desire, causing oppressed persons to believe ideologies that oppress them and to desire the situations, goods, and ways of life that keep them subordinate. By molding the oppressed to desire their position (as well as the privileged to believe they are entitled to theirs), they are made dependent on the desires of the dominant. This is the sense of dependence that we must object to. Dependence on others in the form of reliance on their charity, good will, cooperation, companionship, and good work to make one's own life better is not objectionable. Indeed, such dependence is a part of our sociality that makes human life uniquely wonderful.[2]

The first step toward freedom, then, is to end direct forces of oppression: violence, threats of violence, enslavement, and the blatantly unfair economic practices of invidious wage and hiring discrimination and enforced labor segregation. For women this would be a radical step. Ending violence would mean ending violence against women in the forms of domestic abuse, sexual assault, and sexual slavery. Curtailing direct economic forces would mean ending sex discrimination in hiring and wages, cracking down on sexual harassment, ending the segregation of women into lower paid occupations and jobs, and providing equal opportunities for education and training regardless of sex. But we must recognize that even these enormous steps will not end oppressive dependence, and that there remains a social responsibility on the privileged to do more. The personalities, beliefs, desires of the oppressed and the privileged alike have been formed under conditions of oppression, after all. Changing those conditions will not immediately change the personalities. Future generations will be raised by parents and other adults who retain the personalities of oppressed, oppressor, and privileged. Consider how young women of today are still attracted to positions of sexual, political, and economic submission, despite the advances in economic opportunity that their mothers' and grand-mothers' generations have made. Young men are often resentful of their loss of some privilege and even tend to see themselves as victimized by social efforts to end oppressive practices (Faludi 1999). Psychological progress comes slowly, not only in individuals, but also generationally. The psychology of freedom will not come to us in an instant; it is not an immediate result of the psychology of resistance.

The crucial next step toward freedom is to suggest alternative social practices that would be attractive to a wide variety of persons (not just the oppressed), and yet would help to break the cycle of dependency on the dominant groups. The privileged have to be recruited in the struggle for freedom so that they will not resent and resist change. Large and significant psychological changes will have to be directed also at the youngest members of society. In the United States, single mothers tend to be poor and poor single mothers are less able to equip their children and communities with skills for independence. Low income women tend to need child care in order to get more education, retain their jobs, or move to better ones (Lee 2004). At the same time, quality childcare is costly, which means that poor women cannot afford it. Yet good quality childcare is crucially important to children's health, well-being, and development of capacities for freedom from internal oppression. To fight the eco-nomic forces of poverty for women, by helping make women independent in the economy, and to develop a future of free citizens, broadly available subsidized child care should be socially provided.[3] This step helps to fashion a free society in a variety of ways. It addresses (though does not solve) the problems of women's and poor persons' oppression in our society. It helps develop the capacities for autonomy and independence from domination by the children who receive the good quality care. Furthermore, it is politically feasible even in a society that is not yet free. It appeals to large numbers of men and women across racial and class lines, since people every-where want their children to be well cared for, and for the most part they want other people's children to be well cared for, too. Steps such as this one, which have multiple effects on resisting oppression and developing capacities to internal freedom approach freedom gradually, through small changes that are popularly and demo-cratically adopted. They may not be inexpensive, and so the wealthy will have to be convinced that it is their duty to contribute more for the elimination of oppression. But they do not intrude upon individuals' decisions about how to use what wealth they retain. They make no effort to directly change preferences of any but the children, whose preferences will be formed by some social process or other, and clearly good child care is to be preferred to bad by all rational people of good will. Yet they offer the opportunity for women to take steps toward economic independence, defeating one of the forces of oppression.

These first two steps, while required by justice, will still not bring about a widespread psychology of freedom. There will still be those whose interests are best served by maintaining their position in the existing hierarchy: men who gain eco-nomically, sexually, or psychologically by asserting their dominance and claiming that it is natural for them to do so; women who gain economically or psychologically by selling their sexual subordination, given the current incentives. These people have to be provided incentives to forego those interests and develop new ones. These incentives could be carrots or sticks, but carrots are better for co-opting someone to a progressive cause, and sticks are unwarranted except as punishment for oppressive, not simply privilege-seeking, behavior. Men and women should be given incentives to enter into consensual relations that will enhance women's freedom as well as men's. For instance, small steps that would work through changing incentives to bring about the social provision of child care would include allowing tax credits to employers for providing child care at the work site or awarding block grants to communities for child care centers or for lengthening the school year and the school day to match the working day.[4] Larger steps to undermine economic oppression would include offering scholarship assistance for young women to enter male-dominated professions, tax credits for businesses to hire them or for women to start their own businesses. We must also work toward a vision of freedom at the same time that we undermine the forces of oppression, and social incentives for this vision-work could be offered. Awards might be made available for popular works of art and music that offer visions of a future without oppression. The legal definition of religion might be expanded so that groups who seek to articulate notions of freedom can garner the benefits provided to religions.[5]

Social change will be resisted not only by those who think they will lose their privileges but also by those who are rewarded by the current structures of incentives to continue in their path, even if they do not support its outcome. For example, many people who pursue research on pharmaceuticals are initially motivated to do so by their concern to cure illness. Those persons would presumably be most motivated by research that cures the most disease. Yet they find that the reward structures for drug development are not connected to the numbers of persons whose illnesses they can help to cure, but rather to the amount of wealth that ill persons have. Thomas Pogge (2003) proposes an ingenious solution to the problem of incentives for drug manufacturers to develop drugs for the diseases that primarily and disastrously afflict Third World countries. He proposes a transnational organization that would collect revenues from drug sales and use them to reward inventor firms in proportion to the impact that their inventions have on the global disease burden. The point of doing this is to realign the incentive structures away from just trying to cure the diseases that are relatively trivial in terms of numbers and effects but strike rich persons toward curing the diseases that are life-threatening for masses of persons. The interest of inventor firms and generic drug manufacturers would then come together, and drugs of great significance would be made in great quantities, reaping financial rewards for both types of firms. "Inventor firms would *want* their inventions to be widely copied, mass produced, and sold as cheaply as possible, as these would magnify the impact of these health inventions" (Pogge 2003, 23). This solution requires governmental intervention on behalf of ending oppression (in this case the severe human rights violation of poverty, as argued by Pogge), but the mechanism works through an incentive that makes both the agents of change and the oppressed better off.[6] This is an example of how incentives can be structured to bring together the interests of many in solving problems of oppression.

This third step goes beyond the direct social provision of resources to imagine how society might restructure incentives to bring about envisioned alternative social practices that enhance freedom. Such incentives work through individuals' free choices, rather than through the imposition of beliefs or preferences, and go beyond and improve upon the direct social provision of goods in three ways. First, offering incentives to behave in certain ways is more likely to change beliefs and desires than the previous step (direct social provision to the oppressed) in fashioning freedom. Second, as economists often argue with respect to markets for goods (or bads) subject to externalities (and hence free rider problems), giving incentives for socially beneficial behavior and then allowing individuals to choose the actions that are in their interest is the most efficient way to solve the problem of free riding. A standard example of this is the market for pollution, in which firms are allotted pollution rights that they can trade in the market. The alternative is to put an absolute prohibition on pollution above a certain threshold for each firm. The market solution, it has been argued, works better, by giving firms incentives to innovate where possible and not to cheat, since when they cannot innovate they can still run their business legally by buying the pollution credits from other firms (Varian 1994). The model relies on there being good information about the existing levels of pollution, and since firms have little incentive to provide this information, they have to be monitored by government agencies. The analogy between pollution and oppressive social norms has already been made. What I am arguing here is that there is also an analogy between market-based solutions to pollution problems and incentive-based solutions to changing oppressive social norms. By giving persons incentives to act in ways counter to oppressive social norms, they will choose to do so, and perhaps choose to do so in better ways than could have been devised from those farther removed from the problem. Third, socially structured incentives indirectly change beliefs and desires, in that they entice persons to do things that will enhance their independence. Just as there can be indirect forces of oppression, I am suggesting that there can be indirect forces of freedom enhancement. Joshua Cohen's discussion of the notion of a social ethos and its connection to social institutions supports my claim. By social ethos, a term he takes from G. A. Cohen, he means "socially widespread preferences and attitudes about the kinds of rewards it is acceptable to insist on, and, associated with those preferences and attitudes, a sense about the ways of life that are attractive, exciting, good, and worthy of pursuit" (Cohen 2001, 365). Cohen argues that it is at least plausible that the choice of social institutions causally affects the social ethos, so that, within a Rawlsian framework we can expect justice to require social institutions that instill an ethos conducive to freedom from oppression. If this substantive assumption holds, then people will be led by social institutions that they accept to develop the preferences and attitudes necessary for freedom—not by direct intervention in their lives but by the constitutive shaping of their personalities that must occur through one set of social institutions or another (Cohen 2001, 384).

One might object that such indirect forces are coercive because they manipulate people—indeed, they are specifically designed to manipulate people. But this is just where they differ from indirect forces of oppression. They are not coercive because they do not fit the definition of coercion I argued for in chapter 5: "An institution (economic system, legal system, or norm) is *coercive* if the institution unfairly limits the choices of some group of persons relative to other groups in society." That is, these incentives do not, by hypothesis, *unfairly* limit choices. It is important to reiterate here a point made in the earlier discussion of coercion. I am using coercion in the moralized sense, that is, coercion is lack of choice relative to a set of choices that is deemed fair or moral by some background moral theory. That background moral theory has not been elaborated in this book, and I will not set out to do that now in the final pages of the work. I have in mind a liberal contractarian view of the sort developed by John Rawls in *A Theory of Justice*, or the more libertarian version of David Gauthier in *Morals by Agreement*. The claim that any particular incentive structure that is proposed to take this third step in fashioning freedom is noncoercive stands or falls on the claim that the social institution it seeks to counteract is oppressive. But that claim itself relies on the background moral theory that I am assuming in this book.

A liberal like Berlin might argue that these incentives amount to just the kind of preference re-education project that portends the slide to totalitarianism. But I think that this is not the case, and that a liberal can defend structuring social incentives through government intervention (as well as private incentive provision), or through international quasi-governing institutions. The key to the argument is to see that the government must structure incentives in favor of some set of conditions. It may structure incentives either to maintain the privileges of some social groups or to shift the benefits to others. What makes a totalitarian state evil is that it structures incentives for persons to be coerced into doing what they do not wish, absent that coercion, to do. If a set of incentives do not coerce, then they cannot be part of a totalitarian evil. It is not open to the libertarian to respond by arguing that any set of incentives is totalitarian, since there will be a social structure of incentives regardless. The only argument is over the source and the direction of the incentives.

4. Two Serious Problems for Social Engineering

I have argued that engineering social incentives to change people's beliefs about and preferences for oppressive social norms is not coercive, and that this forestalls Berlin's totalitarian menace objection. There remain two serious problems with social engineering projects that must be addressed. I shall call the first of these problems the problem of unintended consequences and the second the communitarian menace.

4.1. The Problem of Unintended Consequences

One of the basic lessons of the history of macroeconomic policy is that social projects always have unintended consequences (some negative and some positive). There is little reason to doubt that providing incentives for persons to change social norms in the direction of enhancing freedom will sometimes go awry. Consider the record of the World Bank, which has as its main mission to fight poverty by helping people to help themselves.[7] Many well-intended programs have resulted in benign failures or worse. International nongovernmental organizations (NGOs) have had similar experiences (Walley 2004/5). National governments that have tried fiscal or monetary policies have sometimes brought about the reverse of their intended consequences. Sometimes the unintended consequences have been beneficial, such as the building of a railroad in Tanzania that was intended for what we can now see as an unrealistic at best goal, but has resulted in encouraging a thriving trading route.

> The planners of TAZARA [Tanzania's national railway] were not expecting any such transformation when they initiated the project in the late 1960s. They imagined a grand national railway owned by the state that would be used for large-scale regional shipments of copper and other goods from Zambia—a project that would rival Egypt's recently completed, Soviet-funded Aswan Dam. Their primary goal was not to promote rural economic development or improve the lives of rural producers by connecting local markets. But that has been TAZARA's real impact. (Monson 2004/5)

What examples like these tell us is that large-scale social change is to some degree unpredictable and fraught with dangers of making things worse (or better). Yet, just as we cannot shy away from trying to make change in the face of the possibility of totalitarianism, so we cannot shy away from trying to find freedom in the face of failure. What we must do is try to characterize the ways that socially provided incentive structures can fail and try to foresee problems of the same kind from our proposals.

Three kinds of problems are generalizable. First, when incentives are offered and awarded on a competitive basis, then there are incentives for corruption and gaming the system. In many development projects in the Third World, for example, the local government is the intermediary between NGOs and the people in need. It is then easy for the local government officials to skim off a portion of the aid. Another way aid is siphoned off is by apparently legitimate local businesses that supply their services or goods at higher rates than would be required by the market. Corruption and gaming often go in concert, since opening the market to competitor firms should reduce the rents that the businesses can charge to zero. But if the government prohibits or places obstacles in the way of competitor firms, then the system can be successfully gamed. Second, there are incentives for shirking and cheating. This sort of problem arises when there are set rules with incentives for adhering to them and no objective and accurate way of determining compliance. For example, if there are set-asides for minority-owned businesses, but no effective oversight to determine which businesses are minority-owned, then persons from the dominant community can set up businesses that only appear to be minority-owned in order to capture the set-aside. To avoid such problems, incentives should be structured so that either there is little opportunity for cheating or little incentive for it. Third, there may be rent-seeking behavior that relies on an exogenously determined market failure that is ignored by the NGO (Young 2005; Ackerly 2005). For example, micro-credit organizations that make loans to women sometimes fail to benefit those women because the loans are not structured in a way that prevents their male relations from capturing that benefit. In Pakistan, the Grameen Bank often loans money to women who buy rickshaws that have to be operated by their husbands because of the background social norms about what labor women may or may not perform and whom they may work with. The social norm creates a market failure, in the sense that women do not have the freedom to enter the market. Husbands are able effectively to take ownership of the rickshaw and make their wives dependent on them and vulnerable to desertion, violence, and deprivation.

Avoiding such problems is possible by making certain restrictions on the loans to prevent women from getting into a position to be exploited. This requires close attention to how social norms interact to create incentive structures.

What would be some of the potential unintended consequences of the incentive structures that might be proposed to enhance freedom? It seems unlikely that there can be any general answer to that question, beyond the concerns for creating incentives for corruption, cheating, shirking, or rent-seeking. But there is one more kind of bad unintended consequence that can occur with incentives for freedom enhancement. Resistance to oppression is likely to raise backlash on the part of the persons who are losing their privileges (Superson and Cudd 2002, 3–16). Loss of privilege is part and parcel of the end of oppression, though, so it is not possible to avoid the loss of privilege. Individuals must be convinced, then, that they are being compensated for their loss of privileges. In the final section of this chapter I shall complete the argument that the freedom of all is good for all. This argument, if it were generally understood and accepted, would be sufficient to rationally motivate. But because privilege is so difficult emotionally to forego, there need to be appeals at a more emotional and immediate level in order to motivate people even to consider that argument. In some ways the women's movement has been successful at this. Men who are fathers of daughters, or who have sisters or other loved ones who are women, can often be convinced that some loss of privilege to men generally is a worthwhile cost to bear for the benefits of seeing the women they love gain opportunities and succeed. It is commonplace (though sadly not exceptionless) among my female peers that their fathers told them that "they could be anything" when they grew up. And while this was not quite true (professional athletics was almost out of the question but for tennis players and golfers, and there has still never been a female U.S. president), many of these fathers thought that women should have equal opportunity to succeed and perhaps even fought for women's access to equal employment opportunities. Yet it is also the case that progress has been marked by backlash periods. Now, for example, in the United States there is a serious backlash against the Title IX requirements of equal funding for women's and men's educational opportunities when it comes to funding of athletics, despite the fact that this law has been responsible for a ninefold increase in the participation of women in college sports (Brady 2002). While many men see opportunities for their daughters as clearly a good, others (indeed, sometimes the very same men) resent the loss of men's nearly exclusive privilege to playing sports as endangered by having to share the resources for providing opportunities for women. The example nonetheless illustrates how incentives for oppressed individuals to break out of existing oppressive social norms can also appeal to members of privileged groups who have something to lose by that breach. Looking for these alliances, as well as appealing to the sense of justice and good will of the privileged helps to forestall backlash, but does not completely eradicate it.

4.2. The Communitarian Menace

My fundamental political and moral orientation in this book is liberal. That is, I take the individual to be primary morally and ontologically. Thus, I insist that social policies preserve liberal civil rights. Any social policy that is aimed at disrupting one form of oppression must not be unjust in this liberal framework. The communitarian menace is the looming problem that preference re-education might be so successful that it would result in a homogenization of society. Perhaps if the homogenization were complete, this would not be a serious problem, since it might result in social unity and cohesion that would be equally satisfying to each member. But the fact is that there will always be dissidents and persons who just do not fit the social norms, yet who are themselves decent persons.[8] In a homogeneous community they will suffer from ostracization. This threatens the individual, then, in a way that is not oppression, but still a violation of the principle of liberalism. It prioritizes the community's needs and interests over that of the individual. If individuals are going to differ over deeply important matters like sexual preference, religious belief, aesthetic tastes, or philosophical views, or more low-brow matters such as tastes in sports, food, or how their homes should be decorated, then it is best for them if there are a variety of lifestyles from which they can choose. John Stuart Mill wrote eloquently about the value to individuals of living in a society with a variety of experiments in living (Mill 1978, ch. 3). If a society is so homogenous that it does not contain a variety of flourishing experiments in living, then it will not be hospitable for individuals.

Although I take the communitarian menace seriously in general, I do not believe that the incentive-based preference transformation program that I recommend is likely to lead to homogenization of preference or belief. While the incentives will cause individuals to change their behavior to accommodate those incentives, if the incentives act as they are supposed to and enhance freedom, then they are more likely to expand the variety of experiments in living rather than contract them. Still, this concern suggests that something needs to be done to forestall homogenization and its danger of intolerance for diversity. Namely, there must be a background understanding of the advantages of and social support for the value of diversity and tolerance.

Perhaps the greater concern with homogenization, however, comes from the worry that persons who have lived under conditions of oppression will lack the imagination for coming up with diverse lifestyles. Drucilla Cornell's (1998) work on freedom and liberalism helps to illuminate the ways in which society can encourage a variety of experiments in living by supporting the imaginary domain. For Cornell, the imaginary domain is the psychic space that allows a free play of sexual fantasy. She argues that this freedom to explore one's sexual life in imagination lies at the very foundation of self-respect. Although I agree that persons who are constructed under the current oppressions are unable fully to conceive the possibilities for liberation, if we expand the notion to encompass the whole realm of human expression, not only sex but also work, thought, feeling, art, and religion, the imaginary domain offers a glimpse of freedom for individuals. Under conditions of severe enough oppression, persons may be unable to conceive any alternative world at all. But when the bonds of oppression have been loosened to some degree, we can imagine life that is different from what we have known, institutions that are less oppressive.[9] We cannot simply design a future society and take the optimal steps to bring it about. We must be careful what we wish for, as our wishes may unwittingly be for further oppression. Yet, we must continue to wish and strive to make our visions reality. The imaginary domain is our capacity to imagine other ways of being, apart from the social norms that now constrain us.[10] The imaginary domain is the repository from which alternative conceptions of norms and social structures might arise. We are able to imagine them because each of us have different social group memberships, allowing most of us to experience at once privilege and oppression with respect to one or another of them, and giving us experiences of social groups with different ways of life. As I shall argue, the society that succeeds in supporting diversity and tolerance will reap the greatest benefits of freedom, while ensuring the lasting freedom of each individual.

5. The Social Union of Social Unions: Enhancing the Freedom of Others

In examining how oppression happens and how it maintains itself through generations, I have assumed that each person seeks a short-term to medium-term maximum of preference satisfaction, and their interests in the short to medium term account in large part for their behavior. Yet, if freedom is to be possible, it will be necessary for at least some persons to look beyond their short- to medium-term interests and work toward a transformation of society that may be costly over that horizon. What would motivate persons to do this? I have tried to suggest ways that well-intentioned persons can argue, cajole, or bribe their fellows to join them in resisting oppression and seeking gradual enhancements of freedom. At the very least, though, a philosopher should offer a rational argument that would appeal to persons to work toward these ends. I conclude this book with an argument for the claim that the freedom of all is good for each. This claim may seem problematic in two ways. First, it appears to conflict with the argument I have developed throughout that a primary reason that persons, both privileged and oppressed, participate in oppressive social institutions is because it is in their interest to do so. The conflict in this case is merely apparent. One's long-term interest can conflict with one's short- to medium-term interest, with the latter motivating behavior. Indeed, that is one way of explaining the existence of *akratic* behavior. Second, it may appear problematic in that it is utopian to think that we can reach freedom. In the previous chapter and in the first parts of this chapter I have tried to describe how we might make social transformations that lead to freedom. At this point I am only trying to argue for the rationality for each of seeking freedom for all.

In A *Theory of Justice*, John Rawls provides the outlines of the argument. Rawls argues that humans tend to obey a basic generalization of psychology, which he calls the Aristotelian Principle. The principle states: "Other things equal, human beings enjoy the exercise of their realized capacities (their innate or trained abilities), and this enjoyment increases the more the capacity is realized, or the greater its complexity" (Rawls 1971, 426). This principle posits a basic motivational principle that seems to be born out by our everyday experiences. As we grow and mature we often seek out new challenges, and we take pleasure in developing our capacities to enjoy them. Our love of sport, art, craft-making, reading, decorating our homes, cooking food, entertaining our friends, and a thousand other occupations and enjoyments testify to the validity of the principle. The second premise of the argument is supplied by the fact, noted by philosophers from Aristotle to Marx to Rawls that humans are deeply social creatures. As Rawls explains it, "Humans have in fact shared final ends and they value their common institutions as good in themselves. We need one another as partners in ways of life that are engaged in for their own sake, and the successes and enjoyments of others are necessary for and complementary to our own good" (Rawls 1971, 522–523). Humans must join and cooperate with others to carry out projects large and small. Over time our projects deepen in complexity and nuance. The opportunities and ways of life that any individual may choose from are bequeathed by previous generations who themselves built upon those they inherited from and built in cooperation with others. In participating in these projects our achievements are made possible by the achievements of others. The social units that humans form Rawls (following Humboldt) calls "social unions."

The Aristotelian Principle suggests then that individuals find pleasure in the achievements of their social unions, which also means that they find pleasure in the achievements of others in those groups. At its best, participating in social unions effects a transformation of individual psychology that avoids envy and expands our concern for others. Marcia Homiak writes that through shared activity, we

> expand our conception of who we are, thereby making us more continuously active and providing us with more continuous pleasure. When, as members of shared activities, we begin to see ourselves as part of a larger enterprise, our perception of who we are and of what we can do expands to cover the activities of others who are fulfilling other parts of the overall task. (Homiak 1985, 104)

Furthermore, we come to see that by expanding our circle of concern to others who were once excluded we can increase our pleasure.[11]

This idea of finding pleasure in each other's achievements and coming to identify with them is an extremely attractive idea for a political philosopher. Rawls, for instance, argues that the well-ordered society is the "social union of social unions," that is, that the society that is structured by his two principles of justice exemplifies this admirable virtue of each taking pleasure in the achievements, the flourishing, of others. I take it that this is true of the society of free persons, which is not only free of current oppressions, but whose members seek to free all persons of oppression. For such a society the individuals are able to seek their own good with good will toward others as well. They seek to encourage diversity and enhance the freedom of others. They take pleasure in and identify with the accomplishments of others. And further, they come to see their own freedom as connected to that of the others.

We can, I believe, take steps toward a free society because we are able to transform ourselves—make ourselves better—through good willed participation in social unions that are gradually transformed by increasing freedom. A concrete example of how enhancing women's freedom enhances the pleasure of others comes in the achievements of Mia Hamm. She was born in the United States in 1972, the very year that Title IX, which outlawed sex discrimination by federally funded educational institutions, became law. Mia Hamm retired in December 2004 as the most prolific scorer—male or female—in the history of international soccer. At the time of her retirement she was one of the most recognizable people on earth and is a shining example of what determination, hard work, ferocious competitiveness, and athletic talent can produce. But her achievement was an achievement of the social unions of soccer and of democratic society more generally. Mia Hamm's achievements were made possible by a history of soccer players who developed the sport through developing rules and practices of fair play and a game that could highlight and refine certain human abilities and skills, fans who made it popular, and in her case, a long history of women who fought for women's opportunities in sport. More importantly, through taking pleasure in the achievements of Mia Hamm we are able to see how the inclusion of a formerly excluded group (women) from a cherished activity (soccer) makes us all better off. Her achievements were made possible only by these social unions, as well as her natural talents, and in turn they have brought the world much pleasure. We are better for having international women's soccer because Mia Hamm was able to showcase her talents in it. Moreover, we take pride in the very progress of society that allowed Mia Hamm to shine. We can clearly see in this case, as we can see in thousands of other less spectacular cases that we experience closer to home, the enhanced freedom of women has made the world better for all.

In enjoying the achievements of others, we experience freedom from what Marx called the alienation of man from man. We gain valuable information about alternative ways of life that others pursue with interest and devotion. This in turn develops our own capacities, our imaginary domains, which allow each of us the psychic space to enhance our freedom and take pleasure in it. In learning the value of diversity and tolerance, we become motivated to end oppression and privilege, both our own and others. This transformation is not easy; it requires moral character to resist the enticements of privilege or accommodation (Homiak 1991). But at least we can now see that it is rational to seek the freedom of others as well as ourselves. For, to be free is not merely to cast off one's chains, but to live in a way that respects and enhances the freedom of others.

Appendix

This appendix presents a simple game theoretic model of the Larry-Lisa situation. I model their decision first as a two-period noncooperative game as follows. Each of the two must choose a strategy, either M (market work) or H (home work) for each of the two periods, so that each has four possible strategies for the whole game: HH, HM, MH, or MM. Let d_1 be the payoff for either one choosing H in the first period, d_2 the payoff for choosing H in the second period. Let w be the wage rate for men in the first period of work, p the promotion rate ($p < 1$) for a period of work experience, so that $(1 + p)w$ is the wage rate for the second period of work. Let g be the gender wage gap ($g < 1$), so that gw is the wage rate for women in the first period of work and $(1 + p)gw$ for a second period of work.

Now I state some assumptions. Suppose that both Larry's and Lisa's preferences are such that $w > d_1 > gw > d_2$. That is, suppose that they value one parent staying home in the first period (say when their children are 0–5 years old) higher than the gender gap discounted wages, but less than the full men's wages. Also suppose that the second period payoff for domestic work is not as valuable as the gender gap wages (say because the children are in school and their care can be combined with full-time work). Suppose further that Larry and Lisa need to have some income in each period, so that at least one of them must choose M for each period if they are together, and both would have to choose M for each period if they were to split up. Suppose for the moment that they simply wish to maximize the overall payoff (an assumption that I will relax shortly). Then the payoff matrix in figure A.1 represents their feasible options (nf = not feasible). The equilibrium strategy pair given the above assumption about the relative payoff components is either MMHM or MMMM depending on whether the promotion bonus makes up for the wage gap, specifically whether p is greater than, less than, or equal to $(d_1 - gw)/gw$.

Now suppose that we relax the assumption that they wish to maximize the overall payoff, and instead use the Nash bargaining solution to determine the payoffs to each spouse depending on their outside options in each period. Now if we ask

	HH	HM	MH	MM
HH	nf	nf	Nf	$d_1 + d_2 + (2+p)gw$
HM	nf	nf	$d_1 + d_2 + (g+1)w$	$d_1 + (2+p)gw + w$
MH	nf	$d_1 + d_2 + (g+1)w$	nf	$d_2 + w + (2+p)gw$
MM	$d_1 + d_2 + (2+p)w$	$d_1 + (2+p)w + gw$	$d_2 + (2+p)w + gw$	$(2+p)(w+gw)$

FIGURE A.1

whether Lisa will choose HM or MM, we need to ask what her payoffs will be in the relevant boxes. Consider the first period bargain. Then the payoffs she receives will be either $(gw + d_1)/2$ for H or gw for M, while Larry receives $w + (gw + d_1)/2$ if she chooses H or w if she chooses M. Graphically the choice looks like figure A.2.

If we assume then that she chooses HM, their respective payoffs in period two will be $gw + pw/2$ for her and $w + pw/2$ for him and their total payoffs would be $gw + (pw + gw + d_1)/2$ for her and $2w + (pw + gw + d_1)/2$ for him.

Now one might ask whether she would reconsider after seeing how her payoffs will suffer in the second period based on her first period choice not to get work experience. In the second period if she has worked in the first period her outside option is to earn $(1 + p)gw$, and this raises her bargaining power somewhat. So she earns $(1 + p)gw$, but then the assumption is that she has only earned gw for the first period, which is less than she earns if she chooses H in the first period. Her total payoff is $(2 + p)gw$, while Larry's is $(2 + p)w$. Thus, her ultimate decision,

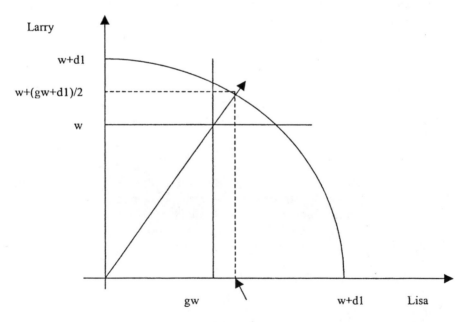

FIGURE A.2

assuming she is planning ahead, depends on whether $(2 + p)gw$ is greater than $gw + (pw + gw + d_1)/2$. Under at least some assumptions about the wage gap, the promotion bonus, and the strength of their preferences for their children to stay home and be cared for by one of them, she will choose HM as her strategy. However, it could be rational for her to choose MM under some assumptions about those values. For some values, it is individually rational for her to choose MM, even though that lowers their overall payoff. Namely when $p < (d_1 - gw)/gw$ and $(2 + p)gw > gw + (pw + gw + d_1)/2$.

It is interesting to note, then, that it would be in Larry's strategic interest to exaggerate his preferences for one parent to care for the children at home (i.e., d_1), since he does better in the bargain in the second period, and overall, if she stays home with the children in the first period. At the same time it is not in her strategic interest to misrepresent her preferences about the care of children, since her payoff depends on her true preference.

Notes

Preface

1. Two recent books may appear to be exceptions to this claim. Harvey (1999) is clearly analytic in style, but not comprehensive, in that it addresses only those cases of "civilized oppression," that is, those not involving violence or serious economic deprivation. O'Connor (2002), on the other hand, focuses on the linguistic practices that contribute to the construction of oppression, neglecting the material manifestations of oppression.

2. There are exceptions here: justification of civil disobedience, and by implication, any violations of his theory of justice.

1. Oppression: The Fundamental Injustice of Social Institutions

1. Namely, we should blame those persons who continue to benefit from the unjust actions of their ancestors, while the ancestors of the victims continue to suffer uncompensated from the original offences. I shall take up issues of responsibility in chapter 7.

2. Wollstonecraft (1989, 43). Compare with her use of "subjection," throughout, and "enslave," p. 32.

3. This reading is consistent with that of Barbalet (1983, 83–85) and Elster (1985, 100). See also Schacht (1994, ch. 2).

4. Of course one might respond that women are themselves a class. But this redefinition of class is not open to Marx, who claims that the economic base of society determines the ideological superstructure. Either women do not constitute a class, in which case women's oppression is not explained by the Marxist account of oppression, or women do constitute a class, in which case sexual domination is equally basic in the explanation of the ideological superstructure of society.

5. See Okin (1979, 226–230) for an insightful elaboration of this claim.

6. Haslanger (2004a) argues very effectively for the claim that the primary source of oppression is institutional. See esp. pp. 104–107.

7. In Cudd (2005) I argue in greater detail for a set of criteria of adequacy that applies to explanatory theories of normative concepts, of which oppression is a prime example.

8. I do not mean to suggest that individuals cannot overcome oppression in the sense of living a meaningful life in spite of or in the face of oppression, or that individuals cannot resist

oppression. By "overcome oppression" here I mean end oppression. Not even Ghandi or Martin Luther King, Jr., could be said to have ended oppression on their own; it was their ability to lead masses to protest the oppression that changed the world.

9. This is to counter the tendency in scholarship on oppression to focus too much on single groups and in doing so to exacerbate the problems of other oppressed groups. Consider, for example, Paulo Friere's conception of oppression as "castration," which he thinks is the ultimate form of dehumanization, or the signs carried by the Memphis Sanitation Workers in the fateful strike of 1968 that read: "I AM A MAN."

2. *Social Groups and Institutional Constraints*

1. Van Fraassen (1980, ch. 5) presents a nice summary of the pragmatic approach to explanation.

2. This is why the proposed "theory of everything" in physics is misnamed; although the theory is supposed to unite the four basic forces in nature, it will surely be silent on questions such as "how do we raise the level of employment without causing inflation?"

3. Kincaid (1994) presents an argument for looking for the microstructure of social phenomena.

4. Elster (1983a) was the first to distinguish these three types of social explanation.

5. This is true of Durkheimian sociology and the semiotic school of anthropology. See, for example, Hanson (1975).

6. Folbre (1994, ch. 2) offers possible sociobiological accounts of oppression based on gender, sexual preference, race, and class. However, she notes that such discussions are "speculative (if not foolhardy)" (74). She then proceeds to offer explanations of both women's subordination and relative equality. Likewise she discusses how sociobiological explanations might account for the origins of oppression or the absence of oppression for different races, classes, and homosexuals. But such speculations are too general to be useful, then, in any one case. At most we can conclude that the existence of oppression within a society has to be compatible with its survival, for a time at least, given its cultural and biological environment.

7. Note that not all feminist scholars accept that women are oppressed in all societies. See, for instance, Omolade (1980).

8. See Davidson (1980, p. 79) for a famous example of how intentional explanations can go awry for such reasons.

9. Gilbert (1989, ch. 3), for example, argues against what she calls the "society-dependence thesis": that meaningful behavior is society dependent. She construes this as implying the transcendental claim that meaningful behavior is inconceivable without society. I merely mean to make the weaker claim that the meaningfulness of human behavior is in fact due to its social nature. Gilbert is willing to grant that the group languages that we speak are essentially social.

10. The term "ascriptive" is sometimes used for "nonvoluntary" by sociologists. Folbre (1994) uses the term "given groups."

11. May (1987) recognizes this defect and tries to remedy it by suggesting that the relations among individuals that constitute their grouphood may simply consist in their being treated similarly by others by virtue of some attribute that they share with other individuals. While this accounts for nonvoluntary social groups, it makes the theory no longer internalist but externalist and strains the use of the term "relation."

12. Elster (1985) offers an externalist account of class, which is one kind of social group: "A class is a group of people who by virtue of what they possess are compelled to engage in the same activities if they want to make the best use of their endowments" (p. 331).

13. It is not quite precise to say that she requires that there actually be common knowledge of joint readiness for appropriate uses of "we." To recognize that this is an idealization that in practice could never be fulfilled by actual persons, Gilbert requires only that the "smooth reasoner counterparts" of the persons included in P, i.e., the ideal counterparts of the persons who are just like them but have infinite time and perfect reasoning capacity, have common knowledge.

14. Tuomela (1995) also presents a theory of social groups that encompasses only what I am calling voluntary social groups. His theory is similar to Gilbert's in that it is an internalist theory, that is, it takes the intentions of the members to be decisive for group membership.

15. Interestingly, Gilbert does not refer to Gould's, DeGeorge's, or May's accounts of social groups.

16. This argument is due to Schelling (1971). See also Schelling (1978).

17. For a compatible view of the role of rational choice theory in structural explanations of behavior, see Satz and Ferejohn (1994).

18. Roger Shiner raised this objection to me.

19. The example was originally used by Michael Bayles (1974).

20. Laurence Thomas, a black Jewish philosophy professor at Syracuse University, tells the story of being in an elevator in Jerusalem with a white American woman whom he did not know. When he got into the elevator with her she looked at him nervously and clutched her purse, despite the fact that he was well dressed, thus obviously professional and upper-middle class, and in an expensive hotel in Israel—hardly matching even the stereotype of a street thug except by his skin color. In Thomas (1990) he writes about this incident and the conversation that he then engaged her in.

21. I am referring here to Thomas Kuhn's (1970) discussion of the misperception of anomalous scientific results as experimental mistakes rather than true counterexamples to a theory.

22. She treats this subject at greater length in (Young 1997, 1999).

23. This condition prevents an objection raised by Tuomela (1995) from telling against my theory of nonvoluntary social groups. There he considers as a sufficient criterion for grouphood [a set of persons who] "are defined by others as belonging to the group" (212). His objection to this is that some persons could define an arbitrary set of persons, and this would not count as a social group "unless trivially, circularly, the social collective here is already presupposed to be a social group" (213). But although this is another conceivable externalist account of social groups, it is not mine, and Tuomela has not envisioned the sort of theory I offer here.

24. Betty Friedan, in *The Feminine Mystique* (1963), wrote about "the problem that has no name," by which she was referring to a series of similar psychological, sexual, and material problems that many middle-class white women in the 1950s faced, but that no one had ever seen as systematic oppression. It may be that women recognized some other common constraints enough to see themselves as a social group at the time, however. An example of a social group that has only very recently been named and become conscious of itself as a social group may be bisexuals. The point is not, of course, that there were not persons who were sexually attracted to both sexes before this consciousness, but rather, that they did not see themselves as having common interests as a result of common constraints (e.g., rejection by both homosexual and heterosexual communities) that formed the basis for grouphood.

25. My view of the continuum of voluntariness of social groups goes something like this. On the far end of the nonvoluntary scale we have NVSGs whose members lack self-consciousness of their grouphood and there is no social consciousness, then moving on toward greater voluntariness we have NVSGs whose members are self-conscious of their grouphood, then NVSGs whose members self-identify or take pride in their group membership, then

NVSGs whose members can rather easily pass in society, so that they need not face the common constraints unless they consciously choose not to pass, then voluntary social groups (VSGs) that are vestiges of formerly NVSGs (such as the Irish Americans discussed in the text), then VSGs whose members bear little costs of membership, and finally on the extreme voluntary end of the continuum we have VSGs with high costs of memberships and low costs of non-membership (e.g., being a female U.S. Marine), so that one has to really want to be a member to do so.

26. It is worth noting that Gilbert, too, thinks that her account of social groups rules out methodological individualism or what she terms "strong analytic individualism." See Gilbert (1989, 434–435).

27. Connolly (1976) uses the John Stuart Mill's *The Subjection of Women* analysis of women's willing participation in their own oppression to argue for the need to postulate what he calls "reference groups," which are social groups in much the same sense as my nonvoluntary groups. Gilbert (1989) also rejects methodological individualism because voluntary social groups bring into being the irreducible concept of the plural subject. I think that she is right and that the refutation of methodological individualism is overdetermined.

28. Spelman (1988, ch. 5) draws here on the work of Davis (1981). I believe that it is a misinterpretation of Davis to read her as endorsing this objection, however.

29. According to a Briefing Paper published in January 1997 by the Institute for Women's Policy Research, Washington, D.C., "The Wage Gap: Women's and Men's Earnings," the wage gap between black men and women 18 years and older, by educational level for 1995 was: high school men $19,514 to women $14,473 (74%); college graduates men $36,026 to women $25,577 (71%); and postgraduates men $41,777 to women $35,222 (84%).

30. For an excellent critique of Spelman's antiessentialist claims using recent empirical evidence of the similarity of women's oppression across races and cultures, see Okin (1994).

31. The Institute for Women's Policy Research statistics, updated in January 1997, report average median earnings as follows: white men $32,172, white women $22,911, African American men $24,428, African American women $20,665. Thus in percentage terms the female/male wage gap for whites is 71.2 percent, for African Americans is 84.6 percent; the African American/white wage gap for men is 75.9 percent, and for women is 90.2 percent.

32. I thank Richard DeGeorge for raising this objection and providing this example.

33. Jones (1999) distinguishes and explicates two senses of group harm. My sense of group harm$_2$ matches, I think, his term "corporate group harm," though I do not draw his distinction between collective and corporate groups in the way he does.

3. Psychological Mechanisms of Oppression

1. Note that there is no discussion of gay men here or how they come to be and little discussion of lesbians—the existence of homosexuals constitutes something of an embarrassment for her theory.

2. Because mothers are of a different sex than boys, they can get pushed into the Oedipus complex at this early age by the instigation of the mother (Chodorow 1978, 107–108). Just what she means by this is not clear to me; it sounds like she is referring to molestation of the boy by the mother, but perhaps she means a fantasy of this somehow induced by the mother? Fact or fantasy is not significant, though, for psychoanalysis, since it is the subjective experience of the individual that matters. In any event, were the boy to come to believe that he had been seduced by his mother, it would cause the boy to be all that much more distant in his relationships, having had to separate himself from his primary caregiver even earlier in life for fear of castration by his father.

3. By "direct evidence" I mean tests of the psychological mechanisms postulated by the theory. I do not include here a set of child development milestones for which there exist competing coherent explanations, the only sort of empirical evidence Chodorow does offer.

4. Hegel writes: "Without the discipline of service and obedience, fear remains at the formal stage, and does not extend to the known real world of existence. Without the formative activity [i.e., working for the master], fear remains inward and mute, and consciousness does not become explicitly for itself. If consciousness fashions the thing without the initial absolute fear, it is only an empty self-centered attitude; for its form or negativity is not negativity per se, and therefore its formative activity cannot give it a consciousness of itself as essential being" (Hegel 1807/1977, 119).

5. This term is Hussein Abdilahi Bulhan's (1985).

6. It should be said that Fanon was not calling for violence for the sake of violence, nor was he unmindful of the dangers to the violent themselves. Unorganized violence and especially violence against one's fellow oppressed is inevitable, insidious, and reflects the pathologies of oppression, namely, "paranoia; and the associated processes of projection, rationalization, and dehumanization" (Bulhan 1985, 153). Fanon writes movingly in the last section of *The Wretched of the Earth* of the patients on both sides of the Algerian struggle for independence of the psychological sufferings of men and women who had practiced or witnessed physical violence. Perhaps he also saw its potential to become a habit.

7. One might think that failing to violently resist oppression is deserving of scorn as an accomodationist strategy or as not sufficiently radical to end oppression. Hence, the strategy would not be resistance at all, and violence could be seen as the only possible form of resistance and so it would not be androcentric to call for it in all cases. While I grant that the situation of colonialism is unlikely to end through nonviolence, there is a significant counterexample in India, and not all forms of oppression are maintained through violence (in my more limited sense). To see violence as the only possibility or the only honorable one in the face of a counterexample is, I must insist, androcentric. I thank John McClendon III for forcing me to consider this issue further, however.

8. Vicki Hearne's (1986) analysis of animal training suggests that the reason for drawing lines and forcing submission at those lines is to give the animal a sense of boundaries that may not be crossed so that when the need arises those boundaries can be enforced immediately and effectively, or so that there are boundaries to lean on, to help to circumscribe the unlimited domain of choice that would otherwise seem present.

9. Specifically she cites Stern (1985).

10. Note that Thomas Hobbes also admitted a role for recognition when he claimed that "glory" is one of the "three causes of quarrel," though the third and least of them (Hobbes 1985, 185).

11. Actually I think that it can be shown to be logically necessary for information processing, since without categorization there are no connections between ideas and so no way to process them. But for the purposes of this paper it is enough to claim that categorization is physically necessary, or necessary for the kinds of physical beings that we are.

12. See Fiske and Taylor (1991, 156–160) for a discussion of the conditions under which people correct their false stereotypic attributions and experimental evidence for them.

13. However, what determines belonging here is a highly theoretical issue, since what constitutes a group is itself a theoretical issue. One aspect of belonging that is systematically conflated in the psychological literature is the issue of whether the perceiver herself determines whether she belongs: Is it her perception that matters? Her commitments? Others' perceptions of her? In experiments this has to be operationalized in some way and is generally done by direct assignment of the subjects to a group in a way that makes it clear and common knowledge to all which group each individual belongs to.

14. This further thought was suggested to me by Branscombe in private discussion.

15. See Fiske and Taylor (1991, 122, and 137–139) for a review of the large literature on the circumstances in which role schemas are disengaged.

16. I thank Beverly Mack for raising this objection.

17. There is a controversy in social cognition theory about whether stereotypes are ever inaccurate (e.g., see Fiske and Taylor 1991, 341–342). What I mean to claim here, is that stereotypes do not present the truth, the whole truth, and nothing but the truth about individuals, and this can plainly be seen by considering the many "effects" and attribution errors that I have referred to here that show stereotyping to be a biased and often false representation of individual attributes.

4. *Violence as a Force of Oppression*

1. By "intragroup violence" I mean violence between members of the same social group. Violence may thus be both intragroup and some other type of systematic violence. I mean to exclude only those cases which are intragroup and not also some other type. For example, violence between white, middle-aged, heterosexual men of the same socioeconomic class. This implies that I am excluding domestic violence between same sex partners who are of the same race and class. Such violence, I contend, would not be a force of oppression. One might wonder how intragroup could be systematic. An example would be the black-on-black violence of the inner city—it is systematic in the sense that such crimes occur to the victims because of institutionally structured facts, in this case the de facto segregation of the inner city.

2. Violence by subordinate groups aimed at dominant groups does not count as oppression, on my view, since it is likely intended to erase the oppression or to protest it. If it were to result in the dominance relations being changed, however, the violence by the first group against the second could turn into oppression. Just because some act is not a part of oppression does not entail that it is not immoral, of course.

3. What one nation sees as a war of aggression might appear to another to be a defensive war. Interventions by third parties appear to some to be defense of an oppressed minority and to others to be imperialist aggression against a nation's sovereignty. Furthermore, there may be differences of opinion among the individuals who make up the aggressor nation as to the motivation or justification of the war. But from the fact that we can misclassify a war it does not follow that there is no truth of the matter. In naming a situation oppressive we take a stand on the facts about the justice or injustice of the cause.

4. According to the FBI crime statistics on murder for 1999, for example, 88% of murders of women in the United States were committed by men. By contrast only 11% of murders of men were committed by women (http://www.fbi.gov/ucr/99cius.htm).

5. Briere (1997, 3), quoting from the *Diagnostic and Statistical Manual of Mental Disorders–IV*.

6. Becker, who works with victims of political repression in Chile, argues that there is no "post" to the ongoing traumatic injuries of his patients, nor is the term "disorder" appropriate, since his patients are displaying a perfectly normal response to the horrors perpetrated by that regime. Furthermore, while stress is a psychological concept that implies an intact self through the duration of the injury, trauma implies a "perceived sense of irreparable tear of the self and reality" (p. 105). Becker's work with patients suggests that ongoing oppression and terrorism cause recurring and sometimes ever-present neurotic and even psychotic states that make life for the patients and their families difficult or nearly impossible to bear.

7. Bartky (1990) discusses the idea that oppressed persons come to internalize an inferiorized self-image, which then leads to a kind of self-oppression. Brison (2002) discusses how this is one of the effects of rape on its victims.

8. Neath (1997) documents statistics showing that male violence against women is a significant cause of disability in women.

9. Darity, Jr. cites Blau and Graham (1990, 321–339) for a study that suggests that inheritance is the major source of wealth and may account for 75% of the enormous wealth gap between whites and blacks.

10. Since women cut across race and class groupings, one might be tempted to argue that women do not suffer from this harm of systematic violence. However, since women control so little of the world's wealth, it is also true that women are economically disadvantaged as a group.

11. The World Health Organization (2000) lists statistics on rates of intimate partner violence in table 4.1, p. 90. According to their statistics (which are not precisely comparable across countries because of differing methodologies), while approximately 22 percent of U.S. women are victims of domestic physical violence, approximately 58 percent of women in Turkey are victimized.

12. Statistics cited on American Bar Association Commission on Domestic Violence website, www.abanet.org/domviol/stats.html, accessed on 9-11-03. This site cites their statistics from the Bureau of Justice and the American Psychological Association.

13. U.S. Department of Justice, Bureau of Justice Statistics, reported on website: www.ojp.usdoj.gov/bjs, tables 91 and 93.

14. According to the National Center for Educational Statistics, there were 2.6 million young people earning high school diplomas or equivalents in 2001, of these just over half were female. See http://nces.ed.gov/pubs2003/snf_report03/table_06.asp (accessed 9-30-03). The statistics on casualties in the Vietnam War can be found at www.vietnam_war_outcome.htm (accessed 9-30-03). The number of total (1959–1975) American casualties is listed as 57,685 killed and 153,303 wounded; there were approximately 2 million Vietnamese killed and 3 million wounded during that time.

15. Evidence for this claim is overwhelming. To cite a few facts supporting it: In much of the world they are less well nourished, less healthy, and less well educated (Lopez-Claros and Zahidi 2005). Everywhere they are vulnerable to violence and abuse by men. It has been estimated that as a result of these facts and the fact that in many places girl babies are disproportionately aborted or killed, there are one hundred million missing women (Drèze and Sen 1989). Many more women in the world lack access to education and many more are illiterate. Jobs that are high paying are much less likely to be held by women. Tedious and menial work is much more likely to be done by women. Women in the workforce are paid less than their male counterparts, more often harassed and intimidated on the job, and far more often are responsible for child care and housework "after work." Independently of their participation in the paying workforce, women suffer from domestic violence at much greater rates, bear primary responsibility for childrearing and housework, and are much more likely to be sick and poor in their old age. In much of the world women do not have access to safe abortion, or sometimes even to contraception, further putting women's health and well-being at risk. Women everywhere bear almost the full burden of unplanned pregnancies. Women in many nations of the world lack full formal equality under the law. Where they have it, they are less likely to be able to access the judicial system and so still lack substantive equality. And almost nowhere in the world do women hold high government offices at anywhere near the rates of men.

16. On the injustice of aggression, see Walzer (1992). When a war is justified, it does not in the first instance constitute a case of oppression. However, wars that conquer a nation, even if justified, can lead to oppressive imperial or colonial domination. An occupation may at first be necessary to secure peace and freedom for a conquered people, but experience shows that occupations can easily go awry.

17. I take this argument up more fully in chapter 5.

18. The argument for reparations is peripheral to the issues addressed in this chapter but still needs to be made. Briefly, my view is that descendants are owed compensation if and because they belong to the same social groups, since the harms to the ancestors are transmitted psychologically and materially to the descendants, while the privileges to the dominant social groups are still enjoyed by their descendants. Thus, there is no level playing field for the competition for current social resources between the two groups, and the disadvantage/advantage stems from an injustice.

19. The massive international condemnation of the rapes caused the Japanese military authorities to outlaw rapes and to institute the infamous "comfort women" program of mass sexual slavery to service the soldiers on other battlefronts. Perhaps they believed that the comfort women in some ways compensated for the prohibition on mass rape, although it can hardly be said that these women were consenting to this "service." See Chang (2000).

20. Salzman (2000, 63) citing UN Economic and Social Council, *Contemporary Forms of Slavery* (Document E/CN.4/Sub.2/1995/38 [13 July 1995]).

21. Enloe (2000, ch. 5) analyzes the many layers of this and other cases of soldier rape.

22. See Burg (1997) for a thoughtful discussion of the complexities in labeling this particular situation a case of genocide.

23. Sex outside marriage is against the law for men, as well, but men are less likely to be accused, less likely to be convicted, and when convicted, less likely to be harshly punished.

24. Estimates of the number of African slaves are very highly contested and range between 10 and 28 million, as reported by the BBC. www.bbc.co.uk/1/hi/world/africa/1523100.htm (accessed on 9-30-03).

25. Of course, this is only male slaves; all females had to wait until the Nineteenth Amendment was ratified in 1920 for their right to vote in federal elections.

26. "Lynch-law" originally referred to extra-legal courts, which were so named after Charles Lynch, a member of the Virginia House of Burgesses, who sat as magistrate over these trials. During the American colonial period, the British rule made it difficult to prosecute crimes efficiently, and petty criminals took advantage of the situation. This caused the colonists to devise their own courts, which were not legally sanctioned by the Crown (White 1969).

27. White is apparently using these quotation marks to refer to Douglas Freeman, editor at the time (late 1920s) of the Richmond *News-Leader* (White 1969, 98–99).

28. This definition is cited on the FBI's website: www.fbi.gov/hq/cid/civilrights/hate.htm (accessed 10-1-03).

29. FBI Press Release, Nov. 22, 2004, found on their website www.fbi.gov/pressrel/pressrel04/pressrel112204.htm.

30. According to the 2003 United Nations Human Development Report, Brazil ranks sixth worst of the 123 countries for which there is data in terms of its Gini index at 60.7. The Gini index is a measure of wealth inequality that ranges from 0 (perfect equality) to 100 (perfect inequality). Brazil is worse on this measure than all of the other countries of all other continents except Africa.

5. *Economic Forces of Oppression*

1. Ezorsky (1991) discusses the "disadvantage of being disadvantaged," by which she means these reinforcing aspects of oppression.

2. It is important to note that the poverty is chosen by the Amish, but their inequality is not. Presumably it is not to be economically inferior to others that they choose a simple life, but that the economic inequality comes along with that choice. If others were to choose a simple life like theirs, they would not choose to be even poorer in order to remain unequal.

3. Parijs (1995, ch. 1) defines pure capitalism and pure socialism as both requiring this property of self-ownership in order to avoid devolving into (morally unacceptable) slavery or collectivism. In this chapter he argues that neither pure socialism nor pure capitalism is the ideal free society, concluding instead that some elements of each, namely ownership of the means of production and some level of provision of social services is necessary for real freedom. I take it that this argument supports my argument that capitalism is not intrinsically oppressive.

4. This is the basic idea of general equilibrium, a proof of which can be seen in Browning and Browning (1989, ch. 17) or just about any contemporary microeconomics textbook.

5. This is not to say that capitalism is incompatible with discrimination, of course. But any other economic system is also compatible with discrimination, and so to indict capitalism as oppressive because it is compatible with other systems of oppression would lead us to indict all economic systems.

6. Some public goods provision should also be included in a full account of a clearly acceptable capitalism. Public goods are goods which are not rival (one person's consumption of the good does not reduce another's) and not excludable (no one can be excluded from consuming the good once it is provided to anyone). Public goods are underprovided in the market and some will be seen as socially necessary. Strategic defense is an example. I thank Neal Becker for this addition.

7. Roemer (1988, ch. 6) gives an analytic argument for this claim.

8. Nozick (1974) argues that coercion is a violation of justice; Raz (1986) argues that coercion is a violation of autonomy. I shall maintain that it can be both or either.

9. Expected utility is just the sum of the products of the utilities of the possible outcomes and their probabilities of occurring.

10. This is not to deny that some psychological states induced by coercion are objective harms, by which I mean harms that are intersubjectively verifiable.

11. Elster (1985, 212–213) implies that there are some purposes for which a moralized theory of coercion or force is necessary, and others for which an empirical theory is adequate. I am claiming that a theory of structural oppression requires a moralized account of coercion, but I would agree with Elster's pluralist position that an empirical theory may be better for other purposes.

12. Martin (1993) argues that not only legal rights are recognized only within the constraints set by background practices but this is also true for theories of moral or human rights. He writes: "social recognition, an actual and appropriate awareness on the part of people in society, is a necessary condition of a morally valid claim's being (or becoming) a moral right" (82).

13. Roth and Sotomayor (1990, ch. 2). The algorithm for producing provably stable matches is quite precisely and formally described there, and differs slightly from the description in my text above, in that the side that accepts or rejects is allowed to keep a proposer engaged while previously rejected proposers make new proposals. The exact details of the algorithm do not matter for my point, though, which is that the structure of the normative practice of marriage proposals can systematically disadvantage a group.

14. Barbara Herman (1991, 796) recognizes this distinction between agent-agent coercion and institutional coercion.

15. Hayek articulates these two criticisms in Hayek (1944) chs. 6 and 7.

16. Such a system would tend to retain the status quo in terms of production and consumption as well as social groups. Innovation may be less likely to occur under such a system than under capitalism. But this lack of innovation does not constitute oppression and may be seen as a worthwhile tradeoff to avoid the economic inequality attendant to capitalism. I thank Neal Becker for discussion on this point.

17. A lack of economic efficiency may, however, entail another kind of injustice, since it means that someone could be benefited without harming anyone else, and I have argued elsewhere that fairness requires that such benefits not be denied to persons (Cudd 1996). The difference between this sort of injustice and oppression is that it need not be group-based.

18. Immigration restrictions may be justified in some cases on grounds similar to the justification of capitalism, by arguing that the existence of national borders allows for political and economic organization that increases the wealth and opportunity for even the worst off outside the borders. It would have to be argued as well that by eliminating such borders there would be a degradation of political and economic rights for all. But just as capitalism must provide a guaranteed social minimum to make the argument that it increases the choices of the worst off, immigration restrictions would have to allow exceptions to provide for the worst off individuals, especially those in immediate danger of violent death.

19. I am referring her to the theory of "compensating differentials," which says that there are jobs whose working conditions are more desirable than others and so will cause workers to choose those jobs for less pay over otherwise similar jobs (in terms of the amount of human capital one needs to get the job).

20. *Robinson v. Jacksonville Shipyards, Inc.,* 760 F. Supp. 1486 (M.D. Fla. 1991).

21. Statistics about inequalities between males and females are available in the U.N. report, *The World's Women 2000: Trends and Statistics,* available on-line at http://unstats.un.org/ unsd/demographic/products/indwm/unpub.htm.

22. By this I mean that if we compare the social inequalities suffered by almost any group that contains both men and women, the women in the group will be inferior or subordinate to the men of that group. This is especially true with respect to economic inequalities. There are certainly some women who are better off than some men, but considered as a group, women are less well off than men, and when economically deprived groups are considered in themselves, the women within them are less well off than the men in them.

23. Think only of the almost legendary status of business leaders like Lee Iaccoca, politicians like Jesse Jackson or Barbara Mikulski, and educators like Thomas Sowell.

24. See Bergmann (1986, 9–10, 63–64) for critical explication of this argument, and for an example of an economics text that argues this, see Fleisher and Knieser (1980, 405–413).

25. Fuchs (1989, 31–32), from Census of Population and Housing, 1980: Public-Use Microdata 1/100 C-Sample, Bureau of the Census, Washington, D.C., 1983.

26. The most important among these laws is the Equal Pay Act of 1963, which made it illegal to pay men and women different wages for "equal work on jobs the performance of which requires equal skill, effort, and responsibility, and which are performed under similar working conditions;" the Civil Rights Act of 1964, which prohibits discrimination in compensation, terms, or conditions on grounds of race, color, religion, sex, or national origin, and which provided for the establishment of an Equal Employment Opportunity Commission to enforce the act (Schmitz 1996, ch. 1).

27. See Okin (1989, 147), who makes a similar point.

28. Hirschman (1970) argues that the feasibility of exit from a relationship determines one's power within a relationship. See also Okin (1989, ch. 7). Formal bargaining theory supports the claim that the opportunities should the relationship fail determine the share of goods in the relationship, since the no-agreement outcome plays a crucial role in determining the outcome of the bargain. Mill in *On the Subjection of Women* (1988) also recognized that differences in bargaining power within a marriage would determine what women would choose to do. See esp. p. 43.

29. Recall here that the model is a rational choice model of behavior. There are surely many non-rational processes that come into play in making a decision to leave a batterer, and

there may also be threats that the batterer uses to assert his power that I have not factored in. This was not meant as a complete explanation of why men batter or why women stay with batterers.

30. In their now well-known sex discrimination lawsuit, Sears tried to defend its actions on exactly these grounds—that women are poor risks for stability and that they (the women) did not really want jobs that would force them to make inflexible time commitments. See Weiner (1985).

31. Mahoney (1995) discusses women's choices of marital partners in light of this bargaining situation. She recommends that women marry "down," that is, that they marry men who have less bargaining power, whether because they are younger or less well educated, in order to avoid this outcome.

32. It may be arguable that an initial natural inequality could be the catalyst for the vicious cycle, though not in any conceivable social arrangement of power. In this case capitalism and the importance of access to wealth in order to have power forms the background that is necessary for the wage gap to play the catalytic role in the cycle.

33. In my home state of Kansas there are on average 26.6 slots in a licensed day care for every 100 children between the ages of 0–5, and in some counties fewer than 20 per 100 children. That leaves parents of 73% of the young children either to share care with others, find caregivers who are not even minimally qualified as daycare providers, or opt out of the workforce to care for the children (Institute for Women's Policy Research, 2002).

6. Psychological Harms of Oppression

1. Rawls (1971) for instance holds that "the basis for self-esteem" is a "primary good"— a good that one wants no matter what else one wants.

2. In January 2005, a large number of debates in a variety of media and forums were waged over statements by Harvard University President Lawrence Summers's claim that women are not successful in science in large part because of a genetic inferiority in mathematical ability. While there exist numerous causes and explanations of women's lack of success in science, some of which are social and under his direct control, it is quite premature and ungenerous, if not to say completely unfair, to chalk it up to the one factor over which none of us have any control.

3. Sadker and Sadker (1994) paint a frightening and depressing picture of sexual harassment by both boys and teachers against girls in America's schools today.

4. Of course, as a female academic, I have experienced this personally.

5. This story was related to me by a colleague of mine, who was the victim.

6. Severely cognitively disabled humans and nonhuman animals may also deserve special treatment on other grounds, but an investigation of that issue is beyond the scope of this book.

7. It is worth noting that abortion laws objectify women even if one holds that abortion is, all things considered, immoral. That is, it objectifies women to prohibit them from severing their ties to a fetus at will by treating them as an object for the use of another.

8. This is a point about the non-foundational nature of our epistemic and moral situation that has been made in a variety of ways by the likes of Wittgenstein, Heidegger, Neurath, Duhem, Quine, Sellars, just to name some of the major twentieth-century philosophers who have done so.

9. Lewis (1969) is the classic account of conventions as solutions to coordination games. In Cudd (1990) I expressed some doubts about the overall aims of the account, but the claim that conventions are solutions to coordination games stands.

10. I owe this analogy to Griffin (1979).

11. I am grateful to Aisha Chaudhri for helping me to see the depth of this problem for religious minorities in the United States.

12. The term "deformed desires" is used by Superson (2005). Other important treatments of adaptive preference or deformed preference include Elster (1983b); Sen (1995); and Agarwal (1997).

13. I argued in chapter 5 that women often face incentives through the social structure to choose ways of life that will further their oppression. The example that I used to illustrate this was a couple deciding on how to allocate unpaid and paid labor between them, and I argued that the gender wage gap (or any of a number of other structural incentives) would make it rational, from a total household perspective at least, for the wife to do the unpaid domestic labor and the husband to do the paid market labor. But, given the exit options that this choice would give each of the spouses, the woman's power to control resources and outcomes in the marriage and in bargaining over goods would be seriously reduced. Hence, the oppressive conditions that give rise to the choices would then tend to be reinforced by those choices. Yet to make an opposite choice might require a degree of power in the marriage that was already precluded by the relative bargaining positions of men and women. Women prefer housework against this background of oppression.

14. I do not mean to suggest here that democracy requires religious intolerance whenever a religion discriminates invidiously against women (or ethnic minorities). At this point, I am simply illustrating the kinds of undemocratic preference deformations that can occur under the influence of religion. In the end I think that the only way to have a justifiable democratic system is to guarantee a set of personal rights that will sometimes conflict with democratic outcomes. Although freedom of religion will be an important right to protect, a democratic society ought to exclude religion from the public sphere. This will be a delicate balance. The details of the balancing process will depend on many local and historical conditions, and are beyond the scope of this book to discuss.

15. I do not mean to suggest here that attacking oppression in these cerebral, cognitive ways is the only or the most effective means. My point is that these are the courses of action that would directly address the oppressive nature of stereotyping itself.

7. Resistance and Responsibility

1. Although in advance it would have been surprising and doubtful to imagine that one individual could have had such an effect, in fact it happened, and thus there must have been some reasonable hope of success.

2. Michael Schwerner was a white Civil Rights worker in Mississippi who was murdered in 1964 by the Ku Klux Klan along with two other Civil Rights workers.

3. McGary and Lawson (1992) discuss the case of African American slaves whose oppression was so long-standing and pervasive that it was as invisible to them as the fact that humans cannot exceed the speed of light is invisible to us, at least most of the time.

4. Sending a message of revolt may be a way of lessening the effects of oppression by making the oppressed person feel better. But it might also make the oppression harsher. Hence we cannot assimilate sending a message of revolt to lessening oppression. Resistance need not have any hope to lessen oppression to still count as resistance. I owe thanks to Mark Lance, Julie Maybee, and Russ Shafer-Landau for discussion of this point.

5. In his *Autobiography* (1873, esp. 79–81), John Stuart Mill briefly discusses his work with the East India Company and what he learned from that experience. But he does not discuss the colonial oppression of India that that firm played such a central role in. In this sense he was blind to his British imperial privilege.

6. Recall Nyla Branscombe's work on privilege discussed in chapter 3 (Branscombe 1998; Branscombe et al. 1999).

7. Frankfurt (1988) poses the possibility of there being moral obligations on the coerced to resist, but considers this the less interesting case than the case in which coercion exonerates the individual of moral responsibility, and so does not discuss it. Wertheimer (1994) agrees and suggests a condition similar to mine for situations in which there is some voluntary choice and exploitation. He writes that "it is plausible to maintain that one is coerced when the background conditions are *unjust*" (82, emphasis in text).

8. The situation is more complex than I have acknowledged here. For example, many women argue that what we should work for is an entire transformation of society such that whether work is paid or unpaid has no bearing on the life prospects, self-esteem, or self-determination of the individual. In the interest of the question at issue I shall ignore this kind of argument.

9. Evidence for this can easily be seen in letters to the editor of feminist and women's magazines such as *Ms.* or *American Baby*. Social conservatives would surely disagree with my examples here, but I think that they could fit some of their own into the category of oppression by choice. For example, a recent commentator argues that poor minorities who have historically been discriminated against, for example, African Americans, can choose to pursue a strategy of self-improvement to get themselves out of poverty rather than relying on government handouts. This would involve some initial hardship and risk of failure, but if pursued in large numbers might forever sever the link between race and poverty (Steele 1990). Another example that I do not discuss in the text might be gay people who can choose to come out or remain closeted. They are oppressed through their choice to remain closeted, and choosing to come out in large numbers might lessen or end the oppression of all, or so one might argue.

10. Heyd adds that the action must be morally good "both because of its intended consequences and because it has intrinsic moral value." But the "and" here seems stronger than is necessary, since one could imagine cases where a good is brought about by unsavory but not immoral ways, or a kind thing is done to someone that does not have morally significant consequences.

11. Some, including Baron (1987) and Hale (1991), have argued that "supererogation" does not refer, in other words, that there are no such things as supererogatory acts. I would disagree, though this is not the place for a sustained argument against them. In any case, since I am arguing that resistance to oppression by choice is not supererogatory, their arguments would not nullify my conclusions here.

12. Calhoun provides a nice discussion of how participation in an oppressive institution tends to strengthen the institution and even justify it from at least the perspective of stability, an important aim of social institutions. Thomas Hill, "Symbolic protest and calculated silence" in his (1991) book, also argues that one might associate oneself with an institution just by refusing to dissociate from it, and that this then lends the institution the honor and prestige of one's association.

13. I say "nearly costless" because it may be that one woman gains by criticizing other women, or at least protects her own position in the social hierarchy. Foregoing that advantage would be a cost in the sense of an opportunity cost.

14. This seems to implicate the oppressed who are at once harmed by the legacy of slavery and genocide while being benefited by the collective social goods produced by the slaves and the stolen wealth. The situation is complicated and some persons may not fit neatly into the privileged/oppressed categories. The test my account offers to sort persons into the oppressed category is this: would a similarly situated (in all respects other than the condition of oppression under consideration) person be better off?

15. The Montgomery bus boycott was marked by violence aimed at the protestors, and remained in effect for over a year before the protestors won the struggle, however.

16. Other such conventions on human rights include: the Convention on the Elimination of All Forms of Discrimination Against Women, the International Convention on the Elimination of All Forms of Racial Discrimination, the Slavery Convention, the Forced Labour Convention, the International Convention on the Protection of the Rights of All Migrant Workers and Members of Their Families, and the Convention on the Rights of the Child. A complete list of these and links to texts are available at the following website: http://www.unhchr.ch/html/intlinst.htm.

17. Although the basic concept of criminal offense thus refers to two individuals, it is obviously often extended to more than two. But it remains individualistic in the sense that each offending individual is held responsible for harms to each victim, and the crimes are added up in that manner. So if I rob three people at gunpoint I have committed three crimes, one against each of my victims.

18. To see that this is the case one need merely consider different societies' legal structures governing sexual relations, kinship relations, spousal obligations, or divorce restrictions.

19. This seems to be the case in our society, given *Beauharnais v. Illinois*, 343 U.S. 250 (1952). However, it may also be argued that this is not settled law, given the subsequent decision in *New York Times v. Sullivan*, 376 U.S. 254 (1964) (Simon 1995).

20. Androcentrism is assuming that the experiences, biology, and social roles of males or men are the norm and that of females or women a deviation from the norm. Androcentrism is to be distinguished from sexism, which is the denigration of one sex or gender. An institution can thus be androcentric without being sexist.

21. While it is beyond the scope of this chapter to argue the point here, I think that it can be shown that the equal individual perspective is similarly ethnocentric, that is, focused on the experience of white Americans of European descent and centered on the experience of the middle class and the able-bodied.

22. This sense of victim-blaming was articulated by Ryan (1976), who was writing about the failures of the War on Poverty programs to substantially alter the situation of poor blacks in America.

23. I mean "normal" in the sense of the psychologists, that is, I am not making a normative judgment about the behavior that I term "normal" but am merely reporting that the behavior is normative, expected, or acceptable in the culture, while other behaviors are less expected or even unacceptable. I mean this sense of "normal" throughout this section.

24. MacKinnon would not, however, agree that any aspect of our lives that involves gender is nonsexual. I find that claim reductionistic, though, and so want to separate my view from it. The point that men dominate women can be made without appeal to sexuality. Unlike MacKinnon, I think that the sex/gender distinction is a crucial one for feminists to maintain, for we may look forward to an ungendered future, but sex will be there as long as we are biological creatures. Since facts about the sexes do not map one-to-one onto facts about gender, it cannot be that they are the same thing.

25. Domestic labor by homemakers is not part of the accounting of the Gross Domestic Product, though if done by paid workers it is counted.

26. Women make up about 96 percent of the labor force in private household service, and in 1999 had a median weekly income for full time work of $244. Source: Labor Force Statistics from Current Population Survey, U.S. Bureau of Labor Statistics.

27. For most employees, time off for pregnancy or infant care must come from unpaid leave. However, the fact that most employees now can take 12 weeks of unpaid family leave is

a result of the Family and Medical Leave Act of 1993; prior to this time, only 18 percent of employees in the private sector could take any form of family leave. Source: Employee Benefits Survey, Bureau of Labor Statistics, 1992, 1996.

28. See http://www.plannedparenthood.org/BIRTHCONTROL/contrachoices.htm.

29. See http://www.plannedparenthood.org/BIRTHCONTROL/YOU_AND_PILL.HTM.

30. In an essay entitled, "The Dark Side of Choice," Gary Bauer invents the following reasoning as typical of women considering abortion: "If your baby is inconvenient for you, if this isn't a good time for you, if the tiny person sucking her thumb, blissfully unaware of how precarious is her claim to life, is too much trouble for you, no big deal. Just dispose of her . . . and go on with your life." http://www.roevwade.org/s3html.

31. Consider the anti-abortion bumper sticker that reads: "Thank your mother for not aborting you."

32. *Planned Parenthood v. Casey*, 505 U.S. 833 (1992), struck down the portion of the Pennsylvania law requiring spousal consent to abortion, leaving it to the discretion of the woman in cases not otherwise proscribed by law. However, the Court also upheld other restrictions on the legal right to abortion, such as a waiting period, and parental consent for minor women provided that there is a possibility for judicial exception.

33. Such laws include required waiting periods, parental notification, and required "counseling" designed to persuade women not to seek abortions.

34. Antioch College attempted to require consent for each sexual act in its date rape policy, and it resulted in a nationwide brouhaha. The policy was even ridiculed in a skit on the television program *Saturday Night Live*.

35. The United Nations Human Development Index, which rates the quality of life of persons in that country on a 0–1 scale, rates the United States at .976, while when adjusted for gender disparity in life outcomes for women it is .824. (UNDR 1993).

36. A particularly insightful male rape victim writes about the distinction between the way that women and men suffer from rape: "The distinction is that while many women and some men are victimized by rape, all women are oppressed by it, and any victimization of women occurs in a context of oppression most men simply do not understand" (Searles and Berger 1995, 255).

37. Again, though I shall not argue the points here, the oppressed group perspective should apply to other crimes that specifically target other oppressed groups and reinforce their oppression.

38. Note that the special circumstance of oppression might also consistently be applied to racially based hate crimes, as well. However, this differs from the so-call hate crimes legislation, which attempts to punish crimes based on their motivation (Freeman and Kaminer, 1994). My proposal to legally recognize the harm of oppression would require that group harm be demonstrated rather than that the motivations of the harm be out of race or gender or sexual orientation bias.

39. That is, conservatives would be forced either to deny that traditional practices that subordinate women are unjust or give up the traditional practices because they are unjust, a move that would make them no longer conservative.

40. There is some evidence to suggest this in the social psychology literature (Branscombe 1998).

41. One might, for example, take this to be an implication of Rawls's claim that it is illegitimate to use state power to decide basic questions of justice as one particular comprehensive doctrine directs (Rawls 1993, 62).

42. This is not to say that he thinks that being a straightforward maximizer is actually rational, however.

43. In 1988, for instance, Felicia Schwartz, a professor at the Harvard Business School, made the headlines with her suggestion that women who wanted to raise children ought to

choose what she called the "mommy track," which would keep women out of the line for corporate promotion. See also Okin (1989) and Bergmann (1986).

8. Fashioning Freedom

1. This is what is going on, I believe, when women criticize feminists for claiming that veiling or female circumcision is oppressive. These women ask feminists to concentrate on what they see as the real issues, such as poverty. But to accept veiling and circumcision is to accept the hierarchy of sex, and that is forfeiting freedom at a basic level.

2. The importance of connection to others has been described particularly well by contractarian thinkers. Rawls, as I will discuss shortly, writes that "In a fully just society persons seek their good in ways peculiar to themselves, and they rely upon their associates to do things they could not have done, as well as things they might have done but did not. . . . It is a feature of human sociability that we are by ourselves but parts of what we might be" (Rawls 1971, 529). Yet contractarians are also quick to insist that shared activities must not be coerced. David Gauthier, writing about the passage of Rawls just cited, states: "if each participant is to find shared activity intrinsically valuable, then it must satisfy the standard of fairness" (Gauthier 1986, 338).

3. An excellent presentation of the argument for and policy plans for providing child care in America, see Helburn and Bergmann (2002).

4. Or even better, perhaps we could shorten the working day and lengthen the school day so that they match, but so that we have more leisure time with our children or other projects. Joan Williams (2000) writes persuasively that the current norms of the ideal worker are bad for both men and women, and that the full commodification of carework would lead to a far worse outcome for individuals and families than reshaping work life altogether. While I appreciate her concerns over the full commodification model, I worry that there will always be a wage-based motivation to be the hardest working worker in a capitalist economy, and hence that attempts to shorten the working day will be thwarted by the collective outcome of the struggles of each individual to have a competitive advantage over the next.

5. Among the benefits provided to religions I would include not only the tax exemptions of the organizations themselves and tax deductions provided to individuals who contribute to them but also social benefits of respect or the benefits of attention by media to the leaders and so on. Generally, religions are regarded as having a special corner on morality. Yet surely those who articulate notions of freedom and seek to achieve them are acting morally and with vision, perhaps even in ways that religious persons label "spiritual."

6. This is not to say that there are no losers here. Drug invention resources will be skewed toward curing more common diseases and away from less common diseases and problems that are described as lifestyle choices, such as those that Viagra or Cialis are meant to combat.

7. Full mission statement available from the World Bank website, www.worldbank.org.

8. John Rawls (1993) accounts for the existence of deep disagreements over social, moral, and religious matters by appeal to what he calls the facts of reason.

9. We can do this because we belong to different social groups, some of which are privileged and some oppressed relative to others. Our multiple identities help us to escape the paradox of social construction, which Hirschmann describes as the puzzle of: "How can we ever figure out who 'we' are or what 'we want' if the language and concepts we must use are antagonistic to the enterprise we seek to carry out, that is, are themselves barriers to women's freedom?" (Hirschmann 2003, 99).

10. Lugones (1990) nicely states the difficulty for theories of oppression that locate oppression in social structures and that want to recommend liberatory strategies.

11. See also Homiak (1990, esp. 175–176).

References

Ackerly, Brooke. 2005. "Comments on Young's 'The Gendered Cycle of Vulnerability in the Less Developed World.'" Presented at the Susan Moller Okin memorial conference, Stanford University, Feb. 4, 2005.

Agarwal, Bina. 1997. "Bargaining and Gender Relations: Within and Beyond the Household." *Feminist Economics* 3:1–51.

Allport, Gordon W. 1979. *The Nature of Prejudice.* 25th anniversary ed. Reading, Mass.: Addison-Wesley.

Arendell, Terry. 1986. *Mothers and Divorce: Legal, Economic, and Social Dilemmas.* Berkeley: University of California Press.

Bailey, Alison. 1998. "Privilege: Expanding on Marilyn Frye's 'Oppression.'" *Journal of Social Philosophy* 29(3):104–119.

Bales, Kevin. 1999. *Disposable People: New Slavery in the Global Economy.* Berkeley: University of California Press.

———. 2002. "The Social Psychology of Modern Slavery." *Scientific American* (April):80–88.

Bar On, Bat-Ami. 2002. *The Subject of Violence: Arendtean Exercises in Understanding.* Lanham, Md.: Rowman & Littlefield.

Barbalet, J. M. 1983. *Marx's Construction of Social Theory.* London: Routledge & Kegan Paul.

Baron, Marcia. 1987. "Kantian Ethics and Supererogation." *Journal of Philosophy* 84:237–262.

Bartky, Sandra L. 1990. *Femininity and Domination: Studies in the Phenomenology of Oppression.* New York: Routledge.

Bay, Christian. 1981. *Strategies of Political Emancipation.* Notre Dame, Ind.: University of Notre Dame Press.

Bayles, Michael. 1974. "Coercive Offers and Public Benefits." *Personalist* 55:139–144.

Becker, David. 1995. "The Deficiency of the Concept of Posttraumatic Stress Disorder When Dealing with Victims of Human Rights Violations." In *Beyond Trauma,* ed. Rolf Kleber, Charles Figley, and Berthold Gersons, pp. 99–131. New York: Plenum Press.

Becker, Gary S. 1991. *A Treatise on the Family,* Enl. ed. Cambridge, Mass.: Harvard University Press.

Becker, Neal C., and Ann E. Cudd. 2003. "Poverty, Wage Slavery, or Bondage? Ethical Dilemmas of Child Labor under Globalization," unpublished manuscript.

Bem, Sandra. 1981. "Gender Schema Theory: A Cognitive Account of Sex Typing." *Psychological Review* 88:354–364.

Bem, Sandra, ed. 1987. *Masculinity/Femininity: Basic Perspectives.* New York: Oxford University Press.

Berger, Ronald J., Searles, Patricia, and Neumann, W. L. 1995. "Rape Law Reform: Its Nature, Origins, and Impact." In *Rape and Society*, ed. Ronald J. Berger and Patricia Searles, pp. 223–232. Boulder, Colo.: Westview Press.

Bergmann, Barbara R. 1986. *The Economic Emergence of Women.* New York: Basic Books.

Berlin, Isaiah. 1969. "Two Concepts of Liberty." In *Four Essays on Liberty*, pp. 118–172. London: Oxford University Press.

Bertrand, Marianne, and Sendhil Mullainathan. 2004. "Are Emily and Greg more Employable than Lakisha and Jamal? A Field Experiment on Labor Market Discrimination." *American Economic Review* 94(4):991–1013.

Blanchard, William H. 1996. *Neocolonialism American Style, 1960–2000.* Westport, Conn.: Greenwood Press.

Blau, Francine, and John Graham. 1990. "Black-White Differences in Wealth and Asset Composition." *Quarterly Journal of Economics* 105(2):321–339.

Boski, Pawel. 1988. "Cross-cultural Studies of Person Perception: Effects of Ingroup/Outgroup Membership and Ethnic Schemata." *Journal of Cross-Cultural Psychology* 19:287–328.

Brady, Eric. 2002. *Major Changes Debated for Title IX.* Online. Available: http://www.usatoday.com/sports/college/2002?12?17?1a?title?ix?cover_x.htm

Branscombe, Nyla. 1998. "Thinking about One's Gender Group's Privileges or Disadvantages: Consequences for Well-being in Women and Men." *British Journal of Social Psychology* 37(2):167–184.

———. 1999. "Perceiving Pervasive Discrimination among African-Americans: Implications for Group Identification and Well-being." *Journal of Personality and Social Psychology* 77: 135–149.

Briere, John. 1997. *Psychological Assessment of Adult Posttraumatic States.* Washington, DC: American Psychological Association.

Brison, Susan J. 2002. *Aftermath: Violence and the Remaking of a Self.* Princeton, N.J.: Princeton University Press.

Brittan, Arthur, and Mary Maynard. 1984. *Sexism, Racism, and Oppression.* New York: Blackwell.

Browing, Joan, et al. 2000. *Deep in Our Hearts: Nine White Women in the Freedom Movement.* Athens, Ga.: University of Georgia Press.

Browning, Edgar K., and Jacquelene M. Browning. 1989. *Microeconomic Theory and Applications.* 3rd ed. Glenview, Ill.: Scott, Foresman.

Bulhan, Hussein A. 1985. *Frantz Fanon and the Psychology of Oppression.* New York: Plenum Press.

Burg, Steven L. 1997. "Genocide in Bosnia-Herzegovina?" In *Century of Genocide*, ed. Samuel Totten, William S. Parsons, and Israel W. Charny, pp. 424–433. New York: Garland Publishing.

Burge, Tyler. 1986. "Individualism and Psychology." *Philosophical Review* 45:3–45.

Burke, Edmund. 2001. *Reflections on the French Revolution.* New York: Collier; Bartleby.com., www.bartleby.com/24/3/.

Calhoun, Cheshire. 1989. "Responsibility and Reproach." *Ethics* 99:389–406.

Chang, Iris. 2000. "The Rape of Nanking." In *War's Dirty Secret*, ed. Anne Barstow, pp. 46–56. Cleveland: Pilgrim Press.

Chodorow, Nancy. 1978. *The Reproduction of Mothering: Psychoanalysis and the Sociology of Gender*. Berkeley: University of California Press.

Churchland, Paul M. 1982. "The Anti-realist Epistemology of Van Fraassen's *The Scientific Image*." *Pacific Philosophical Quarterly* 63(2):226–235.

Clatterbaugh, Kenneth. 1996. "Are Men Oppressed?" In *Rethinking Masculinity*, ed. Larry May, Robert Strikwerda, and Patrick D. Hopkins. Lanham, Md.: Rowman and Littlefield.

Cohen, G. A. 1988. *History, Labour, and Freedom: Themes from Marx*. Oxford: Clarendon Press.

Cohen, Joshua. 2001. "Taking People as They Are." *Philosophy and Public Affairs* 30(4):363–386.

Connolly, John. 1976. "A Dialectical Approach to Action Theory." *Inquiry* 19:427–472.

Copp, David. 2002. "Social Unity and the Identity of Persons." *Journal of Political Philosophy* 10(4):365–391.

Cornell, Drucilla. 1998. *At the Heart of Freedom: Feminism, Sex, and Equality*. Princeton, N.J.: Princeton University Press.

Crafts, Hannah. 2002. *The Bondwoman's Narrative*. New York: Warner Books.

Crocker, Jennifer, and Brenda Major. 1989. "Social Stigma and Self-esteem: The Self-protective Properties of Stigma." *Psychological Review* 96(4):608–630.

Cudd, Ann E. 1990. "Conventional Foundationalism and the Origin of Norms." *Southern Journal of Philosophy* 28:485–503.

———. 1994. "Enforced Pregnancy, Rape, and the Image of Woman." *Journal of Philosophical Studies* 25:22–44.

———. 1996. "Is Pareto Optimality a Criterion of Justice?" *Social Theory and Practice* 22:1–34.

———. 2005. "How to Explain Oppression." *Philosophy of the Social Sciences* 35(1):20–49.

D'Souza, Dinesh. 2002. "Two Cheers for Colonialism." *Chronicle of Higher Education* (May 10, 2002):B7.

Darity, Jr., W. 2000. "Give Affirmative Action Time to Act." *Chronicle of Higher Education* (Dec. 1):18.

Davidson, Donald. 1980. *Essays on Actions and Events*. Oxford: Clarendon Press.

———. 1984. *Inquiries into Truth and Interpretation*. Oxford: Clarendon Press.

Davis, Angela Y. 1981. *Women, Race, & Class*. New York: Random House.

de Beauvoir, Simone. 1971. *The Second Sex*. Trans. H. M. Parshley. New York: Penguin.

De Leon, Brunilda. 1993. "Sex Role Identity among College Students: A Cross-cultural Analysis." *Hispanic Journal of Behavioral Sciences* 15:476–489.

DeBruin, Debra A. 1998. "Identifying Sexual Harassment: The Reasonable Woman Standard." In *Violence against Women: Philosophical perspectives*, ed. Stanley French, pp. 107–122. Ithaca, N.Y.: Cornell University Press.

DeGeorge, Richard. 1983. "Social Reality and Social Relations." *Review of Metaphysics* 37:3–20.

Dhawan, Nisha, Ira Roseman, R. K. Naidu, and S. I. Rettek. 1995. "Self-concepts across Two Cultures: India and the United States." *Journal of Cross-Cultural Psychology* 26:606–621.

Dobb, Maurice. 1947. *Studies in the Development of Capitalism*. New York: International Publishers.

Dobrin, Adam. 1996. *Statistical Handbook on Violence in America*. Phoenix, Ariz.: Oryx Press.

Dollar, David, and Aart Kraay. 2002. "Growth is Good for the Poor." *Journal of Economic Growth* 7(3):195–225.

Downs, Donald A. 1996. *More Than Victims: Battered Women, the Syndrome Society, and the Law*. Chicago: University of Chicago Press.

Dressler, Joshua. 1995. *Understanding Criminal Law*. 2nd ed. United States of America: Legal Text Series, A Times Mirror Higher Education Group Company.

Drèze, Jean, and Amartya Sen. 1989. *Hunger and Public Action*. New York: Oxford University Press.

Dublin, Thomas, and Kerry Harney (n.d.). *How Did Immigrant Textile Workers Struggle to Achieve an American Standard of Living? The 1912 Lawrence Strike*.

Dummett, Michael A. E. 1978. *Truth and Other Enigmas*. Cambridge, Mass.: Harvard University Press.

Elster, Jon. 1983a. *Explaining Technical Change: A Case Study in the Philosophy of Science*. Cambridge: Cambridge University Press.

———. 1983b. *Sour Grapes*. New York: Cambridge University Press.

———. 1984. *Ulysses and the Sirens: Studies in Rationality and Irrationality*. Rev. ed. New York: Cambridge University Press.

———. 1985. *Making Sense of Marx*. New York: Cambridge University Press.

Enloe, Cynthia H. 2000. *Maneuvers: The International Politics of Militarizing Women's Lives*. Berkeley: University of California Press.

Estrich, Susan. 1987. *Real Rape*. Cambridge, Mass.: Harvard University Press.

Ezorsky, Gertrude. 1991. *Racism and Justice: The Case for Affirmative Action*. Ithaca, N.Y.: Cornell University Press.

Faludi, Susan. 1999. *Stiffed: The Betrayal of the American Man*. New York: W. Morrow.

Fanon, Frantz. 1963. *The Wretched of the Earth*. New York: Grove Press.

Felson, Richard B., and James T. Tedeschi. 1993. "A Social Interactionist Approach to Violence: Cross-cultural applications." *Violence and Victims* 8:295–310.

Ferguson, Ann. 1991. *Sexual Democracy: Women, Oppression, and Revolution*. Boulder, Colo.: Westview Press.

Ferraro, Kathleen. 1996. "The Dance of Dependency: A Genealogy of Domestic Violence Discourse." *Hypatia* 11(4): 77–91.

Fiske, Susan T., and Shelley E. Taylor. 1991. *Social Cognition*. 2nd ed. Reading, Mass.: Addison-Wesley.

Flax, Jane. 1981. "Psychoanalysis and the Philosophy of Science: Critique or Resistance?" *Journal of Philosophy* 78:561–568.

Fleisher, Belton M., and Thomas J. Kniesner. 1980. *Labor Economics: Theory, Evidence, and Policy*. Englewood Cliffs, N.J.: Prentice-Hall.

Flew, Anthony. 1985. *Thinking about Social Thinking: The Philosophy of the Social Sciences*. New York: Blackwell.

Folbre, Nancy. 1994. *Who Pays for the Kids? Gender and the Structures of Constraint*. New York: Routledge.

Folbre, Nancy, and Heidi Hartmann. 1988. "The Rhetoric of Self-interest: Ideology and Gender in Economic Theory." In *The Consequences of Economic Rhetoric*, ed. Arjo Klamer, Donald N. McCloskey, and Robert M. Solow, pp. 184–205. New York: Cambridge University Press.

Frankfurt, Harry. 1988. "Coercion and Moral Responsibility." In *The Importance of What We Care About*, pp. 26–46. Cambridge: Cambridge University Press.

Fraser, Nancy. 1995. "From Redistribution to Recognition? Dilemmas of Justice in a 'Post-Socialist' Age." *New Left Review* 212:68–93.

———. 1997. *Justice Interruptus: Critical Reflections on the "Postsocialist" Condition*. New York: Routledge.

Freeman, Steven, and Debbie Kaminer. 1994. *Hate Crimes Laws: A Comprehensive Guide*. Anti-Defamation League.

Freire, Paulo. 1970. *Pedagogy of the Oppressed*. New York: Herder and Herder.

French, Stanley, ed. 1998. *Violence against Women*. Ithaca, N.Y.: Cornell University Press.

Friedan, Betty. 1963. *The Feminine Mystique*. New York: Norton.

Friedman, Marilyn, and Larry May. 1985. "Harming Women as a Group." *Social Theory and Practice* 11:207–234.

Frye, Marilyn. 1983. *The Politics of Reality: Essays in Feminist Theory*. Trumansburg, N.Y.: Crossing Press.

Fuchs, Victor. 1989. Women's Quest for Economic Equality. *Journal of Economic Perspectives* 3(1):25–41.

Gauthier, David P. 1986. *Morals by Agreement*. New York: Oxford University Press.

Gauthier, Jeffrey. 1997. *Hegel and Feminist Social Criticism: Justice, Recognition, and the Feminine*. Albany: State University of New York Press.

Gilbert, Margaret. 1989. *On Social Facts*. New York: Routledge.

———. 1996. *Living Together: Rationality, Sociality, and Obligation*. Lanham, Md.: Rowman and Littlefield.

Gilman, Charlotte P. 1966. *Women and Economics: A Study of the Economic Relation between Men and Women as a Factor in Social Evolution*. New York: Harper & Row.

Gottlieb, Roger S., ed. 1990. *Thinking the Unthinkable: Meanings of the Holocaust*. Mahwah: Paulist Press.

Gould, Carol C. 1978. *Marx's Social Ontology: Individuality and Community in Marx's Theory of Social Reality*. Cambridge, Mass.: MIT Press.

———. 1988. *Rethinking Democracy: Freedom and Social Cooperation in Politics, Economy, and Society*. New York: Cambridge University Press.

Gould, Stephen J. 1996. *The Mismeasure of Man*. Rev. and expanded ed. New York: Norton.

Griffin, Susan. 1979. *Rape: The Power of Consciousness*. New York: Harper and Row Publishers.

Grünbaum, Adolf. 1984. *The Foundations of Psychoanalysis: A Philosophical Critique*. Berkeley: University of California Press.

———. 1993. *Validation in the Clinical Theory of Psychoanalysis: A Study in the Philosophy of Psychoanalysis*. Madison, Conn.: International Universities Press, Inc.

Hale, Susan. 1991. "Against Supererogation." *American Philosophical Quarterly* 28:273–285.

Hamilton, Alexander, Madison, James, and Jay, John. 1961. *The Federalist Papers*. New York: New American Library.

Hampton, Jean. 1991. "A New Theory of Retribution." In *Liability and Responsibility*, ed. R. G. Frey, pp. 377–414. New York: Cambridge University Press.

Han, Gyuseog, and Bonsoon Park. 1995. "Children's Choice in Conflict: Application of the Theory of Individualism-Collectivism." *Journal of Cross-Cultural Psychology* 26: 298–313.

Hanson, F. A. 1975. *Meaning in Culture*. London: Routledge & K. Paul.

Hardy, Amy, and Miles Moffeit. 2004. "Camouflaging Criminals: Sexual Violence in the Military."*Amnesty Now* Spring: 22–26.

Hartmann, Heidi I. 1979. "The Unhappy Marriage of Marxism and Feminism: Towards a More Progressive Union." *Capital and Class* 8:1–33.

Harvey, J. 1996. "Oppression, Moral Abandonment, and the Role of Protest." *Journal of Social Philosophy* 27(1):156–171.

———. 1999. *Civilized Oppression*. Lanham, Md.: Rowman and Littlefield.

Haslanger, Sally. 2002. "On Being Objective and Being Objectified." In *A Mind of One's Own: Feminist Essays on Reason and Objectivity*, ed. Louise M. Antony and Charlotte E. Witt, pp. 209–253. Boulder, Colo.: Westview Press.

———. 2004a. "Oppressions: Racial and Other." In *Racism in Mind*, ed. Michael P. Levine and Tamas Patak. Ithaca, N.Y.: Cornell University Press.

———. 2004b. "What Are We Talking About? The Semantics and Politics of 'Race' and 'Gender.'" Paper presented at Feminist Philosophy in the Analytic Tradition conference, London, Ontario, June 6.

Hayek, Friedrich A. von. 1944. *The Road to Serfdom*. Chicago: University of Chicago Press.

Hearne, Vicki. 1986. *Adam's Task: Calling Animals by Name*. New York: Knopf.

Heberle, Renee. 1996. "Deconstructive Strategies and the Movement against Sexual Violence." *Hypatia* 11:63–76.

Hegel, Georg Wilhelm Friedrich. 1977. *Phenomenology of Spirit*. Oxford: Clarendon Press.

Helburn, Suzanne W., and Barbara R. Bergmann. 2002. *America's Child Care Problem: The Way Out*. New York: Palgrave for St. Martin's Press.

Herman, Barbara. 1991. "Agency, Attachment, and Difference." *Ethics* 101(4):775–797.

Herman, Judith L. 1992. *Trauma and Recovery*. New York: BasicBooks.

Heyd, David. 1982. *Supererogation: Its Status in Ethical Theory*. New York: Cambridge University Press.

Hill, Thomas E. 1991. *Autonomy and Self Respect*. New York: Cambridge University Press.

Hirschman, Albert O. 1970. *Exit, Voice and Loyalty: Responses to Decline in Firms, Organizations, and States*. Cambridge, Mass.: Harvard University Press.

Hirschmann, Nancy J. 2003. *The Subject of Liberty: Toward a Feminist Theory of Freedom*. Princeton, N.J.: Princeton University Press.

Hobbes, Thomas. 1985. *Leviathan*. Ed. C. B. Macpherson. London: Penguin.

Hochschild, Adam. 1998. *King Leopold's Ghost: A Story of Greed, Terror, and Heroism in Colonial Africa*. Boston: Houghton Mifflin.

Hoffman, C., and N. Hurst. 1990. "Gender Stereotypes: Perception or Rationalization?" *Journal of Personality and Social Psychology* 58:197–208.

Hofstadter, Douglas R. 1985. *Metamagical Themas: Questing for the Essence of Mind and Pattern*. New York: Basic Books.

Homiak, Marcia L. 1985. "The Pleasure of Virtue in Aristotle's Moral Theory." *Pacific Philosophical Quarterly* 66:93–110.

———. 1990. "Politics as Soul-Making: Aristotle on Becoming Good." *Philosophia* 20: 167–193.

———. 1991. "On the Malleability of Character." In *Feminist Ethics*, ed. Claudia Card, pp. 52–80. Lawrence: University Press of Kansas.

Hume, David. 1964. *Essays Moral, Political and Literary*. Ed. Thomas Hill Green, Thomas Hodge Grose. London: Scientia Verlag.

Hurley, Susan L. 1989. *Natural Reasons*. New York: Oxford University Press.

Idson, Todd L., and Hollis F. Price. 1992. "An Analysis of Wage Differentials by Gender and Ethnicity in the Public Sector." *Review of Black Political Economy* (Winter):75–97.

Institute for Women's Policy Research. 2002. *The Status of Women in Kansas*. Washington, DC: Author.

Institute for Women's Policy Research. 2003. "Gender Wage Gap Stagnant." News Release. Sept. 26.

International Development Research Centre. 2001. *The Responsibility to Protect*.

Jacobsen, Joyce P. 1994. *The Economics of Gender*. Cambridge, Mass.: Blackwell.

Jones, Peter. 1999. "Group Rights and Group Oppression." *Journal of Political Philosophy* 7:353–377.

Judd, Dennis R., and Susan S. Fainstein, eds. 1999. *The Tourist City*. New Haven: Yale University Press.

Kant, Immanuel. 1969. *Foundations of the Metaphysics of Morals*. Indianapolis: Bobbs-Merrill.

Kernohan, Andrew W. 1998. *Liberalism, Equality, and Cultural Oppression*. Cambridge: Cambridge University Press.

Kincaid, A. D. 1994. *Comparative National Development: Society and Economy in the New Global Order.* Ed. A. Douglas Kincaid and Alejandro Portes. Chapel Hill: University of North Carolina Press.

King, Martin Luther, Jr. 1964. *Why We Can't Wait.* New York: Harper & Row.

Kozol, Jonathon. 1991. *Savage Inequalities.* New York: Crown.

Kuhn, Thomas S. 1970. *The Structure of Scientific Revolutions.* 2nd ed. Chicago: University of Chicago Press.

Kymlicka, Will. 1995. *Multicultural Citizenship: A Liberal Theory of Minority Rights.* New York: Clarendon Press.

Lee, Sunhwa. 2004. "Women's Work Supports, Job Retention, and Job Mobility: Child Care and Employer-Provided Health Insurance Help Women Stay on Jobs." *Research News Reporter.* November.

Lewis, David K. 1969. *Convention, A Philosophical Study.* Cambridge, Mass.: Harvard University Press.

Lipset, Seymour M. 1996. *American Exceptionalism: A Double-edged Sword.* New York: W.W. Norton.

Locke, John. 1980. *Second Treatise of Government.* Ed. C. B. Macpherson. Indianapolis: Hackett Publishing.

———. 1983. *A Letter Concerning Toleration.* Indianapolis: Hackett Publishing.

Lopez-Claros, Augusto, and Saadia Zahidi. 2005. "Women's Empowerment: Measuring the Global Gender Gap." World Economic Forum. Accessed on-line at http://www.weforum.org/pdf/Global_Competitiveness_Reports/Reports/gender_gap.pdf on Oct. 18, 2005.

Lott, Bernice E., and Diane Maluso, eds. 1995. *The Social Psychology of Interpersonal Discrimination.* New York: Guilford Press.

Lugones, Maria. 1990. "Structure/Antistructure and Agency under Oppression." *Journal of Philosophy* 90 (October):500–507.

Lytton, H., and D. M. Romney. 1991. "Parents' Differential Socialization of Boys and Girls: A Meta-analysis." *Psychological Bulletin* 109:267–296.

Mackie, John L. 1965. "Causes and Conditions." *American Philosophical Quarterly* 17:245–264.

MacKinnon, Catharine A. 1983. "Feminism, Marxism, Method and the State." *Signs, Journal of Women and Culture in Society* 7(3):515–545.

———. 1987. *Feminism Unmodified: Discourses on Life and Law.* Cambridge, Mass.: Harvard University Press.

Maguigan, Holly. 1991. "Battered Women and Self-Defense: Myths and Misconceptions in Current Reform Proposals." *University of Pennsylvania Law Review* 140–198.

Mahoney, Rhona. 1995. *Kidding Ourselves: Babies, Breadwinning, and Bargaining Power.* New York: Basic Books.

Mandela, Nelson. 1994. *Long Walk to Freedom: The Autobiography of Nelson Mandela.* Boston: Little, Brown.

Mandelbaum, Maurice. 1955. *The Phenomenology of Moral Experience.* Glencoe, Ill.: Free Press.

Martin, Rex. 1993. *A System of Rights.* Oxford: Clarendon Press.

Marx, Karl. 1964. *Economic and Philosophic Manuscripts of 1844.* Ed. Dirk J. Struik. 1st American ed. New York: International Publishers.

———. 1967. *Capital.* Ed. Frederick Engels. 100th Anniversary Edition ed. Vol. I. New York: International Publishers.

Marx, Karl, and Friedrich Engels. 1978. *The Marx-Engels Reader.* Ed. Robert C. Tucker. 2nd ed. New York: Norton.

Matsuda, Mari J., et al. 1993. *Words That Wound: Critical Race Theory, Assaultive Speech, and the First Amendment*. Boulder, Colo.: Westview Press.

May, Larry. 1987. *The Morality of Groups: Collective Responsibility, Group-based Harm, and Corporate Rights*. Notre Dame, Ind.: University of Notre Dame Press.

———. 1992. *Sharing Responsibility*. Chicago: University of Chicago Press.

McGary, Howard, and Bill E. Lawson. 1992. *Between Slavery and Freedom: Philosophy and American Slavery*. Bloomington: Indiana University Press.

Meyerson, Denise. 1991. *False Consciousness*. New York: Oxford University Press.

Mill, John S. 1873. *Autobiography*. London: Longmans, Green, Reader, and Dyer.

———. 1978. *On Liberty*. Hackett.

———. 1988. *The Subjection of Women*. Indianapolis: Hackett.

Mill, John S., and Harriet Hardy Taylor Mill, eds. 1970. *Essays on Sex Equality*. Chicago: University of Chicago Press.

Miller, Joan G. 1984. "Culture and the Development of Everyday Social Explanation." *Journal of Personality and Social Psychology* 46 (May):961–978.

Mincer, Jacob, and Solomon Polachek. 1974. "Family Investments in Human Capital: Earnings of Women." *Journal of Political Economy*. 82:S76–S108.

Monson, Jamie. 2004/2005. "Freedom Railway: The Unexpected Successes of a Cold War Development Project." *Boston Review*. December–January.

Morris, Herbert. 1968. "Persons and Punishment." *Monist* 52:475–501.

Murphy, Jeffrie G. 1979. *Retribution, Justice, and Therapy: Essays in the Philosophy of Law*. Boston: D. Reidel.

Murphy, Jeffrie G., and Jules L. Coleman 1990. *Philosophy of Law: An Introduction to Jurisprudence*. Rev. ed. ed. Boulder, Colo.: Westview Press.

N.a. 2004. "Female Kicker Says She was Raped." *New York Times*, Feb. 18, D6.

Nafisi, Azar. 2003. *Reading Lolita in Tehran: A Memoir in Books*. New York: Random House.

Neath, Jeanne. 1997. "Social Causes of Impairment, Disability, and Abuse." *Journal of Disability Policy Studies*, 8:195–230.

North, Douglass. 1990. *Institutions, Institutional Change, and Economic Performance*. New York: Cambridge University Press.

Nozick, Robert. 1974. *Anarchy, State, and Utopia*. New York: Basic Books.

Oakes, Penelope, S. Alexander Haslam, and John C. Turner. 1994. *Stereotyping and Social Reality*. Malden, Mass.: Blackwell.

O'Connor, Peg. 2002. *Oppression and Responsibility: A Wittgensteinian Approach to Social Practices and Moral Theory*. University Park: Pennsylvania State University Press.

Oddou, Gary, and Mark Medenhall. 1984. "Person Perception in Cross-cultural Settings: A Review of Cross-cultural and Related Cognitive Literature." *International Journal of Intercultural Relations* 8:77–96.

Okin, Susan M. 1979. *Women in Western Political Thought*. Princeton, N.J.: Princeton University Press.

———. 1989. *Justice, Gender, and the Family*. New York: Basic Books.

———. 1994. "Gender Inequality and Cultural Differences." *Political Theory* 22:5–24.

Omolade, Barbara. 1980. "Black Women and Feminism." In *The Future of Difference*, ed. Hester Eisenstein and Alice Jardiner, pp. 247–256. New Brunswick, N.J.: Rutgers University Press.

Ostaszewski, Pawel, and Leonard Green. 1995. "Self Control and Discounting of Delayed Rewards from an Individual Differences and Comparative Perspective." *Polish Psychological Bulletin* 26:231–238.

Parijs, Philippe van. 1995. *Real Freedom for All: What (If Anything) Can Justify Capitalism*. Oxford: Clarendon Press.

Pettit, Philip. 1993. *The Common Mind: An Essay on Psychology, Society, and Politics*. New York: Oxford University Press.

Pettit, Philip, and Michael Smith. 1996. "Freedom in Belief and Desire." *Journal of Philosophy* 93:429–449.

Piercy, Marge. 1976. *Woman on the Edge of Time*. New York: Knopf.

Piper, Adrian. 1990. "Higher-order Discrimination." In *Identity, Character, and Morality*, ed. Amelie Oskenberg Rorty, pp. 285–309. Cambridge: MIT Press.

Pinto, Amancio. 1992. "Category Norms: Production, Frequency, and Typicality Measures." *Jornal de Psicologia* 10(3):10–15.

Pogge, Thomas. 2002. *World Poverty and Human Rights: Cosmopolitan Responsibilities and Reforms*. Cambridge, UK: Polity Press.

Quine, W. V. O. 1969. *Ontological Relativity and Other Essays*. New York: Columbia University Press.

Rawls, John. 1971. *A Theory of Justice*. Cambridge, Mass.: Harvard University Press.

———. 1993. *Political Liberalism*. New York: Columbia University Press.

Raz, Joseph. 1986. *The Morality of Freedom*. Oxford: Clarendon Press.

Reiman, Jeffrey. 1987. "Exploitation, Force, and the Moral Assessment of Capitalism." *Philosophy and Public Affairs* 16:3–41.

Rhode, Deborah L. 1989. *Justice and Gender*. Cambridge, Mass.: Harvard University Press.

Rich, Adrienne. 1980. "Compulsory Heterosexuality and Lesbian Existence." *Signs: Journal of Women in Culture and Society* 5 (Summer):631–660.

Roemer, John E. 1988. *Free to Lose*. Cambridge, Mass.: Harvard University Press.

Roiphe, Katie. 1993. *The Morning After: Sex, Fear, and Feminism on Campus*. New York: Little and Brown.

Roth, Alvin E., and Marilda A. Oliveira Sotomayor. 1990. *Two-Sided Matching: A Study in Game-theoretic Modeling and Analysis*. New York: Cambridge University Press.

Rousseau, Jean-Jacques. 1987. *Basic Political Writings*. Indianapolis: Hackett.

Ryan, William. 1976. *Blaming the Victim*. New York: Vintage Books.

Sacks, Oliver W. 1989. *Seeing Voices*. Berkeley: University of California Press.

Sadker, Myra, and David Sadker. 1994. *Failing at Fairness: How America's Schools Cheat Girls*. New York: Maxwell Macmillan International.

Salholz, Eloise, and Douglas Waller. 1991. "Tailhook: Scandal Time." *Newsweek*, July 6: 40.

Salzman, Todd. 2000. "'Rape Camps,' Forced Impregnation, and Ethinic Cleansing: Religious, Cultural, and Ethical Responses to Rape Victims in the Former Yugoslavia." In *War's Dirty Secret*, ed. Anne Barstow, pp. 46–56. Cleveland: Pilgrim Press.

Sassen, Saskia. 2002. "Global Cities and Survival Circuits." In *Global Woman*, ed. Barbara Ehrenreich and Arlie Russell Hochschild, pp. 254–274. New York: Metropolitan Books.

Satz, Debra, and John Ferejohn. 1994. "Rational Choice and Social Theory." *Journal of Philosophy* 41:71–87.

Schacht, Richard. 1994. *The Future of Alienation*. Urbana: University of Illinois Press.

Schelling, Thomas C. 1971. "Dynamic Models of Segregation." *Journal of Mathematical Sociology* 1:143.

———. 1978. *Micromotives and Macrobehavior*. New York: W. W. Norton.

Schiller, Bradley R. 1989. *The Economics of Poverty and Discrimination*. 5th ed. Englewood Cliffs, N.J.: Prentice Hall.

Schmitz, Susanne. 1996. *Race and Gender Discrimination across Urban Labor Markets*. New York: Garland.

Schneider, Elizabeth M. 1986. "The Dialectic of Rights and Politics: Perspectives from the Women's Movement." *New York U. Law Review* 61:589.

Schotter, Andrew. 1981. *The Economic Theory of Social Institutions*. Cambridge: Cambridge University Press.

Schultz, Vicki. 1991. "Telling Stories about Women and Work: Judicial Interpretations of Sex Segregation in the Workplace in Title VII Cases Raising the Lack of Interest Argument." In *Feminist Legal Theory*, ed. Katherine T. Bartlett and Roseanne Kennedy, pp. 124–155. Boulder, Colo.: Westview Press.

Searles, Patricia, and Ronald J. Berger, eds. 1995. *Rape and Society: Readings on the Problem of Sexual Assault*. Boulder, Colo.: Westview Press.

Sellars, Wilfrid. 1963. *Science, Perception and Reality*. London: Routledge & K. Paul.

Sen, Amartya K. 1995. "Gender Inequality and Theories of Justice." In *Women, Culture, and Development*, ed. Martha Nussbaum and Jonathon Glover, pp. 259–273. New York: Oxford University Press.

———. 1999. *Development as Freedom*. 1st ed. New York: Knopf: Distributed by Random House.

Shalom, Stephen R. 1981. *The United States and the Philippines: A Study of Neocolonialism*. Philadelphia, Penn.: Institute for the Study of Human Issues.

Sher, George. 1987. *Desert*. Princeton, N.J.: Princeton University Press.

Simon, Thomas. 1995. "Group Harm." *Journal of Social Philosophy* 2:123–137.

Skrypnek, B. J., and M. Snyder (1982). "On the Self-perpetuating Nature of Stereotypes about Men and Women." *Journal of Experimental Social Psychology* 18:277–291.

Smith, Stephanie H., George I. Whitehead, and Nan M. Sussman. 1990. "The Positivity Bias in Attributions: Two Cross-cultural Investigations." *Journal of Cross-Cultural Psychology* 21:283–301.

Snyder, M., E. D. Tanke, and E. Berscheid. 1977. "Social Perception and Interpersonal Behavior: On the Self-fulfilling Nature of Social Stereotypes." *Journal of Personality and Social Psychology* 35:656–666.

Spelman, Elizabeth V. 1988. *Inessential Woman: Problems of Exclusion in Feminist Thought*. Boston: Beacon Press.

Spencer, Steven, Claude Steele, and Diane Quinn. 1999. "Stereotype Threat and Women's Math Performance." *Journal of Experimental Social Psychology* 35(1):4–28.

Steele, Claude. 1997. "A Threat in the Air: How Stereotypes Shape Intellectual Identity and Performance." *American Psychologist* 52(6):613–629.

Steele, Shelby. 1990. *The Content of Our Character*. New York: St. Martin's Press.

Steinem, Gloria. 1983. *Outrageous Acts and Everyday Rebellions*. New York: New American Library.

Stern, Daniel. 1985. *The Interpersonal World of the Infant: A View from Psychoanalysis and Developmental Psychology*. New York: Basic Books.

Stevens, Evelyn P. 1993. "Marianism: The Other Face of Machismo in Latin America." In *Gender Basics: Feminist Perspectives on Women and Men*, ed. Anne Minas, pp. 456–462. Belmont, Calif.: Wadsworth Publishing.

Sunstein, Cass R. 1993. *The Partial Constitution*. Cambridge, Mass.: Harvard University Press.

Superson, Anita. 2005. "Deformed Desires and Informed Desire Tests." *Hypatia* 20(4):109–126.

Superson, Anita M., and Ann E. Cudd, eds. 2002. *Theorizing Backlash: Philosophical Reflections on the Resistance to Feminism*. Lanham, Md.: Rowman & Littlefield.

Tajfel, Henri. 1978. *The Social Psychology of Minorities*. London: Minority Rights Group.

———. 1981. *Human Groups and Social Categories: Studies in Social Psychology*. New York: Cambridge University Press.

Thomas, Laurence. 1990. "In My Next Life, I'll Be White." *Ebony* 46 (December):84.

Thurow, Lester. 1979. "A Theory of Group and Economic Redistribution." *Philosophy and Public Affairs* 9:25–41.

Tomaskovic-Devey, Donald. 1993. *Gender and Racial Inequality at Work: The Sources and Consequences of Job Segregation*. Ithaca, N.Y.: ILR Press.

Troadec, Bertrand. 1995. "Categorisations et Cultures. Approche Interculturalle des Processus Cognitifs de l'Enfant Tahitien." *Bulletin de Psychologie* 48:288–296.

Tuomela, Raimo. 1995. *The Importance of Us: A Philosophical Study of Basic Social Notions*. Stanford, Calif.: Stanford University Press.

Turner, P. J., J. Gervai, and R. A. Hinde. 1993. "Gender-typing in Young Children: Preferences, Behavior and Cultural Differences." *British Journal of Developmental Psychology* 11:323–342.

Tzeng, Oliver C. S., and Jay W. Jackson. 1994. "Effects of Contact, Conflict, and Social Identity on Interethnic Group Hostilities." *International Journal of Intercultural Relations* 18:259–276.

UNDP. 1993. *United Nations Development Report*.

UNICEF. 1997. *The State of the World's Children 1997*.

Van Fraassen, Bas C. 1980. *The Scientific Image*. Oxford: Clarendon Press.

Varian, Hal. 1994. "A Solution to the Problem of Externalities When Agents Are Well Informed." *American Economic Review* 84(5):1278–1293.

Vassiliou, Vasso G., and George Vassiliou. 1974. "Variations of the Group Process Across Cultures." *International Journal of Group Psychotherapy* 24:55–65.

Wade, Francis. 1971. "On Violence." *Journal of Philosophy* 66:369–377.

Waldron, Jeremy. 2003. "Property Rights and Welfare Distribution." In *A Companion to Applied Ethics*, ed. R. G. Frey, pp. 38–49. Malden, Mass.: Blackwell.

Walley, Christine J. 2004/2005. "Best Intentions: The Story of Tanzania's Peoples Park." *Boston Review*. December–January.

Walzer, Michael. 1992. *Just and Unjust Wars: A Moral Argument with Historical Illustrations*. 2nd ed. New York: Basic Books.

Ward, Colleen. 1985. "Sex Trait Stereotypes in Malaysian Children." *Sex Roles* 12:35–45.

Weiner, Jon. 1985. "The Sears Case: Women's History on Trial." *Nation* 241(6):161–169.

Wellman, Christopher H. 2003. "Nationalism and Secession." In *A Companion to Applied Ethics: Blackwell Companions to Philosophy*, ed. R. G. Frey, pp. 267–278. Malden, Mass.: Blackwell.

Wertheimer, Alan. 1987. *Coercion*. Princeton, N.J.: Princeton University Press.

———. 1994. "Coercion and Exploitative Agreements." *APA Newsletter on Philosophy and Law* 94:80–84.

White, Walter F. 1969. *Rope and Faggot*. New York: Arno Press.

Willett, Cynthia. 1995. *Maternal Ethics and Other Slave Moralities*. New York: Routledge.

Williams, Joan. 2000. *Unbending Gender: Why Family and Work Conflict and What to Do about It*. New York: Oxford University Press.

Williams, Patricia J. 1991. *The Alchemy of Race and Rights*. Cambridge, Mass.: Harvard University Press.

Wilson, Glenn D., Paul T. Barrett, and Saburo Iwawaki. 1995. "Japanese Reactions to Reward and Punishment: A Cross-cultural Personality Study." *Personality and Individual Differences* 19 (July):102–112.

Wittgenstein, Ludwig. 1953. *Philosophical Investigations*. New York: Macmillan.

Wollstonecraft, Mary. 1989. *A Vindication of the Rights of Women*. Buffalo, N.Y.: Prometheus Books.

World Health Organization. 2000. *World Report on Violence and Health*. Geneva: World Health Organization.

Young, Iris M. 1990. *Justice and the Politics of Difference*. Princeton, N.J.: Princeton University Press.

————.1997. *Intersecting Voices: Dilemmas of Gender, Political Philosophy, and Policy.* Princeton, N.J.: Princeton University Press.

————. 1999. "Gender as Seriality: Thinking about Women as a Social Collective." In *Feminist Interpretations of Jean-Paul Sartre*, ed. Julien S. Murphy. University Park, Pa.: Penn State University Press.

————. 2000. *Inclusion and Democracy.* Oxford: Oxford University Press.

————. 2005. "The Gendered Cycle of Vulnerability in the Less Developed World." Presented at the Susan Moller Okin memorial conference, Stanford University, Feb. 4.

Zimmerman, David. 1981. "Coercive Wage Offers." *Philosophy and Public Affairs* 10(2):130.

Index

abortion, 213
  laws prohibiting, 42, 167
adaptive preferences. *See* deformed desires
Agency for International Development, 205
alienation, 12–13, 15
  of man from man, 237
Allport, Gordon, 70
American Indians, 203
Amnesty International, 107, 110
androcentrism, 77, 173, 211–212, 256n.20
  Hegel's, 63–64
  of law, 214
apartheid, 206
  in South Africa, 138
Arendt, Hannah, 165
Aristotelian Principle, 235
Aristotle, 5
attribution, 68
  error, 73
autonomy, 129, 225

backlash, 206, 226, 233
Bales, Kevin, 97, 113–114, 161, 170
Bartky, Sandra, 19, 177
battered-woman syndrome, 213
Beauvoir, Simone de, 19
Becker, Gary, 172
Bem, Sandra, 74
Berlin, Isaiah, 224–225
Branscombe, Nyla, 72–73
Browning, Joan, 197
Brown v. Board of Education, 218
Bulhan, Hussein, 67
Burke, Edmund, 8

capitalism, 15, 102, 121–133, 207, 251n.3
  moral defense of, 125
  and strikes, 115
  transnational, 125
capitalists, 131, 182
categorization, 68–71, 74, 81
  social, 71, 222
  theory, 71–73
causation, 190
child care, 258n.3
  social provision of, 229
children, 124, 228
  in brothels, 97
  in debt bondage, 136–137
  as laborers, 205
  in slavery, 136–137
  and women's oppression, 148–151
China, People's Republic of, 134
Chodorow, Nancy, 19, 56–60, 220
choice
  in capitalism, 131–132
  and coercion, 125–131
  individually rational, 151
  of marriage partners, 128, 130
  voluntary vs. involuntary, 125, 127
Civil Rights Act of 1964, 252n.26
Civil Rights Movement, 188, 197, 202
Civil War, U.S., 111
class, economic, 40, 121, 132, 139, 243n.4
Clatterbaugh, Kenneth, 24–25
coercion
  empirical theories of, 126–128
  institutional, 131
  moralized theories of, 126–128